The Ministers Manual for 1979

By the same editor

Holy Holy Land
The Treasure Chest
Words of Life
Our American Heritage
1010 Sermon Illustrations from the Bible
Worship Resources for the Christian Year
Stories on Stone: A Book of American Epitaphs
American Epitaphs: Grave and Humorous
The Funeral Encyclopedia
A Treasury of Story-Sermons for Children
Treasury of Sermon Illustrations
Selected Poems of John Oxenham
Poems of Edwin Markham
Notable Sermons from Protestant Pulpits
Treasury of Poems for Worship and Devotion
88 Evangelistic Sermons
Speaker's Resources from Contemporary Literature
Christmas in Our Hearts (with Charles L. Allen)
Candle, Star, and Christmas Tree (with Charles L. Allen)
When Christmas Came to Bethlehem (with Charles L. Allen)
The Charles L. Allen Treasury
Lenten-Easter Sourcebook
365 Table Graces for the Christian Home
Speaker's Illustrations for Special Days
Table of the Lord
The Eternal Light
Twentieth Century Bible Commentary (co-editor)
Prayers for Public Worship (co-editor)
Christmas (with Charles L. Allen)
A Complete Sourcebook for the Lord's Supper

FIFTY-FOURTH ANNUAL ISSUE

The

MINISTERS MANUAL

(Doran's)

1979 EDITION

Edited by

CHARLES L. WALLIS

Published in San Francisco by

HARPER & ROW, PUBLISHERS

New York, Hagerstown, San Francisco, London

Editors of THE MINISTERS MANUAL

G.B.F. Hallock, D.D., 1926–1958
M.K.W. Heicher, Ph.D., 1943–1968
Charles L. Wallis, M.A., M.Div., 1969–

THE MINISTERS MANUAL FOR 1979.
Copyright © 1978 by Charles L. Wallis. All rights reserved.
Printed in the United States of America. For information
address Harper & Row, Publishers, Inc., 10 East 53rd Street,
New York, N.Y. 10022. Published simultaneously in Canada
by Fitzhenry & Whiteside Limited, Toronto.

FIRST EDITION

The ministers manual; a study and pulpit guide.

    1. Sermons—Outlines. 2. Homiletical illustrations. I. Hal-
lock, Gerard Benjamin Fleet, 1856–   ed.

BV4223.M5   251.058   25–21658 rev*
ISBN 0–06–069024–0

PREFACE

The editor acknowledges with appreciation the contributions of the writers whose homiletic and worship materials are included in this volume of *The Ministers Manual.*

The contributors represent the faith and talent of the worldwide Christian witness including younger and older, male and female, and traditional and experimental writers. Amid a diversity in exegesis and expression is a common commitment of editor and writers to glorify God and especially as we know and experience him through the redemptive life, teachings, death, and resurrection of the Lord Jesus.

Most of the materials have not previously appeared in book form, and much is in print for the first time in these pages. A conscientious effort has been made to include materials that have not been included in previous editions of *The Ministers Manual.*

The editor has attempted to handle responsibly the words and thoughts of the writers by submitting abridgments and condensations of their manuscripts to them for approval.

The Christian heritage is emphasized by the inclusion of writings from earlier generations.

The editor welcomes unsolicited sermons, prayers, and illustrations and makes an effort to add to each new edition of *The Ministers Manual* a considerable number of contributors who have not written for earlier editions.

He also encourages readers to offer comments and criticisms that relate to ways in which the quality and usefulness of *The Ministers Manual* may be improved.

If space permitted, a section devoted to letters to the editor would be interesting and stimulating.

One reader suggests that alternate pages should be blank, thereby providing ample space for notes.

Another letter requests a large-type edition that would make reading easier, and two letters during the past year urge publication in non-English editions.

Several correspondents express appreciation for the various indexes—an arduous task for any editor—and particularly for the newly added indexes identifying materials useful as children's stories and sermons and for use in small groups. A reader writes that he secures a copy of *The Ministers Manual* each year primarily for the sermon title index and adds, "That's all I need to activate my imagination."

Others cite the usefulness of "The Idea Box," the illustrations in Section XI, and the children's sermons.

The listing of anniversaries of hymns and hymn writers has encouraged one pastor to preach a hymn anniversary sermon each month, and another who offers extemporaneous prayers in the pulpit finds the outlines in the "Sermon Suggestions" to provide all he needs to keep his prayers from becoming repetitious.

The editor isn't sure how he should interpret a recent letter from a pastor who says that he has copies of the last twenty-two editions of *The Ministers Manual* and "each copy is as clean as new."

Rev. Charles L. Wallis

Keuka College
Keuka Park, New York 14478

CONTENTS

SECTION I. General Aids and Resources

Civil Year Calendars

1979

JANUARY						
S	M	T	W	T	F	S
	1	2	3	4	5	6
7	8	9	10	11	12	13
14	15	16	17	18	19	20
21	22	23	24	25	26	27
28	29	30	31			

FEBRUARY						
S	M	T	W	T	F	S
				1	2	3
4	5	6	7	8	9	10
11	12	13	14	15	16	17
18	19	20	21	22	23	24
25	26	27	28			

MARCH						
S	M	T	W	T	F	S
				1	2	3
4	5	6	7	8	9	10
11	12	13	14	15	16	17
18	19	20	21	22	23	24
25	26	27	28	29	30	31

APRIL						
S	M	T	W	T	F	S
1	2	3	4	5	6	7
8	9	10	11	12	13	14
15	16	17	18	19	20	21
22	23	24	25	26	27	28
29	30					

MAY						
S	M	T	W	T	F	S
		1	2	3	4	5
6	7	8	9	10	11	12
13	14	15	16	17	18	19
20	21	22	23	24	25	26
27	28	29	30	31		

JUNE						
S	M	T	W	T	F	S
					1	2
3	4	5	6	7	8	9
10	11	12	13	14	15	16
17	18	19	20	21	22	23
24	25	26	27	28	29	30

JULY						
S	M	T	W	T	F	S
1	2	3	4	5	6	7
8	9	10	11	12	13	14
15	16	17	18	19	20	21
22	23	24	25	26	27	28
29	30	31				

AUGUST						
S	M	T	W	T	F	S
			1	2	3	4
5	6	7	8	9	10	11
12	13	14	15	16	17	18
19	20	21	22	23	24	25
26	27	28	29	30	31	

SEPTEMBER						
S	M	T	W	T	F	S
						1
2	3	4	5	6	7	8
9	10	11	12	13	14	15
16	17	18	19	20	21	22
23	24	25	26	27	28	29
30						

OCTOBER						
S	M	T	W	T	F	S
	1	2	3	4	5	6
7	8	9	10	11	12	13
14	15	16	17	18	19	20
21	22	23	24	25	26	27
28	29	30	31			

NOVEMBER						
S	M	T	W	T	F	S
				1	2	3
4	5	6	7	8	9	10
11	12	13	14	15	16	17
18	19	20	21	22	23	24
25	26	27	28	29	30	

DECEMBER						
S	M	T	W	T	F	S
						1
2	3	4	5	6	7	8
9	10	11	12	13	14	15
16	17	18	19	20	21	22
23	24	25	26	27	28	29
30	31					

1980

JANUARY						
S	M	T	W	T	F	S
		1	2	3	4	5
6	7	8	9	10	11	12
13	14	15	16	17	18	19
20	21	22	23	24	25	26
27	28	29	30	31		

FEBRUARY						
S	M	T	W	T	F	S
					1	2
3	4	5	6	7	8	9
10	11	12	13	14	15	16
17	18	19	20	21	22	23
24	25	26	27	28	29	

MARCH						
S	M	T	W	T	F	S
						1
2	3	4	5	6	7	8
9	10	11	12	13	14	15
16	17	18	19	20	21	22
23	24	25	26	27	28	29
30	31					

APRIL						
S	M	T	W	T	F	S
		1	2	3	4	5
6	7	8	9	10	11	12
13	14	15	16	17	18	19
20	21	22	23	24	25	26
27	28	29	30			

MAY						
S	M	T	W	T	F	S
				1	2	3
4	5	6	7	8	9	10
11	12	13	14	15	16	17
18	19	20	21	22	23	24
25	26	27	28	29	30	31

JUNE						
S	M	T	W	T	F	S
1	2	3	4	5	6	7
8	9	10	11	12	13	14
15	16	17	18	19	20	21
22	23	24	25	26	27	28
29	30					

JULY						
S	M	T	W	T	F	S
		1	2	3	4	5
6	7	8	9	10	11	12
13	14	15	16	17	18	19
20	21	22	23	24	25	26
27	28	29	30	31		

AUGUST						
S	M	T	W	T	F	S
					1	2
3	4	5	6	7	8	9
10	11	12	13	14	15	16
17	18	19	20	21	22	23
24	25	26	27	28	29	30
31						

SEPTEMBER						
S	M	T	W	T	F	S
	1	2	3	4	5	6
7	8	9	10	11	12	13
14	15	16	17	18	19	20
21	22	23	24	25	26	27
28	29	30				

OCTOBER						
S	M	T	W	T	F	S
			1	2	3	4
5	6	7	8	9	10	11
12	13	14	15	16	17	18
19	20	21	22	23	24	25
26	27	28	29	30	31	

NOVEMBER						
S	M	T	W	T	F	S
						1
2	3	4	5	6	7	8
9	10	11	12	13	14	15
16	17	18	19	20	21	22
23	24	25	26	27	28	29
30						

DECEMBER						
S	M	T	W	T	F	S
	1	2	3	4	5	6
7	8	9	10	11	12	13
14	15	16	17	18	19	20
21	22	23	24	25	26	27
28	29	30	31			

Church and Civic Calendar for 1979

JANUARY

1 New Year's Day
   Festival of the Christening
5 Twelfth Night
6 The Epiphany
14 Missionary Day
15 Martin Luther King, Jr. Birthday
18 Confession of St. Peter
18–25 Week of Prayer for Christian Unity
19 Robert E. Lee Birthday
25 Conversion of St. Paul

FEBRUARY

1 National Freedom Day
2 Presentation of Jesus in the Temple
11 Race Relations Sunday
12 Lincoln's Birthday
14 St. Valentine's Day
18–25 Brotherhood Week
19 Presidents' Day
22 Washington's Birthday
24 St. Matthias, Apostle
25 The Transfiguration
27 Shrove Tuesday
28 Ash Wednesday

MARCH

2 World Day of Prayer
4 First Sunday in Lent
11 Second Sunday in Lent
17 St. Patrick's Day
18 Third Sunday in Lent
25 Fourth Sunday in Lent
   The Annunciation

APRIL

1 Fifth Sunday in Lent
   Passion Sunday
8 Palm Sunday
   Passion Sunday (alternate)
8–14 Holy Week
12 Maundy Thursday
13 Good Friday
15 Easter
22 Easter (Orthodox)

   Low Sunday
25 St. Mark, Evangelist

MAY

1 Law Day
   Loyalty Day
   May Day
   St. Philip and St. James, Apostles
6–13 National Family Week
13 Mother's Day
19 Armed Forces Day
20 Rural Life Sunday
21 Victoria Day (Canada)
24 Ascension Day
28 Memorial Day
31 The Visitation

JUNE

3 Pentecost (Whitsunday)
9 Corpus Christi Day
10 Children's Sunday
   Trinity Sunday
11 St. Barnabas, Apostle
14 Flag Day
17 Father's Day
24 Nativity of St. John the Baptist
25 Presentation of the Augsburg Confession
29 St. Peter and St. Paul, Apostles

JULY

1 Dominion Day (Canada)
   Independence Sunday
2 The Visitation (alternate)
4 Independence Day
15–21 Captive Nations Week
22 St. Mary Magdalene
25 St. James the Elder, Apostle

AUGUST

6 The Transfiguration (alternate)
15 Mary, Mother of Our Lord
24 St. Bartholomew, Apostle
26 Women's Equality Day

SEPTEMBER

2 Labor Sunday
3 Labor Day

17   Citizenship Day
17–23   Constitution Week
21   St. Matthew, Evangelist and
        Apostle
28   American Indian Day
29   St. Michael and All Angels

OCTOBER

1   Child Health Day
7   World Communion Sunday
8   Columbus Day
      Thanksgiving Day (Canada)
12   Columbus Day (alternate)
14   Laity Sunday
18   St. Luke, Evangelist
24   United Nations Day
28   Reformation Sunday
      St. Simon and St. Jude, Apostles
31   National UNICEF Day
      Reformation Day

NOVEMBER

1   All Saints' Day
2   All Soul's Day
      World Community Day

4   World Temperance Day
11   Stewardship Day
      Veterans Day
18   Bible Sunday
      Thanksgiving Sunday
22   Thanksgiving Day
30   St. Andrew, Apostle

DECEMBER

2   First Sunday in Advent
6   St. Nicholas Day (Orthodox)
9   Second Sunday in Advent
10   Human Rights Day
15   Bill of Rights Day
16   Third Sunday in Advent
21   Forefathers' Day
      St. Thomas, Apostle
23   Fourth Sunday in Advent
25   Christmas
26   St. Stephen, Deacon and Martyr
27   St. John, Evangelist and Apostle
28   The Holy Innocents, Martyrs
31   New Year's Eve
      Watch Night

Lectionary for 1979

The following scripture lessons, with occasional alterations according to denominational preferences, are commended for use in public worship by various Protestant churches and the Roman Catholic Church and includes first, second, and gospel readings according to Cycle B from January 1 to November 25 and according to Cycle C from December 2 to December 30.

CHRISTMASTIDE

January 1 (New Year's Day): Eccl. 3:1–13; Col. 2:1–7; Matt. 9:14–17.

EPIPHANY

January 6 (Epiphany): Isa. 60:1–6; Eph. 3:-1–6; Matt. 2:1–12.
January 7: Isa. 61:1–4; Acts 11:4–18; Mark 1:4–11.
January 14: I Sam. 3:1–10; I Cor. 6:12–20; John 1:35–42.
January 18–25 (Week of Prayer for

Christian Unity): Isa. 35:3–10; I Cor. 3:-1–11; Matt. 28:16–20.
January 21: Jonah 3:1–5, 10; I Cor. 7:29–31; Mark 1:14–22.
January 28: Deut. 18:15–22; I Cor. 7:32–35; Mark 1:21–28.
February 4: Job 7:1–7; I Cor. 9:16–19, 22–23; Mark 1:29–39.
February 11: Lev. 13:1–2, 44–46; I Cor. 10:31 to 11:1; Mark 1:40–45.
February 18: Isa. 43:18–25; II Cor. 1: 18–22; Mark 2:1–12.
February 25: Hos. 2:14–20; II Cor. 3:17 to 4:2; Mark 2:18–22.

LENT

February 28 (Ash Wednesday): Isa. 58:-3–12; Jas. 1:12–18; Mark 2:15–20.
March 4: Gen. 9:8–15; I Pet. 3:18–22; Mark 1:12–15.
March 11: Gen. 22:1–2, 9–13; Rom. 8:-31–39; Mark 9:1–9.
March 18: Ex. 20:1–3, 7–8, 12–17; I Cor. 1:22–25; John 4:19–26.

March 25: II Chron. 36:14–21; Eph. 2:-1–10; John 3:14–21.

April 1: Jer. 31:31–34; Heb. 5:7–10; John 12:20–33.

HOLY WEEK

April 8 (Palm Sunday): Zech. 9:9–12; Heb. 12:1–6; Mark 11:1–11.

April 9 (Monday): Isa. 50:4–10; Heb. 9:-11–15; Luke 19:41–48.

April 10 (Tuesday): Isa. 42:1–9; I Tim. 6:-11–16; John 12:37–50.

April 11 (Wednesday): Isa. 52:13 to 53:12; Rom. 5:6–11; Luke 22:1–16.

April 12 (Maundy Thursday): Deut. 16:-1–8; Rev. 1:4–8; Matt. 26:17–30.

April 13 (Good Friday): Lam. 1:7–12; Heb. 10:4–18; Luke 23:33–46.

EASTERTIDE

April 15: Isa. 25:6–9; I Pet. 1:3–9; Mark 16:1–8.

April 22: Acts 4:32–35; I John 5:1–6; Matt. 28:11–20.

April 29: Acts 3:13–15, 17–19; I John 2:-1–6; Luke 24:36–49.

May 6: Acts 4:8–12; I John 3:1–3; John 10:11–18.

May 13: Acts 9:26–31; I John 3:18–24; John 15:1–8.

May 20: Acts 10:34–48; I John 4:1–7; John 15:9–17.

May 24 (Ascension Day): Acts 1:1–11; Eph. 1:16–23; Luke 24:44–53.

May 27: Acts 1:15–17, 21–26; I John 4:-11–16; John 17:11–19.

PENTECOST

June 3 (Pentecost): Joel 2:28–32; Acts 2:-1–13; John 16:5–15.

June 10 (Trinity Sunday): Isa. 6:1–8; Rom. 8:12–17; John 3:1–8.

June 17: Deut. 5:12–15; II Cor. 4:6–11; Mark 2:23 to 3:6.

June 24: Gen. 3:9–15; II Cor. 4:13 to 5:1; Mark 3:20–35.

July 1: Ezek. 17:22–24; II Cor. 5:6–10; Mark 4:26–34.

July 4 (Independence Day): Isa. 26:1–8; I Thess. 5:12–23; Mark 12:13–17.

July 8: Job 38:1–11; II Cor. 5:16–21; Mark 4:35–41.

July 15: Gen. 4:3–10; II Cor. 8:7–15; Mark 5:21–43.

July 22: Ezek. 2:1–5; II Cor. 12:7–10; Mark 6:1–6.

July 29: Amos 7:12–17; Eph. 1:3–10; Mark 6:7–13.

August 5: Jer. 23:1–6; Eph. 2:11–18; Mark 6:30–34.

August 12: II Kings 4:42–44; Eph. 4:1–6, 11–16; John 6:1–15.

August 19: Ex. 16:2–4, 12–15; Eph. 4:17–24; John 6:24–35.

August 26: I Kings 19:4–8; Eph. 4:30 to 5:2; John 6:41–51.

September 2: Prov. 9:1–6; Eph. 5:15–20; John 6:51–59.

September 9: Josh. 24:14–18; Eph. 5:21–33; John 6:60–69.

September 16: Deut. 4:1–8; Jas. 1:19–25; Mark 7:1–8, 14–15, 21–23.

September 23: Isa. 35:4–7; Jas. 2:1–5; Mark 7:31–37.

September 30: Isa. 50:4–9; Jas. 2:14–18; Mark 8:27–35.

October 7: Jer. 11:18–20; Jas. 3:13 to 4:3; Mark 9:30–37; (World Communion Sunday) Isa. 25:6–9; Rev. 7:9–17; Luke 24:13–35.

October 14: Num. 11:24–30; Jas. 5:1–6; Mark 9:38–48.

October 21: Gen. 2:18–24; Heb. 2:9–13; Mark 10:2–16.

October 28: Prov. 3:13–18; Heb. 4:12–16; Mark 10:17–27; (Reformation Sunday) Gen. 12:1–4; II Cor. 5:16–21; Matt. 21:-17–22.

November 4: Isa. 53:10–12; Heb. 5:1–10; Mark 10:35–45.

November 11: Jer. 31:7–9; Heb. 5:1–6; Mark 10:46–52.

November 18: Deut. 6:1–9; Heb. 7:23–28; Mark 12:28–34.

November 22 (Thanksgiving Day): Deut. 26:1–11; Gal. 6:6–10; Luke 17:11–19.

November 25: I Kings 17:8–16; Heb. 9:-24–28; Mark 12:38–44.

ADVENT

December 2: Jer. 33:14–16; I Thess. 5:1–6; Luke 21:25–36.

December 9: Isa. 9:2, 6–7; Phil. 1:3–11; Luke 3:1–6.

December 16: Zeph. 3:14–18; Phil. 4:4–9; Luke 3:10–18.
December 23: Micah 5:1–4; Heb. 10:5–10; Luke 1:39–47.
December 24 (Christmas Eve): Zech. 2:-10–13; Phil. 4:4–7; Luke 2:15–20.

CHRISTMASTIDE

December 25: Isa. 52:6–10; Eph. 1:3–10; John 1:1–14.
December 30: Isa. 45:18–22; Rom. 11:33 to 12:2; Luke 2:41–52.

Four-Year Church Calendar

	1979	1980	1981	1982
Ash Wednesday	February 28	February 20	March 4	February 24
Palm Sunday	April 8	March 30	April 12	April 4
Good Friday	April 13	April 4	April 17	April 9
Easter	April 15	April 6	April 19	April 11
Ascension Day	May 24	May 15	May 28	May 20
Pentecost	June 3	May 25	June 7	May 30
Trinity Sunday	June 10	June 1	June 14	June 6
Thanksgiving	November 22	November 28	November 26	November 25
Advent Sunday	December 2	November 30	November 29	November 28

Forty-Year Easter Calendar

1979 April 15	1989 March 26	1999 April 4	2009 April 12
1980 April 6	1990 April 15	2000 April 23	2010 April 4
1981 April 19	1991 March 31	2001 April 14	2011 April 24
1982 April 11	1992 April 19	2002 March 31	2012 April 8
1983 April 3	1993 April 11	2003 April 20	2013 March 31
1984 April 22	1994 April 3	2004 April 11	2014 April 20
1985 April 7	1995 April 16	2005 March 27	2015 April 5
1986 March 30	1996 April 7	2006 April 16	2016 March 27
1987 April 19	1997 March 30	2007 April 8	2017 April 16
1988 April 3	1998 April 12	2008 March 23	2018 April 1

Four-Year Jewish Calendar

	1979	1980	1981	1982
Purim	March 13	March 2	March 20	March 9
Passover	April 12	April 1	April 19	April 8
Shabuoth (Revelation of the Law)	June 1	May 21	June 8	May 28
Rosh Hashanah (New Year)	September 22	September 11	September 29	September 18
Yom Kippur (Day of Atonement)	October 1	September 20	October 8	September 27
Sukkoth (Thanksgiving)	October 6	September 25	October 13	October 2
Simhath Torah (Rejoicing in the Law)	October 14	October 3	October 21	October 10
Hanukkah	December 15	December 3	December 21	December 11

Holidays begin at sunset on the evening before the date given.

Traditional Wedding Anniversary Identifications

1 Paper	7 Wool	13 Lace	35 Coral
2 Cotton	8 Bronze	14 Ivory	40 Ruby
3 Leather	9 Pottery	15 Crystal	45 Sapphire
4 Linen	10 Tin	20 China	50 Gold
5 Wood	11 Steel	25 Silver	55 Emerald
6 Iron	12 Silk	30 Pearl	60 Diamond

Colors Appropriate for Days and Seasons

White. Symbolizes purity, perfection, and joy and identifies festivals marking events, except Good Friday, in the life of Jesus: Christmas, Easter, Eastertide, Ascension Day, Trinity Sunday, All Saints' Day, weddings, funerals.

Red. Symbolizes the Holy Spirit, martyrdom, and the love of God: Pentecost and Sundays following.

Violet. Symbolizes penitence: Advent, Lent.

Green. Symbolizes mission to the world, hope, regeneration, nurture, and growth: Epiphany season, Kingdomtide, Rural Life Sunday, Labor Sunday, Thanksgiving Sunday.

Black. Symbolizes mourning: Good Friday.

Historical, Cultural, and Religious Anniversaries in 1979

Five years (1974). *February 13:* Alexander Solzhenitsyn deported from Russia. *May 14:* Donald Coggan succeeds Michael Ramsey as archbishop of Canterbury. *June 3:* Supreme Court rules that women must receive equal pay as men for same work. *August 9:* President Richard Nixon resigns and on September 8 is given an unconditional pardon.

Ten years (1969). *April:* first overland crossing of the North Pole. *July 20:* astronaut Neil A. Armstrong first man to set foot on the moon. *October 15:* Vietnam Moratorium Day emphasizes national war protest. *December 18:* British abolish death penalty for murder.

Fifteen years (1964). *February 4:* twenty-fourth amendment to the Constitution abolishes poll tax. *February 17:* Supreme Court rules one man one vote. *May 27:* Nehru dies. *July 2:* President Johnson signs civil rights bill. *August 5:* United States begins bombing of North Vietnam.

Twenty years (1959). *January 1–3:* Castro overthrows Batista in Cuba. *January 3:* Alaska becomes forty-ninth state. *April 25:* St. Lawrence Seaway opened. *July 21:* first atomic-powered merchant ship launched. *August 21:* Hawaii becomes fiftieth state.

Twenty-five years (1954). *January 21:* first atomic-powered submarine launched. *March 17:* Supreme Court declares racial discrimination in public schools to be unconstitutional. *September 8:* SEATO proclaimed. *December 2:* Senate votes condemnation of Senator Joseph R. McCarthy.

Thirty years (1949). *January 7:* cease-fire in Palestine following first Arab-Israeli war. *January 20:* President Truman proposes Point Four program to assist world's less developed peoples. *March 18:* NATO established. *September 23:* announcement of Russia's first atomic bomb test. *October 1:* Mao Tse-tung establishes Chinese People's Republic.

Forty years (1939). *March 15:* Germany seizes Czechoslovkia. *March 29:* Franco victor in Spanish civil war. *April 20:* first commercial television broadcast by RCA. *April 30:* New York World's Fair opens. *September 3:* Britain and France declare war on Germany.

Fifty years (1929). *January 31:* Trotsky expelled from Russia. *June 7:* Vatican becomes independent state. *August 8–29:* "Graf Zeppelin" flies around the world. *September 14:* United States joins International Court. *October 24:* collapse of New

York Stock Market signals beginning of the Great Depression.

Seventy-five years (1904). *February 6:* Russo-Japanese War begins. *May 4:* construction of Panama Canal undertaken. *October 27:* New York subway opened.

One hundred years (1879). Northeast Passage navigated. *October 21:* Edison invents incandescent electric light.

Two hundred years (1779). *September 23:* John Paul Jones on *Bonhomme Richard* defeats *Serapis* in British North Sea waters.

Two hundred and fifty years (1729). Bach composes "St. Matthew Passion."

Three hundred and fifty years (1629). English settlements in Massachusetts. Sixth Crusade restores Jerusalem, Nazareth, and Bethlehem to Christians.

Four hundred years (1579). Sir Francis Drake claims California for Britain.

Four hundred and fifty years (1529). *May 17:* Publication of Luther's "Small Catechism."

Five hundred and fifty years (1429). May 1–3. Joan of Arc liberates Orleans.

Six hundred years (1379). New College, Oxford, founded.

Six hundred and fifty years (1329). *June 7:* Robert Bruce, liberator of Scotland, dies.

Nine hundred years (1079). Construction of Winchester Cathedral begun.

Nineteen hundred years (79). Eruption of Mt. Vesuvius destroys Pompeii.

Anniversaries of Hymns, Hymn Writers, and Composers in 1979

10 years (1969). Death of Harry Emerson Fosdick (b. 1878), author of "God of grace and God of glory" and "O God in restless living."

25 years (1954). Death of William P. Merrill (b. 1867), author of "Rise up, O men of God."

50 years (1929). Writing of "Eternal God, whose power upholds" by Henry Hallam Tweedy; "Remember all the people" by Percy Deamer. Death of Katharine Lee Bates (b. 1859), author of "O beautiful for spacious skies"; Robert Henry Earnshaw (b. 1856), composer of hymn-tune ARIZONA ("Lord of all being"); Elisha A. Hoffman (b. 1839), author of "Leaning on the everlasting arms" and author-composer of "I must tell Jesus" and "What a wonderful Savior"; Frederick Lucian Hosmer (b. 1840), author of "God that madest earth and heaven," "O thou in all thy might so far," "Thy kingdom come, on bended knee," etc.; J. Alfred Jeffery (1854), composer of hymn-tune ANCIENT OF DAYS ("Ancient of days, who sittest throned"); Arthur H. Mann (b. 1850), composer of hymn-tune ANGEL'S STORY ("O Jesus, I have promised"); Lelia N. Morris (b. 1862), author-composer of "Let Jesus come into your heart," "Sweeter as the years go by," etc.; William H. Parker (b. 1845), author of "Tell me the stories of Jesus"; G. A. Studdert-Kennedy (b. 1883), author of "When through the whirl of wheels"; Edward S. Ufford (b. 1851), author-composer of "Throw out the life-line"; John H. Yoakley (b. 1860), composer of hymn-tune ALL SOULS ("Lead us, O Father, in the paths of peace").

75 years (1904). Writing of "O beautiful for spacious skies" by Katharine Lee Bates; hymn-tune CHRISTMAS TUNE ("There's a song in the air") by Karl P. Harrington; hymn-tune PARRAT ("I need thee every hour") by Walter Parrat; tune-tune INTERCESSOR ("O brother man, fold to thy heart") by C. Hubert H. Parry; hymn-tune ENGELBERG ("All praise to thee, for though") by Charles V. Stanford. Death of John White Chadwick (b. 1840), author of "Eternal ruler of the ceaseless round"; Henry Hiles (b. 1826), composer of hymn-tune ST. LEONARD ("The shadows of the evening hours"); Jeremiah E. Rankin (b. 1828), author of "God be with you"; William T. Sleeper (b. 1819), author of "Jesus, I come."

100 years (1879). Writing of hymn-tune ABERYSTWYTH ("Jesus, lover of my soul" and "Watchman, tell us of the night") by Joseph Parry; "O Master, let me walk with thee" by Washington Gladden; hymn-tune PENITENCE ("In the hour of trial") by

Spencer Lane. Birth of John Haynes Holmes (d. 1964), author of "The voice of God is calling"; J. Edgar Park (d. 1956), author of "We would see Jesus"; Geoffrey Turton Shaw (d. 1943), composer of hymn-tunes GRESHAM ("Ten thousand times ten thousand") and LANGHAM ("Father Eternal, ruler of creation"). Death of Frances R. Havergal (b. 1836), author of "Another year is dawning," "I gave my life for thee," "Lord, speak to me," "Take my life and let it be," "True-hearted, wholehearted," etc.; Henry Thomas Smart (b. 1813), composer of hymn-tunes LANCASHIRE ("The day of resurrection" and "Lead on, O King Eternal"), REGENT SQUARE ("Angels, from the realms of glory" and "Praise, my soul, the King of heaven"), and REX GLORIAE ("Praise the Lord! ye heavens adore him").

150 years (1829). Writing of "Our blest Redeemer" by Harriet Auber; "Spirit divine, attend our prayers" by Andrew Reed. Birth of Louis M. Gottschalk (d. 1869), composer of hymn-tune MERCY ("Holy Spirit, truth divine" and "Softly now the light of day"); Priscilla Jane Owens (d. 1907), author of "Jesus saves"; Frederick Whitfield (d. 1904), author of "Oh, how I love Jesus." Death of Carl G. Glaser (b. 1784), composer of hymn-tune

AZMON ("O for a thousand tongues to sing").

200 years (1779). Publication of *Olney Hymns* including "Sometimes a light surprises" by William Cowper and "Amazing grace," "Glorious things of thee are spoken," "How sweet the name of Jesus sounds," etc., by John Newton. Writing of "All hail the power of Jesus' name" by Edward Perronet. Birth of Robert Grant (d. 1838), author of "O worship the king"; Thomas Moore (d. 1852), author of "Come, ye disconsolate"; Dorothy A. Thrupp (d. 1847), author of "Savior, like a shepherd lead us."

250 years (1729). Harmonization of hymn-tune PASSION CHORALE ("O sacred head, now wounded") by Johann Sebastian Bach from his *St. Matthew Passion.* Writing of "God himself is with us" and "Thou hidden love of God" by Gerhardt Tersteegen.

450 years (1529). Writing of "A mighty fortress is our God" by Martin Luther.

550 years (1429). Writing of "O Jesus Christ, our Lord most dear" by Heinrich von Laufenberg.

900 years (1079). Birth of Peter Abelard (d. 1142), author of "Alone thou goest forth, O Lord" and "O what their joy and their glory must be."

Quotable Quotations

1. The distance a man has got on his journey is of less consequence than the direction in which his face is turned.—Alexander Maclaren.

2. Everything that is done in the world is done by hope.—Martin Luther.

3. What life does to us in the long run depends upon what life finds in us.—E. Stanley Jones.

4. Before religion can be known as sweet communion, it must first be known as answered summons.—John Baillie.

5. In the life of a true believer there are no accidents.—Corrie ten Boom.

6. The difference between present day Christianity and that which we find in the Bible is that today for the majority the Christian life is a performance, but to the

early believers it was the real thing.—J. B. Phillips.

7. Hell is a place where no one believes in solutions anymore.—Ingmar Bergman.

8. Evangelism is one beggar telling another beggar where to find bread.—D. T. Niles.

9. A world without prayer is fundamentally a world without meaning.

10. Sunday clears away the rust of the whole week.—Joseph Addison.

11. I have never met a man who has given me as much trouble as myself.—Dwight L. Moody.

12. To believe in God means to know that there is somebody who knows us through and through and loves us.—Joseph Pintauro.

13. Through our feelings we are linked to each other's joys, sufferings, and dreams; and through our creativeness we are linked to the creator of all, to our Lord himself.—Jacques Lipschitz.

14. Love is what we do to people who irritate us.—Ray C. Stedman.

15. The Christian ethic flows from the agony of the cross, repeated continually in the life of man.—Kenneth E. Boulding.

16. Be too large for worry, too noble for anger, too strong for fear, and too happy to be submerged by trouble.—William O. Douglas.

17. To learn how to be good to oneself is often more difficult than to learn how to be good to others.—Joshua Liebman.

18. Christianity's home is in the world; and to know what it is, we must seek it in the world and hear the world's witness of it.—John Henry Newman.

19. He was made what we are that he might make us what he is himself.—Irenaeus.

20. It was not the outer grandeur of the Romans but the inner simplicity of the Christians that lived through the ages.—Charles A. Lindbergh.

21. Any ruler can rule, but only a king can die for his people.—St. Basil.

22. The story of the Christian is the story of many resurrections.—John Calvin.

23. When people are free to do as they please, they usually imitate each other.—Eric Hoffer.

24. Our relationship to Christ determines the kind of light the world sees in us—Vivencio L. Vinluan.

25. The Christian life that is joyless is a discredit to God and a disgrace to itself.—Maltbie D. Babcock.

26. Before we set our hearts too much upon anything, let us examine how happy they are who already possess it.—Ross C. Crighton.

27. Life in Christ Jesus, in the new being, and in the Spirit means having no absolutes but his love and being totally uncommitted in every other respect but totally committed in this.—John A. T. Robinson.

28. Forgiveness is the wonder of being trusted again by God in the place where I disgraced him.—Rita F. Snowden.

29. Palm Sunday dramatized in unforgettable fashion the impossibility of neutrality on great issues.—Harry Emerson Fosdick.

30. Though every believer has the Holy Spirit, the Holy Spirit does not have every believer.—A. W. Tozer.

31. Christ's residence was for thirty-three years here on earth, but it did not naturalize him as a citizen of earth.—Henrietta Mears.

32. He that lives in the spirit and temper of devotion and whose heart is always full of God lives at the top of human happiness.—William Law.

33. There are too many people who depend on the church but upon whom the church cannot depend.—Ross C. Crighton.

34. God is love. And in every moment of genuine love we are dwelling in God and God in us.—Paul Tillich.

35. History is a vision of God revealing himself in actions to persons who are sincerely seeking him.—Arnold Toynbee.

36. There falls no shadow where there shines no sun.—*Christian Herald.*

37. The greatest treason is to do the right thing for the wrong reason.—T. S. Eliot.

38. It is not flesh and blood but the heart which makes us fathers and sons.—Friedrich von Schiller.

39. If we have learned one thing from our past, it is that to live through dramatic events is not enough. One has to share them and transform them into acts of conscience.—Elie Weisel.

40. Believing on God is really receiving what God gives.—John Hunter.

41. So long as man is capable of self-renewal he is a living being.—Frederic Amiel.

42. The Christian community is fashioned by the Holy Spirit for the specific purpose of accomplishing God's mission in the world.—Wallace Fisher.

43. When I read the Bible, I get the impression that God expects each one of us to be a giant.—Soren Kierkegaard.

44. Left to ourselves we tend immedi-

ately to reduce God to manageable terms.—A. W. Tozer.

45. Christ came not to be ministered to but to minister, and our first duty is to be ministered to by him.—P. T. Forsyth.

46. The bird of paradise alights only upon the hand that does not grasp.—John Berry.

47. Only he who is already loved can love; only he who has been trusted can trust; only he who has been the object of devotion can give himself.—Rudolf Bultmann.

48. The best definition of radiant, inspired prayer is the soul singing in the presence of God.—Glenn Clark.

49. The nearer I approach the end, the plainer I hear around me the immortal symphonies of the world to come.—Victor Hugo.

50. If God sends us on stony paths, he provides strong shoes.—Corrie ten Boom.

51. To keep alive the pain of being a person is the first task of the educator in our time.—Martin Buber.

52. The wise man thinks about his troubles only when there is some purpose in doing so.—Bertrand Russell.

53. God often gives in one brief moment that which he has for a long time denied.—Thomas a Kempis.

54. Originality is simply a fresh pair of eyes.—Woodrow Wilson.

55. Many times a day I must realize how much my own inner and outer life is built upon the labors of my fellow men.—Albert Einstein.

56. This is the world Christ loved, and men must be saved where they are, not where they ought to be.—Pope John XXIII.

57. You cannot teach a man anything; you can only help him to find it within himself.—Galileo.

58. The forgiveness of God is the foundation of every bridge from a hopeless past to a courageous present.—George Adam Smith.

59. If God could turn some of us inside out he might send us to turn the world upside down.—Leonard Ravenhill.

60. There are as many ways of climbing to the stars as there are people to climb.—George Russell.

61. When by mutation a new rose is born in a garden, all the gardeners rejoice. They isolate the rose, tend it, foster it. But there is no gardener for men.—Antoine de Saint-Exupery.

62. What you call hindrances, obstacles, and discouragements are probably God's opportunities.—Horace Bushnell.

63. In dreams begin responsibilities.—Delmore Schwartz.

64. The average man's idea of a good sermon is one that goes over his head and hits one of his neighbors.—Ross C. Crighton.

65. We promise according to our hopes and perform according to our fears.—Francois Duc de la Rochefoucauld.

66. Every particular thou is a glimpse through to the eternal thou.—Martin Buber.

67. Each relationship trembles with the promise of the realization of the presence and power of God.—Reuel L. Howe.

68. Now is the nick of time in matters which reach into eternity.—Ralph Waldo Emerson.

69. The pity is that the church can be so harmless that it would not be worthwhile to take the trouble to crucify it.—William Barclay.

70. Everyone must sacrifice a portion of his own life for others.—Albert Schweitzer.

71. Religion is what you do in your solitariness. If you are never alone, you can never be religious.—Alfred North Whitehead.

72. He who labors as he prays lifts his heart to God with his hands.—St. Bernard of Clairvaux.

73. The way a pastor thinks about the church which he serves determines what that church is to become.—Richard C. Halverson.

74. Life must be lived forwards, but it can only be understood backwards.—Soren Kierkegaard.

75. How would you like your thoughts printed in tomorrow's newspaper?—Ross C. Crighton.

76. Relying on God has to begin all over again every day as if nothing had yet been done.—C. S. Lewis.

77. Like stupid cattle we keep our heads to the grass and rarely contemplate the infinite.—Jenkin Lloyd Jones.

78. Prayer is not an easy way of getting what we want but the only way of becoming what God wants us to be.—G. A. Studdert-Kennedy.

79. There is no fit search after truth which does not begin to live the truth which it knows.—Horace Bushnell.

80. Without prayer there can be no religion or only a dumb one.—Thomas Carlyle.

81. A man is simple when his chief care is the wish to be what he ought to be, that is, honestly and naturally human.—Charles Wagner.

82. Everybody thinks of changing humanity and nobody thinks of changing himself.—Leo Tolstoy.

83. Happiness is living by inner purpose, not by outer pressures.—David Augsburger.

84. True charity is the desire to be useful to others without thought of recompense.—Emanuel Swedenborg.

85. Every saint has a bee in his halo.—E. V. Lucas.

86. No person is strong enough to carry a cross and a prejudice at the same time.—William A. Ward.

87. That man is great and he alone who serves a greatness other than his own.—Owen Meredith.

88. We take for granted that for which we should give thanks.—George W. Wiseman.

89. Some people complain because God put thorns on roses, while others praise him for putting roses among thorns.

90. I believe that God should be the daily companion of the common way and not only the refuge in emergency.—William Barclay.

91. Character is not made in a crisis; it is only exhibited.—Ross C. Crighton.

92. The Christian is a person who makes it easy for others to believe in God.—Robert Murray McCheyne.

93. Man without God is no longer man.—Nicholas Berdyaev.

94. God has two dwellings, one in heaven and the other in a meek and thankful heart.—Izaak Walton.

95. The fact of Jesus' coming is the final and unanswerable proof that God cared.—William Barclay.

96. When one person lights his torch at the altar of God, hundreds of persons will take their light from that person.—Walter Rauschenbush.

97. It is possible to give without loving, but it is impossible to love without giving.—Richard Braunstein.

98. No one ever regarded the first of January with indifference.—Charles Lamb.

99. We must stop planning our future on the basis of the defeats of the past.—Peter McNee.

100. We live in an unfinished world, but it's a finishable world.—William T. Watkins.

Questions of Religion and Life

These questions may be useful to prime homiletic pumps, as discussion starters, or for study groups.

1. How does the Mormon teaching differ from mainstream Christian faith?

2. Which hymns are most frequently sung in our churches?

3. How may the church minister to members who have been divorced?

4. Which scriptural passages are most persuasive in Christian witnessing?

5. What is the continuing legacy of Dr. Martin Luther King, Jr.?

6. How would you characterize the Christian church in the 1970s?

7. Explain the meaning of biblical prophecy.

8. In what differing ways is the Lord's Supper observed in various denominations?

9. Is there a Christian point of view regarding abortion?

10. What benefits are found in Christian symbolism?

11. Is the church increasing or decreasing missionary effort?

12. What guidance does the Bible offer regarding tithing?

13. Has the church a dialogue with organized labor?

14. How accurately can the books in the New Testament be dated?

15. What have scientists told us regarding life after death?

16. Which of our contemporary novelists interpret life according to Christian perspectives?

17. Is growing up more difficult for young people today than in former generations?

18. Should church property be taxed?

19. In what ways are the letters of the apostle Paul most relevant to our generation?

20. What are the biblical bases for ordination to the ministry?

21. Why do Christians participate in public worship?

22. What lessons can Christians learn from Jewish beliefs?

23. What does the word "sacrament" mean?

24. What particular talents do Sunday school teachers need?

25. How can I encourage my family to participate in family devotions?

26. Has anyone ever suggested that the Surgeon General label alcohol as being injurious to health?

27. Do statistics show a relationship between church membership and successful marriages?

28. How good were "the good old days"?

29. What distinguished major from minor prophets?

30. Can Christians do anything to improve the moral standards of television programs?

31. What Christian beliefs are not expendable?

32. How can we love our enemies?

33. What books should be in every Christian home?

34. What influence does a belief in immortality have on Christian living?

35. Explain the temptations of Jesus in Matthew 4:1–11.

36. Is homosexuality a sin?

37. Should a Christian marry a non-Christian?

38. How can we avoid the practice of stereotyping people and races?

39. In what ways do civil laws reflect the Mosaic law?

40. Is the Old Testament antifeminist?

41. Do public schools have an obligation to teach moral education?

42. What are the values of a sermon in a worship service?

43. Why was Jesus baptized?

44. Do world religions share any common teachings and practices?

45. What is the unpardonable sin?

46. How important is individualism in our over-populated world?

47. Why are the people in so many nations apparently satisfied with communism?

48. What is "believer's baptism"?

49. How can my faith conquer my fears?

50. What alternates are there to war among nations?

51. Are Christians expected to make sacrifices that affect their standards of living?

52. How can a young Christian withstand the pressures of his peer groups?

53. Does God know us individually?

54. What is the appeal of violence in sports?

55. What is the responsibility of government in regard to the moral and physical welfare of the people?

56. How can the church reach young people who are seemingly lost in various subcultures?

57. Who were the patriarchs?

58. Interpret the divine trinity?

59. What progress has been made in race relations during the past twenty years?

60. Should churches sponsor games of chance such as bingo?

61. How can prayer change my life?

62. Show the difference between Christian hope and wishful thinking.

63. Has secularism destroyed the Lord's Day?

64. What is the Last Judgment?

65. Is the grace of God without limitation?

66. What is the role of emotion in religion?

67. Where is the need for Christian missionaries most urgent?

68. Why do we persist in using the words "thee," "thou," and "thy" in our prayers?

69. What words from the Bible would you most wish to hear at the time of your death?

70. Is the conversion of the world possible?

71. Relate our use of energy to Christian stewardship.

72. What is the meaning of the phrase "post-Christian man"?

73. Could a united effort of all Christians change American life?

74. Define "the simple gospel."

75. What clues does the Bible give us regarding Christ's second coming?

76. Is participation in Holy Communion a privilege or an obligation?

77. Who are the most influential spokesmen of the American church?

78. Are human beings incurably religious?

79. What controls should be put on the use of drugs?

80. How can I experience the presence and guidance of the Holy Spirit?

81. Are churches effectively using the time and talents of senior citizens?

82. What makes a Christian college "Christian"?

83. What are the most persuasive arguments against premarital sexual relationships?

84. Has the church been sufficiently aggressive in working for meaningful equality between the sexes?

85. Why do some churches grow and others decline in membership?

86. Why do some Bibles include the Apocrypha and others do not?

87. Do most Christians who hold public office find it necessary to compromise their Christian convictions?

88. What can the local church do to alleviate world hunger?

89. What must I do to be saved?

90. Is faith healing a gift which God bestows on a chosen few?

91. What is the ministry of the Holy Spirit?

92. Why should children be encouraged to memorize Bible verses?

93. Are there any Christian martyrs in the twentieth century?

94. Has the church too greatly accommodated itself to the world?

95. Should we expect or encourage sincere Christians to interpret Christ's teachings differently?

96. Should the church exclude known homosexuals from membership?

97. What achievements has the church made in our century?

98. Will God forgive my sins?

99. Can the mercy and wrath of God be reconciled?

100. How has the incarnation of Jesus Christ altered the course of history?

The Idea Box

TABLEAU. Thirteen men of the North Dade Community Church in Miami, Florida, on Maundy Thursday presented a living Lord's Supper. In a tableau suggesting da Vinci's painting, each disciple in turn told of his first meeting with Christ and of what that meeting meant to him. Then the pastor, portraying the role of Christ, offered communion to all worshipers.—*The Church Herald.*

BIRTHDAY PARTY. To celebrate Pentecost the members of the Central United Protestant Church in Richland, Washington, hold a birthday party for the church and invite those attending to wear something red, provide red stoles and bright helium balloons for everyone, serve birthday cake, and extend a warm welcome to members received into the church fellowship during the preceding year.

TAPE EXCHANGE. To emphasize the character of world Christianity on World Communion Sunday, exchange a cassette tape with a congregation in an overseas mission church. The tape might include a prayer, choral selections, or the serving of the bread and wine in the native language of the exchange churches.

THINKING GLOBALLY.   How may the breadth of the Christmas commitment be made more vivid on World Communion Sunday?

Place a large globe of the world on the communion table or suspend a globe above the altar.

Display in the chancel flags representing the nations native to members of the congregation. A rack of small flags from world nations might be borrowed from the local Rotary Club.

Invite exchange students from area schools and colleges to participate in communion worship.

Select and identify hymns and choral numbers representative of overseas Christian talent.

THANK YOU LETTERS.   Members of the First United Church of Christ in Richmond, Virginia, were invited to write letters to persons to whom they wished to express gratitude. The letters, placed in offering plates in the narthex before the Thanksgiving day service, were later carried to the altar and dedicated before being mailed.—*A.D.*

SEED MONEY.   To involve personal involvement in missions the Southside United Protestant Church in Richland, Washington, gives each cooperating member "seed money," a dollar bill, which he is to invest in an activity that will make it grow. One person bought a fishing license and sold the fish he caught. Another purchased cleaning supplies for a car wash. Other projects included back yard sales, handcraft items, banners, and paintings. At harvest time, the first Sunday in Advent, the average yield was tenfold. "Seed money" represents mission monies above and beyond the regular support to missions.

CHRISTMAS HOMES.   Prepare for next year's Christmas program by having an amateur photographer in your church visit members' homes this Christmas to take pictures showing how families make Christ central at Christmas in their households. Add an appropriate narration and a musical background, and next Christmas you will have a program of particular appeal.—*The Preacher's Magazine.*

PRAYER PARTNERS ANONYMOUS.   Members of the First Baptist Church in Arkansas City, Kansas, are invited to sign up for one-month periods as participants in "Prayer Partners Anonymous." The list of volunteers is included each month in the church newsletter, and anyone may call a person listed and ask that his special need become a matter for intercessory prayer. The caller need not reveal his identity to the prayer partner, he may ask that the partner pray with him, or he may request a relationship in prayer that continues for several weeks. The prayer partner honors all confidences shared with him and reveals to no one the names of those contacting him.

SHEPHERDING.   A number of women in the West Side Cumberland Presbyterian Church in Nashville, Tennessee, serve for thirteen-week periods as "shepherds" who check each Sunday on the attendance of members on their individual lists and contact those who are absent, not to discipline or to criticize but to let them know they were missed and to encourage their attendance.

LOVE PANTRY.   A room in the education building of the Carrollton Avenue Church of Christ in New Orleans, Louisiana, has been designated as the "Children's Love Pantry" where the youngsters in the Sunday school learn of God's concern for the needy in the community by collecting and arranging on the shelves canned goods which are brought to each church service.

SECOND MILE CORNER.   The newsletter of the Church of Christ in Catlin, Illinois, includes a "Second Mile Corner" that tells of persons in the congregation who render outstanding service for the cause of

Christ. Anyone may suggest names of "second milers."—*Lookout.*

GUEST DAY. To encourage those who have been intending but delaying in inviting neighbors and friends to attend church with them, the Westwood Hills Christian Church in Los Angeles, California, each year schedules a Guest Day. Following worship an informal brunch is served, and an opportunity is provided for friends and strangers to meet one another.

MISSION MISSIVES. On a bulletin board in the foyer of the First Covenant Church in Minneapolis, Minnesota, are posted letters and other communications from missionaries whose work is supported by the congregation. News and letters are displayed and kept up-to-date by members of the missionary committee of the church.

BACKYARD CLUBS. Following the close of Vacation Bible School, the Northwest Baptist Church in Austin, Texas, reached out to other children in the community through "Backyard Bible Clubs" which were conducted in backyards, parks, and vacant lots, each club meeting for ninety minutes on five successive weekdays.

INTERPRETATION. The First Baptist Church in Seattle, Washington, provides participation by the deaf in Sunday worship through the interpretation of ritual and sermon in sign language.

SCRIPTURAL RESPONSE. The nominating committee of the First United Baptist Church in Lowell, Massachusetts, circulated the following list of common alibis and scriptural responses:

(a) "I'd rather not do anything this year. I've done my share, and now it's someone else's turn." Rev. 2:10.

(b) "I know plenty of people who never help. Call them." Rom. 14:12.

(c) "There are many people better qualified than I am." John 21:20–22.

(d) "You won't catch me serving on another committee. People do little more than find fault." Eph. 6:5–7.

(e) "I've decided to take this year off."

Ask me next year." Luke 9:23.

(f) "I'm not trained for the job." II Cor. 12:9.

PRAYER CHAIN. Do you have a special need in your church? Set up a prayer chain. List the people of the congregation at random, telling the first person when he has prayed for that special need to call the next person on the list. Urge everyone to keep the chain going.—Asa H. Sparks.

AGAPE. On the agape bulletin board of the First Church of the Nazarene in Lansing, Michigan, are posted lists of specific items requested by missionaries, and those attending church are invited to initial individual requests. In this way the whole church is given an opportunity to share in the work of the mission emphasis groups.

INTERCESSION. At regularly scheduled hours the sanctuary of the Groce United Methodist Church in Asheville, North Carolina, is open for those wishing to engage in intercessory prayer. Available near the altar are 3 x 5 inch cards on which prayer concerns may be written so that others may read them and offer supportive prayers.

FOLLOW UP. On Bible Presentation Sunday all third graders attending the worship services of the Central United Protestant Church in Richland, Washington, are given copies of *The Living Bible* designed especially for children and are invited to attend a special class on subsequent Sundays in which they are helped to discover ways of using the Bible.

CARTOON BOOK. Adding imagination to its evangelistic ministry in Harlem, the Church of the Master in New York City sponsored a contest featuring black-oriented cartoons based on episodes in the book of Genesis. Fifteen young people were selected as having talent and engaged in a summer-long artistic endeavor under the guidance of professional writers and cartoonists to prepare panels for publication.

SUPPORTING MISSIONS. How many Christmas cards are exchanged among members and friends in your church? The total would be hundreds and perhaps thousands and the expense, including postage, proportionately high. The Community Presbyterian Church in Malverne, New York, provides an alternative in which no one is overlooked in exchanging greetings and mission giving is enhanced. The people in the parish are invited to send a card to the church. The cards are displayed in the nave, and members are asked to donate the savings to the mission causes of the church.

ADVENT ASSIGNMENT. During Advent, members of the First United Presbyterian Church in Alliance, Ohio, were asked to complete the statement, "If I could live my life over again, I would—" More than fifty responded. Representative replies: "develop my natural talents," "be more thoughtful of others and less critical," and "enjoy Christ more in daily living." The anonymous answers formed the basis of the pastor's New Year communion meditation on the text: "I don't do the good I want to do; instead I do the evil I do not want to do. . . . Who will rescue me?" (Rom. 7:19, 24, GNMM.)

MAYFLOWER SERVICE. On Thanksgiving Eve members of the United Church of Christ in Merton, Wisconsin, held a shipboard service similar to those of the Pilgrims during their two-month voyage on the *Mayflower*. The congregation crowded into a twenty-foot area, the approximate size of the *Mayflower* cabin, and each wore a name tag of a passenger who remained in the new land. The service followed the Separatist form, and the sermon was a compilation of extracts from the sermons and letters of Pastor John Robinson. In the background a tape recorder provided the sound of water splashing against the hull of a ship.

HELP WANTED. The Community Church at the Circle (UCC) in Mount Vernon, New York, solicited new choir members by including the following in the church newsletter:

Positions open. In soprano, alto, tenor, and bass sections. No others need apply.

Physical qualifications. Must be able to carry hymnal, folder, and musical notes, must have sufficient vision to see the director, and must hear well enough to listen to other choir members.

Age limit. All whose voices have matured.

Experience. Singing or humming in the shower or elsewhere.

Wages. Guaranteed satisfaction and joy in serving the Lord.

Advancement. Members who demonstrate unusual ability and courage may sing solo parts.

Hours. Approximately one hour on Wednesday nights and seventy-five minutes on Sunday mornings.

Retirement. When the voice begins to sing two notes at the same time, the musician is gratefully permitted to sit in a pew and enjoy the God-given talents of others.

PLANT TABLE. In the narthex of the Westbrook Park United Methodist Church in Canton, Ohio, is a "plant table" where members may leave plants and cuttings for distribution to shut-ins, the hospitalized, and others.

Daily Bible Reading Guide for 1979

JANUARY.   *Theme: Our one prayer. 1:* John 17:11–26; *2:* John 11:1–44; *3:* John 14:-12–24; *4:* John 15:1–11; *5:* John 16:16–33; *6:* Matt. 6:1–18; *7 (Sunday):* Matt. 7:1–12; *8:* Matt. 8:1–13; *9:* Matt. 18:15–35; *10:* Matt. 23:1–14; *11:* Mark 11:12–25; *12:* Mark 14:32–42; *13:* Luke 6:12–38; *14 (Sunday):* Luke 9:18–27; *15:* Luke 9:28–43; *16:* Luke 11:1–13; *17:* Luke 18:1–14; *18:* Luke 18:31–43; *19:* Luke 21:29–38; *20:* Acts 1:12–26; *21 (Sunday):* Acts 4:23–37; *22:* Acts 10:1–8; *23:* Acts 10:9–33; *24:* Acts 12:1–17; *25:* Rom. 8:22–39; *26:* Eph. 3; *27:* Eph. 6; *28 (Sunday):* Phil. 4; *29:* Col. 4; *30:* I Thess. 5; *31:* I Tim. 2:1–8.

FEBRUARY. *Theme: The Lord's people. 1:* Lev. 19:1–18; *2:* Lev. 19:30–37; *3:* Prov. 22; *4 (Sunday):* Prov. 25; *5:* Mal. 2:1–10; *6:* Matt. 5:21–48; *7:* Matt. 25:31–46; *8:* Mark 3:19–35; *9:* Mark 12:28–44; *10:* Luke 10:25–37; *11 (Sunday):* John 13:31–38; *12:* Acts 11; *13:* Acts 17:22–34; *14:* Rom. 12; *15:* Rom. 13; *16:* Rom 14; *17:* Rom. 15:- 1–13; *18 (Sunday):* I Cor. 8; *19:* I Cor. 13; *20:* Gal. 3; *21:* Col. 3:1–17; *22:* I Thess. 3; *23:* I Thess. 1; *24:* Heb. 13:1–8; *25 (Sunday):* I Pet. 1; *26:* I Pet. 4:1–11; *27:* I John 2:1–11; *28:* I John 4.

MARCH. *Theme: Our one call. 1:* Deut. 6; *2:* Deut. 30; *3:* Joshua 24:14–28; *4 (Sunday):* Ruth 1:1–18; *5:* I Kings 18:21–39; *6:* Ps. 119:1–24; *7:* Ps. 119:25–48; *8:* Isa. 2:- 1–4; *9:* Isa. 6:1–8; *10:* Isa. 45; *11 (Sunday):* Isa. 55; *12:* Jer. 29:1–14; *13:* Ezek. 33:- 1–16; *14:* Joel 2:12–32; *15:* Matt. 22:1–22; *16:* Mark 1:14–28; *17:* Mark 10:17–31; *18 (Sunday):* Luke 12:1–12; *19:* Luke 14:1–14; *20:* Luke 14:15–35; *21:* John 4:1–26; *22:* Acts 8:26–40; *23:* Acts 16:1–18; *24:* Rom. 5; *25 (Sunday):* II Cor. 5; *26:* II Tim. 2; *27:* Titus 2; *28:* I John 5; *29:* Rev. 1; *30:* Rev. 20; *31:* Rev. 22.

APRIL. *Theme: Our one atonement. 1: (Sunday):* John 19:1–29; *2:* Col. 1; *3:* Heb. 2; *4:* Heb. 9; *5:* Jude; *6:* Rev. 5; *7:* Luke 19:- 1–28; *8 (Palm Sunday):* Luke 19:29–48; *9:* Luke 20:1–47; *10:* Luke 21:1–28; *11:* Luke 22:1–13; *12:* Luke 22:14–53; *13 (Good Friday):* Luke 23:1–38; *14:* Luke 23:39–56; *15 (Easter):* Luke 24:1–35; *16:* Acts 2:14–36; *17:* Acts 3; *18:* Acts 10:34–48; *19:* Acts 17:1–15; *20:* Acts 26:1–23; *21:* Rom. 3; *22 (Sunday):* Rom. 10; *23:* I Cor. 1; *24:* Eph. 1; *25:* Eph. 2:11–22; *26:* Ps. 31; *27:* Ps. 111; *28:* Isa. 35; *29 (Sunday):* Isa. 43:1–13; *30:* Isa. 53.

MAY. *Theme: Our one hope. 1:* Ps. 49; *2:* Ps. 51; *3:* Ps. 71; *4:* Ps. 74; *5:* Dan. 12; *6 (Sunday):* Matt. 6:19–34; *7:* Matt. 28; *8:* Mark 12:13–27; *9:* Luke 3:15–22; *10:* John 3:1–21; *11:* John 3:22–36; *12:* John 5:19– 30; *13 (Sunday):* John 9; *14:* Acts 2:1–13; *15:* John 10; *16:* John 16:1–15; *17:* John 20:19–31; *18:* Acts 2:37–47; *19:* Acts 24:-

10–27; *20 (Sunday):* Rom. 1:1–17; *21:* Rom. 4; *22:* I Cor. 15: 1–34; *23:* I Cor. 15:35–58; *24:* II Cor. 4; *25:* Eph. 4:17–32; *26:* I Thess. 4; *27 (Sunday):* I Tim. 6:12– 21; *28:* I John 1; *29:* I John 2:12–29; *30:* I John 3; *31:* Rev. 21.

JUNE. *Theme: Our one goal. 1:* II Kings 23:1–25; *2:* Ps. 1; *3 (Sunday):* Ps. 40; *4:* Ps. 66; *5:* Ps. 84; *6:* Ps. 92; *7:* Matt. 7:13–29; *8:* Matt. 10:16–33; *9:* Matt. 16:13–28; *10 (Sunday):* Mark 2:1–2; *11:* Luke 6:39–49; *12:* Luke 12:13–40; *13:* Luke 15:11–32; *14:* Luke 18:15–30; *15:* John 4:27–42; *16:* John 6:47–71; *17 (Sunday):* John 15:12–27; *18:* John 17:1–10; *19:* Acts 1:1–11; *20:* Acts 4:1–22; *21:* Acts 20:17–38; *22:* Acts 22:1–21; *23:* Rom. 8:1–21; *24 (Sunday):* I Cor. 10:1–15; *25:* I Cor. 14:1–20; *26:* Eph. 1:15–23; *27:* Eph. 2:1–10; *28:* Eph. 4:1– 16; *29:* Phil. 2:1–13; *30:* Phil 3:8–21.

JULY. *Theme: The one God. 1 (Sunday):* Exod. 19:1–9; *2:* Exod. 20:1–17; *3:* Deut. 32:1–14; *4:* I Chron. 29:10–20; *5:* Ps. 24; *6:* Ps. 89:1–18; *7:* Isa. 61; *8 (Sunday):* Isa. 64; *9:* Ezek. 18:1–23; *10:* Ezek. 18:24–32; *11:* Dan. 3:1–18; *12:* Dan. 3:19–30; *13:* Dan. 6:1–18; *14:* Dan. 6:19–28; *15 (Sunday):* Jonah 1; *16:* Jonah 2; *17:* Jonah 3; *18:* Jonah 4; *19:* Matt. 25:14–30; *20:* Luke 4:- 31–44; *21:* John 8:25–36; *22 (Sunday):* Rom. 6; *23:* Rom. 7:15–25; *24:* I Cor. 6; *25:* Gal. 5:13–26; *26:* Gal. 6; *27:* II Tim. 1; *28:* Heb. 12:1–13; *29 (Sunday):* Heb. 13:- 9–25; *30:* I Pet. 2:1–10; *31:* I Pet. 2:11–25.

AUGUST. *Theme: Our own discipline. 1:* Job 23; *2:* Ps. 94; *3:* Prov. 3:1–12; *4:* Isa. 1:1–20; *5 (Sunday):* Isa. 40:18–31; *6:* Isa. 44:21–28; *7:* Ezek. 3; *8:* Zech. 4:1–10; *9:* Mal. 3; *10:* Matt. 19:16–30; *11:* Matt. 20:- 1–16; *12 (Sunday):* Mark 8:31–38; *13:* I Cor. 11:23–34; *14:* II Cor. 12:1–10; *15:* Titus 3; *16:* Heb. 10:19–39; *17:* Heb. 11:- 1–16; *18:* Heb. 11:17–40; *19 (Sunday):* James 1; *20:* James 2; *21:* James 3; *22:* James 4; *23:* James 5; *24:* I Pet. 4:12–19; *25:* Rev. 2:1–8; *26 (Sunday):* Rev. 2:8–11; *27:* Rev. 2:12–17; *28:* Rev. 2:18–29; *29:* Rev. 3:1–6; *30:* Rev. 3:7–13; *31:* Rev. 3:- 14–22.

SEPTEMBER. *Theme: Our one work. 1:* Gen. 1; *2 (Sunday):* Gen. 2; *3:* Deut. 10:-12–22; *4:* I Chron. 28:9–21; *5:* Ps. 34; *6:* Ps. 37:1–22; *7:* Ps. 37:23–40; *8:* Eccl. 9:-7–18; *9 (Sunday):* Hag. 2:1–9; *10:* Matt. 5:1–20; *11:* Matt. 21:18–32; *12:* Matt. 24:-36–51; *13:* Mark 10:32–52; *14:* Mark 13:-24–37; *15:* Mark 14:1–9; *16 (Sunday):* Luke 6:1–11; *17:* Luke 10:38–42; *18:* Luke 12:-41–48; *19:* John 6:16–29; *20:* John 21:-14–25; *21:* Acts 9:1–9; *22:* Acts 9:10–31; *23 (Sunday):* Acts 9:32–43; *24:* I Cor. 3; *25:* I Cor. 4; *26:* I Cor. 16; *27:* II Cor. 1; *28:* II Cor. 6; *29:* II Cor. 8; *30 (Sunday):* II Tim. 4:1–8.

OCTOBER. *Theme: The one word. 1:* Deut. 4:1–14; *2:* Deut. 8:1–20; *3:* Deut. 11:-18–32 *4:* Joshua 1:1–9; *5:* I Kings 8:1–21; *6:* I Kings 8:22–36; *7 (Sunday):* I Kings 8:37–53; *8:* I Kings 8:54–66; *9:* Ps. 119:-49–72; *10:* Ps. 119:73–96; *11:* Ps. 119:-97–120; *12:* Ps. 119:121–144; *13:* Ps. 119:145–176; *14 (Sunday):* Jer. 15; *15:* Jer. 23:18–32; *16:* Ezek. 2; *17:* Ezek. 12:17–28; *18:* Ezek. 37:1–14; *19:* Matt. 22:23–46; *20:* Matt. 24:1–35; *21 (Sunday):* Mark 4:1–20; *22:* John 1:1–18; *23:* John 5:31–47; *24:* John 12:20–50; *25:* John 14:1–14; *26:* John 17:10–26; *27:* Acts 18; *28 (Sunday):* Gal. 1; *29:* I Thess. 2; *30:* II Tim. 3; *31:* Heb. 4.

NOVEMBER. *Theme: The one thanksgiving. 1:* Exod. 23:1–13; *2:* Exod. 23:14–25; *3:* Lev. 26:1–13; *4 (Sunday):* Deut. 28:1–13; *5:* I Chron. 16:7–36; *6:* Neh. 8:1–12; *7:* Ps. 11; *8:* Ps. 33; *9:* Ps. 35; *10:* Ps. 50; *11 (Sunday):* Ps. 65; *12:* Ps. 67; *13:* Ps. 68; *14:* Ps. 100; *15:* Ps. 107:1–22; *16:* Ps. 116; *17:* Isa. 12; *18 (Sunday):* Isa. 42:1–12; *19:* Jer. 33:1–11; *20:* Matt. 9:1–17; *21:* Matt. 9:-18–38; *22 (Thanksgiving):* Matt. 11; *23:* Mark 6:30–44; *24:* Luke 17:1–19; *25 (Sunday):* Luke 24:36–53; *26:* John 6:1–15; *27:* II Cor. 9:1–15; *28:* Eph. 5; *29:* I Tim. 4; *30:* Rev. 7.

DECEMBER. *Theme: The one Savior. 1:* Ps. 46; *2 (Sunday):* Ps. 118; *3:* Isa. 9:1–7; *4:* Isa. 11:1–10; *5:* Isa. 25; *6:* Isa. 40:1–17; *7:* Isa. 52; *8:* Isa. 59; *9 (Sunday):* Jer. 23:1–8; *10:* Jer. 33:12–26; *11:* Dan. 2:1–30; *12:* Dan. 2:31–49; *13:* Nahum 1; *14:* Zech. 9:-9–17; *15:* Zech. 11; *16 (Sunday):* Zech. 12; *17:* Zech. 13; *18:* Zech. 14; *19:* Mal. 4; *20:* Luke 1:1–25; *21:* Luke 1:26–38; *22:* Luke 1:39–56 *23 (Sunday):* Luke 1:57–80; *24:* Matt. 1:18–25; *25 (Christmas):* Luke 2:1–20; *26:* Matt. 2:1–12; *27:* Matt. 2:13–23; *28:* Luke 2:34–52; *29:* Mark 9:1–13; *30 (Sunday):* I Tim. 1:1–17; *31:* I Pet. 3:18–22.—Prepared by the American Bible Society.

Biblical Benedictions and Blessings

The Lord watch between me and thee, when we are absent one from another.—Gen. 31:49.

The Lord bless thee, and keep thee; the Lord make his face shine upon thee, and be gracious unto thee; the Lord lift up his countenance upon thee, and give thee peace.—Num. 6:24–26.

The Lord our God be with us, as he was with our fathers: let him not leave us, nor forsake us: that he may incline our hearts unto him, to walk in all his ways, and to keep his commandments, and his statutes, and his judgments, which he commanded our fathers.—I Kings 8:57–58.

Let the words of my mouth, and the meditation of my heart, be acceptable in thy sight, O Lord, my strength, and my redeemer.—Ps. 19:14.

Now the God of patience and consolation grant you to be likeminded one toward another according to Christ Jesus: that ye may with one mind and one mouth glorify God, even the Father of our Lord Jesus Christ. Now the God of hope fill you with all joy and peace in believing, that ye may abound in hope, through the power of the Holy Ghost. Now the God of peace be with you all. —Rom. 15:5–6, 13, 33.

Now to him that is of power to establish you according to my gospel, and the preaching of Jesus Christ, according to the revelation of the mystery, which was kept secret since the world began, but now is manifest, and by the scriptures of the prophets, according to the commandment of the everlasting God, made known to all nations for the obedience of faith: to God only wise, be glory through Jesus Christ for ever.—Rom. 16:25–27.

Grace be unto you, and peace, from God our Father, and from the Lord Jesus Christ.—I Cor. 1:3.

The grace of the Lord Jesus Christ and the love of God, and the communion of the Holy Ghost, be with you all.—II Cor. 13:14.

Peace be to the brethren, and love with faith, from God the Father and the Lord Jesus Christ. Grace be with all them that love our Lord Jesus Christ in sincerity.— Eph. 6:23–24.

And the peace of God, which passeth all understanding, shall keep your hearts and minds through Christ Jesus. Finally, brethren, whatsoever things are true, whatsoever things are honest, whatsoever things are just, whatsoever things are pure, whatsoever things are lovely, whatsoever things are of good report; if there be any virtue, and if there be any praise, think on these things. Those things, which ye have both learned, and received, and heard, and seen in me, do: and the God of peace shall be with you.—Phil. 4:7–9.

Wherefore also we pray always for you, that our God would count you worthy of this calling, and fulfill all the good pleasure of his goodness, and the work of faith with power: that the name of our Lord Jesus Christ may be glorified in you, and ye in him, according to the grace of our God and the Lord Jesus Christ.—II Thess. 1:11–12.

Now the Lord of peace himself give you peace always by all means. The Lord be with you all. The grace of our Lord Jesus Christ be with you all.—II Thess. 3:16, 18.

Grace, mercy, and peace, from God our Father and Jesus Christ our Lord.—I Tim. 1:2.

Now the God of peace, that brought again from the dead our Lord Jesus, that great shepherd of the sheep, through the blood of the everlasting covenant, make you perfect in every good work to do his will, working in you that which is well-pleasing in his sight, through Jesus Christ, to whom be glory for ever and ever.— Heb. 13:20–21.

The God of all grace, who hath called us unto his eternal glory by Christ Jesus, after that ye have suffered a while, make you perfect, stablish, strengthen, settle you. To him be glory and dominion for ever and ever. Greet ye one another with a kiss of charity. Peace be with you all that are in Christ Jesus.—I Pet. 5:10–11, 14.

Grace be with you, mercy, and peace, from God the Father, and from the Lord Jesus Christ, the Son of the Father, in truth and love.—II John 3.

Now unto him that is able to keep you from falling, and to present you faultless before the presence of his glory with exceeding joy, to the only wise God our Savior, be glory and majesty, dominion and power, both now and ever.—Jude 2:24–25.

Grace be unto you, and peace, from him which was, and which is to come; and from the seven Spirits which are before his throne; and from Jesus Christ, who is the faithful witness, and the first begotten of the dead, and the prince of the kings of the earth. Unto him that loved us, and washed us from our sins in his own blood, and hath made us kings and priests unto God and his Father; to him be glory and dominion for ever and ever.—Rev. 1:4–6.

SECTION II. Vital Themes for Vital Preaching

January 7. To Bethlehem and Home Again (Epiphany)
SCRIPTURE: Matt. 2:1–12.

I. The wise men followed the star and knelt down and worshiped the newborn king of the Jews.

(a) Our thoughts of the wise men usually end quite abruptly at this point. But the departure of the wise men from the Christ Child is actually one of the most mysterious and important aspects of the story. For as they were preparing to leave, God informed them in a dream that they were to return to their homeland by another way.

(b) With our treasures for the king, we make our trek across the deserts in our spiritual life. Whatever the conditions or problems of our journey, we move forward with great faith and hope. For the holy desire to worship is the key reason for our visit, and it is only becoming for us, like the wise men, to worship when we choose a king.

II. In our search for Christ we are likely to meet with deceptive minds such as Herod's. For Herod possessed the desire for earthly power and glory and for worldly rule. The Herod-consciousness will destroy our hope of reaching the king. Thus we must continue to be spiritual-minded in our choices. To guide mankind in his search God has placed in the sky a star which causes men to lift up their eyes above the vain world's glory and keeps them from confusing their high, lofty aims with inconsequential distractions.

III. To worship God is our highest desire. To accomplish this we must give to Christ our talents, time, and substance, which represent the three treasures of the wise men. When we give our treasures to the king, we grow in spirit and are enlightened, inspired, and filled with new wisdom.

IV. After we have worshiped, a voice within says that we must return to our home, our work, and our everyday associations by taking a new way. The road on which we came to Bethlehem is our past filled with selfishness, greed, envy, malice, and pride. Since traveling this road, we have received new joy, and our lives have been touched by the divine. We have been reborn, for Christmas gives us a new vision, a new perspective, and a new view of life. We no longer desire the old way. (See II Cor. 5:17.)—Harold A. Schulz.

January 14. The First Christian Missionary (Missionary Day)
TEXT: John 1:41–42 (NEB).

This Johannine cameo of the way in which Andrew anticipated his Lord's command tells us three things about the missionary work of the church.

I. It tells us something about the priority of mission: *"The first thing he did* was to find his brother Simon." Andrew had his priorities right. He did not say to himself, "Next time I see Simon I'll have to tell him that we've found the messiah." He went

20

straight away to look for Simon and to fetch him to Jesus. For Andrew the mission to Simon was not something to put off until time and a suitable opportunity were available; it was an urgent call, requiring immediate action.

II. The text tells us something about the proximity of mission: "The first thing he did was to find *his brother Simon.*" Andrew did not have to go far away to become a missionary. He started at home with his own family.

III. The story of Andrew's first venture in missionary activity illustrates what may be called the productivity of mission: "He brought Simon to Jesus, who looked him in the face, and said, 'You are Simon . . . you shall be called . . . Peter, the Rock.'" Andrew could hardly have foreseen what Jesus would be able to make of his brother Simon.

(a) The fruits of the church's missionary endeavor may often seem to us meagre or even at times nonexistent. We may not be able to see what good can possibly come out of it and so very often we just don't bother or we give up. But when we do that we reckon without Jesus. Again and again in the history of the Christian mission he has produced the most incredible results out of the most insignificant and unpromising of situations, provided his servants have been ready to do and to offer what they could.

(b) The church must never despise the poor and meagre efforts of its humblest witnesses. Peter was destined to become the outstanding figure among the apostles of Christ. Yet he might never have come to the Master at all had it not been for his far less prominent brother Andrew.—Owen E. Evans.

January 21. When Prayer Is Difficult (Week of Prayer)
TEXT: Matt. 5:23–24.

I. If we did what the text instructs, the church would be empty at the hour of worship. Wrong relationships with our neighbors, which we have not tried to correct, are one of the difficulties of prayer. We cannot get close to the Father when we stand far off from our neighbor. The elder brother would not or could not come into the Father's house while he was at odds with his brother.

II. The principal difficulties result from wrong relationships with ourselves. We are critical of others. We sit too often in the seat of the scornful. We allow wrong thoughts to crowd into our minds. The "wicked whisper" drives out our emotion of reverence. When we want to pray, our minds run into far countries where we would waste our substance.

III. Our greatest difficulty is the unforgiving spirit. To forgive means more than to refrain from retaliation; it means to restore trust and to be freed from resentment. The unforgiving spirit cancels out our forgiveness. Hate and love do not mix. Before we can invite love in, we must cast out the other.—Roy L. Minich.

January 28. The Spirit of Thanksgiving
TEXT: Ps. 92:1.

I. Thanksgiving is a total response of heart, mouth, mind, and life by a man or woman, boy or girl who has seen what God has done for him or her.

II. Thanksgiving is a reciprocal expression of love and indebtedness that comes naturally after a person has confronted the blessings of God and has had his desposition changed by God's grace.

III. Thanksgiving is the praising, blessing, and worshiping attitude of life that is trying in every action, in every service, and in every work and word to say thank you to God for his abundant blessings.

IV. Thanksgiving is an attitude always aimed at God but in the process expressed as well to the instruments of his blessings —other people.—Larry James.

February 4. Fourteen Ways to Kill a Church
TEXT: Heb. 10:25.

I. Don't come.

II. If you do come, come late.

III. When you come, come with a grouch.

IV. At every service ask yourself, "What do I get out of this?"

V. Never accept office. It is better to stay outside and criticize.

VI. Visit other churches about half the time to let your minister know you are not tied to him. There is nothing like independence.

VII. Let the pastor earn his money by doing all the work.

VIII. Sit pretty well back and never sing. If you do sing, sing out of tune and behind everybody else.

IX. Never pay in advance. Wait until you get your money's worth, and then wait a bit longer.

X. Never encourage the preacher. If you like a sermon, keep mum about it. Many a preacher has been ruined by flattery. Don't let his blood be on your head!

XI. It is good to tell your pastor's failings to any strangers that might happen in. They might be a long time finding them out.

XII. Of course you can't be expected to get new members for the church with such a pastor.

XIII. If your church unfortunately happens to be harmonious, call it apathy or indifference or lack of zeal or anything under the sun except what it is.

XIV. If there happen to be a few zealous workers in the church, make a tremendous protest against the church being run by a clique.—Robert Freeman.

February 11. Are You in Love? (St. Valentine's Day)

SCRIPTURE: I Cor. 13.

I. How do we use our time, our talents, our possessions for God? Do we think mostly of what we can get from him?

II. How about our attitude toward our fellow creatures? Do we use them for our advantage or seek ways to make life better and brighter for them?

III. Whom are you in love with? Yourself? Your neighbor? God?

IV. How do you tell when you are in love? Is your love of God pure enough to endure when disaster strikes? When disappointments loom? When frustrations dominate? When it costs something of self?—E. Paul Hovey.

February 18. The Church's Calling

TEXT: Eph. 1:24.

I. God calls his elect to show forth Christ's earthly life, his love, his faithfulness, his healing, and his hope to the nations.

II. God calls his church to remember that even though we live by grace there is no such thing as moral neutrality.

III. God calls his elect to proclaim the Lord's death until he comes.

IV. God calls his church to pattern its life upon Christ's resurrection and promised coming again.—William F. Keesecker.

February 25. The Absence of God

TEXT: Amos 8:11–12.

Several attitudes on the part of people cause God to absent himself.

I. One is apathy. Have you ever tried to have a conversation with someone who makes it quite evident he wished you'd leave? Better that he'd argue and scream at you. Many people have no time for God. They are too busy with work, pleasure, crusades, careers, and any number of valid activities. God is absent because there is little desire to have him present. Time and time again the biblical witness insists that only those who seek God find God. He doesn't come where he isn't wanted. He forces no man.

II. A second attitude is human pride. There is a scene in Paddy Chayefsky's play *Gideon* in which the protagonist is running around the stage calling, "Where are you, Lord?" To which the angel of the Lord replies, "O Gideon, do not forsake me." As long as Gideon retained his sense of dependence upon God, he sensed God's presence. But when pride took over and Gideon began to think he had achieved his victories on his own, he could not see or hear God.

III. A third attitude is a neglect of moral principle. People can't play fast and loose with God and expect him to carry on business as usual. This is the note struck by Amos. God has refused to speak because man has refused to walk with moral integrity.—Kenneth Barker.

March 4. Lenten Adventure

TEXT: II Tim. 1:7.

I. Lent can be an adventure in knowing God. We can come to understand our Lord better; we can read more about him in books; we can speak more to him in prayer; we can deepen our love for him in worship. Through definite Lenten work for him and for his cause we can learn more of his purposes. We learn of him as we try to do his will.

II. Lent can become an adventure in coming to know ourselves better. It is a time of self-examination. It is a season for painful but purifying honesty with ourselves about ourselves. We need to face our sins, our bad habits, and our shortcomings. Lent should drive us to our knees in repentance.

III. Lent can lead us to new hope and confidence in ourselves through Christ. Unsuspected possibilities for spiritual growth may be stirred up in us. We may come to see more clearly not only our sins but also whatever good qualities we have through Christ.—William Paul Barnds.

March 11. Living in Christ (Lent)

TEXT: Phil. 1:21.

What did the apostle Paul mean?

I. Christ was the author of his life. It was as though he had written, "To me to live at all is Christ."

II. Christ was the sustainer of his life. "To me to continue to live is Christ."

III. Christ was the law of his life. "The conditions in which I live my life are summed up in Christ."

IV. Christ was the product of his life. "To me to live is to reproduce Christ."

V. Christ was the aim and influence of his life. "To me to live is to lead men to Christ."

VI. Christ was the impulse of his life. "To me to live is to be swept along under the compassion of the Christ."

VII. Christ was the finisher and the crown of his life. "To me to live is at last to be what he is and to find the crowning of all my manhood in him."—Bill Duncan.

March 18. Are You Ready? (Lent)

TEXTS: Rom. 1:15; Acts 21:13; II Tim. 4:6.

In writing to the Romans Paul expressed himself as ready to preach the gospel in the Imperial City. When he came to Caesarea and a prophet foretold the inevitable experiences which would await him in Jerusalem, his friends tried to persuade him not to go, but he said that he was ready not only to be imprisoned but also to die there for the name of the Lord Jesus. From his prison in Rome he sends this brave word to Timothy, "I am now ready to be offered."

I. Paul was ready to preach. Paul was eager to visit Rome only because he was eager to preach there the gospel of Christ. Every other ambition of his life had passed into this, "to preach to the gentiles the unsearchable riches of Christ." When Silas and Timothy came down from Macedonia, Paul was "constrained by the word" or as William Ramsay renders it, "wholly absorbed in preaching." The urgency of his message burned like a fire in his bones. His passion to win men for Christ was a divine constraint which gave him no rest.

II. Paul was ready to suffer, "not only to be bound but also to die at Jerusalem for the name of the Lord Jesus." He was ready to encounter the penalties for preaching the gospel. Anyone who preached Christ in that day took his life in his hands. Paul was ready to suffer the loss of all things and to count them as trash if he might only gain knowledge of Christ and advance his cause. He was ready to suffer for the sake of him who in the form of a slave was led forth to prison and judgment that men everywhere might be freed from the bondage of their sin.

III. Paul was ready to die. "I am now ready to be offered and the time of my departure is at hand." As he sits in prison waiting for the day which is coming near, Paul likens what remains of life to him to the drops which are not yet poured out upon the altar. The rest he has given gladly and gratefully. Now he is an old man, and to the last drop he is ready to be poured out on the same altar.—John Bishop.

March 25. Key Words (Lent)

TEXT: Luke 19:48.

I. *A word of judgment.* People need a prophetic voice to tell them what is wrong with them. This is done, as Jesus did so often, by asking questions that probe our nature. In this way the speaker avoids setting himself up as a stern judge. Moreover a word of judgment alone can generate cynicism and negativism. But if the question uncovers a need it is an open-ended judgment and the possibilities become endless. It is here that "possibility thinking" has merit and integrity.

II. *A word of redemption.* The word of judgment exposes our need as in the poet's words, "Thou ailest here and here." But care must be taken to avoid setting these words over against a situation and thereby leaving it worse than at first. There are always the clergy who preach at their people rather than to and for them. In every encounter Jesus had with both enemies and seekers, his words, though often judgmental, were also redemptive. This is why he left every situation better than he found it.

III. *A word of nurture.* When Jesus told Peter on the shore of the Sea of Tiberias, "Feed my sheep," he meant nourishing people with the good news. Paul said, "Feed the church of God." No Christian can be sustained by only an initial introduction to an experience of Christ. Every day demands fresh nourishment from one spiritual source. The word of truth must be heard again and again. This is a strong argument in favor of worship and preaching. "Sing them over again to me, wonderful words of life." So many words we hear are tidings of human failure, rebellion, brutality, and death. When good news comes, however, people hang upon the words of the messenger for they receive assurance that the universe is on the side of goodness, and the will to make it their own is theirs for the asking.—Donald Macleod.

April 1. The Shape of the Cross (Passion Sunday)

TEXT: Mark 12:29–31.

What is the issue of life? Is it to be upwardly related to God or outwardly related to persons? Surely it is both, but the record indicates that he who made of his life a balance between the two became a plague on both their houses until they joined a common chorus shouting "Crucify him!"

I. Jesus was crucified on a cross because it was the death method then in use for criminals.

(a) It had been invented long before the time of Christ, probably in Carthage, as a means of inflicting maximun suffering upon the dying victim. Instant death was to be avoided in favor of slow, lingering pain. With such an assignment, men devised an implement of torture in the shape of a cross, a horizontal across a vertical, from which the victim was suspended.

(b) This is irony that history should have ready such an instrument of death for the man who was condemned because his life was expressed in the shape of a cross: a horizontal against a vertical and an outreach against an upreach.

II. The cross was firmly anchored in the earth. The vertical pointed upward. How realistic that was for the one who looked up to pray, "Father, forgive them." The arms were stretched as the horizontal seemed to extend the victim's reach. How realistic for the one who was still reaching far out toward friend and foe and embracing a criminal with the words, "You will be with me." Those who assigned Jesus Christ to a cross wanted for him only pain, but this position, so natural for him, became a base from which he continued both his God-reach and his man-reach until the shape of the cross became the shape of hope.

III. Two marks of quality stand out in this life. One, the balance between the vertical and the horizontal. With sensitive insight he fulfilled the injunction, "You shall love God, and your neighbor." A second was his personal commitment to this two-directional love. He borrowed no lives to save his own. The way of the world is to enlist armies to do the dying. In contrast Jesus began with himself: "I lay down my life."

IV. Surely the beauty that sprung from this life to live through centuries resulted from tension. In contrast to the notion that we must be free from tension, life is made for stress. We get "up-tight" over the wrong things, maybe because we try to avoid the healthy tension of love expressed. The horizontal across a vertical is a picture of love in tension without which beauty's grandeur will be missed. The violinist knows that true notes are sounded only when the strings are under tension.

V. The New Testament contains two definitions of eternal life. (a) One without the other is incomplete. John's gospel says, "This is eternal life, that they know thee, the only true God, and Jesus Christ whom thou hast sent" (17:3). The eternal always has an upward reach.

(b) The second definition is in the parable of the last judgment. Here the judge of life says to the chosen, "Come . . . inherit the kingdom . . . for I was hungry and you gave me food . . . I was a stranger and you welcomed me" (Matt. 25:34–35). The eternal always has an outward reach.

VI. To spend one's life loving God and people is to know the stress of a horizontal against a vertical, but this is the tension that makes music possible. To move with balance in both directions, up and out, is to know something of the resurrection.—Wesley P. Ford.

April 8. From Olivet to Calvary (Palm Sunday)

SCRIPTURE: Matt. 21:1–11.

What kind of a king was he? What did he want? What did he offer? What was his greatest desire?

I. He was a king of righteousness. He wanted goodness to be in the hearts of people and in the city over which he wept. (a) He went to the temple on the great Day of Atonement and drove out the moneychangers. The clamor in the house of prayer concerned Jesus, so he turned over the tables, scattered the money, and drove them out.

(b) The crusading Jesus is with us yet and still makes us uncomfortable. Much better to have the praying Jesus, the healing Christ, and the Christ of the children, but Palm Sunday shows us the prophetic, disturbing Christ. The poor, the needy, and the dispossessed heard him. They were there in the temple after others had been driven out. Naturally they would receive him, but those of us who have plenty might miss his prophetic message and even resist it.

II. He came as the king of truth. There are two things about truth. It hurts and it helps.

(a) Jesus was crucified because he told the truth about people, and they couldn't take it. He stormed the citadels of the vested interests, and they fought back as they always do. He realized that this same truth that cuts and hurts can be redemptive and saving. (See John 8:32.)

(b) Self-interest has stained this globe in blood and separated nations from each other. It's about time this world tried the message of him who rode into the heart of the city and offered himself to mankind. Even an approximation of his life has brought some healing.

III. He was the king of love. This was really his role. He rode a lowly beast of burden, a king coming in peace. There was no pomp and glory. From Olivet to Calvary he went in love.

(a) This love gives meaning to the life we all seek. No one likes to be separated from a meaningful interpretation of this life. "What is this world all about?" he wants to know. "Where did it start and where will it end? Are we isolated on a little ball of mud in this universe, or is there someone who cares?" Jesus comes to say that there is a God who loves us. He gives status to every human being who turns toward him. We are not alone in a silent universe.

(b) This is made plain in that journey from Olivet to Calvary and his death on the cross when he looked in love upon the worst that men could do and cried out, "Father, forgive them for they know not what they do." God loves us and redeems and fills our life with meaning and hope.—Thomas A. Whiting.

April 15. Design for Living (Easter)

TEXT: I Cor. 15:58.

I. This Easter conviction is the faith in which we can struggle undiscouraged for a better world, the faith that ultimately justice and right will triumph, and the faith that when we labor for justice and right we are working with and not against the grain of the universe. It is made that way.

(a) The universe is on the side of truth, goodness, and love. When we move in their direction, we can work with confidence.

(b) How desperately we need just now the assurance that we are on God's side, that justice, right, and love are God's side, and that when we labor for them we may be certain of the ultimate outcome.

II. This is the faith that keeps us on our feet in the struggle for individual, personal goodness. What normal person does not at times have misgivings? Is goodness worth what it costs in struggle and sacrifice?

(a) This Easter assurance is that human decency, goodness, and love are rooted in the universe. When I live for them, I am like the farmer and physician working with and not against the very nature of things.

(b) Easter says: "Don't be ashamed of decency, mercy, and goodness. They are eternal values. When you live for them, you are cooperating with the universe. When you spurn them, you are defying God."

(c) Through the cross and an open tomb see God's design for living. Fix life's loom so as to weave the hours and days into an eternal pattern. He lives, and we too shall live. The universe is friendly to man's deepest insights.—Frank B. Fagerburg.

April 22. Human Sin and Divine Forgiveness

SCRIPTURE: Rom. 7:25–8:1 (RSV).

We all know right from wrong, and we all fail repeatedly to obey God's laws. By all rights we deserve only condemnation. God's fatherly love however is great enough to forgive us and accept us into eternal life in spite of our repeatedly hurting him. He sets us free from the law of sin and gives us a spirit of life. He bends the rules, so to speak, making an exception for us and allowing his own Son's death to balance the scales of justice. (See Rom. 8:3–4.) How does one respond to that kind of generosity? Paul gives several answers.

I. "We may bear fruit for God" (Rom.

7:4). In Gal. 5:22 he lists some of the fruits of the Spirit. Examine your life. Do the fruits of the Spirit make clear to those around you that Christ has given you something special?

II. Paul says we respond to God's gift of freedom by setting our minds "on things of the Spirit" which lead to "life and peace." As one thinks, so he lives. (See Phil. 4:8.) If you focus your mind on things pleasing to God, your life is more likely to show the fruits of the Spirit.

III. Paul urges us to "put to death the deeds of the body" so that we shall live (Rom. 8:13). It is up to each of us through worship, study, and discussion to determine those "deeds of the body" which are harmful to us and which lessen our influence with others.

IV. In our efforts to live the Christian life, we constantly backslide. However, if we sincerely repent and intend to do better, God will forgive us. If we are open to God's Spirit, our failings will be less frequent and our transgressions less serious as we go on to perfection in Christ our Lord.—David B. Lewis.

April 29. God's Acceptance of Sinners

SCRIPTURE: John 4:5–30, 39–42.

I. *My child, I love you.* I love you unconditionally, good or bad, with no strings attached. I can love you like this because I know all about you. I have known you ever since you were a child. I know what I can do for you and what I want to do for you.

II. *My child, I accept you.* I accept you just as you are. You don't need to change yourself. I'll do the changing when you are ready. I love you just as you are. Believe this, for I assure you it is true.

III. *My child, I care about you.* I care about every big or little thing which happens to you. Believe this. I care enough to do something about it. Remember this. I will help you when you need me. Ask me.

IV. *My child, I forgive you.* I forgive you, and my forgiveness is complete. It is not like that of humans who forgive but cannot forget. I love you, and my arms are open with love that pleads, Please, come here to me! I forgive you. Do not carry your guilt another moment. I carried it all for you on the cross. Believe this. It is true. Rejoice and be glad.—Rosalind Rinker.

May 6. Ten Commandments for the Modern Home (National Family Week)

I. Thou shalt honor the Lord thy God, and him shalt thou reverence in thy home, and him shalt thou worship in his church that thy home may be blessed with his constant presence.

II. Thou shalt live "in honor preferring one another" that honor and understanding shall characterize all your home life.

III. Thou shalt recognize Christ as "the unseen guest at every meal, the quiet listener at every conversation."

IV. Thou shalt have the best religious books and magazines in thy house.

V. Thou shalt each one share the duties of the home that the joy of each member may be complete in the home which the Lord thy God has given thee.

VI. Thou shalt make thy home a rendezvous for fellowship where friends shall delight to come for wholesome fun and uplifting conversation that others may share the joy that is thine.

VII. Thou shalt rejoice and make gladness to resound in thy house that happy memories of home shall ever be an inspiration to the lives of all who live therein.

VIII. Thou shalt cultivate cooperation, family loyalty, and appreciation of each other that harmony, goodwill, and love may ever prevail in thy home.

IX. Thou shalt always speak with gentle voice and in tones of calmness, and with kindness shalt thou call to each other.

X. Thou shalt seek to make thy home attractive and inviting, a place of beauty which shall be a joy forever that thy home may be a blessing to all who enter.—Roy C. Helfenstein.

May 13. Christian Conscience and World Hunger

TEXT: Isa. 58:9–10.

I. Peter Van Breeman says: "When you eat a piece of bread, the bread ceases to be bread and becomes a part of you. It rises to a new life." We then like bread are consumed in the gift of ourselves to our fellow men and women and rise with them.

II. If we are really serious about God and his action in Jesus Christ, we realize we are commanded to recognize the solidarity of all peoples, their right to life, and their absolute worth.

III. All of the prophets and Jesus make inexorable demands on us for social justice and compassion.

IV. Our neighbor as defined in the parable of the good Samaritan is Everyman. Van Breeman says that Christ compels us to identify neither with the one who comes to help nor with the one who refuses to help, but with the one who needs help and then causes us to ask, "Who is my neighbor?" We are not at the center, but rather the one who needs help.

V. The earth and its fulness is lovingly given for all. We are stewards of the earth's food and resources given in trust by God for the good of the many and not the few.

VI. We are called to live fully in this world, engaging reality and acting responsively and responsibly. We are called to see things as they are and then to act to make things what they ought to be in the name of Christ.

VII. We are a people under the orders of a servant.

VIII. Because Christ identified himself with us and with the poor, the hungry, the sick, and the imprisoned, we are brought into an unavoidable face to face identification with them.

IX. We are reminded always that we are a part of the brokenness of the world and that we cannot be isolated from its pain.

X. We are called to work for justice even when the possibilities seem remote and the ambiguities great. The imponderables can be left to God and to the fulness of his time.

XI. All the actions and inactions of persons and nations are subject to judgments. Persons like nations are accountable for their behavior. When they behave irresponsibly, they become sick. In Prov. 21:13 we are told that he who closes his ear to the poor will himself cry out and not be heard.

XII. Structures, institutions, and patterns that are dehumanizing or which rob people of their basic rights bestowed in love by the Creator need to be changed.

XIII. Faith without works is dead. In the case of hunger the works that are fitting and proper are well defined throughout the New Testament.

XIV. The hungry are as near to us as is Christ. They are, as Edna St. Vincent Millay wrote, only "a Christ distance away."

XV. Our own self-interest and our own well-being are served as we seek to serve. —James M. Dodson.

May 20. The Ascended Christ (Ascension Sunday)

TEXT: Heb. 2:9 (NEB).

The writer argues from Ps. 8 that man was made but "a little lower than the angels." When he thinks of Judas selling Jesus for thirty pieces of silver, the mob shouting "Crucify," and the persecution and torture of Christians since the crucifixion, he feels that man is more of a devil than an angel. We may see only disorder created by man, but through the clouds of confusion we see also the ascended Christ. Here lies our hope.

I. Jesus has moved away from men's sight; he has not vanished into the "beyond" absorbed into a vague world of spirits. He has not left the world. He has moved to the center of existence at the "right hand of God." Jesus is the point of reference for us, and the burning center of creative love and truth. We are saved from a vague spirituality and a mystical woolliness. All insights lead to Jesus at the heart of things, the point of light and illumination and of inspiration and healing.

II. Jesus is not only a living, continuous existence, but also he is Lord. The symbolism "going up" implies "over" us and "above" us in authority, one to be looked up to because of his worth. The symbolism "the right hand of God" means he shares God's honored place. Here is one whom we adore when we truly see him as he is, "full of grace and truth." The essence of the right response to the ascension is adoration before the moral and spiritual grandeur of Jesus. We acknowledge gladly his kingly rule at the heart of all things, at the heart of his church, and

at the heart of our personal life.

III. In moving to the center of all things he has become available to all generations, all mankind, and all people. He has broken through the limitations of one point in time. He is more than ever the contemporary Jesus.—Wilfred H. Bridge.

May 27. Let the Roof Fall!

TEXT: Heb. 10:25.

To cover their embarrassment for not attending church, some people say, "If I come to church the roof will fall in." The usual reply is, "I don't think so, so why don't you come and see what does happen?" The truth is "The roof will fall in."

I. The roof will fall in on your house of self-righteousness, and you will see yourself as you are.

II. The roof will fall in on your house of selfishness, and you will see the heartaches and needs of others and in turn will absorb strength for your own needs.

III. The roof will fall in on your procrastination, your dishonesty with yourself, and your belief that you can be as good a Christian out of the church as in it.

IV. The roof will fall in on your belief that the church is full of hypocrites, posers, and self-righteous people. Instead you will find real men and women making an honest attempt to worship and serve God. You will find them trying to cooperate in the fight against wrong and trying to make a positive contribution to the right.

V. The roof will fall in, but when it does you will be able to see clearly the overarching sky of God's love which has been hidden these many years by the roofs you have built.—Alvin D. Johnson.

June 3. The Holy Spirit (Pentecost)

SCRIPTURE: Acts 19:1–7.

I. The Holy Spirit is a real spirit. To see lives transformed, to see homes recreated, to see men and women living with a new sense of direction and with new zest and enthusiasm, and to see churches set on fire is to know that the Holy Spirit is a real spirit.

II. The Holy Spirit is a willing spirit. He is more willing to give than we are to receive. He is more willing to bless and empower than we are to accept. Lancelot Andrewes wrote, "It is the will of God that our life should be an everlasting Whitsuntide."

III. The Holy Spirit is a sensitive spirit. James Stewart has written, "Pentecost is God's answer to a soul's surrender to Jesus; it comes after the surrender, not before." The Holy Spirit does not come where he is not wanted, is not invited, and is not expected. Pentecost did not happen in a vacuum. It happened in an atmosphere of faith and expectation. Those men and women were waiting, looking, and longing for the coming of the Spirit. What is it that hinders the outpouring of the Spirit today? Not only our pride and our prayerlessness but also our lack of expectancy. The Spirit of God is a sensitive spirit, and he does not come where men have ceased to look for him and where they fail to prepare for his coming.—S. Robert Weaver.

June 10. One God (Trinity Sunday)
Text: Eph. 2:18.

There is one question which each of us may fittingly ask himself: Am I truly worshiping one God? I do not mean that we are likely to be worshiping several gods. If we look at our text we may see the point of this question.

I. We read that it is through Christ that we have our way to the Father. This is not necessarily a true account of how you first began to believe in God; it is a description of all truly Christian faith in God. It is not difficult for us, even as Christians, to think about God in ways which are incompatible with our own understanding of Jesus. Even the thought of God as Father is only securely founded if he is for us primarily the father of Jesus, the perfect example of "like father, like Son." Michael Ramsey wrote, "We need continually to Christianize our idea of God."

II. We read that it is "in the one Spirit" that we have our way to the Father. This means that we should never forget that the God whom we worship works within us and that we "have our way to him" only if and when he has his way in us. This also means that whenever we believe that the

Spirit is at work we must test that belief by the conviction that he is the Spirit of Jesus. Wherever God the Holy Spirit is at work, the marks of Christ's work are to be seen.

III. Let us look again at the phrase "our way to the Father." No New Testament writer speaks about us all being God's children; they write about us becoming his children. Paul can even write about our need to be adopted by the one who is our Father. That is one reason why the word "brother" in the New Testament always refers to a Christian brother. Much that we now say about all men being "brothers" is said in the New Testament about all men being "neighbors," and when you think what it means to live as brothers and as children of the Father-God it becomes clear why the New Testament authors wrote as they did. The gospel of Trinity Sunday is that we and all men may not only believe that God is Father and learn what kind of father he is but may also live as his children and as members of his family. His love can be "spread abroad in our hearts."—Frederic Greeves.

June 17. Making Life Worthwhile (Commencement)
Text: John 10:10.

I. We make life worthwhile by the set of our minds. Ella Wheeler Wilcox wrote: " 'Tis the set of the sails and not the gales which decides the way to go." Sailors with skill and proficiency can move a ship in any direction, although driven by the very same winds. The same winds of adversity that blow and beat around these lives of ours can destroy some of us, or they can push others of us to the top. The difference is found in the way we think.

II. We make life worthwhile by the intensity of our struggle. I am not saying that you ought to set up mountains just for the sheer purpose and enjoyment of climbing mountains. But I am saying, never retreat when the way is hard, when it's all uphill, or when it's pull and climb and tug and fight to get to the top. You will discover when you reach the peak that life is more satisfying because of your struggle.

III. We make life worthwhile when we

show affection and self-giving love. We need to be persons who care and who show tenderness and concern to our family, to our community, and to the world at large.

IV. We make life worthwhile through an abiding faith in God. You can only deal with the outside world with an inside faith. With him you can be a match for any experience under the sun, but without him you are going to be knocked down more than once. You need always a higher hand to bring you out at the right place.—Russell T. Cherry, Jr.

June 24. What Is Right with the Church?
TEXT: Eph. 5:27.

I. The foundation of the church is right. Jesus Christ is the foundation. "Other foundation can no man lay."

II. The message of the church is right. Jesus Christ saves us from our sins and provides the way of life.

III. The mission of the church is right. Like its Master it goes about doing good by helping people and changing the world.

IV. The fellowship of the church is right. We are his body. We belong to each other as brethren in Christ. We fulfill the law of love and belong to a fellowship which even death does not sever.—Gaines M. Cook.

July 1. A Christian Bill of Rights (Independence Sunday)
TEXT: Mal. 2:6.

I. Every child should find itself a family housed with decency and dignity, so that it may grow up as a member of that basic community in a happy fellowship that is unspoiled by underfeeding or overcrowding, by dirty and drab surroundings, or by mechanical monotony of environment.

II. Every child should have the opportunity of an education till years of maturity, so planned as to allow for his peculiar aptitudes and to make possible his full development. This education should throughout be inspired by faith in God and find its focus in worship.

III. Every citizen should be secure in possession of such income as will enable

him to maintain a home and bring up children in wholesome conditions.

IV. Every citizen should have a voice in the conduct of the business or industry which is carried on by means of his labor and the satisfaction of knowing that his labor is directed to the well-being of the community.

V. Every citizen should have sufficient daily leisure with two days of rest in seven and, if an employee, an annual vacation with pay to enable him to enjoy a full personal life with such interests and activities as his tasks and talents may direct.

VI. Every citizen should have assured liberty in the forms of freedom of worship, of speech, of assembly, and of association for special purposes.—William Temple.

July 8. John Calvin on Stewardship
TEXT: I Pet. 4:10.

I. We are not our own; therefore neither our reason nor our will should predominate in our deliberations and action.

II. We are not our own; therefore let us not presuppose it as our end to seek what may be expedient for us according to the flesh.

III. We are not our own; therefore let us, so far as possible, forget ourselves and all things that are ours.

IV. We are God's; to him therefore let us live and die.

V. We are God's; therefore let his wisdom and will preside in all our actions.

VI. We are God's; toward him, as our only legitimate end, let every part of our lives be directed.—*Institutes of the Christian Religion.*

July 15. Escaping from Loneliness
TEXT: Heb. 13:5.

I. Reaffirm the unalterable fact that you are a worthwhile human being in your own right; God loves you; Christ died for you.

II. Assert to yourself the promise of Christ for a more abundant life in spiritual blessings even when sparse in material and physical qualities.

III. Seize the day and create your own best opportunities and environment; admit that no one else can do this for you.

IV. Determine to submit to the discipline of loneliness insofar as it is unavoidable in the human condition and to make it a vehicle for becoming a better Christian.

V. Take advantage of the opportunity loneliness affords for extensive prayer and meditation. Getting close to the heavenly Father will strengthen you. He is always available even when we feel most alone.—June McEwen.

July 22. A New Awareness
Text: II Cor. 4:6.

I. We need a fresh awareness of God's presence when we pray if we are to truly talk with God. This can be worth more in terms of spiritual blessings and power than any other aspect of prayer. We are never the same when we have been with God.

II. We need to be aware of God's power. If we were aware of whom we were talking to in prayer, look at the power to which we would have access.

III. Our God is none other than the creator of the universe, the omnipotent, omniscient, omnipresent one, my heavenly Father. God wants us to prove his greatness. The writer of Hebrews tells us to come boldly to the throne of grace. "Whatsoever you ask, believing, you will receive" (Matt. 21:22). God does not want us to limit him by our disbelief. Neither must we limit God by supposing that we know what he can do. We need to expect the unexpected. He "is able to do far above all that we think or ask" (Eph. 3:20).

IV. Each time you pray, be quiet first and then worship God in his glory. Be aware of his presence. Then think of what he can do, and expect great things.—Carol Pharris.

July 29. Reading the Bible
Text: Luke 4:16, 20.

I. The Bible reveals man as he is. The Bible makes no attempt to distort the facts of human nature and experience. It spells out the message of the darker side of humanity. It reports the mistakes and foibles, the errors and primitive misunderstandings of the human race.

II. The Bible reveals God as men knew him. The Bible is all about God. He comes in at the first verse, and on the last page he speaks of himself as "the beginning and the end."

(a) This is not just any kind of God. It is a very particular God. He is a God who acts, who loves, and who judges. He is a God who speaks, who directs, and who reveals himself to man. In other words, throughout the Bible we have a dawning knowledge of a personal God.

(b) Throughout the Bible we have a developing sense of what God was like and a heightened appreciation that something big was going to happen. Groping through the darkness of the Old Testament men came upon the light, Jesus the Christ.

(c) Men came to realize that in the man of Nazareth was some distinctive attribute which they couldn't quite describe in the usual terms. They came to see that he was something more. They began to call him Master, Lord, the Christ, and in the crisis of the cross and the resurrection they saw God in action in a unique way.

III. The Bible reveals life as it can be. The Bible is about God's life for man and the way life, both personal and social, should be ordered according to his plan. It offers illustrations and examples, but above all it offers the words of life, for the message of Jesus is the kernel of the whole book. And this is the word that changes men.—Ivor Bailey.

August 5. The Originality of Jesus
Text: John 1:14.

I. The originality of Jesus was found in his passionate dedication to moral principles even at the cost of alienating those who would in the end put him to death. He broke the bonds of the law and did so in the name of more fundamental moral principles. If the religious leaders had been wise, they would have seen that his approach would have saved their institutions by putting them on a solid foundation.

II. The originality of Jesus was found in the freshness of his approach. Not only had religion of his time become encased in meticulous legal regulations, but it had also become stale, lifeless, and platitudinous. A platitude is a truth which has lost power to change lives. In the content of his teaching Jesus was not much different from the prophets. He and they taught social righteousness, accountability to God, forgiveness, judgment, the need of compassion, and the claims of love. It was in the realm of the freshness and vitality of his approach that Jesus differed so much from the religious leaders of his time.

III. The originality of Jesus is seen most of all in his having lived what he taught. It is seen in his example. God's truth became flesh. It lived and walked on earth in the form of Jesus of Nazareth. It was not a mere academic statement or philosophical proposition. It became enshrined in the person of Jesus of Nazareth so that by seeing him men and women knew that they had seen God's truth.—Arthur W. Mielke.

August 12. The Christian Perspective
Text: Rom. 15:13.

I. God is sovereign in his universe. Men may and do rebel against him, disobey him, and ignore him, but they do not overthrow him, and the last word will be his.

II. Nothing can separate us from the love and concern of God, neither our sinning, our suffering, nor our dying.

III. The central purpose of the gift of life is to grow a soul and to grow in our love for God and in our love for our fellowmen.

IV. Whether or not we can see it or feel it, the supporting strength of God is present in every effort to fulfill that central purpose.

V. Nothing can happen to us that cannot in some way be made to serve the purposes of God.

VI. The only judgment that ultimately matters is not the judgment of our fellowmen but the judgment of God.—Richard Lancaster.

August 19. A Lesson from David
Text: I Sam. 30:6 (lb).

I. There is the posture of the soul which determines destiny. It is man's part to acknowledge his need and God's part to meet it. David stood at attention before God.

II. There is the promise that invites us onward. There is always a promise from God that his presence is available. David had lived enough with God to know this.

III. There is a plan which takes us to tomorrow. And that plan always includes an open, obedient heart and a strengthening, shepherding heart.—C Neil Strait.

August 26. Christianity and Sex
Text: I Cor. 6:20.

There are principles in our Christian religion that protect us both from too rigid and too permissive attitudes toward sex. They need to be affirmed positively and clearly lest in an effort to free our bodies we enslave our souls.

I. The pursuit of happiness may be a legal right, but it is not the chief goal of human life. Sexual fulfillment may be earth's greatest physical delight, but it is not humanity's highest joy.

II. When a man and a woman come together in sexual union, it is not just a bilateral arrangement but one in which society has a stake and over which God's laws must hold sway.

III. Any attempt by one person to exploit another for his or her own selfish enjoyment—whether heterosexual or homosexual—by rape, seduction, solicitation, prostitution, or enticement is immoral and cannot be approved.

IV. To a Christian all life is holy and is lived in God's presence, and all are urged to find this out if they can. But for those who cannot, and none of us can completely in this world, we are taught by our Savior to be instruments of God's compassion, not closing our eyes to his judgment but being ourselves instruments of his forgiving and healing love.

V. The sexual drive is, next to thirst for water and hunger for food, the strongest natural drive. When controlled by spirit and used responsibly in a relationship involving total personal commitment of two people to each other, it can minister to great physical and spiritual wholeness. When uncontrolled, it can be a destructive demon. God, who created it, will help us control it.—Nathanael M. Guptill.

September 2. Why Sunday School? (Rally Day)

TEXT: Eph. 4:14–15.

I. *From the standpoint of Godliness.* It teaches the Bible, which is the basis of our faith in God and leads to Christ as personal Savior and Lord.

II. *From the standpoint of education.* It trains your mind and heart along the lines of things eternal.

III. *From the social standpoint.* It enables you to enjoy the friendship and fellowship of genuine Christians.

IV. *From the standpoint of the personality.* It helps you to devote the Christian character necessary to face life's problems victoriously.

V. *From the standpoint of character.* It is the chief aim of the Sunday school to teach us to be examples of the believer in word and deed.

VI. *From the standpoint of interest.* It presents interesting programs for your delight and culture.

VII. *From the standpoint of the family.* It has a class for every age, and the whole family can go together and profit by its teaching.

VIII. *From the standpoint of service.* It affords ample opportunity to serve God and the church in activities that are not open elsewhere.

IX. *From the standpoint of immortality.* It turns our eyes heavenward and makes us realize that we must prepare for a life beyond the mortal grave.

X. *From the practical standpoint.* The hour or so spent in Sunday school each Sunday could not be expended more profitably.

September 9. The Christian Ideal in Marriage

TEXT: Mark 10:9.

Christians need periodically to reexamine the concept of a Christian marriage and reaffirm its principles in their own lives. The Bible is the textbook for family life.

I. The Christian ideal is that both per-sons come to the marriage with the intention of permanency. The two become one. This attitude is in opposition to the surge toward attachments on the basis of congeniality instead of commitment. Both persons must want the marriage to succeed. They must recognize that imperfect people working toward a perfect ideal will often fail in the task and need the forgiving love of God and of each other.

II. The Christian ideal involves parent-child relationships. Children are taught, "Honor thy father and thy mother." Respect is to be given even if one must stand against some acts and attitudes of parents. On the other hand parents should live so that their children can respect them, not only for whom they are but also for what they are.

III. The Christian ideal includes a training responsibility. Children are to be raised "in the nurture and admonition of the Lord." Parents must instill Christian principles. This is in opposition to the modern parents who say, "We will let our children grow up and then decide for themselves about their religion." This is ridiculous, for it assumes that the rest of society will not influence the child either. Society is piling a mass of ideas daily on impressionable young minds. If parents think Christian faith so unimportant that they do nothing to help a child decide for it, then he is most likely to decide against it. When children are taught by example and word that Christ is life, they most often choose life.—Earl Ray Jones.

September 16. The Marks of the Fellowship

SCRIPTURE: Rom. 15:1–7.

This passage gives us a wonderful summary of the marks which should characterize the Christian fellowship. They deal with the duties of those within the Christian fellowship to one another and especially the duty of the stronger to the weaker.

I. The Christian fellowship should be marked by the consideration of its members for each other.

II. The Christian fellowship should be

marked by the study of the scriptures whereby the Christian can draw encouragement.

III. The Christian fellowship should be marked by fortitude that gives triumphant adequacy with which one can cope with life.

IV. The Christian fellowship should be marked by hope in God's power for strength to endure anything.

V. The Christian fellowship should be marked by harmony in order to solve the problems of living together.

VI. The Christian fellowship should be marked by praise.

VII. Our Christian fellowship should take its pattern and example from Jesus Christ. He did not seek to please himself. —Bill Duncan.

September 23. Condemning the Do-Gooders

Text: I Thess. 5:21 (rsv).

I. The term "do-gooder" is a term of derision. The do-gooder is not to be admired or emulated. He is to be shunned or at best tolerated with condescending suspicion. But is "doing good" something to be ashamed of? What makes a do-gooder an object of contempt? To the extent the term makes us aware of dangers, it has validity. Religious prophets long ago warned of the sin which could be committed in the name of good.

(a) One danger is self-righteousness. A man may do good in order to build up his own ego or to draw attention to himself. As Martin Luther remarked, "He who does good to another in order to catch him and make him his own does him more harm than good." (See Matt. 23:15.)

(b) A second danger in doing good is the danger of limiting goodness to the outward display. This was an issue which caused tension between Jesus and some of his contemporaries. Jesus condemned the goodness which was superficial and gave the outward impression of goodness but failed to ring true. (See Matt. 23:27.)

(c) A third danger in doing good is the possibility of engaging in a good cause with the best of intentions but with insufficient foresight. The do-gooder can often

do great harm if his zeal is not matched by wisdom. And the world has witnessed many programs or crusades, undertaken with the best intentions, which have done great harm.

II. Unfortunately the criticism often oversimplifies the issue. The do-gooder is damned without serious consideration of the alternatives. If we are not going to be do-gooders, what are we going to be? If we are not going to seek the genuine welfare of those in serious need, what are we going to do? If the do-gooder is no longer to be the cultural or moral hero, who is to fill the void?

(a) One alternative is to glorify the evildoer, and there are those who promote this alternative. In some circles the new hero is the happy drug pusher, the jolly raper, the antisocial rebel, or the destructive anarchist.

(b) There is a second alternative to the do-gooder. People may decide to do nothing. They may "cop out." And whether this withdrawal from life's responsibilities be the stylish cop out of the mod young or the more traditional cop out by their parents who have decided to live for number one and the rest of the world be damned, the results may be equally disastrous.

(c) To those who look with contempt upon the do-gooder, flirt irresponsibly with evil, and retreat to the comfort of a self-centered existence, the counsel of Paul to the early Thessalonian Christians remains valid: "Test everything, but hold fast what is good."—Kenneth S. Barker.

September 30. Seven Social Sins

Text: I Cor. 12:26.

I. Politics without principles.

II. Wealth without work.

III. Pleasure without conscience.

IV. Knowledge without character.

V. Commerce without morality.

VI. Science without humanity.

VII. Worship without sacrifice.

October 7. Three Perspectives of the Lord's Supper (World Communion)

Text: I Cor. 11:24–26.

I. The words of institution bid us to look backward: "This do in *remembrance* of me."

The New Testament word for remembrance is *anamnesis* and means "the activity of calling to mind." At the Lord's Supper we deliberately gather to look back, to call to mind, and to remember Jesus.

II. The words of institution summon us to the present: "This *do* in remembrance of me." In the original Greek the force of this is not simply "do this" but "keep on doing this." It is a command to perpetuate the sacrament. So the instruction of Jesus is that now and for all time, as long as the faithful gather, they are to take bread and wine and "do this."

III. The sacrament has a future perspective: "For as often as you eat this bread and drink this cup, you proclaim the Lord's death, *until he come.*" The suggestion is that a time is coming when there will no longer be a need for this sacrament which calls us to remember him, for he will come and we shall be with him. There is a triumphant eschatological note here, and we miss the full significance of the Lord's Supper unless we sound it. Its strains speak of a day when Christ's people will no longer need a memorial of one who is present with them in person and of a day when the words of Jesus at the very first communion table will be fulfilled: "I will see you again, and your hearts will rejoice, and no one will take your joy from you." —Ian MacLeod.

October 14. The Committed Christian (Laity Sunday)

TEXT: Luke 10:1.

I. A committed Christian will have an urgent concern for man's lostness.

II. The committed Christian will have the conviction that Jesus' way is the only way.

III. A committed Christian will come to see that the church exists to minister, not to be ministered to, and to give itself for the sake of the world. Mission to the world is our calling. We are to take his healing and saving message to the world near and far.

IV. The committed Christian will make room for the work of the Holy Spirit. The Holy Spirit seeks to renew and bless all those who bear the name of Christ. It is through the Holy Spirit that Jesus Christ reaches out to us today.—W. Wallace Fridy.

October 21. Have You Not Read?

TEXT: Matt. 12:3.

I. On five different occasions Jesus suggested that the trouble with people was that they had not read their Bible.

(a) Some Pharisees criticized the disciples for plucking and eating some ears of corn on the Sabbath. Jesus said in effect that if they had read about David in I Samuel and about the priests in the book of Numbers they would have known that the spirit of the law is more important than the mere letter. (See Matt. 12:3, 5.)

(b) On another occasion the Pharisees pounced a trick question on him about divorce. He replied that if they had read the first two chapters of Genesis they would have understood the real nature and purpose of marriage. (See Matt. 19:4.)

(c) On Palm Sunday, when some boys in the temple started shouting hosanna to the Son of David, the religious leaders were indignant. He replied that if they had read the Psalms more closely they would have known that sometimes children get things right when their elders do not. (See Matt. 21:14.)

(d) A day or two later when he was having a rough passage with the authorities Jesus told against them the parable of the vineyard and rounded it off by saying that if they had read Ps. 118 they would have understood that initial neglect and rejection of someone can be followed by great prominence and importance. (See Matt. 21:42.)

(e) About the same time the Sadducees tried to trap him with a question about a much-married widow. Jesus made it clear that if they had really read their Bibles they would not have asked the question because they would have known that even after people die they are still in the care of God. (See Matt. 22:31.)

II. Each time Jesus made his point by asking the question, "Have you never read?" He had every reason to expect them to have read these passages. The Jews were very concerned about education. Josephus said, "Our principal care is to educate our children well." This began in the home when it was probably the father's duty to teach his son to read and write. Then attached to every synagogue there was a school at which (after 75 B.C.) attendance was made compulsory for boys. The center of this education was their Bible. The school was often called "the house of the book." Yet in spite of this opportunity Jesus identified people's trouble as either not having read or not having noticed what they read in the Bible.

III. It is the same today. It may even be worse. When we have nearly 100 percent literacy in this country and Bibles readily available, at point after point of people's need it is clear that they have not read what the Bible says about it. If Jesus were to talk with us today, it would not be very long before he would say to us, "Have you not read?" and we might well have to admit that we had not.—Tom Houston.

October 28. Who Is a Christian? (Reformation Sunday)

TEXT: I Cor. 1:9.

I. A Christian puts Jesus Christ central in his religious devotion. He sees in Jesus the perfect revelation of the nature and character of God.

II. The Christian takes the New Testament as his guide to understanding of the life, teaching, and real meaning of Jesus Christ. What Jesus said about God, the way he trusted God, the way he sought to do the perfect will of God, and the way he held God first in all his considerations become the Christian's standard for his own knowledge of the nature and character of God and his goal for his own relationship to God.

III. A Christian takes the way, the truth, and the life of Jesus Christ as the basis for determining how he should live with and relate himself to his fellow men. He finds himself captivated by the moral majesty of Jesus, seeing in him one who revealed a depth of understanding for those who are striving to make the most of their lives.

IV. The Christian reads of the way in which Jesus transformed the lives of ordinary people, and then he strives to emu-

late those fishermen, tax collectors, and others who followed Jesus because they found in him a friend who, while condemning sin, had an inexhaustible love for the sinner himself.

V. As the Christian seeks to work out a living relationship with God and his fellows, he discovers that it involves what is termed "forgiveness." He learns that he can be forgiven of God only insofar as he forgives those who wrong him.

VI. Christians are appealed to buy the basic idea that Jesus made so real, namely, that the human soul is the most precious thing in the world and that every person has the capacity to become a being of such dignity that he is worthy of being called a son of God.

VII. The Christian, like Jesus, loves God with all his heart, soul, mind, and strength, and then, following further the example of Jesus, he seeks to love his neighbor as himself.

VIII. The Christian trusts in Christ so implicitly that he entrusts to him his very life, daring to believe that this way will lead to a quality of living which is eternally right and satisfying.

IX. The Christian obeys and follows Christ, not asking "Why should I take the narrow road when the wide road is more attractive?" but asking only for strength to travel the way Jesus has gone before, believing that Christ will lead his loyal followers to the castle splendid.

X. The Christian continually strives to make applications of the social philosophy of Jesus in terms of feeding the hungry, giving wholesome drink to the thirsty, clothing the naked, visiting the sick, showing hospitality to strangers, and giving help to all who are downtrodden and oppressed. He takes seriously the words of Jesus in Matt. 25:40–41.—Homer J. R. Elford.

November 4. Drugs and the Christian Family (World Temperance Day)

SCRIPTURE: I Cor 6:9–20.

Paul suggested three guidelines for making ethical decisions which speak to our concern for responsible drug usage. Paul was talking about decisions made by each individual in regard to his own life, but I think these are also applicable to the family unit. A definitive yes or no is not a realistic answer to the use of drugs and alcohol in our society. But even a situational ethic demands love as its motivating force. The family must decide if its use of drugs is interfering with the development of loving relationships between its members and God.

I. *Is it helpful?* (See v. 12.) Does the use of alcohol or drugs enhance the relationships within your family? Or are these substances used to avoid the demands that are made upon responsible parents and youth?

II. *Does it enslave?* (See v. 12.) Any family member who is addicted to a drug not only surrenders his own personal freedom but also sells the entire family into a life of servitude. All family activities and relationships become dependent upon his habit. One person's periodic "highs" can create consistent "lows" for the other family members.

III. *Does it glorify God?* (See v. 20.) A family finally must decide where its priorities lie. Does it seek to be in mission to God and to others or is each member content to indulge his own self-gratification?—Marion B. Crooks, Jr.

November 11. Giving as Christians
SCRIPTURE: II Cor. 9:6–9.

I. Christians should give generously. The more God's children give to him the more abundantly he will bless them. If any Christian expects to enjoy God's favor and blessing, by all means he must be faithful in the realm of his stewardship. If we want an abundant harvest of spiritual blessings from our Christian stewardship, we must sow bountifully.

II. Christians should give purposefully. God would have Christians to give deliberately and systematically. Christian giving should never be a hit-or-miss proposition. Giving certainly should be universal among Christians. Not a one is excluded from this privilege. In all probability no two will have an equal amount to give, but none should be deprived of the privilege or lose out on the blessing of giving something.

III. Christians should give cheerfully. Their gifts should be presented with the full and hearty consent of their will and never as a matter of duty or in a grudging manner. They should give in such a way that they would never regret their gifts as though they had been wrung from them. "God loveth a cheerful giver."—H.C. Chiles.

November 18. Christian Thanksgiving
TEXT: Eph. 5:20.

Christian people know that giving thanks is the basic response to God by any person whose faith in Christ is meaningful. The giving of thanks is deeply rooted in the faith we claim.

I. Christian thanksgiving is not the following: (a) A warm, sentimental glow which comes upon us once a year in late November when we are reminded of the Pilgrims who invited new-found friends to dinner.

(b) A seasonal or occasional event observed as a national holiday.

(c) A national holiday when one can overeat and still maintain a good conscience about it.

(d) Something which we human beings conjure up to capture God's attention on special occasions.

II. Christian thanksgiving is the following: (a) God's gift to us of a right spirit within our hearts.

(b) Part of that power by which God enables us to respond to his love in ways which please and give glory to him.

(c) A way of life by which we continually "show forth God's praise not only with our lips but in our lives."

(d) Our essential motivation as we identify as members of Christ's body and break the bread of thanksgiving.

(e) An attitude cheerfully accepted toward the whole of life.—Herbert M. Barrall.

November 25. The Challenge of Being a Remnant
TEXT: Mic. 4:7.

Throughout the Bible the theme is repeated that God never leaves himself without his remnant. Some of the phrases used are "remnant of Israel," "holy remnant," and "tiny remnant." Yet because of the nature of the living word of God, remnant is not a static and sterile concept, but as the Israelites experienced afresh the responsibility and challenge of being the people of God, the whole idea of being God's remnant gains a richer, deeper dimension. In Israel's spiritual pilgrimage there are three dominant notes that remnant expresses.

I. *Remnant means judgment.* It is a far cry from the promise of God to Abraham that his seed should be like the dust of the earth for number to the passionate outburst of Amos to a rebellious people: "As the shepherd rescues from the mouth of the lion two legs, or a piece of an ear, so shall the people of Israel be!" The scene changes in Isaiah, but the theme of devastating judgment is renewed a century later. The prophet likens the remnant that will remain after God's deserved judgment to a few stray ears of corn or a couple of leaves and berries on a treetop, four or five solitary remnants of foliage on a bare branch. The message of the remnant is judgment. Only a remnant will remain.

II. *Remnant means hope.* When we reach the spiritual watershed of the Exile and listen to the insistent voices of Jeremiah and Ezekiel, we hear another note.

(a) Jeremiah pleads with the remnant of exiles to settle in a foreign land and wait with confident hope, not fatalistic despair. "For I know the plans I have for you," says the Lord, "plans for welfare not for evil, to give you a future and a hope." So Jeremiah, himself a prisoner, affirms the future that God guarantees for his people.

(b) Ezekiel brings a ray of light into an atmosphere of gloom and doom. To his searching question addressed to God, "Ah, Lord God! wilt thou make a full end of the remnant of Israel?" the answer comes, "I will give them one heart, and put a new spirit within them!"

(c) It is essential to note that it is God himself who will take the initiative. What we shall witness is renewal through God's spirit, not reformation through man's striving. Here the idea of remnant has changed and deepened. Not only a remnant will remain, but always a remnant shall remain. The very fact that there will always be a remnant is an invitation to hope. We have moved from the shadows to the dawning light of the continuing covenant-love of God.

III. *Remnant means mission.* The writer Second Isaiah, used by God to bring hope, the other side of judgment, to the exiles, also brings challenge: "I have given you as a covenant to the people, a light to the nations." A remnant they may be, but it is too trivial a view of God that he shall restore a remnant to their homeland just for them to lord it over others as God's elect or to start a Preserve Jerusalem Society! The saving purpose of God must reach the ends of the earth. This is the role of the remnant. It becomes identical with the role of the suffering servant.—Edgar Jones.

December 2. In the Fulness of Time (Advent)

TEXT: Gal. 4:4.

The year 1809 was a desperate and depressing year throughout the world. Yet in that year Lincoln, Poe, Gladstone, Tennyson, and Oliver Wendell Holmes were born.

I. God's timing is always adequate and accurate. "In the fulness of time" is a phrase that can be applied to more than Christ's birth. In a very real sense it is an adequate description of God's work in the context of history.

II. God's mighty hand guides us in a steady, sure manner. There are times when we see nothing. Yet underneath are taking shape the forms of victory which will be unveiled in the fulness of time.

III. God's dependable work amidst the clamor of history is a comfort to his children. It is a reminder that hope never fades with the crumbling of the present but awaits some final, appropriate work from God before writing its verdict. Into the record of history must always go the phrase, "When the time had fully come." To have faith in God is to hope for a better tomorrow.—C. Neil Strait.

December 9. The Difference His Coming Makes (Advent)

TEXT: Luke 1:51–53.

I. The first Christmas split time into two parts: B.C. and A.D., Before Christ and Anno Domini (in the year of our Lord). This separation of events in history has long been rather universally recognized.

II. The coming of Christ split the heavens open and revealed the character of God to man. Jesus was the man from God come on earth and the word made flesh. (See John 1:14.)

III. The coming of Christ split righteousness and unrighteousness distinctly, definitely, and irreparably apart. God and evil, right and wrong, and holiness and sin can forever be determined by the measure of Christ.

IV. The coming of Christ split humanity in two: those who are for him and those who are against him. (See Matt. 12:30.)—Herschel T. Hamner.

December 16. Why We Love Christmas (Advent)

TEXT: Matt. 4:16.

I. Christmas is a time of *giving* unselfishly to those you love and respect. Its spirit goes beyond self to others. Instead of thinking of how much of my goods I can lavish on myself, I think of others and try to bestow on them as much of my wealth as possible as an expression of love. Such a program is universally approved by all.

II. Christmas is a time of *joy.* Too many of our people and too much of our time are filled with sadness and sorrow. We need to climb out of the slough of despair and scale the heights of optimism by singing, "Joy to the world! The Lord is come." No one objects to joy. It is a common desire.

III. Christmas is a time of *peace.* Even armies have refused to fight on Christmas. Hardened criminals declare a moratorium on December 25, for less crime is committed on this day than on any other day of the year. All normal persons abhor war and desire peace. No wonder Christmas strikes a responsive chord universally.

IV. Christmas is a time of *love.* Hatred is a cancer in the soul producing all kinds of evil acts. Love heals, unites, and impels good deeds.

V. Christmas is a time of *goodwill.* At this season we look for the best in people, extend our good wishes, and curb ill will.

VI. Christmas is a time of *benevolence.* We not only give to our loved ones and friends, we also give to strangers who are unfortunate and needy. Food and clothing and toys are freely bestowed to bring well-being and joy to others.

VII. Christmas is a time of *music.* We sing and play, blow horns, clang bells, and rejoice. Everyone prefers harmony to discord, joy to sorrow, and life to death.

VIII. Christmas means *salvation* from sin and its effects. This is its supreme meaning. All men are sinners. Christmas signifies deliverence.—J. D. Wadley.

December 23. Wise Men Worship (Advent)

TEXT: Matt. 2:1–2.

I. The wise men were students, seekers for the truth.

II. The wise men believed their life to be lived under the light of a guiding star. They knew they were not free agents. Their life was conditioned by forces beyond their own control.

III. The wise men sought answers, and the gifts of life come to those who remain seekers as long as they are alive.

IV. The wise men were intellectual adventurers, always seeking to know more and challenged by the adventure of life.

V. When they found the Christ Child, they offered to him their gifts and they worshiped. Warned in a dream they returned by another way. Always after we worship we should return by another way, the way of inner peace, the way of inner strength, the way of joy, and the way of a Christ-filled life.—Frank A. Court.

December 30. The God of Promise (Watch Night)

SCRIPTURE: Exod. 3:13–17.

God is the God of promise. A promise is about the future; it is about something we have not yet received. Because it is about things which are to be ours in the future, we have a special interest in and concern for that future. We live in hope of the future of the promise that has been made to us.

I. When scripture and our Christian faith speak of God as the God of promise, they are relating very closely to this quality in us. When we confess God to be the God of promise, we are saying something about our future and our hope about that future. Because we have a hope for the future, this makes a real difference in the way we live our lives in the present.

II. The story embodies a conviction, born of experience and of recollection on that experience, about the meaning of man's life and about his destiny.

(a) Moses is bothered because he can't see the people of Israel listening to his account of how he came to be seized by the conviction that he should lead them out of their slave conditions in Egypt. They do not want a burning bush that doesn't burn for them! That sort of thing might be all right for some but not for hardheaded people like them! So Moses has the problem of how he is to persuade them that what he proposes is God's will.

(b) Much ink and more words have been used in attempts to make intelligible to us the answer, "I am who I am." Perhaps it is sufficient to suggest that the clue to their meaning may be found in the words of our text.

(c) This enslaved people will come to know God not because he makes every-thing true in the present but because he has a future in which his promise will be put to the test. They must trust that promise now and commit themselves to that future now. This will inevitably mean a stance of a distinctive kind in their present situation and also an attitude of an equally distinctive kind toward the possibilities of that present being changed.

(d) Scripture does not linger over the burning bush. It is not the burning bush which matters but the response to it which led to the word of promise being heard. And the impact of the word of promise is that those who hear it become dissatisfied with their present. When the God of promise speaks to them about his future, the present will no longer do.

III. Our Christian faith commits us to God's future. (a) We are people of hope in a God who has promised a future. We need to take more seriously than we do that God is the God of promise.

(b) He has promised a future and guaranteed that future in Christ in raising him from the dead. It is this hope of God's future which should shape how we live today and how we react to the situations and problems created by today's world and by tomorrow's world. There is much in the past and in the present to which we should thankfully recognize that we are in debt, yet our chief characteristic as Christians should be that we believe in the future of God's promise when his righteousness rules all life.—D. J. Harris.

SECTION III. *Resources for Communion Services*

SERMON SUGGESTIONS

Topic: Dimensions of the Lord's Supper
SCRIPTURE: I Cor. 11:23–32.

I. The Lord's Supper is a *commemorating* ordinance. That night in the upper room, when Jesus had given the bread and the cup to his disciples, he said to them, "Do this as a memorial of me." At the holy table we do this as a memorial of what God did for us when he came into our history in a unique and decisive way in the person of Jesus Christ.

II. The Lord's Supper is a *confessing* ordinance. The word "confessing" is used here in the old-fashioned way, not as meaning primarily an acknowledgement of one's sins but rather as a public declaration of faith. Because we remember the Lord Jesus Christ we must declare him to the world.

III. The Lord's Supper is a *communicating* ordinance. In and through the sacrament, when we approach it in faith and commitment, Jesus Christ communicates himself to us. In our remembering and in our confessing we do come to an awareness of Christ as Lord. And here we come to the traditional notion of "the real presence," the presence of Christ at the sacrament, the Lord whom we experience in faith when we come to his holy table.

IV. The Lord's Supper is a *covenanting* ordinance. When Jesus passed the cup to his disciples, he said, "This cup is the new covenant sealed by my blood." The disci-ples immediately recognized here a familiar note out of their Hebrew religious tradition. It was of the very heart of that tradition that God enters into a covenant with man and that God responds with mercy and grace to man's faith and commitment. Every time we come to the holy table we are enabled to renew our covenant with God and to ratify our commitment to him in faith in the assurance that he will accept us despite our weakness and failure and sin.—J. A. Davidson.

Topic: Enough and to Spare
TEXT: Luke 15:17.

The bread and wine of communion with all their deep and rich symbolism demonstrate the ample provision of the Father. There is nothing stinting in his giving and no poverty in his providing. This table speaks of the Father's abundance and of the Father who gives "enough and to spare."

I. "Enough and to spare" of the father's *forgiving love*. (a) This is what the prodigal discovered as he rounded the corner and caught his first distant glimpse of the old homestead. Any fears which he might have nourished about his reception were dispelled immediately. "For while he was yet afar off his father saw him, and ran and fell on his neck and kissed him." And these visible tokens of the father's love and these tangible signs of the father's forgiveness were all the assurance the prodigal needed.

(b) No one is ever worthy to come to this table, but we cannot doubt our reception as we do come, for the symbols of the feast are the visible, tangible tokens of the Father's forgiving love.

II. "Enough and to spare" of the father's *restoring grace.* (a) How well the prodigal had prepared himself for that moment of meeting, and doubtless all the way home he was rehearsing that speech about his unworthiness to be a son and his plea to be accepted as a hired servant. But the plea was never made, for the father interrupted him. This pitiful creature standing before him, beneath the wrinkles of high living and the marks of sin, is still recognizable to the father as his boy. He is a son, however dim the bedraggled resemblance may be, and the symbols of sonship will be restored to him.

(b) This sacrament means that God not only accepts us with his pardon but also with his restoring grace. However weak, foolish, and unworthy we are, he welcomes us to the table in his house, still seeing in us a resemblance to himself—high hopes, perhaps, aspirations for cleanness and wholeness, so that the Father's features, although eroded, are not altogether eradicated. And with the robe of his righteousness he covers the rags of our unrighteousness, accepts us at the table of his Son, and receives us not as slaves but as children and heirs.

III. "Enough and to spare" of the father's *continual sustenance.* (a) This also the prodigal discovered on his return. His hope was to return as a hired servant. That is, in the capacity of a servant who was simply hired on a day-to-day basis. And while such a prospect was better than feeding on carob pods, it was nevertheless a hand-to-mouth existence with no guarantee of regular provision. But accepted as a son, the whole outlook changes, and like the elder brother he will enjoy the father's abundance.

(b) This table speaks of the Father's provision of continual sustenance. We take the bread and hear the words, "This is my body, which is for you," and remember also those other words of Jesus: "I am the bread of life. He who comes to me shall

never hunger." And down the ages men have found it so wherever this sacrament has been celebrated.—Ian MacLeod.

Meditation: One Table

TEXT: John 13:2.

"Supper being ended" Jesus took a towel and began to wash his disciples' feet. If they were under the spell of the mystical union created by his words and actions at the table, it was to be rudely broken. From the table to the towel is the movement of this story of the upper room. It tells us what kind of Lord we worship and what kind of Lord we try to serve. Belief and action, piety and service, devotion and duty—what God hath joined together let no man put asunder.

We do try to put them asunder. Some want the Church of the Table, a place where they can forget the ledger-books and the dishcloths and concentrate on the holy communion with their Lord and Savior. Others want the Church of the Towel, a community that is devoted to cleaning up the dirt in the world around us. With our passion for finding labels, we call the one group pietists and the other activists and think we have sliced the church neatly down the middle. Surely here in the upper room we can learn that the Church of the Table is the Church of the Towel.

Jesus went straight from the table that is the symbol of his sacrifice for us to the towel that is the symbol of our sacrificial service in his name. How could he more plainly say that communion with him is not something that takes place in the recesses of the soul when we meet around the table but a response of our whole being, with all that we possess, to his self-giving love? He saw nothing incongruous in passing from the solemn breaking of the bread and pouring of the wine to a basin and a towel and from instituting the holy sacrament of his body and blood to scrubbing the dirty feet of his bewildered disciples. And he is saying in almost identical words: "This too do in remembrance of me." "If I then, your Lord and Master, have washed your feet; you also ought to wash one another's feet." To call this Jesus "Master and Lord" involves at once the practical, humble, and costly service of our fellowmen.—David H. C. Read.

Topic: Is It I, Lord?
TEXT: Matt. 26:1.

Three facts of Christian experience are implied in the anxious question.

I. It reveals *how little I know myself.* It may be that the disciples ask the question in part to justify themselves: "Surely, it could not be I!" But the defense soon breaks down into deeper anxiety. No man is sure of himself. The scene epitomizes what modern psychology is realizing increasingly—the unconscious, hidden self that lies within each of us.

II. The question reveals *how little I know my Lord.* That is our deeper problem. These men love their master, but they understand him so little. They want him to fit their plans, and they have not learned to surrender their plans for his. Even in the sanctity of this upper room their failure to understand is painfully apparent. Even at the table they quarrel as to who will be greatest. Even when Jesus has washed their feet, he must ask, "Do you know what I have done to you?" All through that evening their questions continue to reveal how little they know him: "Lord, we do not know where you are going; how can we know the way?" "Lord, show us the Father, and we shall be satisfied." Jesus' reply is full of pathos: "Have I been with you so long, and yet do you not know me?"

III. The question reveals *how deeply my Lord knows me and how deeply he loves.*

(a) Look at the scene once more. "The Lord Jesus on the night when he was betrayed took bread." W. M. Clow wrote that the apostle here is not only making a point in time, but he is also pointing a contrast between sin and grace and between our treachery and Christ's faithfulness. Think of it! On the night when he was betrayed, Jesus took bread and gave it, saying, "This is my body which is broken for you."

(b) How well he knows us! He welcomes us to his table of fellowship and forgiveness. This is what turns the judgment of the supper into salvation. It is precisely because he knows me so well that he

comes to me. It is because he loves me so deeply that he takes my sin.—John Frederick Jansen.

ILLUSTRATIONS

INNOVATION. In the days of fierce denominational rivalries in Scotland W. B. Robertson of Irvine was approached by a particularly bigoted member of another fellowship. She commented, "I hear you are introducing some terrible innovations into your church service." "Indeed," replied Dr. Robertson, "and what do you have in mind?" "I hear that you read the commandments at the communion." "Is that all you hear. We've introduced a far greater innovation than that." "What's that?" queried the lady in some alarm. "We try to keep them," he said with a twinkle.—Henry Hutchison.

THE CREATOR'S ACT. The holy communion is the creator's act through his people of binding the wounds and healing a broken humanity. Participation signals your desire to take on hope. Therefore all people confessing their frail humanity and yearning for a greater life are welcome to come to the altar and receive the holy communion.—Corita Kent.

COMMUNION AND HUNGER. The Lord's table is at the center of the Christian community. It is the source of our spiritual strength, just as the dinner table is the source of our physical strength. I can think of no better time for pastors to stress the need to commit Christians to the hungry people of the world than when the congregation comes to eat this sacred meal. And I think of no better place for Christians to commit themselves to feeding the hungry than at our Lord's table.

There is no longer time for us to hesitate about sharing what we have with the world. Lazarus is at our door now, and he is very near death. If we play the part of the rich man and do not reach out to help him, then we will eat and drink judgment upon ourselves. Our Lord will not accept our excuses. We have the power to move mountains, if need be, to feed this hungry world. If we do not start using that power, then the bread of life and the cup of the new covenant will surely choke us.—Michel D. Yonts.

RECEIVING AND EMBRACING.	The sacraments are God's message for the eye, for the whole body. One eats and drinks, and the whole man partakes of the sacrament. It is however not eating and drinking alone but surely solely and simply permitting God to say what he wants to impart to us, which is just nothing but the gospel laid hold upon at its heart in the message of the cross. To receive and embrace God's word in the sacrament, this alone matters. God acts upon us in the Lord's Supper.—Emil Brunner.

INVITATIONS TO COMMUNION

The Lord's Supper is a memorial of the person of Jesus Christ. As such it holds a unique place. It was instituted by Christ not merely as a means of conveying his gifts to us but for the specific purpose of bringing us into his holy of holies where we come into his own presence. "This do in remembrance of me." We come to the holy table not merely to remember things about Jesus' life or death or recall his teaching or give thanks for his example but primarily that we may meet with him. To come to the Lord's Supper is just like a person going to Jesus while he was on earth. To those who went without any intention of obedience he could not reveal himself. To those who went with a real difficulty he gave light. To the penitent he gave forgiveness. To the weak he gave strength. To the sorrowful he gave comfort. May you find that which you need in his presence today.

The Lord's Supper is the central act of Christian worship. Wherever the church takes root, there its life is quickened, nourished, and manifested in the celebration of the Lord's Supper. It is central in worship because it gathers up, expresses, and makes effective the whole meaning of the spiritual life. It proclaims the Christian gospel. In it God comes to us with his for-

giveness and his strength. One by one as we partake we respond to him with gratitude and awe. As one person has said: "It is the richest, the most appealing, the most mysterious, and the tenderest of all. It gathers into its fathomless depths the unsearchable riches of Christ." So may it be to you today.

Only as we receive Jesus Christ and allow him to enter into us are we able to live the Christian life. Jesus said, "Apart from me, ye can do nothing." It is the spirit that we receive from him that gives us the victory over our sins, helping us to conquer our bad temper, irritability, and pride, as well as to reject the grosser temptations of life. It is our fellowship with him that helps us to act toward one another in the spirit of love. The deepest secret of the Christian life is found not in fighting against our temptations nor in struggling to do our duty but in receiving strength to do these things. Jesus says, "Receive me." Do that today in the communion.

From that upper room in the long ago stretches an unbroken chain of light down the centuries to our own day. Through all the changes of life it stands, like a great rock, unchanging amidst all the changes of light and shade, night and day, fair weather and foul. In this supper the whole of what our religion means is expressed. Here we realize that we are dependent upon our God for everything, and we render thankful adoration to him. God loves us. He comes to us. He offers us forgiveness. All he wants in return is our love. It is all there in the Lord's Supper.

You have examined yourself. You have confessed your sins. Now is the time to express your intention to lead a new life. Be specific about it. Have you been unkind and uncharitable? Henceforth with God's help you will be kind and charitable. Have you been lazy? Henceforth, God helping, you will be diligent. Have you been self-indulgent? Henceforth by God's grace you will be self-controlled and self-denying. You alone can see the old self you are casting off and the new self you are taking on. If you honestly feel you do not want this new life strongly enough, pray this prayer: "O Lord, make me want to be the person you want me to be."

In no other service of the church does the remembrance of those once with us but now gone before come so near to us as at the table of the Lord. We are conscious of a great cloud of witnesses by which we are surrounded, and the fellowship of those whom we have known and loved is never more real than when we join in this act of communion with our Lord and Savior at the Lord's table. We are one family in heaven and on earth, one household of faith and love. Thank God for eternal life and the assurance that our loved ones are in his presence as we commune today.—Myron J. Taylor.

PRAYERS

BLESSEDNESS OF COMMUNION. O God, lead us into the blessedness of the mystery of communion with thee. Help us to bow in reverence before thy majesty, yet lift us up into a sense of kinship with thyself. Send the spirit of thy Son into our hearts that from the heart we may call thee our Father. Bestow upon us the peace that quiets every misgiving and the trust that fills the soul with joy and gladness. Since we so readily forget that it is so, remind us that we cannot have the consolations of faith without its commitments and that its satisfactions are known only to those who have imposed on themselves its disciplines.—Robert J. McCracken.

CONFESSION. We are utterly unworthy of so beautiful an hour as this. Every one of us can only say, "God be merciful to me a sinner." Thou hast given to no man the measure of any sins but his own, and we know how we have broken our vows and dishonored our sacraments. Greatly blessed, we have been ungrateful. Greatly trusted, we have been disloyal. Greatly forgiven, we have been unforgiving. We have not done justly, nor loved mercy, nor walked humbly with thee. Nor have we sought first thy kingdom and righteousness. We have put our bodies before our souls, our rights before our duties, our desires before our needs, and the praise of men before the truth about ourselves. Neglecting thee, we have made only small uses of great things and starved in the land of thy plenty. We who might have lived in glorious liberty as thy true children have lived too often as slaves of selfish passion and besetting sins. For the wrong desires we have cherished and for the evil we have done and the good we failed to do, O God of all compassion, whose name from of old is redeemer, and without whom we have nothing to hope for, by the mighty power of thy Spirit, bring us now to true repentance and of thine unwearied, immeasurable grace and bring home to our very hearts thy full forgiveness, through the merits of him who died that we might live, even Jesus Christ our Lord.—Adam W. Burnet.

TO SEE ARIGHT. Once more let the bread be broken before us, Lord; again let the cup be poured out; and grant that, remembering the Master's death for our sake, we may comprehend thy will for man. Create in us the heart to see aright what things are great and what things small, what ends deserve our sacrifice and what other goals, though prized on earth, are still no more than folly in thy sight. Save us from selling our souls for a larger home, a newer automobile, a bigger bank account, or a higher standing in the social circles. Vouchsafe that we may have the grace to live the life which, being most truly simple, is most surely profound and which, most surely denying the self, most truly gives the self-fulfillment. Increase the days when thou dost back us out of harness and when thou dost teach us how to rest and how to wait; and in the meeting of our daily problems remind us often that the word made flesh still dwells among us and that the day is yet unknown when thou art not the Lord.—Roy Pearson.

FOR MAUNDY THURSDAY COMMUNION. Almighty and everlasting God, who art the Lord of heaven and of all the earth, in whose eternity our little times are held and in whose service there is perfect freedom: we come to thee with grateful hearts on this day of quiet remembrance, and we yearn for thy Spirit of peace to find a large place in our souls. We thank thee for this Holy Week when the pilgrim church follows the footsteps of its Lord along the hard and lonely way of the cross. We come not with noisy acclaim or sounding brass or tinkling cymbals but with faces fixed on him with awe and adoration. Grant, O God, that during this brief pause in the business of our day all of us may respond in true devotion to the strength and beauty of thy sanctuary.

O thou Father of all humanity, who sent thy Son to be the savior of the world and through whose victory our life has never been the same again, help us to hear his voice calling us to watch with him one sober and silent hour. Help us to follow the pattern of his costly obedience, to enter into the fellowship of his sufferings, and to receive within our souls the power of his eternal sacrifice, so that in sharing his anguish in the garden we may in the end share his eternal glory.

O God in heaven, who did so love the world as to give thine only Son to die upon the cross, pour out that same love into our waiting hearts today; claim our wills for new ventures in thy service; and being redeemed by thee, may we walk in the light of that same love until our traveling days are done.—Donald Macleod.

SECTION IV. Resources for Funeral Services

SERMON SUGGESTIONS

Topic: Heaven According to Jesus
TEXTS: Matt. 6:9–10, 20.

The most impressive thing of all in the way Jesus speaks about heaven is the casual nature of his references. He never talks defensively about eternal life as if it were something to be debated. You can't miss the note of quiet certainty about an eternal realm with which we shall all have to do. He just assumed that this present life is not the end and took for granted that how we live now has its repercussions in the life beyond. Out of the huge number of references to heaven in the gospel there are more than fifty in Matthew alone. I have selected three.

I. The first occurs in the opening of the prayer we repeat every week: "Our Father who is in heaven." Did you ever wonder why in a prayer that is stripped down to the absolute essentials, a masterpiece of brevity, these words "who art in heaven" should be added? Jesus, who clearly found his Father everywhere, found it natural to speak of "our Father who art in heaven." He thus accepts the belief that the God who is everywhere has yet a special home, an environment we might say, but at the same time teaches us that this home is not a place to be located in the physical universe but is another sphere of existence called "heaven."

II. What had Jesus to say about what heaven is like? It is not from him that we have the metaphors of golden streets and pearly gates. If we must have some kind of definition of heaven, the only one he offers is in this same prayer: "Thy will be done on earth as it is in heaven." Heaven is the environment where nothing happens that is not God's will. Obviously Jesus did not believe that everything that happens in this world is according to the will of God. With reference to the dangers that threaten children, he specifically said, "It is not the will of your Father who is in heaven that one of these little ones should perish." Heaven is where nothing whatever happens contrary to the will of God.

III. We come to the third of these glimpses of heaven from the sermon on the mount: "Lay up for yourselves treasures in heaven." In his blunt way he makes very plain that there are two kinds of treasures: those that we accumulate in the service of mammon and those we accumulate in the service of God. To base our lives ultimately on the treasures of the world, whether money, power, or fame, is to arrive at the end of our earthly days empty-handed. "You can't take it with you," as we say. To base our lives ultimately on those heavenly qualities of love, generosity, gratitude, and trust is to find fulfillment on the other side. For you can take them with you.—David H. C. Read.

Topic: Tell Me about Heaven
TEXT: Mark 4:11.

I. Heaven will be *life with Christ:* "that

47

where I am you may be also. If it were not so I would have told you."

II. Heaven will be *an instantaneous transition*. Remember the word to the penitent criminal on the cross: "Today you shall be with me in paradise."

III. In heaven we shall *live in spiritual bodies*. The bodies we use now are to be maintained at maximum efficiency and treated with respect and care. Our physicians, surgeons, and other medical scientists do well to help us live in them long and well. It is our Christian faith that our present bodies are temples of the Holy Spirit. But one day we shall move out and on. "Flesh and blood cannot inherit the kingdom of heaven," asserted the apostle Paul.

IV. Heaven will be *life in fellowship*. "After this I saw a vast throng, which no one could count" (Rev. 7:9, NEB). It would not be heaven without those we love and who love us. There will be recognition. It would be meaningless to the penitent thief to be told he would be with Christ that very day if he could not recognize him. Christians believe in the communion, the comminity, and the fellowship of the saints.

V. Heaven will be *unlimited opportunity for growth* in character and skill, in love and life eternal. The unfinished symphony of your life will be completed. There will be opportunities unlimited. Life in heaven and now is marked by growth and by development. So will it be in the next phase of life eternal.

VI. Heaven will be *a time of adventurous service*. Don't be put off by those old pictures of a static heaven with golden streets, an endless symphony concert, and playing a harp for eons.

VII. In heaven will be *unquenchable peace*, the peace which follows pain, God's peace. "God will wipe away every tear."(See Rev. 21:4.)—David A. MacLennan.

Topic: The Good News

TEXT: John 11:25.

In the economy of God the two greatest events of human history occur within a time span of some forty hours—the cross and the resurrection. What do these re-

deeming events, later called the "good news," mean for our day?

I. The good news solves the riddle of life. Men have been asking for a long time, "What is it all about?" One says that life is a dead-end street. Another says it is a poor joke. Cynics say that it is an essential absurdity and that all men lead lives of quiet desperation. The good news solves this riddle in the one who says, "I am the way, the truth, and the life." Christ not only enables us to get it all together; he also enables us to keep it all together.

II. The good news solves the mystery of death. Death has been a shadow haunting mankind for eons. A possum will not go down into a hole unless he sees tracks coming up out of the hole. Man felt this way about the grave until Jesus. Before Christ the grave was a one-way street. Christ took care of our dilemma. He solves the mystery of death as he says, "I am the resurrection and the life: he that believeth in me, though he were dead, yet shall he live." The grave could neither hold Jesus nor yet can it hold his followers. Those who are born twice die only once.

III. The good news solves the question mark of eternity. Eternity is no longer the "grand perhaps." It is in our Father's house. I have always enjoyed going home, whether it is going home to my parents or going home to my family. One of these days when we have "hoed our rows" God is going to take us home. The good news solves the question mark of eternity in the words of Jesus, "I go to prepare a place for you."—Bill Sherman.

Topic: A Triumphant Farewell

TEXT: II Tim. 4:6–8.

In both Romans and I and II Corinthians, Paul compares a Christian's death to the death and resurrection of Jesus as he testifies to his ultimate faith that our Lord has broken the bonds of death asunder. It is out of this kind of faith that Paul describes his own death as a simple departure. And yet "simple departure" might not be quite appropriate. In the way Paul puts it, it's more of a triumphant farewell.

I. The first thing we see is that Paul had completed his task. Having finished the course of life laid out for him, he had also kept the faith entrusted to him.

II. Paul knew where he had been, but he also knew where he was going. He had run the race and had kept the faith, but now he is going to see the Lord, whom he describes here as being "the righteous judge."

III. Paul knew the award waiting for him when he reached the Father's house. "Henceforth there is laid up for me a crown of righteousness which the Lord will award to me on that day," he said.—Roy T. Sublette.

Topic: Taking the Life out of Death

TEXT: II Tim. 1:10.

Christ has abolished death. Can we really believe that? Look at the Greek word translated "abolished." It means "to make barren," "to take the heart out of," "to put down," "to conquer," "to devitalize." That is the astounding claim which Paul makes. Christ has devitalized death. He has taken the life out of it. How has the prince of life done this?

I. Christ devitalized death by his teaching. Read your New Testament with a view to noticing how our Lord uses the word "death." Only once does he use it where we would have used it. Normally where we use the word "death" he uses the word "sleep." He used it with such consistency and discrimination as to exclude the fact that it was for him a figure of speech. To the mourners standing around the breathless body of the daughter of Jairus he said: "She is not dead. She sleepeth." To the disciples concerning Lazarus already laid in the tomb he remarked, "Our friend Lazarus is fallen asleep, but I go that I may awake him out of sleep." They were so slow to understand their Master's mind that they said, "Lord, if he is fallen asleep, he will recover." Then as a concession to their dullness of mind he used the word "death" as they would use it. "Then Jesus said unto them plainly, Lazarus is dead." Where we would use the word "death," he used the word "sleep." He took the dread out of the thing by changing the word. He devitalized death in his teaching by refusing to regard the end of our physical ac-

tivities as something final.

II. Christ devitalized death by his cross. The great cause of human misery is sin. The vital principle of death is sin. Most of Paul's letters bear witness to that, and we do not understand the gospel at all if we do not know that the cross and sin were somehow for our redemption most intimately related. Paul says so plainly. "Christ died for our sins," and he died that we need not die. No man can save himself from his sins, from the guilt of past sin, nor yet from the consequences of sin in death. Only Christ can do that. He devitalized death because he dealt with sin in his cross.

III. Christ most completely devitalized death by his rising again. The cross would have been all darkness had not the light from the empty tomb streamed back upon it and lit up that darkest hour in human history to make it the brightest hour of all. Shakespeare called death "that undiscovered country, from whose bourne no traveller returns." But one traveller did come back. Christ would not stay dead but went striding through death like somebody blazing a trail through undiscovered country, carrying the frontiers with him, heading straight for the lands beyond the sunset, and bringing back with him the title-deeds.—John Bishop.

Topic: Facing Death

I. The first element in a philosophy of death would be a proper appreciation of life as a good gift of God. The most appealing gravestone inscription I ever saw was in a village in Ireland. It consisted of three words: "Thanks for everything." A delight in life should not prevent us from reflecting that we are not here on this earth forever. The true end of life is to know the life that never ends.

II. The next thing is to put the visitation of death, whether to ourselves or those near to us, in the hands of God long before it happens. We can only make sense of life by making sense of death, and the only way to make sense of death is to let God in upon it.

III. The third element in a philosophy of death is that as Christians we must get firmly fixed in our minds that death is nothing to be afraid of.

(a) It is nothing to be afraid of physically. Many ministers and doctors would confirm this. Medical science assures us that what we normally call the "agony of death" is felt much more by the bedside watcher than by the person passing over.

(b) For most of us the fear of death is the fear of loneliness and the unknown. Many experiences of life are tolerable because they can be shared. We could perhaps face with calmness the thought of death if we had not to venture into the unknown alone.

(c) Perhaps the process of being born into this world may be something like the experience of being born into the other world. If a little child could speculate, would he hate being born as much as we hate dying? He is carried, kept warm, loved, and suddenly there is a demand to go out into this cold, horrible world. But what happens? He is received with open arms, surrounded by love, and everything is done to make his entry into this world happy. Does not God know that you will be timid and shy, a little frightened, and a little bit lonely, and you shrink back from death? But there will be arms to receive you, a heart that loves you, and eyes that gaze into yours. If we have lived with Christ in this life and have known the meaning of communion with him, we are sure that he will not leave us when we bid farewell to the last earthly friend. He will go with us through the gates of death. He has said: "I will never leave thee nor forsake thee" and "I go to prepare a place for you that where I am there you may be also."

IV. The fourth element in our philosophy of death is the thought of getting ready.

(a) We smile at the old Victorian text, "Prepare to meet thy God!" But that is eminently sound advice and not morbid in the least. If we know we are bound for a different country and a different climate, it is common sense that we should prepare ourselves.

(b) The great essential of life is that a man should fit himself for entry into the presence of God. This may sound presumptuous. How can men and women like ourselves talk about living in God's presence? But this is what we can talk about, if for us to live is Christ. Christ gives us the certainty that God will welcome us. "He suffered . . . that he might bring us to God" (I Pet. 3:18). For the Christian to die is to be with Christ and to be taken by him into the Father's presence.—D. W. Wright.

ILLUSTRATIONS

PATTERN. When certain Oriental rugs are made, the foundation threads are put on a frame which is then set up in a vertical position. Small boys, sitting at various levels, work on the back side of the frame. The artist stands on the front of the rug, the side people will see and eventually walk on. From there he shouts his instructions to the boys. Sometimes a boy will make a mistake, but the really creative artist leaves the so-called mistake and weaves it into the pattern. Just so with the irregularities of life. The great master artist weaves them into the pattern. Sometimes, to be sure, it is difficult for us to believe at the time that anything good can come out of it. The pain is too great. But many are the people who look back upon some illness or even some great sorrow and say: "That was the turning point in my life. That was the time that I learned the really important lessons of life."—Homer J. R. Elford.

ACQUAINTED. One day a friend said to Horace Bushnell, "Dr. Bushnell, do you know I think that when you come to heaven at last and are walking up the street it is not unlikely that one of the archangels, or someone else near the master, will say to him, "Master, there comes a man you know." It is said that the grand old man bowed his silver head and replied, "I trust so, but I also hope that when I come to see him I shall not be altogether unacquainted with him either."

AS A FATHER. Peter Marshall told of an eight-year-old boy who had an incurable disease. Although his parents never told him, the child somehow instinctively realized he was dying. One day he asked his mother, "Mommy, what is it like to die?" The mother, overwhelmed with the tension and emotion of his impending death, rushed to the kitchen on the pretext of tending to something on the stove. Leaning against the doorpost, she prayed for wisdom and words to explain death to her eight-year-old darling. She wiped away her tears and went back to the child. "Son," she said, "do you remember when you were a wee little lad you would fall asleep down here in the living room? Yet, when you woke up in the morning, you would be upstairs in your own bed. How did you get there?" The child responded, "My daddy carried me up to my room." "Yes," the mother continued, "your father with his strong loving arms picked you up when you were asleep and carried you up to your bedroom and tucked you in bed. That is what it's like to die. God comes and with loving care tenderly carries you home with him to your room in heaven."—William R. Clark.

GLORIOUS JOURNEY.   Sir William Osler was for many years chief physician at Johns Hopkins Hospital and later regius professor of medicine at Oxford University. Among other accomplishments, he trained the Mayos. Sir William's son was wounded in action while fighting with the British Forces in World War I. Army doctors tried in vain to save him; the boy died. It was a severe blow to Osler, but he found relief in his Christian faith. During his own fatal illness in 1919 Sir William was observed writing something on a piece of paper. Later that same day he died with the paper in his hand. He had written: "And so the voyage is nearly over and the harbor is in view. It has been a glorious journey with such good companions along the way. But I go gladly, for my boy will be waiting for me over there."—Jerry W. Hopkins.

REJOICING.   Aristeides, a Greek, in 125 A.D. wrote to one of his friends about the new religion, Christianity, trying to explain its success. A sentence from one of his letters reads, "If any righteous man among the Christians passes from this world, they rejoice and offer thanks to God, and they escort the body with songs and thanksgiving as if he were setting out from one place to another nearby." What a description of Christian faith in immortality!—Arlena Hasel.

LOVE AND DEATH.   As he was dying, Michelangelo said: "I have loved marble and paint. I have loved architecture and poetry too. I have loved my family and friends. I have loved God and the earth and the heavens. I have loved life to the full, and now I love death as its natural termination. God did not create me to abandon me. The forces of destruction have never overcome creativity."

HAND IN HAND.   A small boy late one afternoon built an entire city of sand on the seashore. He built skyscrapers, service stations, homes, farm lands, animals, barns, and fences. He was so engrossed in his work he did not realize that the tide was coming in. Suddenly a mighty wave swept in over his creation, and it was all washed out to sea. The child was terrified and ran toward home as hard as he could. But all the while overlooking him was his older brother standing high on the bluff. As the tearful child ran for the bank the brother reached down and helped him up. Through the gathering gloom they walked toward the gleaming lights of home where waited rest and refreshment, further discipline, and high achievement. So at last Jesus who called himself a brother will lead us beyond the sands of time and place to our Father's house to undertake other tasks for which life has been both discipline and preparation.—Roy A. Burkhart.

PRAYERS

TREASURED HOPE.   Our Father, who in Christ didst bring us the power of an endless life and who hast given us our loved ones, we trust thee though the music of life is stilled in a soul dear to us. Thou didst inspire the affection, joy, and faith we shared so intimately. Only thou canst understand our broken hearts and dost measure our grief. Thou, O Christ, hast known the darkness of death and the anguish of forsakenness. Thou hast heard our joint prayers in happier days. Speak thy word of resurrection and life unto us. Assure us of thy conquest over death and of the vigil of thy everlasting love for dear ones. Make the light of faith to shine through blinding tears. Let the echo of heavenly music in the gospel cause us to listen for thy unending song of triumph.

Lord of time and eternity, we thank thee for precious years and enriching companionship which united heart, mind, and endeavor. Let the hope we treasured shine down the future's broadening way. Cause the night of sorrow to be transformed into a waiting for the dawn of thy kingdom. Sanctify these hours of bereavement with thy presence that we may follow thy leading through the valley of the shadow and rejoice in the glory of thy house forever. Let our dismay be changed into an awareness of a holy and wise will encompassing our own. May the comfort of friends become a mutual witness of an invisible fellowship. As we contemplate the brevity of life, may we use our remaining days in reverence and obedience, looking to thy grace to heal our wounds and to reunite us in the joy of life everlasting.—Samuel J. Schmiechen.

CALLED INTO THY PRESENCE.   O God of all the living, we thank thee for the happy memories of those whom thou hast called out of this transitory life into the external joy of thy presence. Thine they were upon earth, and thine they are still. We thank thee for their lives of devoted service, for the happy days spent in their companionship, for the example of their faith and patience, the inspiration of their words and deeds, and for their share in heaven's new opportunities of service. Help us so to live that they may welcome us with joy when thou shalt call us to thyself.

LEGACY.   Whatever we have known and loved is ours while life shall last. Help us to see, O God, that what we love becomes a part of us, interfused with our lives, blended with mind and memory, and joined to our souls. Strengthen us in resolve that the good we knew in those who have passed from us shall live in ourselves and be passed from one generation to another, immortal both with God and men. —A. Powell Davies.

SECTION V. Resources for Small Groups

DISCUSSION SUGGESTIONS

Topic: The Miracles of Christ

I. The miracle of forgiveness. (See Mark 2:1–12.)

II. The miracle of worship. (See Mark 3:1–6.)

III. The miracle of peace. (See Mark 4:-35–41.)

IV. The miracle of life and death. (See Mark 5:21–24, 35–43.)

V. The miracle of blessing. (See Mark 6:35–44.)

VI. The miracle of faith. (See Mark 9:-14–27.)

VII. The miracle of grace. (See Mark 10:46–52.)—M. Edgar Burch.

Topic: Love: The Greatest Thing in the World

RESOURCE: I John 4:7–11.

I. Love the essence of religion. (See Matt. 22:34–40; 5:43–44.)

II. Love that surpasses knowledge. (See Rom. 8:26–39.)

III. Unfailing love. (See John 17:6–15.)

IV. Love the sign of true discipleship. (See Col. 3:12–24.)

V. Deep-rooted in love. (See Eph. 3:-14–19.)

VI. Love the test of Christian loyalty. (See John 21:15–19.)

VII. The truth in love. (Jas. 3:1–13.)

VIII. The measure of love. (John 15:-1–11.)

IX. The incentive to love. (I John 3:-11–18.)

X. Love the method of redemption. (See John 12:27–33.)

XI. Love the motive in redemption. (See Eph. 1:3–10.)

XII. The persuasive power of love. (See II Cor. 5:11–15.)

XIII. The bond of mutual love. (See Eph. 2:11–16.)

XIV. Love's greatest expression. (See John 15:18–27.)

XV. God's unlimited love. (See Acts 2:-5–11.)

XVI. Let love be your aim. (See Rom. 14:10–20.)—T. Raymond Allston.

Topic: Keys to a Happy Life

I. *Face reality.* Keep in mind that happiness is a state of mind and a quality of life. There can be no happiness for the person who denies reality. Problems are not solved when we merely deny their existence. Face life as it is, and find ways of coping with it.

II. *Adapt to change.* Change is inevitable, and many people resist it. But if there is to be a measure of happiness for us, we must find ways to adapt.

III. *Control anxieties.* No responsible person can be totally free from anxiety, but methods may be found by which he may become relatively free. Control your anxieties, and do not permit them to control you.

IV. *Give of yourself.* We come into the

world completely on the receiving end. Some people find difficulty in moving to a position of giving. They ask, "What's in it for me?" They need a cause, a mission, and an aim in life. Jesus reminds us that we find life by losing, that is, by giving.

V. *Consider others.* Self-seekers are among the most miserable of persons. If life is to have meaning, we must enlarge our hearts and our hands to embrace others. We are our brother's keeper.

VI. *Curb hostility.* A surprisingly large number of problems and much unhappiness stem from self-hate. And this in turn is directed toward others. We must learn to curb such feelings.

VII. *Learn to love.* The Lord said, "Love one another for love is of God." To love and to master the other keys will lead to happiness in the highest sense.—Adapted from William C. Menninger.

Topic: The Miracle Power of Life

I. The power of loving. (See I Cor. 13.)

II. The power of giving. (See Mark 12:41–44; 14:3–9.)

III. The power of believing. (See Mark 11:20–24; John 14:12–14.)

IV. The power of trusting. (See Ps. 37:1–5.)

V. The power of confession. (See I John 1:5–9.)

VI. The power of saying yes. (See Jas. 1:2–8, 17–18.)

VII. The power of praising. (See Ps. 135:1–3; Acts 2:42–47.)

VIII. The power of blessing. (See Deut. 28:1–6.)—Harold A. Schulz.

Topic: After This Manner Pray

RESOURCE: Matt. 6:9–13.

I. The children: "Our Father" (v. 9).

II. The worshipers: "Hallowed be thy name" (v. 9).

III. The subjects: "Thy kingdom come" (v. 10).

IV. The servants: "Thy will be done" (v. 10).

V. The suppliants: "Give us this day" (v. 11).

VI. The confessors: "And forgive us our debts" (v. 12).

VII. The dependents: "Deliver us from evil" (v. 13).—*Pegs for Preachers.*

Topic: The Prophets Speak to Our Times

I. Jeremiah speaks to our spiritual charade.

II. Hosea speaks to our wandering affection.

III. Joel speaks to our inner discouragement.

IV. Amos speaks to our affluence.

V. Jonah speaks to our persistent prejudice.

Topic: The Kinds of Service the Lord Requires

I. Serve the Lord with a perfect heart. (See I Chron. 28:9.)

II. Serve the Lord with all your heart. (See Deut. 10:12.)

III. Serve the Lord without fear. (See Luke 1:74.)

IV. Serve the Lord in holiness. (See Luke 1:75.)

V. Serve the Lord with a willing mind. (See I Chron. 28:9.)

VI. Serve the Lord faithfully. (See Dan. 6:20; also Dan. 1:8; 6:4–5, 10; 10:11–14.)

VII. Serve the Lord with a pure conscience. (See II Tim. 1:3.)

VIII. Serve the Lord acceptably with reverence. (See Heb. 12:8.)

IX. Serve the Lord with all humility. (See Acts 20:19.)

X. Serve the Lord with gladness. (See Ps. 100:2.)

XI. Serve the Lord all the days of your life. (See Luke 1:75.)

XII. Serve the Lord in hope of his return. (See Matt. 24:46–47; Luke 19:13.)

Topic: To God Be the Glory

RESOURCES: Rom. 1:23; 3:23; 4:20; 5:2; 6:4; 8:17–18; 9:23; 15:5–7; 11:36; 16:27.

I. The God to whom glory is to be given.

(a) He is the God of patience and endurance. (See Rom. 15:5–12.)

(1) The source of this unity: God. (See v. 5.)

(2) The example of this unity: the mind of Christ. (See v. 5.)

(3) The degree of this unity: one heart and mouth. (See v. 6.)

(4) The object of this unity: to glorify God. (See v. 6.)

(5) The result of this unity: mutual acceptance. (See v. 7.)

(6) The motive of this unity: as Christ accepted you. (See v. 7.)

(7) Scriptural confirmation of the results. (See vv. 8–12.)

(b) He is the God of hope. (See Rom. 15:13.)

(1) God is the source of our hope.

(2) God will fill us with great joy and peace.

(3) The degree of our fulness with joy and peace is determined by our trust.

(4) Our experience: overflowing with hope.

(5) The power of this filling is the Holy Spirit.

(c) He is the God of peace. (See Rom. 15:33.)

(1) Peace is essentially a part of the divine character.

(2) If the God of peace is with us, then peace will pervade our spirit and life.

(d) He is the only wise God. (See Rom. 16:27.)

(1) Hear about the wisdom of God. (See Ps. 104:24; Prov. 3:19; Dan. 2:20; Rom. 11:33; I Cor. 1:25.)

(2) God's wisdom is revealed in the world through Jesus Christ.

II. Alternatives to giving glory to God.

(a) We may appropriate God's glory to ourselves.

(b) We may appropriate God's glory to the church.

(c) We may appropriate God's glory to the nation.

III. The manner in which we must glorify God.

(a) We must glorify God through our humility.

(b) We must glorify God through our good works. (See Matt. 5:16.)

(c) We must glorify God through our fruit-bearing. (See John 15:8.)

(d) We must glorify God through our stewardship.

(e) We must glorify God through our entire consecration.

(f) We must glorify God through our faithfulness.

(g) We must glorify God through the fulfillment of the great commission.—Ralph M. Dornette.

Topic: How Can We Help Our Church?

I. Extend a warm welcome to all who come. We can give our church a reputation for friendliness and genuine concern by letting all worshipers know that we are glad to see them and that we sincerely care.

II. Be aware of all new families within the perimeter of the church's ministry. Be among the first to welcome them to the neighborhood and invite them to the worship services, Sunday school, and other activities.

III. Witness to the meaning of your faith in Christ and to your commitment to the ministry of the church every day by the quality and character of the work you do, by your relationships with the people you meet, and by what you say. Be light and salt in the world.

IV. Pray daily for your church. Remember the ministerial staff, your fellow Christians, and especially those whose need is greatest for intercessory prayer.

V. Demonstrate an enthusiasm for your church and its program. Avoid faultfinding and unproductive criticism. Your commendations and praise create a contagious goodwill.

VI. Remember that your Christian life includes family associations and your use of leisure time. Show that a Christian can enjoy all facets of his life.

VII. Set a worthy example by regularly attending services and by participating in the various church activities. Your example is more persuasive than your words.

VIII. Use your telephone to invite friends to church and to let those who were absent know that they were missed.

IX. Be positive, optimistic, and thankful. Expect great things from God. Praise him daily for what he has done through you and your church.

X. Show your concern for a Christian world by supporting the local church and national and foreign missions with your tithes and offerings and by investing your time, talent, and contributions in worthy community projects.

Topic: Where the Spirit of the Lord Is
I. Where the Spirit of the Lord is, there is a manifestation of his presence.
II. Where the Spirit of the Lord is, there are healings and miracles.
III. Where the Spirit of the Lord is, there is divine direction.
IV. Where the Spirit of the Lord is, there is Holy Spirit conviction.
(a) There is conviction of truth.
(b) There is conviction of the manner of living.
(c) There is conviction of sin.—Wade H. Horton.

Topic: God's Word in a Personal Context
I. What God's word does for me. (a) It quickens me. (See Ps. 119:25.)
(b) It sanctifies me. (See John 17:17.)
(c) It cleanses me. (See Ps. 119:9.)
II. What God's word is to me. (a) Precious. (See I Sam. 3:1.)
(b) Penetrating. (See Heb. 4:12.)
(c) Powerful. (See Jer. 23:29.)

(d) Purifying. (See Jer. 23:29.)
(e) Protecting. (See Eph. 6:17.)
III. How God's word should be treated by me.
(a) I am to love it. (See Ps. 119:97.)
(b) I am to search it. (See John 5:39.)
(c) I am to feed on it. (See Jer. 15:16.)
(d) I am to hold fast to it. (See Tit. 1:9.)
(e) I am to preach it. (See II Tim. 4:2.)
(f) I am to meditate on it. (See Ps. 119:-15.)
(g) I am to delight in it. (See Ps. 119:16.)
—Charles Inglis.

Topic: The Promise of Advent
I. Advent is promise. (See Luke 3:21-22.)
II. Advent promises more than . . . (See Luke 4:1–4.)
III. Advent promises newness. (See Luke 3:36–39.)
IV. Advent promises freedom. (See Luke 1:68–79.)
V. Advent promises generosity. (See Luke 7:36–50.)
VI. Advent promises wholeness. (See Luke 8:43–48.)
VII. Advent promises victory. (See Luke 9:23–25.)—Pinckney C. Enniss, Jr.

SECTION VI. Resources for Lenten and Easter Preaching

SERMON SUGGESTIONS

Topic: Church Goals for Lent
TEXT: Matt. 7:7.

I. We seek to love people and to lead them to new or renewed commitment to Jesus Christ so that they are gathered into the church, the body of Christ.

II. We seek to encourage and enable persons who are members of the church to deepen and broaden their faith and to discover and use their spiritual gifts so that they may grow in faith and love.

III. We seek to respond to the needs of persons and groups with practical and specific ministries of service and compassion.

IV. We seek to affirm a scriptural style which brings inspiration, healing, faith, hope, love, and practical guidance for daily living.

V. We seek to rejoice in the diversity of worship, education, and service styles within our congregation.—Joe A. Harding.

Topic: The Relevance of the Cross
TEXTS: Mark 10:32; I Cor. 1:23.

I. Jesus is relevant because he did not avoid suffering. He chose openly to move into the heart of the nation's life, to challenge it by all that he was and stood for as the only way to bring deliverance to men, and to set men at the doorway to freedom whatever cost in human agony.

II. The cross is relevant because here is direct confrontation with evil which causes so much of the tragedy. In the events leading to the cross Jesus took evil by the throat and shook off its shams and disguises and left it naked for mankind to see it in its horror.

III. The cross is relevant because it embodies the victory of agonizing love over the assaults of evil. Evil has met its master. Mark tells us that Jesus prepared his friends not only for suffering and death, confrontation and conflict but also for victory—"and after three days he will rise again."—Wilfred H. Bridge.

Topic: The Unattractive in Jesus
SCRIPTURE: Isa. 53:1–5.

I. *There is no beauty that we should desire him.* Isaiah speaks of him as growing up as a tender plant. There is a suggestion of gawkishness. He is described as a root growing up out of dry land. One thinks of the desert. A root growing up in a desert is usually an ugly thing. Isaiah emphasizes the picture when he says there is no form nor comeliness. There is no beauty. We do not like to face the ugliness of the cross. We like to dress it up, gild it, and make it attractive. Likewise we do not like to face the unattractive in Jesus.

II. *He was despised and rejected.* He came from a lowly family. He lived in a despised town. It was said no good thing could come from Nazareth. "He was despised and we esteemed him not." When he came, men turned their backs on him.

57

They forsook him and fled. He became a lonely figure upon a cross.

III. *We hid our faces from him.* Though he hath borne our griefs and carried our sorrows, though he was wounded for our transgressions and bruised for our iniquities, though the chastisement of our peace was upon him and with his stripes we are healed, yet "we thought him suffering from a stroke at God's own hand" (MOFFATT). In spite of the lack of comeliness and esteem and in spite of the fact that he was despised and rejected, "he was wounded for our transgressions, he was bruised for our iniquities."—J. Manning Potts.

Topic: A Theological Approach
TEXT: Mark 11:9.

The value of Good Friday is largely determined by the way we approach it, and the proper approach is along the avenue of Palm Sunday, a profoundly theological roadway. This is what Palm Sunday says about the figure on the cross on Good Friday.

I. He is the Lord, the sovereign, the one with the right to command. We are wrong if we think of Jesus as some impractical idealist caught up in the eddies of some political maelstrom. Palm Sunday was planned to show the world that the crucified was no pathetic victim to be pitied but a master riding upon the backs of the untamed political forces of his day to accomplish a purpose greater than his opponents could ever conceive. The man on the cross is the Lord of all. He holds us in his hands.

II. The man on the cross is the coming one. This again is brought out by the crowds crying, "Blessed is he that cometh in the name of the Lord." Palm Sunday prepares us for Good Friday. It says, when on Good Friday you see Jesus on the cross, say to yourself: "This is the longed-for messiah. Here is deliverance being accomplished." The cross is not the fading out of Christ's work but the zenith of his work. Here is fulfillment. Here is what Christ came to do. Here is the counterpart of all those failure messiahs of the centuries past. In the crucifixion of Christ we are to see instead complete success.

III. Palm Sunday advises us that the great paradox of the Christian gospel is that life comes through death, gaining through giving, and victory through sacrifice.

(a) Go back once more to those pilgrims lining the triumphal route to Jerusalem and hear their chorus, "Hosanna, blessed is he that cometh in the name of the Lord." It was a liturgical refrain. It comes from what is called "the Great Hallel" from Ps. 118:25 and would be sung at the Passover festival while the lambs were being slaughtered for the great temple sacrifice.

(b) It would be sung therefore while Jesus was being sacrificed on a cross of wood outside the temple, even outside Jerusalem's walls, an outcast from so-called civilized life, dying on a gibbet stuck up on a patch of bare rocky ground, the macabre shape of a man's skull.

(c) The crowds anticipated that sacrificial liturgy by chanting it to Jesus as he rode that colt that Sunday into Jerusalem, unwittingly testifying to the great truth about Jesus that he would soon be a sacrifice himself, and this would be his great work on behalf of all mankind.

(d) At Calvary, the Lord, the king, the longed-for messiah would come into his own through self-giving. The triumphal procession on Palm Sunday was in fact the pathway to his kingdom. On the cross on Good Friday he established it.—D. W. Cleverley Ford.

Meditation: Second Thoughts

I've often heard it said that the same people who made up the crowd that welcomed Jesus when he showed himself to them on Sunday also made up the crowd who, when Pilate showed him to them on Friday, shouted, "Crucify him!" I don't think there is any solid evidence to back that up, and what is more, it seems to me to go against the grain of what the gospels tell us did happen to Jesus. The gospels all agree that it was the authorities—the local political authorities and the local religious authorities—who plotted Jesus' death, mainly because of envy and because they feared for the security of their own positions in the face of his overwhelming popularity with the rank and file of the citizenry. The gospels also all agree that the plot against Jesus had to be carried out by stealth by means of secret informers, an arrest under cover of darkness while the city slept, a midnight trial with witnesses bribed to give false testimony, and a hasty sentence under which the prisoner could be turned over to the Romans for immediate execution before the news of what had happened could become generally known. The reason for this is stated plainly. The authorities did not dare to act publicly because they were afraid that, if they moved against Jesus openly, the result would be a popular uprising. So I do not think we can put much stock in the oft-repeated statement that it was the fickle crowds who were responsible for Jesus' death.

Nor do I think we can put much stock in another rather shallow commonplace that one hears fairly frequently, namely, that if Jesus were to come into the world again today the same thing would happen all over again. I don't believe that. No doubt there would be those who would not welcome him, and some of them no doubt would be in positions of authority. But they would have a harder time in putting Jesus out of the way than did the men of old who encompassed his death with such apparent ease because the fact that Jesus lived has not been without its effect on the world. His teaching has deepened the dimensions of our moral thinking, and his life and death and resurrection have broadened the horizons of our understanding of the things of the spirit. We have changed because he walked among us. And if he came again today, I think he would find many more men and women who would be ready not only to welcome him but also to stand beside him to the end.—Charles H. Buck, Jr.

Topic: King Eternal
TEXT: Matt. 27:37.

I. The sign said the crucified man was a king. It said so in three languages. It said it in Greek, the language of culture; in Latin, the language of power; and in Hebrew, the language of religion. Pilate paid Jesus the compliment of saying he was the king of man's mind, will, and heart. All of man was his kingdom.

II. Jesus wants to be king of the whole man. The clever man, unredeemed, may be dangerous. The strong man, unrestrained, may wreck life. The kind man, undirected, may be only a sentimentalist. Partial commitment is always dangerous. The saints yielded all and gained all. The calculating man yields a part and loses all. The life of total commitment is the only one which does not end in frustration.

III. We are not naturally good, bad, weak, or strong. We become what we love. Through communion with Christ we become the body in which we have shared. "Lead on, O King Eternal." We follow in faith. Thou art our king.—Roy L. Minich.

Topic: The Living God
TEXT: Rev. 1:18.

I. Easter assures us that God is not dead. God in Christ returned to life on earth. God raised up Jesus who came out of the cave on an early Easter morning in all power, might, and glory. Death could not hold him. We worship, love, and serve a living God, for the very essence of God is life.

II. If God lives, then there is an ultimate victory for the cause of God. Easter assures us that there is a basic rightness in the fabric of the world. We live in an evil world which oppresses us at times. We wonder why things happen to us when we try to live with God and do his will.

III. Because God lives, we can be sure of eternal life. As we get older the question becomes more important to us, "If a man die, will he live again?" What is the answer? What answer can really make us sure of life eternal? At this Easter time we hear many suggestions. We are told that we can be sure there is no death because of the fragrance of a hyacinth or the song of a bird or the beauty of a snowflake or the renewal of Spring. These evidences of nature are only suggestions of immortal life. The real and only basis for faith in eternal life is the resurrection of Christ. He literally, truly, and realistically came out of the tomb where he lay three days. He was real enough to speak, to eat, and to be touched. He was material enough to be seen and to be recognized. It was a resurrection of the body. As Jesus came back from death, we are told by the scriptures that we too shall rise again.

IV. Is God dead or alive for you personally? It is quite possible that God is dead in your life. You may be a nominal church member. Your religion may be all a matter of rites, customs, and ceremonies. Does God really live inside your heart? If he does not, then you are experiencing only disillusionment, despair, and ultimate death. On the other hand, is God alive in your heart and mind? If he lives in you by your faith in Jesus Christ, your life is full and free. Because God lives, you too truly live. Your life is one of matchless beauty in the Lord. Life for you is vibrant and victorious because God is not dead.—John R. Brokhoff.

ILLUSTRATIONS

RENEWAL.   I shall keep this Lent and hope to refresh my soul. It is like a clock all out of order. I must take it to pieces, and after cleansing it I must somehow put it together again that it may strike correctly and once more give the right time. —Francis of Sales.

CROSS ON FIFTH AVENUE.   Fifth Avenue in New York City is an open textbook for studying the meaning of the cross. Strolling along this busy thoroughfare, you see, for example, a great cathedral with numerous crucifixes showing Jesus in various attitudes of pain. Move farther up the avenue, and there is another magnificent church with a cross originally meant to bear a crucified body but for one reason or another is left vacant. A bit beyond is a church whose cross is illuminated and gives no indication that it ever bore a body. At the end of your walking tour, opposite Central Park, you come to the true cathedral of Fifth Avenue: Tiffany's. In its jewel cases on the mezzanine are more crosses than in all the churches put together. Some flash silver and some are

chased in gold; some are sprinkled with diamonds instead of nails; some have little rubies to represent the blood. It is true that the empty cross is the sublime symbol of the resurrection, but it is not true that Jesus rose from the dead on the mezzanine of Tiffany's. In our walking tour we have paralleled the Christian understanding of the cross from a realization of the true love of Christ with its terrible sacrifice to sentimentalism, from sentimentalism to revisionism, and from revisionism to superstition. Every cross is a symbol of Christ, but what we are doing with the cross says a great deal about what we have done to Christ.—George William Rutler.

"I THIRST."   Thirty years ago there came to Calcutta a plain, rugged Yugoslav nun. Moving among the living and the dying along the streets of that city of poverty she became an angel of mercy. Presently in a derelict Kali temple she opened a home of charity. There she began to love deserted babies back to life and gave tenderness to the dying. Today there are Houses of Charity in sixty-seven countries, where hundreds of women and men toil among the poor. That nun, Mother Teresa, has become one of the saints of the twentieth century.

Mother Teresa places two words above the door of every House of Charity. They are the moving words of Jesus: "I thirst."

On the cross of Calvary Jesus spoke seven times, seven precious sentences wrung from his lips during the agony of crucifixion. One was the very human cry: "I thirst."—Alan Walker.

A LIGHT ON HIS WAY.   Paul may not have known Jesus in the flesh, he may never have heard his voice or felt the touch of his hand, but he knew the Lord Christ who in a blinding light on the road to Damascus confronted him, laid hold upon him, possessed him, demanded his life completely, changed and recreated his whole character, and set him upon a new and untraveled way. For Paul the resurrection was no theoretical speculation. When he said that Jesus is alive, he was talking about someone he had met not casually the way one meets a friend on the street but catastrophically, dynamically, the way one meets overpowering truth or overwhelming love.—Theodore P. Ferris.

BEYOND THE CROSS.   C. T. Itty visited an ashram near Delhi and asked to see the chapel. Afterward he wrote: "I sat and looked, and it was strange. There was a small wooden cross hanging on thin wire. Behind the cross there was no wall. I am used to thick walls behind the cross, but in this chapel as I looked at the cross I could look beyond. What I saw was some dirty linen hanging in the bathroom. I could see bedrooms and people with brooms dusting the path. And I could see cattle roaming around—cows and sheep and everything. Actually the smell comes right into the chapel. I could see people walking on the streets beyond. For heaven's sake, how can I pray in this place? The man behind me said: 'We want you to pray with your eyes wide open. That's what we do in this place.' How can I adore God without looking right through and seeing people and the rugged reality of things? I need to see them so that I can lift them up before the throne of grace."

DAILY ENCOUNTER.   For me Easter is a personal, daily encounter with the healing, enlivening, transforming power of the Spirit making me know, beyond the shadow of a doubt, that there is life after death, and it is for this that I am now being readied.—Elisabeth Kubler-Ross.

EASTER BELLS.   An unusual incident occurred, we are told, during Napoleon's Austrian campaign in the spring of 1813. His army had advanced to within six miles of the village of Feldkirch. The Austrian army was some distance away, and it looked as if Feldkirch would be occupied without resistance. But as the emperor's troops advanced by night the Christians of Feldkirch gathered in their little church to pray. Hour after hour they besought God to save their village. It was Easter eve. Next morning at sunrise the bells of the village church pealed out across the countryside. Napolean's officers, not realizing

it was Easter Sunday, suspected that the Austrian army had moved into Feldkirch during the night and that the bells were ringing in jubilation. They ordered a retreat, and the occupation of Feldkirch never took place. The bells of Easter had brought peace to the Austrian countryside. Billy Graham.

WITHOUT SUSPICION.   Easter is the one day in the year when anyone may attend church without incurring any suspicion that he is deeply committed to Christian faith and life.—Angus Dun.

PRAYERS

FOR A PURE AND HOLY LIFE.   O God, thou great redeemer of mankind, our hearts are tender in the thought of thee, for in all the afflictions of our race thou has been afflicted, and in the sufferings of thy people it was thy body that was crucified. Thou has been wounded by our transgressions and bruised by our iniquities, and all our sins are laid at last on thee.

We pray thee, O Lord, for the grace of a pure and holy life that we may no longer add to the dark weight of the world's sin that is laid upon thee but may share with thee in thy redemptive work. As we have thirsted with evil passions to the destruction of men, do thou fill us now with hunger and thirst for justice that we may bear glad tidings to the poor and set at liberty all who are in the prison house of want and sin.

And if the evil that is threatened turns to smite us and if we must learn the dark malignity of sinful power, comfort us by the thought that thus we are bearing in our body the marks of Jesus Christ our Lord. —Clifford L. Stanley.

QUICKEN OUR FAITH.   O almighty God, who didst bring again from the dead our Lord Jesus, we confess that through worldliness of spirit we have not discerned his presence among us. Blinded by our sorrows, we have not known him though he spoke with us. Through disappointment of mind and dejection of soul our hearts have not burned within us as we have heard his word. Forgive us that we have been so dull. By the indwelling of thy Holy Spirit wilt thou quicken our faith so that in every circumstance, in our homes and daily work, in our duties and opportunities, and in our strength and in our weakness, we shall know the presence of the living Savior? Even so come, Lord Jesus, as thou didst come to thy disciples long ago. Be our companion on life's journey and our friend who sticketh closer than a brother. Fulfill now thy promise, "Lo, I am with you always," and we shall rejoice with unutterable and exalted joy.— Leonard Griffith.

DEFEND US.   O God our Father, because we are men and women with human hearts and human minds and human emotions, there is no escape for us from temptation.

Defend us from the temptations of the world, from lowering our standards and abandoning our ideals, from the cautious conformity that fears to be different, and from the materialism which really believes that a man's life does consist in the abundance of the things he possesses, defend us, O God.

Defend us from the temptation of the flesh, from the passion which can wreck life, from the impulses which can bring regret to follow, from the too strong emotions which can sweep us to disaster, and from the freedom which has become licence and the love which has become lust, defend us, O God.

Defend us from the temptations of the devil, from the yielding to any seduction to sin, from the power of the fascination of the forbidden thing, and from forgetting that in the end our sin is bound to find us out, defend us, O God.

Give us by your grace hearts so pure that they love only the highest and minds so clean that they seek only the truth. And grant that nothing may lure us from our loyalty and nothing deflect us from our path, and so help us in all our days ever to follow you and never to turn back and never to lose our way. —William Barclay.

SECTION VII. Resources for Advent and Christmas Preaching

SERMON SUGGESTIONS

Topic: On the Road of Curiosity
TEXT: Luke 2:15.

I. Curiosity is a road that can lead us to the Christ Child because curiosity says, "Come and see." We Christians make many wonderful claims about Christ. We say that he is the fairest of ten thousand. We say that God was in Christ. In him was the fulfillment of prophecies given over many centuries. This Jesus, we say, is the savior of mankind. Who would believe us? The claims are too good to be true. They are remarkable, unbelievable, and out of this world. The doubting, indifferent, and cynical should have their curiosity aroused. If so, we say to them: "Come and see for yourselves. Seeing is believing."

II. Curiosity is a road to Bethlehem because it says to us, "Come and try it." Curiosity may convince us of the nature of Christ and Christianity, but will the teachings of Christ and his church work? We make tremendous claims: Christ is the answer to every problem, Christ can save the human soul, and peace on earth is possible through Christ. How can we convince the world of the truth of these claims? There is only one way: arouse curiosity to the point where the world will be willing to come and try Christianity.

III. While curiosity takes us down the road to the Christ Child, it is not enough. Curiosity does not necessarily keep us there. Curiosity took the shepherds to Bethlehem, but soon they returned to the hills. That is the last we hear from the shepherds. As far as we know they did not become disciples of Jesus, they did not stand at the foot of the cross, and they did not become members of the original church. Curiosity must turn into commitment. Jesus said to John's disciples, "Come and see." They came out of curiosity, but they never left him. They committed themselves to him.—John R. Brokhoff.

Topic: Word and Flesh
TEXT: John 1:14.

I. The word became flesh so that God can speak to us in language we understand. The key problem of all religions is how do we get in touch with God and how does he communicate with us. The Christian claims the word became flesh: truth investing in personality.

II. The word became flesh to weld God and his world together. Word and flesh: God without the world is an enigmatic abstraction and the world without God is a terrifying fiction.

III. The word became flesh to signify the dependence of God. (a) Christianity shares many truths with other great religions, but one truth is unique to it. While other religions make great play of man's dependence upon God, only Christianity dares to speak of God's dependence upon man. The word becomes frail human flesh to symbolize the truth that God puts him-

63

self at our mercy and entrusts himself into our hands.

(b) Does he not need human hands to wield the instruments through which he heals, a human voice to bring comfort to the distressed and distress to the comfortable, human eyes to look in compassion on the lonely, a human presence to stand beside the outcast, human brain power to help make deserts fertile and feed the hungry, and human political skills dedicated to beneficent ends to create a more just and humane social order?

IV. The word made flesh is a stupendous demonstration of faith. Not our faith in God that flickers and fades, waxes and wanes but God's faith in us, entrusting himself and the fate of his kingdom into our shaky, treacherous hands. God puts himself at our mercy and commits himself into our hands to exalt or humiliate, proclaim or neglect. Is not this the supreme cosmic wager—the ultimate gamble—God taking the chance that we will not let him down?—Colin Morris.

Topic: Glad Tidings to All People
TEXT: Luke 2:10.
I. Christmas brings us the glad tidings that the best is true; that this universe is so made that goodness, kindness, decency, integrity, and moral character will be sustained by it; that God who creates it and keeps it going intended that there should be peace; that men of integrity should be in places of leadership; and that there should be goodwill. We do not work in a universe that is against us or indifferent to us but one made for us and for our best.
II. Christmas brings the glad tidings that we need not be alone and that the blessed companion has been born and has grown to manhood. In Christmas is found all the life of Christ.
III. We should not have heard these glad tidings if the first receivers of them had not heard the words "to all peoples" and said to themselves, "We must not keep these glad tidings as if they were meant for us exclusively."
IV. The ultimate glad tidings is the belief that man is essentially decent and that he has capacity for hearing, believing, and

being transformed by the spirit and power of God. The good tidings leads to the ultimate conclusion and possibility that if we all do our part to own him as lord and master, one day every knee shall bow and every tongue shall confess him lord.— Richard C. Raines.

Topic: Immanuel
TEXT: Matt. 1:23.
I. The word "Immanuel" tells us something about God. In Christ we discover that God is knowable and that he is with us. This is the primary truth of the incarnation. This is the center round which circles all Christian instruction, all our hopes for the present, and all our ambitions for the future.
II. This word "Immanuel" tells us something about Christ. It not only means that God is knowable; it goes farther and says that the messiah is available. Not only is God with us; he is also among us.
III. This word "Immanuel" not only tells us something about God and something about Christ, but it also indirectly tells us something about ourselves. "Immanuel" means that God is knowable, that the messiah is available, and that mankind is redeemable. This too is the significance of the incarnation. God is with us, among us, and for us.—J. Gordon Jones.

Topic: Christmas: A Down-to-Earth Faith
TEXT: Matt. 4:16.
I. Christmas gives us a *down-to-earth understanding of God.* What is more commonplace than this familiar Christmas scene: a mother, a baby, and shepherds gazing into a manger bed? Here, says Christmas, God is to be found; he is near, he is accessible, and he is available to mankind. He speaks to us from within human experience.
II. Christmas gives us a *down-to-earth joy.* Joy is the central mark of Christmas. On that first Christmas day the angels proclaimed good tidings of great joy. In our carols we sing, "Joy to the world" and "Good tidings of comfort and joy" and " 'Tis the season to be jolly." Our most-used Christmas greeting is "Merry Christmas." Joy and happiness are the predomi-

nant themes and moods of the Christmas season. Christmas is a time to be merry, and the Christian unashamedly lets that spirit invade his life.

III. One other aspect of the faith of Christmas is the *down-to-earth concern for people* that the season brings. At the very heart of Christmas is the proclamation of God's love for us: "God so loved the world that he gave his only begotten Son." One of the fruits of God's great act of love is to make his followers persons who have love and concern for other people. Jesus underscored this in his parable of the last judgment. His redeemed people were those who had responded with loving care for the stranger, the hungry, the thirsty, the sick, naked, and imprisoned ones.—Russell W. VandeBunte.

Topic: The Highest in the Lowest
TEXT: Luke 2:14.

I. Glory to God in the highest means accepting the priority of God the highest. This is where so much "religion" has gone wrong. Through the ages men have tried to enlist the sacred authority of God to sanctify their own schemes and to add respectability to plans which are sectional and selfish. One single note running through the whole Bible is that God demands obedience from men if they are ever to enjoy a society which is stable and progressive with its projects held in balance by goodwill.

II. The angels' song continues with an acknowledgement of the presence of God "in the lowest."

(a) Some, like Dr. Goodspeed, punctuate the song to read, "Glory to God in the highest and on earth." Full stop. The message continues, "Unto you is born a Savior . . . and you shall find the babe lying in a manger." The highest was found in the lowest. Stephan Hopkinson's corrective is worth repeating: "The gospel sets out a tough and realistic attitude to life. It grew up in the dirt of a stable floor and is nourished by the blood of a dying man."

(b) Glory, an intriguing word in Jewish religious thought, was used to describe the presence of God in the pillar of fire and smoke which preceded the Israelites wandering in the wilderness. They called this the *shekinah*—God coming to men in their humble tents and camping with them. St. John accepted this picture when he wrote, "The Word was made flesh and tented with us, full of grace and truth."

(c) The angels saw the shekinah of God in a child, cradled amid the filth of a cattle stall, and ultimately rejected and crucified. In the lowest life God revealed himself to men. Confidently the angels bring God's salvation, "Peace to men of goodwill," using the very phrase with which a Jew would greet his neighbor, "Shalom!"—peace. Those who have been captured by the spirit of Jesus will find the highest glory of God in the lowest circumstances and situations.—John H. Withers.

Topic: The Day after Christmas
TEXTS: Matt. 2:12-15; Luke 2:20.

Do you remember as a child experiencing a mild melancholy the day after Christmas? There had been such a build up of wonder, but with all the presents open and the tree a bit dismantled the only wonder seemed to be how to straighten up the mess. It is appropriate that we should be worshiping together after Christmas for it is always on that side of Christmas that the real wonder of Christ's coming needs to be encountered.

I. Consider what it must have been like for the wise men the day after Christmas. It has been a long and exciting trip, but now they must return to a society that did not believe in the possibility of something genuinely new happening. But this is also the world to which we return. The magic of Christmas gives most people an aura of joyfulness which lasts as long as the glitter is present. But the time in which we have to live is the day after Christmas. Like the wise men, it is then that we need to live lives that demonstrate a freedom from fatalism and despair.

II. Consider the shepherds who had to return to the same old fields. Anyone who works with people knows how persistent human problems can be. Hate, fear, suspicion, and jealousy are not wiped out by the birth. It is there in the fields, even more than at the manger, that we have to discover that the gift of Christ is not an elimination of problems but a claim on our lives. It is really giving us our lives as a brand new gift.

III. Consider Joseph and Mary for whom post-Christmas was a refugee journey into a strange and alien land. Their experience makes our after Christmas blues seem silly. From them we learn that the coming of Christ does not take away the problems, but it does give us the capacity to live with them without defeat.—Robert B. Wallace.

ILLUSTRATIONS

THE ACCEPTABLE YEAR. God may be ready for the acceptable year, but are we? There is much of Advent in this idea of the jubilee year, much of the "fullness of time," much of God's action in spite of human unreadiness or unwillingness. Read the Magnificat and tremble! Mary had the *joy* ("good news for the poor") and the *freedom* ("release to the captives") and the *vision* ("recovery of sight to the blind") and the *liberation* ("liberty to the oppressed") to accept God's word to her with celebration! She was ready for the acceptable year of the Lord.—Jane Parker Huber.

THREE WONDERS. There are three wonders here: one, that God should become a man; another, that a virgin should bear a child; and the third, that Mary believed. And the greatest of these is that Mary believed.—Martin Luther.

HOW DOES CHRIST COME? We know how he first came among men, born of Mary. I believe Christ's birth was the miraculous breakthrough, but I believe also that his entering our lives in this present age is equally miraculous as God uses our particular abilities to receive his gift of redemption. Some may come about it intellectually, using a well thought out theological system to come to a rational conclusion. Others are led by the mystery, the wonder, and the overpowering sense of awe to accept the gift of the word made flesh. Still others are convinced by their inner feelings of love, adoration, gratitude, and joy at the very idea. Your own experience of Christ coming may be a combination of these, for we all have some measure of intellect, mysticism, and emotion. What matters most is that this year, perhaps as never before, we commit all we have and all we are to receive Christ and to serve him joyfully.—Herbert M. Barrall.

HIS BIRTH IN US. He came once in the flesh that he might come forever in the spirit. He was born once in the city of David that he might be born in every man who will receive him. If he has been born in us, even though he can find no room in us but a manger and no swaddling clothes but the few and tender spiritual truths we have learned in childhood, we can have our Christmas. We can join our voices with the angels in singing, "Glory to God in the highest!" We can welcome him to such homes as we have in our hearts. They are poor homes, it is true, and scantily supplied with the heavenly furniture of holy affections. But he will come wherever there is a place to lay his divine head.—Chauncey Giles.

WHERE PEOPLE MATTER. Christmas is a festival which brings us together in small groups, a family group if we are lucky. We are not just nameless people in a crowd. We meet as friends who are glad to be together and who care about each others' happiness. Nowadays this is a precious experience. So much of the time we feel that our lives are dominated by great impersonal forces beyond our control. Then Christmas comes and once again we are reminded that people matter, and it is our relationship with one another that is important. Jesus showed that what people are and what they do does matter and does make all the difference.—Elizabeth II.

CHRISTMAS PERSPECTIVES. Christmas is yesterday: the memories of childhood, the miracle of Santa Claus, the singing of carols, and the glow of being remembered.

Christmas is today: the presence of absent ones, the reminder of the generous act, the need to love, and the need to be loved.

Christmas is tomorrow: the miracle of faith, the fulfillment of ancient hopes, the reign of God, and the dying of death in the land.—Howard Thurman.

PRAYERS

A NEW PILGRIMAGE. O God, eternal and unchangeable, in whom and through whom all things consist and without whom no one of us can truly live, we thank thee for this season of the year and for the annual rememberance of the visit of the dayspring from on high. We thank thee for every intimation of thy presence whereby the faith of thy people has been sustained through ages of hoep and despair, of peace and war, and of triumph and disaster. Especially do we praise thee for the light which shone into the darkness to guide forever the life of people everywhere.

O God in heaven, whose love and mercy brought to us the child of Bethlehem, we lift before thee today a larger world than ancient seers and lowly shepherds could ever know. Yet we confess that the home of our souls is still far away from thee. Help us to set out afresh on a new pilgrimage of mind and heart, and by following the star of our faith may we come finally to the place where we are constrained to kneel.

O thou who has loved us with an everlasting love, help us so to pray and serve that the fruits of Christ's coming may become real in the midst of this world's darkness and pain. Keep us from making a comedy of this holy season of the year. Direct us to find places where we can work deeds of mercy and kindness and thereby bring joy back to our world again. Purify our celebration of the advent of the king of kings and subdue the noisy prattle of our preoccupation with jingles and things so we may hear the glad sounds of the song of peace on earth and goodwill to all people.—Donald Macleod.

MOOD OF WONDER. Almighty God, who hast revealed the glory of thy love in the face of Jesus Christ and hast called us through him to live with thee as children, help us to welcome him with gladness and to make room for him in our lives. Grant us the glow and thrill of great hours. Quicken in us the mood of wonder and the joy of expectancy. As we gather around our festive boards may we not forget the deeper meaning of the manger. In the gladness of our giving may we remember those who are no longer present to receive and those of all lands who live in the shadow of fear and want. Let those who are offended forgive and those who have offended repent, so that all thy children may live together as one family, praising thee for the great redemption which thou has wrought for us.—Ralph W. Sockman.

CHRISTMAS DEVOTION. Gracious God, who hast revealed thyself to mankind through the child of Bethlehem, accept the devotion that now we offer. May the spirit of this Christmas season so possess us that we may worship thee in the beauty of holiness. The dayspring from on high hath visited us and revealed thy glory, and we bow before thee in gratitude. We glorify thee for the divine mystery of Christmas and rejoice in its tidings of redemption. We thank thee for the human tenderness of Christmas and rejoice in its tidings of love. We magnify thy name for the glorious promise of Christmas and rejoice in its tidings of peace on earth and goodwill to men.

We confess our waywardness and impatience. Our hearts have often been busy inns that had no room for thee. Our ears have been closed to the song of the angels, and our eyes have dimmed to the splendor of Bethlehem. Forgive our blindness. Quicken our spirits. Make us sensitive to the everlasting presence of him who is the light of the world.

Unto thy gracious keeping we commend ourselves. The light of the Christmas star illumines our way. Sustain us in days of routine. Guide us in all new adventure. Keep us on the highway of Christian truth. And give us grace to lay before our king the gold of obedience, the incense of lowliness, and the myrrh of healing friendship. We offer our prayer in the name of the babe of Bethlehem, our Savior and Lord.—Carl A. Glover.

COME AGAIN, O LORD. Thou who has come so many times to thine own and found no resting place, forgive us for our overcrowded lives, our vain haste, and our preoccupation with self. Come again, O Lord, and though our hearts are a jumble of voices and our minds overlaid with many fears, find a place, however humble, where thou canst begin to work thy wonder of peace and joy with us. If in some hidden corner or in some out-of-the-way spot we can clear away the clutter and shut out the noise and darkness, there be thou born again, and we shall kneel in perfect peace with the wisest and humblest men. Help us to guard our affections well, lest the powers of this world assault our new-found hope and leave us bereft of this sign under heaven. Give us Christmas from within, that we may share it on all sides.— Samuel H. Miller.

CRADLE AND ALTAR. We thank thee, O Christmas Christ, that thy cradle was so low that shepherds, poorest and simplest of all earthly folk, could yet kneel before it and look into the face of God. We thank thee that thy cradle was so high that kings of knowledge and of wealth could not miss it in starry altitudes where it was their wont to gaze and that they were not ashamed to hazard their wisdom's store into thy baby hands. We thank thee that, having grown in statute and being a carpenter, thou didst fashion a Christmas altar like unto thy cradle, which should be the possession of the ages. Like thy cradle, thy Christmas altar is as high and as low as all human necessity so that all knowledge, all simplicity, all wealth, all poverty, all joy, all sorrow, all righteousness, and all sin may find an answer there. Be this our Christmas haste, O Christmas Christ, to seek that altar, and at this season of thy birth, unafraid of the time's complaint, may we be found kneeling still.—Robert Nelson Spencer.

SECTION VIII. Evangelism and World Missions

Topic: Elements of Evangelism
TEXT: Rom. 1:16.

Evangelism is sharing the good news of the gospel in deeds and words of love. It is the joyous proclamation of a God who involves himself with us in life. It is the announcement of grace and of meaning for life as we know it in Jesus Christ.

I. Faith in the master means holistic identification. Evangelism is calling for the total self to be committed to Jesus Christ, the mind, the volition, and the psychic aspects of a person's life. This is calling for total discipleship. An evangelism which overlooks obedience and emphasizes instead subjective experience is missing the meaning of New Testament discipleship. Dietrich Bonhoeffer said, "Only he who obeys truly believes, and he who truly believes obeys."

II. Faith that identifies means authentic participation. The risen Christ makes reconciliation immediate so that we are now involved in a relationship with God. This is an actual righteousness, a right relatedness with God, which has superseded the righteousness of the law. Such identification with Christ means that we relate to the whole Jesus, what he said, what he did, and what he was. Participation with him means that the total life is brought under his lordship and that one's expression of Christian faith is a life-style of discipleship. Being saved means that one already

participates in the kingdom of Christ. Paul writes that we are "citizens of heaven" here and now.

III. Faith that is authentic will articulate itself. While the expression of faith is in deeds as well as words, an authentic faith will articulate itself. There is no way that persons can hear the good news without our verbalizing it. And the Bible says, "Faith cometh by hearing and hearing by the word of God." In the midst of a secular society it is important that we verbalize our faith not with the old cliches but in ways which apply the truth to the vocabulary and life of the present.—Myron S. Augsburger.

Topic: Dimensions of Evangelism

I. *Assurance.* This is derived from and is the result of faith in God through Jesus Christ and is further constituted of repentance and a knowledge that God has forgiven and continues to forgive our sins. There is a witness of the Spirit with our spirit that we are heirs of God. We have been accepted.

II. *A new relationship.* This dimension adds to life and makes for effective living in the kind of world that is ours. Such an experience makes it easier for others to live with us.

III. *A new inspiration.* New ideas, new approaches, and a new and deeper devotion to helping others in the day-to-day routines.

IV. *A transformation.* Here is where the

69

uniqueness of Christianity is strongest in its evangelical nature.—John L. Sandlin.

Meditation: Parable

Picture a dangerous and rocky sea coast where storms frequently rage and ships often lose their way and are wrecked. A series of lighthouses and lifesaving stations have been established along this coastline in the name of and at the inspiration of one who came to be the light of the world. Over the years a tremendous work of rescue has been done from these stations with their small boats patrolling the coast and picking up the shipwrecked seamen. Those who man the stations are those who have themselves been rescued,' joining in glad gratitude their rescuers in this work of saving others. And through the years tales of heroic rescues and stories about the more notable heroes of the stations have been treasured and told again when the members of the rescue communities gather to go out on a new mission.

But with the years certain changes began to take place. More time and effort came to be expended in enlarging and beautifying the rescue stations. Stained glass windows were placed in the stations to commemorate their heroes. More and more comfortable quarters were built for the residents of the rescue communities, and there was even a feeling sometimes that those bedraggled and dirty seamen who were brought in from shipwrecks ought to be sent elsewhere so that they would not crowd and even soil the facilities that were properly set aside for the rescue community itself.

The building and beautifying of the rescue stations became such an absorbing activity that the rescue service itself was increasingly neglected. Traditional rescue drills and rituals were carefully carried on, but the actual launching out into ocean storms became something that a paid staff was expected to do along with a few volunteers. The result was that even though there were now a great many rescue stations along the coast—indeed it was crowded with them—there were simply not enough rescue boats at work and numbers of unfortunate seamen were lost in the continuing storms.—Theodore Wedel.

Topic: From Doubt to Faith

I. Any one of us may have honest doubts. The truth of it is he who has never doubted probably has never reached any great faith. It is only as we doubt and then verify that we come into a living faith.

II. Doubt may but bring us closer to God. Doubt often comes from disappointment and disillusionment and sometimes from sorrow and misunderstanding and persecution. On one occasion John the Baptist said, as he looked upon Jesus, "Behold, the lamb of God that taketh away the sin of the world." But when he was cast into prison he sent a messenger to Jesus asking if he were the messiah or were they to look for another. John knew the prophecy concerning Jesus, and Jesus told him to observe that the blind had their eyes opened, the deaf were made to hear, the sick were healed, and the poor had the gospel preached unto them. That was the ultimate answer.

III. The best way to dispel doubt is to do the will of God. Doubt sometimes arises because we live self-centered lives and sometimes even self-indulgent lives. The man who is living sinfully is likely to question the Christ, whose life is a rebuke to his own. Jesus said, "If any man willeth to do his will, he shall know the teaching."

IV. The best way to build a faith that is unshaken is to consecrate ourselves to the work that pleases others and pleases God.—Fred R. Chenault.

Topic: Where Faith Begins

Text: Rom. 8:38.

I. Without self-respect we cannot respect God. Unless we believe in ourselves we cannot believe in God. We miss great faith not because of the keenness of our intellect but because of the shallowness of our lives. Whenever a man in his private life runs counter to his highest ideals, he throws his system of values out of gear, and life loses its moral and spiritual significance. How can one believe in God whom he has not seen unless he first believes in himself with whom we lives daily?

II. Faith begins with a searching, doubting process by which we separate the wheat from the chaff, the real from the sham, and the petty from the significant. There are many serious and important questions troubling our world today, and for Christians to ignore or evade them, taking refuge in strong stands on petty, trivial issues, is a denial of the Christian faith. Great faith begins when the things that matter most are not sacrificed for the things that matter least.

III. Great faith begins when we earnestly and sincerely desire to express in our own lives the love of God which we have found in Jesus Christ. Concerning any proposed decision or action, we shall not ask, as does the world, "How will this affect my interests and my security?" but rather, "How can I best express my devotion and loyalty to God?" When we are truly governed by the love of God we have found in Jesus Christ, we can risk all the material things of life and life itself.—Ivan B. Bell.

Topic: Journey to Faith
SCRIPTURE: Matt. 15:21–28.

I. We have to start out afresh from where we are right now if we are going to make the road that leads somewhere in particular. That road which leads somewhere in particular leads to God, not to dull and dreary despair but to God in whom all joys are found. At every fork, including the one where you are right now, there is the road to God. Set your foot on the road to God, and it takes you at once on a new and always exciting journey to faith, which makes all of life worth living.

II. The journey to faith is not easy. It has to take the rough road, rough enough to give a real workout to the mind and muscle of any man or of any woman. The word of God tells us that the journey to faith in God is tough to take. Taking it is worth the time and the effort.

III. The journey to faith begins by turning away from one's self to God. This turning from one's self to God, whether it occurs dramatically or undramatically, is

called repentance in the scriptures. The unrepentant never turn to God. They would rather depend upon themselves, citing their record, such as it is, to justify their way of life.

IV. The first step is to cross the barrier with complete confidence in God, leaving the old road and going down the new one, crossing the boundary that marks the end of the old state and the beginning of the new state. It was not easy then, and it is not easy today.

V. Jesus had a heart for this woman, as he has a heart for all. In all the goodness of his heart he led her forward on the long, hard, rough journey to faith. When he was finished with her, no one around could any longer take faith for granted as if it is easy come and easy go.

VI. Having faith in Christ, refuse to be disappointed! Final and irreversible refusal to be disappointed in Christ is the journey's end. Christ himself speaks to the trusting heart of everyone who follows him in true faith: "Be it as you will" or better still, "Be it to you as I will."—Oswald C. J. Hoffman.

ILLUSTRATIONS

BURIED FEARS. Columba, a sixth-century missionary, set out with twelve men to evangelize northern Scotland. The task was dangerous because of the ferocious Picts who lived there. Upon arriving at the Island of Iona, the first thing they did was to bury their boat. Filling their boat with rocks was the missionaries' way of burying their fears and saying we have come to stay.—Wesley F. Ford.

SUCCESS STORY. An old minister in Scotland was nearing the end of a long ministry in an obscure parish. He felt dreadfully disappointed about the results of his work because he could point to no seemingly clear-cut conversions. He was telling the disappointment to a very distinguished minister whose work had appeared so fruitful. The famous preacher listened till the old man had finished. Then he said, "Do you remember a young woman who used to worship in your church some twenty years ago?" When he had described her, the old minister said: "Yes, I remember her. She came for quite a while, but she never joined the church." "Well," replied the great man, "that young woman had a younger brother who was rapidly becoming a drunkard. She would come home from church and talk to him about your sermons until finally she changed his habits. That young man was myself."—Ralph W. Sockman.

ARM IN ARM. Billy Graham has said that there are three things involved in any decision for Christ. Up in your head, imagine three little men sitting on a bench. One is named Intellect; another, Emotion; and another, Will. Intellect says, "I know that I am a sinner; I recognize my condition before God." Emotion says, "I am sorry that I am a sinner; I don't like sinning against God." Will is sitting in the middle, and he takes Intellect with one arm and Emotion with the other and says, "Come on, fellows, let's do something about it!"

LIFE'S BURDENS. One late afternoon Sadhu Sundar Singh, a Hindu convert to Christianity who became a missionary in India, was traveling on foot through the Himalayas with a Buddhist monk. It was bitter cold, and with night coming on the monk warned Sadhu that they were in danger of freezing to death if they did not reach the monastery before darkness fell.

Just as they were traversing a narrow path above a steep precipice, they heard a cry for help. Down the cliff lay a man, fallen and badly hurt. The monk looked at Sadhu and said: "Do not stop. God has brought this man to his fate. He must work it out for himself. Let us hurry on before we too perish."

But Sadhu, the Christian, replied: "God has sent me here to help my brother. I cannot abandon him."

The monk made off through the whirling snow, while the missionary clambered down. The man's leg was broken, and he could not walk. So Sadhu took his blanket, made a sling of it, and tied the man on his back. Then, bending under his burden, he began a body-torturing climb. By the time

he reached the narrow path again, he was drenched with perspiration.

Doggedly he made his way on through the deepening snow. It was dark now, and it was all he could do to follow the path. But he persevered, and though faint with fatigue and overheated from exertion, he finally saw ahead the lights of the monastery.

Then for the first time Sadhu stumbled and nearly fell. But not from weakness. He had stumbled over some object lying in the road. Slowly he bent down on one knee and brushed the snow off the object. It was the body of the monk, frozen to death.

Years later a disciple of Sadhu's asked him, "What is life's most difficult task?" Without hesitation Sadhu replied, "To have no burden to carry."—*The Michigan Christian Advocate.*

CONTRAST. One evening more than a century and a half ago, the westering sun was casting long shadows into the crooked streets of the little down of Leicester, England. A young man, about twenty-five years of age, hurried homeward, carrying under his arm a roll of leather. We follow him into his humble abode. Looking around, we see in a corner his cobbler's bench and a pile of shoes in need of repair. A table stands in the center of the room and beside it a couple of well-worn stools. In a quaint-looking cabinet against the wall is a copy of the English Bible, *Captain Cook's Voyages,* a Dutch grammar, and a few other books. This show of learning is not amiss, for the young man is not only a cobbler but also a schoolmaster and a minister.

On the wall of the room is a map of the world. It is made of leather and brown paper, and it is the cobbler's own workmanship. The crude map appears to fascinate him, for he is haunted day and night by the vision of a world in need. The great proclamation of Jesus sounds incessantly in his soul: "Go ye into all the world and preach the gospel to every creature."

One unforgettable day from the pulpit of his little church this youth, known to history as William Carey, laid bare his soul to his people. As a result there was set on foot one of the greatest missionary movements of modern times. Carey himself set out for India, and within the next three decades, with the help of a couple of colleagues, he prepared numerous grammars and dictionaries and translated portions of the scriptures into nearly forty languages and dialects. William Carey did most of this literary work.

It is not surprising that so unusual a man should have participated in one of those startling contrasts with which history abounds. On November 11, 1793, the very day on which the French revolutionists tore the cross from Notre Dame Cathedral in Paris and smashed it in the streets below, proclaiming the final defeat of God, on that day William Carey sailed up the Hooghly River to Calcutta and claimed a new continent for Christ and his kingdom.—John Sutherland Bonnell.

CHANGING SOCIETY. Some years ago a man by the name of John Richard Green went down in East London, where men and women drank, gambled, and sinned away their lives. He opened libraries and taught classes; he cleaned the streets, improved the homes, and fed the hungry. After ten years, however, he gave up in despair and said: "It's no use. They will go on drinking and gambling to the end of time." Then he went back to Oxford University and wrote his *History of the English People.*

But down into that very same section of London went a man of God named William Booth and his wife Catherine. There they preached Jesus Christ and gave themselves in sacrificial service. As a result drunkards were made sober, prostitutes were made pure, gamblers were transformed into honest men, and homes were remade.

The problems of East London were basically spiritual. Booth knew that until a spiritual change took place in the hearts of the people of East London their social conditions would never really improve. He also knew that the only possible way that this spiritual change could take place was by preaching Jesus Christ. He did just

that, and the social problems of East London were greatly reduced because of it.—John S. Jennings.

DREAMS AND DESIGN. In the African desert Livingstone made a highway that became safe for civilized man. Dr. Grenfell opened up a way through the snow for 2,000 miles along the stormswept coast of Labrador to visit the sick and suffering. Mary Reed opened a way among the lepers of India. John Eliot made the "Jesus way" plain to the red man. Sheldon Jackson tramped the snowy regions of the North to reach the hearts of the Alaskans. What was the lure that led these men and women to give up wealth, family, position, and pleasure? What music divine did they hear that we are not attuned to hear? What vision celestial did they see that our eyes are too dim to behold? What gleams of glory set them singing songs of sacrifice? Love and God and heaven were painted into the landscape that loomed ever before them, enticing them onward. Their dreams followed a design. They found God's purpose and pursued it.

SPIRIT OF LOVE. When David Livingstone started out for Africa, he knew it would take years of study to learn the dialects of the people there. He didn't feel he could possibly wait to do that, so he resolved to simply serve them in the spirit of love. One who traveled there years later wrote, "In the heart of Africa, among the lakes, I have come across black men and women who remembered the only white man they had ever seen—David Livingstone; and as you cross his footsteps in that dark continent, men's faces light up as they speak of the kind doctor who passed three years ago. They could not understand him; but they felt the love that beat in his heart."

TRANSFIGURED. Christopher Mayhew questioned representatives of all the major religions of the world concerning the ways in which they sought God and how they thought he could best be revealed to men. The Muslim took him to a mosque at the time of praying as the masses bowed in that attitude of submission which is the literal meaning of the word "Islam." The Hindu showed him the ritual of sacrifice within the temple. The Jew read to him in a synagogue the sacred writings of the prophets. Then came the turn of the Christian, an Indian. He took Mayhew not to a church nor even to the Bible but into a leprosy home where the deformed and disfigured patients who had once been discarded by society were now gathered into a community. In those faces he saw the beauty of Jesus transfiguring them and changing them "from glory into glory" not only as they received healing but even more as they knew themselves loved and accepted for Jesus' sake.—Pauline Webb.

NEW METHODS.   John Wesley had to break with conventional ways and to go out into the fields and the public squares to preach. Today we believe that we must look constantly for new ways not for the sake of being unconventional but in order to be effective.—Ronald Mann.

FULFILLMENT.   When I get up to give my testimony and to sing to the Lord, I seem to gain new strength. The more you witness, the more you commit yourself. I feel such fulfillment and freedom that I never experienced in the entertainment industry.—Dale Evans Rogers.

RADICAL CONTRADICTION.   A central weakness of many contemporary doctrines of salvation is that they produce a sole concern for personal redemption and justification before God apart from any reference to the kingdom of God. The common failing of many evangelistic proclamations comes when there is a concentration upon getting one's heart right with God, which predominates over a primary concern for the meaning and coming of the kingdom. Christ the atoning sacrifice for sins is stressed to the exclusion of Christ the bringer and bearer of a new order in history that is in radical contradiction to the standards and structures of the present world.—Jim Wallis.

SECTION IX. Children's Stories and Sermons

January 7. Seven Days Plus One (New Year's Sunday)

In the manse we have a grandfather clock. It keeps splendid time, although it is nearly 200 years old. I wind it every Saturday night, just as my father and my grandfather used to do. After it is wound, it keeps going for a week. One Saturday I forgot all about it. Do you know what happened? Nothing! It just kept on going. The old clockmakers knew that people could sometimes forget to do the things they ought to do, so they made their clocks to go after they were wound, not just for a week, but for a week and a day. Perhaps you and I could learn from the old clock to do just a little more than we are forced to do, to give a little more than we must give, and in helpfulness to go just a little further than we have to go.—John R. Gray.

January 14. Gifts That Make a Difference

Can you recall the gifts you received last Christmas? You may remember one or two, but if you received as many as five or six, you have likely forgotten some of them. Unless your birthday was very recent, you have possibly also forgotten some gifts you were given on your special day.

And what about the gifts you do remember? They may be things which were costly, but what is their real worth? Do you still have them, or have they been used up or worn out? If you had not received them, what real difference would it make in your life? Could you live without them?

Every day God showers us with gifts that make a difference. Life itself heads the list. Take a moment to think of other gifts of God you may have forgotten or taken for granted.—James D. McGuire.

January 21. His Hand on Ours

On one of his canvases the French painter Emile Ranouf has depicted an old man dressed in a fisherman's garb and seated in a boat with a little girl beside him. Both the elderly gentleman and the child have their hands on a huge oar. He is looking down fondly and admiringly upon her. Apparently he has told her that she may assist him in rowing the boat, and the child feels she is doing a great share of the task. It is easy to see however that it is his strong, muscular arms which are actually propelling the boat through the waves. In this painting, called "A Helping Hand," one may trace a parable. Christ has granted us the privilege of sharing his work, but we must never forget that it is only as God works in and through us that we are able to perform our task. While he directs us to put our hand upon the oar, we must always be aware of the source of our power.—Richard Sutherlin.

January 28. The Little Flame

High on a rock along the New England coast there was once a lighthouse which sent its beam of light forty miles out to sea. This was long before present-day electronic devices were perfected. The source of light was a small flame provided by an oil-burning wick. However, the little flame was set in front of some 1600 separate pieces of glass which were so perfectly related to each other and to the flame that they reflected the light as a powerful, life-guiding, and life-saving beacon.

Jesus told people like ourselves, "You are the light of the world" and "Let your light so shine before men that they may see your good works and so glorify your Father who is in heaven." It is not uncommon for us to say that our little light is insignificant. The world is depending on illumination from us, it will walk as in the dark. But we overlook the fact that if we simply put ourselves in right relationship with other people—as those pieces of glass were put in right relationship with one another—we can help produce a light which is great enough to lead and guide others.—Homer J. R. Elford.

February 4. Volunteers

The commander of a unit of the Coldstream guards, the famous old British regiment, addressed his troops. "Men," he said soberly, "I need two volunteers for an especially hazardous mission. I am going to turn my back and if you are willing to volunteer, take one step forward." But when the commander turned to face his troops again, the line was perfectly straight. Apparently not a man had moved. "Men," said he, "I don't understand this. You are members of the Coldstream guards, noted for courage. Surely one of you should be willing to volunteer. Now I'll give you one more chance." Again he turned his back, but this time he turned more quickly to face the men. To his pleasant surprise, he saw that the whole company in perfect unison had taken a step forward to volunteer.

Centuries before, in a similar fashion, Joshua called for the people of Israel to step forward as volunteers for hazardous service in the name of God. We are not told how many volunteered, but we do know that Joshua, along with his house, set the example.—John W. Wade.

February 11. "I Love You" (Valentine's Day)

According to legend, the valentine takes its name from a young Christian who once lived in ancient Rome. Like so many of the early Christians, Valentine had been imprisoned because of his faith. Often and longingly he thought of his loved ones and wanted to assure them of his well-being and of his love for them.

Beyond his cell window, just within reach, grew a cluster of violets. He picked some of the heart-shaped leaves, pierced them to spell the words "Remember your Valentine," and sent them off by a friendly dove. On the next day and the next he sent more messages that simply said, "I love you."

Thus did the valentine have its beginning. On Valentine's Day people of all ages remember those they love by sending valentines. God loves us and he sends us gifts to show his affection. Not once a year but every day, he sends us many blessings—love, joy, peace, health, seasons of sunshine, and showers of rain. Best of all, he sent heaven's fairest jewel down to earth to become our savior. Respond to God's great love by accepting his Son as your personal savior. Send him a valentine—your grateful heart—to show him that he has not loved in vain.—Edith Brock.

February 18. The Echo (Brotherhood Sunday)

A small boy was introduced to the echo. "Hello," the boy shouted across the valley. "Hello" came back the reply. "Who are you?" he asked. "Who are you?" was the reply. This annoyed the small boy. It sounded as if he were being mocked. "Why don't you come out?" he shouted. "Come out" came the answer. Quite exasperated, the boy challenged this unseen voice, "Come out or I'll fight you." And the voice replied, "Fight you." That sent the young lad back to his mother with his tale of a mean boy in the valley who mocked him and threatened to fight him. But the mother was wise and suggested the boy run back and shout, "I love you," and see what answer came back. So the boy ran back and shouted, "I love you."

And back came the reply, "I love you."—Alfred T. Davies.

February 25. The Patron Saint's Prescription

If you visit schools in Wales on St. David's day, which is March 1, you would see boys and girls wearing the leet or the daffodil in honor of their patron saint.

Dewi, as he is known in Welsh, was born in Pembrokeshire some 1500 years ago to a lady named Non. He became a missionary and founded a monastery on the site of the present St. David's Cathedral. When he is remembered in the annual celebrations, his last words to his followers will be recalled. They are the patron saint's prescription to Christians. His exhortation was "Be cheerful, keep the faith, and do the little things which you saw me do, and of which you heard me speak."

Be cheerful. It is important to remember that Jesus never intended his followers to put on a sad, long face. His church was a happy band of people.

Keep the faith. This is why reading the Bible, praying, and worshiping are so important to us all. They help us to keep the faith.

Do the little things. Some people may imagine that it's the big things that matter most—the sensational and the spectacular. But didn't our Lord speak of being faithful in the least? Didn't one of the prophets urge his people to "despise not the day of little things?"—Raymond Williams in *The Expository Times.*

March 4. Zero (Lent)

A zero means nothing by itself, but when it is combined with another number it can have considerable value. Three zeros after one, for instance, make a thousand. If you think your life doesn't count for much, if you feel like a zero, combine your life with that of Jesus, and you will have great value. This multiplication of value by the presence of Christ in a life is one of the great values of Christianity. Talents and abilities are created and also intensified by his presence.

The apostles were simple men. They probably were zeros in the community. But when they accepted the invitation of Jesus, "Follow me," they became men of power sufficient to launch a movement that will transform the world. Never feel like a zero. Put Jesus ahead of you in your life.—L. Wendell Fifield.

March 11. God's Face (Lent)

Suppose that God had a face like ours. And suppose we could see his face. What do you think it would look like? Would he have a frown? A scowl? Would he look angry? Happy? Sad? Of course God doesn't have a face like ours. But the Bible sometimes speaks as if God looked angry or pleased or happy. Jesus says that God has a joyful face when even one sinner repents. He means that whenever a man realizes how little he loves God and his fellow man and asks forgiveness, then God is pleased. When a man prays, "O God, forgive my many sins, and help me to trust in you," then God is pleased. When a man prays, "God forgive me for thinking only of myself, and make me more sympathetic toward people who are suffering," then God has a happy face. He rejoices over every sinner who repents.—Leroy Norquist.

March 18. Philippine Incident (Lent)

A twelve-year-old-orphan boy, living with his grandmother, peddled *puto,* a native bread, around the neighborhood. Two days before All Saints' Day he went early to an urban bus station to sell *puto.* At that time many city residents were going back to their homes in the provinces to observe the holiday. As the boy zigzagged his way among the crowd, three young men, rushing to board the first bus trip, accidentally knocked the boy down. His basket was dropped and the contents scattered on the platform. As the boy carefully picked up the *puto,* an old man with two suitcases in his hands saw his predicament. He laid aside his luggage and helped. When all the bread was accounted for, the boy approached the old man and humbly asked, "Sir, are you the Christ?"—Buenafe T. Manongdo.

March 25. Three Books (Lent)

I once visited the British Museum, and among its treasures I found the biggest book in Britain and the smallest.

The biggest is a giant atlas made in the time of King Charles II. And you'll never guess its size—5 feet 9½ inches high and 3 feet 2½ inches wide! So big is it that it takes two tall men, one on either side, to hold it steady and turn the pages.

I also saw the smallest book in the museum. You'll find it just as hard to imagine its smallness as to imagine the big one's bigness. It is just one thirty-second of an inch! It was made by a young soldier in his spare time. Each tiny page is stitched on with a strand of the finest silk; each page is only big enough to print one letter of the alphabet. Its cover is of soft Persian leather. It is plain that Sergeant Alfred Howman had clever fingers to create such a book.

But size is not the only way to judge a book. In the same museum are copies of the most precious book in the world. Yes, it's the Bible which is precious not for its size or its cost. Each Bible, whether quite new or your own small cheap copy, is precious to its faithful reader. It carries the message of God's creative power and love, unmistakably shown in the coming of Jesus.—Rita F. Snowden.

April.1. Strength and Guidance (Passion Sunday)

John Muir, the great naturalist, was a bold explorer of mountains and forests. With no equipment except a stout pair of hiking boots, he set out to conquer Mount Ritter in the High Sierras. Climbing across a great glacier, he encountered a precipice going almost straight up. He began the dangerous climb, but halfway to the top he came to a dead stop, arms outspread, clinging close to the face of the rock, and unable to move. He knew he would fall to the glacier below. His mind was filled with indecision and uncertainty. Suddenly he became possessed of new strength. His muscles grew firm, and his eyes became like microscopes. He could see tiny cracks and crevices, and his fingers and limbs moved almost instinctively. Soon he stood on the topmost crag in blessed light.

Daily we need to draw upon God's strength and guidance so that we are prepared to deal with insurmountable difficulties and to fulfill God's purposes.—Sterling W. Schallert.

April 8. Hands (Palm Sunday)

Palm Sunday surely is an appropriate occasion for inspecting our hands. (See Luke 9:44.) Are your hands the hands of Judas? His were *cupped* hands. We may think of Judas as the militant nationalist, who saw in Jesus the potential leader of an armed uprising against the Roman occupying armies, perhaps even the future dictator of a new Israel. When the truth slowly dawned on him that Jesus had a different mission—to transform the hearts of men of all nations—his bitter disappointment led him to liquidate this false messiah. He had cupped his hands to receive Jesus as a tool for his political ambitions.

Are your hands the hands of Peter? These are the *cold* hands of denial. After the arrest of Jesus, Peter tried to lose himself among the soldiers around the brazier in the yard, holding out his cold hands to the warm glow. Suddenly, as more dry fuel is thrown on the fire, the sparkling flame lights up his face and a serving maid recognizes him: "You were with him." Impulsively Peter throws out his cold hand in blank denial: "I know him not." He dissociated himself from the very best friend he had ever had.

Are your hands the hands of Pilate? These are the *washed* hands of abdication from responsibility. Pilate believed that the prisoner before him was innocent and twisted and turned in every direction to secure his release. But in order to placate the mob he delivered Jesus into their hands. Taking a basin of water, he "washed his hands before the multitude and said, 'I am innocent of the blood of this just man: see ye to it!' " He washed his hands of all responsibility for this miscarriage of justice.

Are your hands the hands of the crowd? These are the *counted* hands. As Pilate puts the proposal to the meeting and says, "All in favor will raise their hands," the crowd is not satisfied with hands but shouts out with full voice, "Crucify him!" Every hand is counted. Their votes were cast for Barabbas, and Christ was sent to his cross. —John H. Withers.

April 15. Jesus Within Us (Easter)

Four-year-old Linda enjoyed looking at the big picture of "Jesus and the Children" which hung in the kindergarten room. One day the minister came and sat on a low chair. Taking one of the children on his knee, he talked with the group. When Linda went home, she said: "Jesus was at school today. He came and talked with us just like the picture!" This was an exciting moment for Linda.

The disciples on the way to Emmaus did not recognize Jesus until he blessed and broke the bread. We are often unaware of Christ in the lives of those about us until some act alerts us. In a very special sense Christians reflect Christ's presence—his heart and body, his hands and feet.—Ruth H. Short.

April 22. Two Friends

Susie has an imaginary friend. In some ways he is the best friend anyone could ever have. He always wants to play. He is never too busy. He listens to everything Susie wants to say to him. Wherever she wants a friend he is close at hand. All she has to do is imagine him.

In some ways God is like Susie's friend, only better, because he is not imaginary. But, like her friend, he too is always close at hand, ready to listen to our concerns, and never too busy to know what matters to us.

Of course God is different from Susie's friend too. Since he is not imaginary, he has a mind of his own. He will not always do what we want him to do. Instead he does what he knows is best. That's what makes God a real friend to us.

Sometimes people treat God like an imaginary friend, someone they can call upon to serve their own selfish needs and wants, but that is very wrong. When we treat God as a real friend, we learn to be

thankful for his wisdom, which is greater than our own.—Allan M. Fluent in *Family Devotions.*

April 29. The Boomerang

An Australian friend gave me a boomerang. It is made of hard wood, is about three feet long, and is curved almost through a right angle. It weighs about half a pound. It is thrown by holding it upright behind the head and then sending it forward, spinning it as much as possible. It will travel for about fifty yards upright and then it will flatten out. This is because one side is flat and the other side is curved and the edges are sharp. It will begin to rise and can do three or four circles, going up to 150 feet and as far as 100 yards away. Then because it has a skew in it, this piece of wood does something which is strange. When you throw a flat piece of wood it falls to the ground as far away as your strength can make it, but when an Australian throws a boomerang, it comes back.

Some things in life are like a boomerang. The way you speak and act toward others will often be the way they speak and act toward you. If you treat others with kindness, you will find that kindness will be shown to you by most of them. If you are not very nice to others, then you will find that most will not have much to do with you. Jesus said: "Blessed are the merciful, for they will receive mercy" and "Forgive and you will be forgiven." St. Paul put it another way: "A man reaps what he sows." What we are and what we do to others comes back to us in what people are and what they do to us—just like a boomerang.—Ian Haile.

May 6. Home Building (National Family Week)

"I hear that the carpenters and the painters have finished and that you've moved into your new home," said one of Kevin's friends. "Oh, we still have the same home," the boy replied. "It's just in a new house." Kevin was thoughtful beyond his years. He knew that a home is much more than the building which contains it. Stone and cement, lumber and nails go into the building of a house. People who are bound together by love make a home.—Doris Davis.

May 13. The Guest (Mother's Day)

A traveler crossing a desert at nightfall came to a small tent where he sought food, rest, and shelter. The tent dweller asked the traveler, "What do you call your god?" "I do not believe in a god," the traveler responded. And thereupon the tent dweller cast the stranger out of his tent. During the night the Lord appeared to the owner of the tent in his troubled sleep and asked him, "Where is your guest, my son?" The man answered, "I put him out of the tent because he had no god." Then the Lord directed the tent dweller to go outside and said to him: "Look up and see by the light of the stars a sky far greater than the roof of your tent. I have not shut anyone out because he did not know as much as he ought to know. If I can give shelter to the unworthy in my vast world, could you not give your unworthy guest a little shelter in your tiny tent?"—R. Lofton Hudson.

May 20. A Mountain Through a Pinhole

I can see all your faces, boys and girls, and you can see my face. If however I put this sheet of paper right in front of my face, you cannot see me anymore, but I can still see you. For in the middle of my sheet of paper I have made a hole with a pin, and even though it is a tiny hole, looking through it I can see you all. You can actually see through the pinhole something as far away as a mountain.

There is something even more wonderful, and it is that God is very, very great. None of us can see him, not face to face. Yet he has let us see what he is like in the life of Jesus of Nazareth. As we read about what Jesus said and what Jesus did, we can look through that one short life and see quite clearly the greatness and goodness and glory of God. That's what St. John meant when he said: "No one has ever seen God. The only Son . . . has made him known." That is what Jesus meant when

he said, "He that hath seen me hath seen the Father."—John R. Gray.

May 27. Telling the Truth

Twelve-year-old Bobby came home from school in tears. He explained to his mother that a classmate had told some other students that he had cheated on a test. The class had gotten their papers, and Bobby had made the top grade. The other boy had become jealous. "Did you cheat?" asked his mother. "Of course I didn't!" Bobby replied. "Then why are you upset?" she asked. She then suggested that truth never needs defense. Lies seem destructive for a short time, but in the end truth wins. Bobby decided to return to school the next day, head up.—W. Wayne Price.

June 3. The First Strawberries

When man and woman first came to earth, so the story goes, they lived happily for many years learning the mysteries of the woods and water and sky. Then one day they quarreled, and the wife left the house and walked away into the land toward the east. The husband was sad at her leaving and followed her for a long time, but he could not catch up to her because an angry woman walks too fast. He became discouraged and sat down on a rock to rest, and then an angel of God heard his thoughts, took pity on him, and said to him, "Are you still angry with your wife?" "No, I am not angry," the man said, "But how can I tell her I am no longer angry because she has gone so far ahead and she travels so fast." "Get up and continue your journey," the angel said, "and I will cause her to walk more slowly so that you can overtake her."

The angel caused a new kind of fruit to grow close to the ground that would invite her with its color and its delicious odor. As the woman hurried along, she walked on some of the new plants and crushed some of the ripe fruit. She smelled its fine fragrance and glanced at the ground to see what she had stepped on. She saw the first strawberries. She bent down and picked some. She ate some and found them delicious. Out of the leaves she made a bowl and filled it with the largest berries she could find. "I must take some of these berries to my husband," she said. "I will not be selfish for God has been so good."

She had forgotten all about the quarrel, and she thought no longer about running away to the east. And as many people do when picking berries, she walked in a circle and ended up going back toward her home in the west. She found more and more berries growing in that direction. With her bowl full and her hands full, she looked up and saw her husband coming toward her along the trail. She hurried to meet him and held out to him a bowl of fragrant strawberries. "See the fine fruit I have picked for us to enjoy," the woman said. "It is the finest fruit that grows in all our country." They ate the berries together and went back to their home by the river and forgot that they had ever talked in anger. To this day it is hard for people to quarrel when strawberries are ripe in their fields.—Winfield S. Haycock.

June 10. O.F.S.T. (Children's Day)

Two mothers were standing before a window watching a group of small children at play in the yard. A small boy began tormenting one of the smallest little girls, and her young brother joined in the fun. The mother watched silently for a few minutes, then called out, "Remember, O.F.S.T." Abruptly the little brother changed sides, sticking up for his little sister. "What in the world are the magic letters O.F.S.T.?" asked the neighbor. "That is our family call to arms," explained the mother. "The letters stand for OUR FAMILY STICKS TOGETHER, and the letters have a real meaning to every member of our family."

June 17. He's My Father (Father's Day)

A Roman emperor was enjoying a well-earned triumph. He had the privilege which Rome gave to her great victor of marching his troops through the streets of Rome with all his captured trophies and his prisoners in his parade. So the emperor was on the march with his troops.

The streets were lined with cheering people. The tall legionnaires lined the boulevards to keep the people in their places. At one point on the triumphal route there was a little platform where the empress and her family were sitting to watch the emperor go by in all his pride.

On the platform with his mother was the emperor's youngest son, a little boy. As the emperor came near, the little boy jumped off the platform, burrowed through the crowd, and tried to dodge between the legs of the legionnaires to run out onto the road to meet his father's chariot.

A legionnaire stooped down and stopped him. He swung him up in his arms and said: "You can't do that, boy. Don't you know who is in the chariot? That's the emperor. You can't run out to his chariot." Then the little boy laughed, "He may be your emperor, but he's my father."—Mark Trotter.

June 24. Christ's Faithfulness

On the slopes of the Sierra Nevada Mountains in California grow the famous Sequoia trees. One of them, the General Sherman tree, is classed as the largest and oldest living thing on earth. Supposedly it was beginning to grow about the time of Moses' birth. At the time when Christ was born, the General Sherman tree was already 1500 years old. If scientific figures are correct, it has been growing for 3500 years. Even the Sequoias do not last forever. Sometimes they fall in a storm or are burned in a fire. But the faithfulness of Christ is without end. He is always there waiting to help us in our time of need.—Janice Pauls.

July 1. Quiet Worship (Independence Sunday)

In his book *God's Smuggler*, Brother Andrew tells how people in Yugoslavia wait until dark and then walk slowly across the fields by twos and threes as if they were going to visit neighbors. Actually they are going to a home being used as a church. Their government frowns on group worship, so they carry their lanterns low to keep their faces in the shadows.

Many congregations find it desirable to dispense with hymn singing and even to preach very softly. Otherwise the police could come and take them away. One group of believers found this out the hard way. When police heard the hymn singing, they barged in, stared at the faces, recorded names, and left.

Later the punishments came. The woman who had allowed them to meet in her home no longer had a home, one man was exiled from the country, some had large fines levied against them, and others lost their jobs.—Delores F. Cork.

July 8. Living Water

Along the border between England and Scotland are many old castles now reduced to ruins by the ravages of time. These castles were built hundreds of years ago by English landlords as a protection against the marauding Scots who frequently swept down out of the highlands to raid the English countryside. Important to the defense of each castle was a good source of water. Often the only water available was in a spring some distance from the castle. Such a spring was sometimes secretly piped into the castle to provide water. But the clever Scots sometimes discovered the source of water and cut it off. Then all they had to do was surround the castle and wait for its surrender. But some of the castles had made more adequate provisions. Either they had a spring inside the castle or they dug a well or cistern inside its walls. Thus they had no fear that a seige would cut off their water supply.

Strong Christians are like these castles. Weaker men place their trust in springs that can be cut off, but strong Christians under constant seige from worldly enemies need not fear. They trust in Christ from whom comes a never-ending supply of living water.—John W. Wade.

July 15. Learning Obedience

In a certain province in Arabia there is a highly trained cavalry, known as the King's Guard. Only the very best horses are chosen for the assignment. The way the horses are trained is fascinating. They are put through very difficult routines, and one thing is absolutely essential: they must

obey. The trainer has a whistle, and whenever he blows it, the horses must come to him immediately. When the training is nearly over and the final group is to be selected, the horses are taken to the edge of the desert and put in a corral at the top of a hot, sandy hill. Just below, at the foot of the hill, is a fresh lake which the horses can see at all times. The temperature in the corral rises high during the day, and the horses are left there without food or water for forty-eight hours. Then on the evening of the second day they are released. They rush for the lake of water. Just at the last moment, when they have almost reached the lake, the trainer, standing by the corral, blows his whistle. Only those horses that turn back from the lake without drinking are considered worthy to serve in the King's Guard.—Homer J. R. Elford.

July 22. God's Creatures

Have you ever taken modeling clay or a piece of wood and tried to fashion a dog, a horse, or maybe an elephant? It's great fun trying to shape the lines that make one animal different from another. God must have enjoyed making the animals, planning some for our food, some to give milk, some to be used for work, and even some for pets.

Then God created people, similar in some ways to the animals, but one scientist tells us that man's brain is different in the way in which it grows from that of any animal. And all this God planned. Then, the scripture says, he made people masters over all animals, fish, and birds. That means that people are to use properly, protect, and care for the other creatures of the world. What a duty!

Sometimes we forget this. Sometimes we don't protect them from weather conditions and willful killers until the species becomes "endangered," and few are left on the earth. Fortunately we are now protecting the snow leopard, the whooping crane, and bald and golden eagles. We were too late for the beautiful passenger pigeons. The last one of those died more than fifty years ago.—Eleanor P. McCann.

July 29. The Other Side of the Fence

There were beautiful, fat red raspberries growing beside the fence but in the next dooryard. The owner, Mr. Rhodes, saw little five-year-old Kim looking at them. He walked over and said: "Kim, there are berries growing through on your side of the fence. Take them. They're yours." Kim's daddy, hoeing nearby, joined them at the fence. "That was nice of Mr. Rhodes, Kim. Remember, take only the berries on our side of the fence. The others belong to Mr. Rhodes." Later he noticed Kim looking longingly beyond the fence. He said quietly: "I'm glad you didn't take those others. No one might have seen you, but God would have."—William F. Wills.

August 5. An Attractive Weed

There is an attractive but little-known plant called the feverfew that has fooled a great many people. It resembles the oxeye daisy. Each blossom has a flat, disklike head of yellow or white florets surrounded by one or more rows of flat, white petals. The flowers are lovely and last long after they are picked.

Sometimes persons dig up a few to transplant to their own yards or gardens. They are usually quite pleased to find that the new plants thrive and blossom quickly. But the feverfew is a weed. It multiplies until it crowds out all other flowers and plants. Before the property owner realizes what has happened, the weed has taken over and is extremely difficult to eradicate.

Little faults transplanted to our own lives sometimes take hold so firmly that they cannot be wiped out. They end up controlling our lives. A small sin is still a weed, attractive as it may seem.—Max L. Batchelder.

August 12. Climbing the Stairs

It is a big moment when a child first ventures to climb the stairs. Parents stand nearby to see how he makes out. Invariably the toddler will reach the top safely if he just keeps going. The last step is just as easy as the first. Trouble comes only if the child begins to wonder what business he has so high. Then if he turns back he is in for a tumble.

As Christians pressing toward the goal, we can take some hints from the toddler. First, our heavenly Father is standing by. Secondly, the struggle is not greater the higher we get; in fact it is easier because we have experience behind us. Thirdly, it is dangerous to look back. Too often we follow our gaze. It is a big adventure for a child to climb the stairs. It is the greatest possible adventure for any of us to ascend to God and live eternally with him.

August 19. A Family of Scolders

Imagine living in a family where each time a person saw some fault in another member of the family he would point out that fault and scold the person for it. Most people have plenty of faults, so there would be lots of scolding. You probably wouldn't have time to talk about anything else. Would you like to live in that kind of a family? God has told us to accept people as they are. We should not always be trying to correct them. God does not box our ears every time we are unkind or selfish. He gives us room to live. And he continues to treat us kindly. So we too must be kind and forgiving. In the long run this will be more helpful than if we are always pointing out other's faults. Besides, how well can we judge other people's faults when we have so many of them ourselves?—Leroy Norquist.

August 26. On Being Real

"What is real?" asked the Rabbit one day. "Does it mean having things that buzz inside you and a stick-out handle?"

"Real isn't how you are made," said the Skin Horse. "It's a thing that happens to you. When a child loves you for a long long time, not just to play with, but REALLY loves you, then you become Real."

"Does it hurt?" asked the Rabbit.

"Sometimes," said the Skin Horse, for he was always truthful. "When you are Real, you don't mind being hurt."

"Does it happen all at once, like being wound up," he asked, "or bit by bit?"

"It doesn't happen all at once," said the Skin Horse. "You become. It takes a long time. That's why it doesn't often happen to people who break easily, or have sharp edges, or who have to be carefully kept. Generally, by the time you are Real, most of your hair has been loved off, and your eyes drop out, and you get loose in the joints and very shabby. But these things don't matter at all, because once you are Real you can't be ugly, except to people who don't understand . . . (And) once you are Real, you can't become unreal again. It lasts for always."—Margery Williams in *The Velveteen Rabbit.*

September 2. The Man Who Stayed in London

Thomas John Barnardo went to London to train as a missionary for service in China. During his free time he ran a meeting for boys in a little back street mission. One night, when the meeting was over, one lad was lingering behind. Barnardo told him to go home. "Please, sir, I haven't got a home to go to." Barnardo was shocked, but there was nothing he could do. He was going to China. Some time later he met Lord Shaftesbury at a dinner party and told him of the needs of the East End. Shaftesbury was unwilling to believe the story, and so after dinner the two got into a cab and drove to Whitechapel. Among a pile of packing cases in a shed they found a little boy. They comforted the lad and told him they were looking for homeless boys, and in a few minutes he had rounded up seventy-three children. Lord Shaftesbury turned to Barnardo and asked, "Are you sure God is sending you to China?" You know the rest of the story. Barnardo gave his life for homeless children in London's East End.—Ivor Bailey.

September 9. The Choice Is Yours

How many choices have you made so far today? Decisions and choices are constantly before us. We must decide where to go, what to wear, how to act, what to say, and what to do.

When we are young, the choices are relatively simple, though still important. A little child must choose what to play, where to play, whom to play with, and when to go home.

As children move into school-age years,

more and more choices are presented to them—choices such as what friends to choose, what courses to select, and what clubs and activities to participate in.

In high school and young adult days, the choices become increasingly more demanding. We must ask ourselves: What will I do with my life? How must I prepare myself? Where can I get this training? Whom shall I date? And, eventually, whom shall I marry?

But the most important question every individual must face concerns the purpose to which he will give his life. Jesus said that we cannot serve two masters. (See Luke 16:13.)

The choice is yours. You must choose one or the other. There is no such thing as indecision. Not to decide for is to decide against.—Ann Pollard Williamson.

September 16. Trust and Confidence

The hummingbird is the smallest of all birds. It gets its name from the fact that when flying its wings beat so rapidly that they produce a humming sound.

Hummingbirds live upon nectar and tiny insects obtained from flowers. When feeding, this tiny, colorful bird does not perch but rather hovers in front of a blossom. Its wings beat so rapidly that they appear only as blurred outlines.

When searching for food, hummingbirds do not fly blindly in every direction. Rather they depend upon the sharp-eyed skill of a few scouts to locate the food supply. Then, if the scouts find, for example, a honeysuckle patch, large numbers of hummers move in to feed from the flowers.

Even though the world of nature is in many ways very complicated it is also simplified by the trust and confidence each creature has in other members of its species.—Janice Pauls.

September 23. Somebody's Nobody

A man in his thirties adopted three children over a period of time. He had had great difficulty with the second boy. The boy had been born of a mother who didn't know who the father was. Nor did she want the child. The boy was finally taken from the mother by the welfare agency and placed in a foster home. That proved to be a happy experience for the boy. But it didn't last. He was taken out of that happy setting and put up for adoption.

The young man in his thirties, anxious to have a companion for his first son, was allowed to adopt this boy. The child was full of hurt and pain. He was confused by the constant moves. As the months went by, it was apparent that he wasn't adjusting to his new home. His new father tried in so many ways to reach out to him but without success. One day he did succeed in having a long conversation with his adopted son. Finally the boy with real bitterness said that he was a "nobody." After a long silence, the father said to his new son, "Yes, but now you are somebody's nobody." The boy thought about that for a while. Then, as he realized what his father had said, he broke into a smile, grabbed his father's neck, and hugged him tightly. The hurt and the pain started to go away as the healing balm of love was beginning its miracle of rebuilding a life.—William C. Heffner.

September 30. Listening to God

Let us imagine now that I want to telephone my friend, Willie, whom I haven't seen in a long time. I dial his number and the conversation goes like this: "Hello, Willie. This is Tommy here. I am just phoning you because I haven't been able to see you for a while, but I can tell you that life here is all right except for school and homework and things like that, but we're hoping to go for a holiday sometime soon. That's all in the meantime. Goodbye."

I can see by the expression on your faces that you thought that that was a crazy telephone conversation. Poor Willie never got the chance to say a word. So it wasn't a real conversation at all.

Yet that is what can happen when we speak to God in our prayers. It is so easy to pray, and we chatter on until suddenly we end it all with "Amen." We have never given God a chance to say anything.

Learning to spend a little time listening to God in our prayers is very important.

We can look to no better an example than Jesus who loved to spend quiet times in God's presence. The reason is simply this. If we don't learn to listen, how else will we ever know what God wants of us?

I wonder if God gave to us two ears but only one mouth so that we were meant to listen twice as much as we speak.

The best time to learn is when we are young. One of the greatest of the leaders of God's people in the Old Testament times was a man called Samuel. You can read for yourself in I Sam. 3 how Samuel learned as a boy to say his prayers, "Speak, for thy servant heareth."—E. R. D. Smart.

October 7. Love Story (World Communion)

A. J. Cronin told of a friend, Henry Adams, an average white collar worker who took an average pride in his modest Connecticut home and garden, his wife, and his three children—two girls and a boy. The boy was his "assistant" in the garden, and many a happy hour they had together. When the storm clouds of World War II were gathering, the Adams decided to take in a refugee child for the duration, although Henry wasn't too wild about the idea. So a little Central European by the difficult name of Paul Pietrostanalski came to live with them.

Paul was half-starved and bony, had close-cropped hair and frightened eyes, and could not speak a word of English. But he took an immediate liking to Sammy, the boy in the family.

As the weeks passed the Adams began to taste disillusionment. Perhaps because of the terrors of war and privation and uprooting, Paul was hard to handle. He had confused ideas about honesty and obedience. As he acquired English he proved to be adept at stretching the truth to suit his convenience. Sometimes he was withdrawn, secretive, and evasive.

One day he fell sick. Against strict orders he had gone swimming in a creek known to be polluted. His fever rose. He had to be isolated, and not even his beloved Sammy could be allowed to see him. Then one morning Henry Adams found that Paul had crept from his room in the night and crawled in bed with Sammy. A week later Sammy was dead from the virulent infection.

Sometime later Cronin paid a visit to the Adams' home. To his surprise Paul was helping Henry in the garden. "You still have him?" he asked, nodding toward the boy. "Yes," came the answer, "and he's improved quite a bit. They're giving him some gland tablets. He's quieter and brighter." Then with a quiet smile Adams added: "You won't have any trouble pronouncing his last name any more. He's Paul Adams now. We've adopted him."—Joe A. Harding.

October 14. One Flesh and One Blood

When William Penn summoned the Indians of the region which is now Pennsylvania and made his famous pact with them, he said: "The Great Spirit rules in the heavens and on earth. He knows that we have come here with a hearty desire to live with you in peace. We use no hostile weapons against our enemies. Good faith and goodwill toward men are our defenses. We believe you will also deal kindly and justly with us. I will not call you children, for parents sometimes chide their children severely; nor brothers only, for brothers differ. The friendship between me and you, I will not compare to a chain, for that the rains might rust or a falling tree might break. We are the same as if one man's body were to be divided into two parts. We are all of one flesh and one blood." At every sentence all the Indians shouted a response in their own language. At the end the chief replied for all his people, "We will live in love with William Penn and his children, as long as the sun and the moon shall shine."—Winfield S. Haycock.

October 21. The Get Better Card

Boys and girls, what's this? It's not a Christmas card. It's not an Easter card. It's not a birthday card. It's a get well card. I have often thought a happier name for it would be a get better card. If you are really ill, you can't just get well in a day. But no matter how ill you are you can feel a little bit better every day. It is nice to know that our friends are sorry when we are not well and that they want us to get better.

There is one friend we all have when we are ill. He not only wishes us to get better, but he also does something about it. He gives us a very special get better card that actually helps us to be well again. Here is one. There are no flowers on it and no nice little poems. There is a lot of dull printing and some very bad writing, but it really helps us to get well. What is it called? A prescription. And it is our friend, the doctor, who gives us one when we need it.

In a way the Bible is a sort of get better card. It tells us how we should get better. It tells us not to tell lies, not to cheat, not to hurt anyone. It tells us that we ought to get better every day. But it is not very easy. God knew that it was not easy, and so he did more than send us a get better card; he sent his Son to help us to grow better every day, to become more like him, and finally to be perfect as he is.—John R. Gray.

October 28. Standing on the Cord

The other evening I tried to close the venetian blinds in front of our large door. Despite all my efforts I was not able to lower them. Finally I gave up and turned away. I then discovered I had been standing on the cord. The trouble was not with the blinds but with me. How often we feel that the troubles we encounter are outside of us when their cause is within us. Jesus realized this truth. It led to his frequent teaching concerning the importance of having life right within. He expressed it in simple terms. "Cleanse first the inside of the cup and the platter," he said. Every woman who heard him knew exactly what he meant. Many men did also.—L. Wendell Fifield.

November 4. Christian Love in Action

On Christmas Eve, 1909, a young seminary student moved his belongings into a tiny house in the dirtiest, smelliest, most crowded slum in Kobe, Japan. He had decided that he would never really understand the people of the slums unless he lived with them. And they would never believe his Christian preaching unless he identified with them. His name was Toyohiko Kagawa.

So Kagawa began living with the poor and friendless in their wretched, noisy, and dangerous part of town. It wasn't long until he had taken in various homeless, starving men. Soon he rented two more houses so he could help more needy ones. The little children of the slums loved him too.

Kagawa's whole adult life was spent helping the poor and oppressed in his country. No sacrifice was too great to make. His life showed the people of Japan and of the world that for a Christian love is the law of life.—Rhoda Cressman.

November 11. Building a Church

As a Korean missionary walked with a friend through the country, the friend was amused to see a young man instead of an ox pulling a plow. "They must be very poor," commented the friend. "Yes," was the reply. "When the church was being built, they wanted to give something, so they sold their ox and gave the money. That is why this spring they have to plow like that." "What a sacrifice!" exclaimed the friend. "They did not call it a sacrifice," replied the missionary. "They were glad to have an ox they could sell." —Arlena Hasel.

November 18. Fresh Water (Thanksgiving Sunday)

On the *Mayflower* fresh water was scarce by the time the Pilgrims arrived in the New World. Water is a precious commodity that can only be appreciated when it is scarce. Is it any wonder that there is today a marker to point out the site where the Pilgrims first found fresh water? Visitors to the Cape follow a footpath to this very spot.

The spring of water found by the Pilgrims was a blessing to be sure. But their thirst in coming to the New World was deeper. They knew of the "spring of water welling up to eternal life." The God who had guided them across miles of treacherous ocean would provide for their needs, both material and spiritual.

That finding of fresh water for weary travelers is much more than an historical marker. It is the affirmation recounted again and again in the Bible that God provides for his own.—Bruce O. Breuer.

November 25. Each One a Helper

Karen called Bonnie, a member of her Sunday school class, to see why she had been absent the previous week. Bonnie replied that her father was in the hospital and her mother had just gone to the hospital to have a baby. "I'm taking care of my three little brothers," Bonnie explained, "and I just couldn't get there."

The next Sunday Karen related to the class what happened to Bonnie's family. "We must do something," one member said. "But what can we do? Their problem is so big," another said.

After a moment of silence, one girl offered to go help Bonnie clean the house. Another said, "I'll take vegetables from our garden." Someone else volunteered: "My mother is a nurse. I know she would help them." Another offered: "I can sew. I'll make some gowns for the baby." "And I'll ask my husband to go and cut their lawn," the teacher said. "I'd love to go and help take care of the other children," someone offered. Others chimed in with offers of help.

When the teacher reminded the class of the memory verse for the day, they smiled joyfully. Now they understood it: "So the believers decided to send relief to the Christians in Judea, each giving as much as he could" (Acts 11:29, LB).—Marion Bond West.

December 2. God and Man (Advent)

A scientist kept a colony of ants under glass. While marveling at their industry and orderliness, he detected a weakness in intelligence. A scout ant discovered food and led others to the spot. Later food was placed in a new position and nearer the nest. This was discovered only by first traveling along the original route and then on around the table. The professor hoped they would be intelligent enough to take a new shortcut. He even built obstacles to divert them, but these they laboriously surmounted, crawled over and around, and so persisted in their original route. Said the scientist: "How stupid they are! How I wish I could tell them! If only I could become an ant and show them. But then on becoming an ant I should only have an ant's limited intelligence. I should have to become both ant and man!" Then flashed into his mind a phrase he remembered about our Lord from the Nicene Creed: "Truly God and truly man."—Warren A. Nyberg.

December 9. A Happy Song (Advent)

One day a happy song danced into the heart of a little boy just ten years old. His name was Edmund Hamilton Sears. He lived with his father and mother on a farm away up on the hills of Massachusetts. It was a busy farm where everybody in the family had to help.

Each morning, before they set off, Edmund's father read aloud something out of the Bible. Little Edmund loved the stories of Joseph and David and others, the songs of happy hearts called psalms, and the stories of Jesus.

Under the blue sky while doing his farm work, little Edmund had plenty of time to think over them. One day a little song came dancing into his mind. After he had sung it over and over, his first thought was to write it down so that he would never forget it.

Now that was a problem because out there on the hillside he had no pencil and no paper. What was he to do? Then suddenly an idea came to him. All about his feet, lying almost hidden in the grass, were pieces of soft white limestone. He picked up one very slender one to be his chalk and took off his black hat to be his blackboard.

That night when little Edmund got home, he read the words of his song to his father and mother. They couldn't believe that he'd done it all by himself. But there and then he wrote another verse just as good, and that proved it.

In time Edmund went away to school, but he never forgot to sing. For a year he served as a missionary, sharing with others some of those interesting things his father had read aloud on the farm. Next Edmund became a minister of a church, preaching, telling stories, and visiting and helping everybody. But he never forgot to write songs. It was a long time since he had written his first, but the story of the world's first Christmas that he learned when he was very small he never forgot.

And one day he wrote a happy song that no one had ever heard before. Now lots of us know it and love it. It says with great happiness, "It came upon the midnight clear."—Rita F. Snowden.

December 16. Her Best Gift (Advent)

Lucy heard the missionary tell about the children of India. "They don't have dolls. Their parents wouldn't have any money for dolls. All their money goes for food to keep them from starving." The next day Lucy's mother saw her wrapping her newest doll and questioned her. "I'm going to give it to the missionary for a little girl in India." Lucy explained. "Why don't you give one of your older dolls?" suggested mother. "No," said Lucy, "I'm giving my best one."

The wise men did not bring the leftovers to Jesus. Gold, frankincense, and myrrh were first-rate gifts that would be given to any king. They were the best that anyone could offer.—Winifred Paul.

December 23. Parable of the Birds (Advent)

Once upon a time there was a man who looked upon Christmas as a lot of humbug. He wasn't a Scrooge. He was a very kind and decent person. But he didn't believe in the incarnation which churches proclaim at Christmas. And he was too honest to pretend that he did. He simply could not understand the claim that God became man. It didn't make any sense to him.

On Christmas Eve, his wife and children went to church for the midnight service, but he stayed home. It began to snow. "If we must have Christmas," he thought, "it's nice to have a white one." He sat down by the fire to read the newspaper. A few minutes later he heard a thudding sound, followed by another and another.

Birds, caught in the storm and in a desperate search for shelter, had tried to fly through his window. Now they lay huddled miserably in the snow. "I can't let the poor creatures lie there and freeze," he thought. "But how can I help them?"

He thought of the barn. It was a warm shelter. He put on his coat and overshoes and tramped through the deepening snow to the barn. He opened the doors wide and turned on a light.

But the birds didn't come in. "Food will bring them in," he thought. So he sprinkled a trail of breadcrumbs from the birds to the sheltering barn.

To his dismay the birds ignored the crumbs and continued to flop around helplessly in the snow. He tried shooing them into the barn. They scattered in every direction except that of the warm and lighted barn. "They find me a strange and terrifying creature," he said to himself, "and I can't seem to think of any way to let them know they can trust me. If only I could be a bird myself for a few minutes, perhaps I could lead them to safety."

Just at that moment the church bells began to ring. He stood silently for a while, listening to the bells pealing the glad tidings of Christmas. Then he sank on his knees in the snow. "Now I do understand," he whispered. "Now I see why you had to do it."—Louis Cassels.

December 30. Bridge Builders

A guild in southern France during the twelfth century was called "Bridge Building Brothers." It was made up of nobles, clergymen, and artisans and was approved by Pope Clement III in 1191 A.D. The purpose of this guild was to clear difficult and dangerous roads, to assist pilgrims, and to build all sorts of bridges over rivers, brooks, treacherous precipes, and dangerous ravines. In a real sense this guild could well describe Christians, for we should all be Bridge Building Brothers.—W. Wallace Fridy.

SECTION X. Sermon Outlines and Homiletic and Worship Aids for Fifty-Two Weeks

SUNDAY: JANUARY SEVENTH

MORNING SERVICE

Topic: Frontiers of Our Faith (New Year's Sunday)

TEXT: Gen. 13:14.

I. *The frontier of trouble.* Trouble has been many a man's frontier of faith. Life goes on in a settled fashion with all the securities of moving in familiar ways. Then one day trouble comes, and suddenly you are in frontier country. What does your faith have to say then?

(a) Suffering is always new. The pain of today will be just as new as the first pain man ever had. The great experiences of trouble never grow old. They are repeated anew in every life. The sorrow of a family today is just as real as the sorrow which David felt for the loss of his son. The remorse that was born this morning is just as fresh as that which the prodigal knew in the far country. We are all confronted with frontiers of faith, and each man has to claim them anew for himself.

(b) What do you do when you have to enter that frontier country of a new trouble that has come? Let us face the alternatives for a moment.

(1) You can let your trouble get you down, become increasingly cynical about life, and fall into that state which is probably the unhappiest known to men—self-pity. That's one alternative, and some men choose it.

(2) There is a way of faith. It confesses that trouble is a mystery. You do not know why it comes. But trouble handled faithfully and with the courage you can call out can be a source of new victory and experience.

(c) Some of you stand surrounded by this unknown and fearful territory of trouble. The alternatives are practical and yet profound. At such a frontier God's word often comes clearest, "Lift up your eyes, and look from the place where you are."

II. *The frontier of restlessness.* A frontier of faith is often restlessness in the spirit of a man.

(a) To my mind the spiritual significance of this restlessness has not been sufficiently understood by many of us. It is a growing conviction that it is somehow a frontier of the soul if we but see it. We are restless because we need to move out into understanding and experience the meaning of God in our lives. Can it be that it is God's constant reminder that we need to find our peace in him?

(b) There are some of us who have been putting off that moment when we could, as it were, come face to face with the God of Jesus Christ. We have offered him so many things in advance including our intentions, our words, and our little virtues. Yet all of these have been lesser gifts. What a surprise awaits some people today who have been restless and fearful, for they will learn that God does not need to be persuaded. He has been seeking out of love and forgiveness and contrition to bring you face to face with him.

(c) That restlessness, that feeling of being driven, that fretful flitting from one thing to another, what can it be? The very dissatisfaction it reflects may be the evidence that you stand at a frontier where God says, "Lift up your eyes, and look from the place where you are."

III. *The frontier of doubt.* Many a man has had intellectual doubt because God was thereby calling him to lift his eyes and look from the place where he was. His doubt has been the preface to a deeper faith than he knew before.

(a) This is not to pass lightly over the matter of religious doubt. Sometimes it is not a frontier at all; it is a dead-end. Actually there is a great difference in the spirit a man carries into his times of doubt. It is the difference as to whether you are using doubt as a means of getting away from God or as something to be overcome in getting to him.

(b) This is a plea for a man to respect the intellectual struggle. You will not out-think God. And if by chance you find your inherited idea of God too little, do not for a moment think that a newer understanding is closed. "Lift up your eyes, and look from the place where you are."

IV. *The frontier of social struggle.* No man in this generation could speak of frontiers without turning for a moment to the social struggle as another.

(a) Here in America we look upon 1890 as the year when the geographical frontier closed. At that point we thought we became a settled country. But what new frontiers have opened since! They are those questions which lie at the point of our human relationships. That frontier is here. It cannot be escaped. Someone is going to claim the social areas of our lives. My daily prayer is that it may be Jesus Christ.

(b) We are confronted by overwhelming questions. How shall peace be found? How shall justice be served? How shall a society be secure and yet free? How shall

we use power that is ours without being corrupted by it? Can you see how any Christian can live in our time without becoming a frontiersman of faith in these matters?

(c) My concern is that at a time when a frontier is open and many of every belief are moving into it, we shall never cross the border. Ray S. Baker, who was with the State Department under Woodrow Wilson, looked at the rise of hope for peace and asked whether it was all in vain. Answering those who thought the failure was final he said: "Nothing is ever accomplished without an excess of faith. I am for the ultimate fling of this glorious excess. There is too little passion upon this earth, too little glorious and unrepentant living, too little faith in that which is beautifully impossible. It is a wonderful age we live in, one that will never be forgotten. I thank God that I am a part of it." That's the spirit of a frontiersman, unafraid of the new opportunities for a better world.—Gene E. Bartlett.

Illustrations

FULL OF PURPOSE. This has been a long year, a memorable year. I have seen many novel and some horrible things and gone far over God's earth and feel stronger than ever that there is certainly purpose in the world and that it is God's purpose and that men are the responsible agents. I do not know just what he has in mind for me or just what for you. But there is nothing trivial or unimportant in any of it. It is full of purpose. My prayer on this last day of the year is that God may bless you, strengthen you, and protect you with the wings of his love.—Henry Zylstra.

GOD IN HISTORY. The futurists talk about "when we will use up energy sources, when we will blow ourselves up, and when there will be a revolution, and they ask how we can intervene." But the religious person anticipates the working of God in history and asks how we can act now as if the future of God's new age were already present.—Letty Russell.

Sermon Suggestions

LIFE AS PILGRIMAGE.   Text: Heb. 11:8, 13. (1) For the Christian, life is perpetual pilgrimage. (2) Pilgrimage is the inexorable law of our life. (3) Pilgrimage is the central temper of faith. (4) Pilgrimage is all along the way and at the end God's summons, God's invitation.—Henry P. Van Dusen.

CHRISTIAN PARADOXES.   (1) Seeing the invisible. (See Heb. 11:27.) (2) Knowing the unknowable. (See Eph. 3:19.) (3) Believing the unprovable. (See Heb. 11:1.) (4) Doing the impossible. (See Mark 9:23.) —Henry Osborne.

Worship Aids

CALL TO WORSHIP.   "Both young men, and maidens; old men, and children: let them praise the name of the Lord: for his name alone is excellent; his glory is above the earth and heaven." Ps. 148:12–13.

INVOCATION.   Grant, O God, that because we meet together this day life may grow greater for some who have contempt for it, simpler for some who are confused by it, happier for some who are tasting the bitterness of it, safer for some who are feeling the peril of it, more friendly for some who are feeling the loneliness of it, serener for some who are throbbing with the fire of it, and holier for some to whom life has lost all dignity, beauty, and meaning.

OFFERTORY SENTENCE.   "This is the thing which the Lord commanded, saying, Take ye from among you an offering unto the Lord: whosoever is of a willing heart, let him bring it, an offering of the Lord." Exod. 35:4–5.

OFFERTORY PRAYER.   Our Father, we bow in humble gratitude that as a new year dawns we may call on thee to guide, strengthen, bless, and forgive, and that through these gifts we may share thy love with all who call upon us and thee.

PRAYER.   O God, we thank thee for the gift of another year. May we meet the hours that lie ahead with brave heart and unfailing hope as those who put their trust in thee and, trusting, are unafraid.

May our every thought be pure and every purpose holy. Make us generous in spirit, tolerant in judgment, and unselfish in all human relations. May nothing that we do or say harm another. Whatever comes, may we meet life courageously, bearing with patience the hope deferred and the dream unrealized.

With simple faith and unerring constancy may we seek thy holy will, ever growing in a knowledge of thy truth and walking with joy in the ways of peace.— Alfred Grant Walton.

EVENING SERVICE

Topic: God Leads the Gentiles to Their Shepherd-King (Epiphany)
SCRIPTURE: Matt. 2:1–11.

In the leading of the magi God demonstrates the sincerity of his promise that he would have all men to be saved. We rejoice in the visit of the magi to Christ, for by it God enables all mankind to be included as "the people of his pasture and the sheep of his hand."

I. God leads the gentiles. (a) He led the magi. They shared a common expectancy. In faith they "knew" when they saw the star. They came seeking Christ to pay homage.

(b) In them God keeps his promises to us. All nations shall come to God's light. (See Isa. 60:3.) In him shall all the gentiles hope. (See Rom. 5:12.) He is a light to lighten the gentiles. (See Luke 2:32.)

II. To their shepherd-king. (a) As shepherd he rules and governs, guiding, guarding, folding, and feeding, and as ruler, he "leads the way" to a people God has chosen for himself.

(b) He lays down his life as the true king, as the perfect high priest, and as the savior of men.

(c) He enables a response of faith and obedience by the magi and by us in the totality of life.—Norbert Mueller.

SUNDAY: JANUARY FOURTEENTH

MORNING SERVICE

**Topic: World Mission Still Makes Sense
(Missionary Day)**
TEXT: Matt. 24:14.

Does Christian mission around the world make sense enough to call for our sacrificial giving in the latter half of the twentieth century? I believe it does.

I. World Christian mission makes sense because today, more than ever before, it focuses on people and Christian leaders of and in other lands, not on missionaries.

(a) Without denigrating the missionaries, past or present, it is only realistic to recognize that their task today is supportive and supplementary. The major work and responsibility is in the hands of able and dedicated Christian leaders of other nations.

(b) These leaders are a human lot, fallible as all human beings. Yet across the world one cannot help being impressed with the caliber and faithfulness of men and women whose lives are given over completely to the church of Jesus Christ. Some match the best of Christian leadership of any place or age; some face persecution, jail, and torture for their faithfulness; some sacrifice for Jesus Christ far beyond what most of us in the West realize; some in their own cultures are exceedingly effective evangelists, church administrators, nurses, doctors, teachers, craftspeople, and vocationalists.

(c) Most live on resources far below those we take for granted in the West. The movements and institutions they represent struggle on with a dearth of resources that we, by God's providence, are privileged to help provide. To support world Christian mission today is not to support our work overseas but to help people of other nations to better do their work in faithfulness to Jesus Christ.

II. World Christian mission makes sense because today, more than ever before, it focuses on causes rather than on symptoms.

(a) Churches throughout the world minister to the suffering of multitudes, but increasingly these churches are unwilling merely to pick up the broken victims of war, injustice, oppression, and hatred. The churches probe deeply into the questions of cause.

(b) The church visits the sick and ministers to them, but simultaneously it develops public health programs and planned parenthood programs and promotes integral health development. The prisoners are visited, but more and more the church challenges racism in governmental structures, privilege that ignores the poor, and pride that concentrates rather than distributes power. To support world Christian mission today is to participate in a worldwide attack on the causes of human misery, not just in ministry to its most obvious symptoms.

III. World Christian mission makes sense today because, more than ever before, it is ecumenical in nature.

(a) There is still plenty to do through denominational channels, but it is increasingly evident that erstwhile patterns of narrow denominationalism make no sense on much of the globe. A growing unity in mission, however, makes a great deal of sense.

(b) In recent years the Christian forces have come together in new ways. There is no guarantee that an ecumenical project will be perfect. However, there is much evidence that exceedingly important tasks for the Christian community are beyond the potential of any single church or denomination and that together Christians of many churches can accomplish tasks that would be impossible if attempted alone. Ecumenicity in its finest expressions is taken for granted in many areas of the world, usually far more so than in North America and Europe. For this very reason we should support it and the widespread ministries it embodies.

IV. World Christian mission makes sense because today, more than ever before, the mission is multidimensional and multidirectional.

(a) There is no other channel of giving on earth that provides opportunity for participation in such a wide spectrum of assault on human need. This ministry reaches from personal spiritual struggle to the development of nations and international community relations.

(b) It is likewise heartening that in impressive numbers the former "mission lands" are sending people and resources to other countries. Their mission comes from their commitment to Jesus Christ and their understanding of stewardship.—Eugene L. Stockwell.

Illustrations

LINK.   What is the link which binds St. Polycarp refusing to worship the emperor as Lord, St. Bernard of Clairvaux purifying European monasticism, St. Catherine rebuking pope and prelate, St. Charles Borromeo pioneering a new style of episcopacy at Milan, John Bunyan writing of his pilgrim in Bedford jail, John Wesley proclaiming scriptural holiness, and Mother Teresa tending the dying in the slums of Calcutta? Surely their shared secret is devotion to Jesus, for Christianity in the end is not a system of doctrine nor an organization, important though these may be. It is a person, Jesus Christ, whose living body we are.—J. Munsey Turner.

RELEVANCE.   People say that we must adopt the language and culture of the day to be relevant to today. That is a mistake. If the church marries itself to the spirit of the times, it will be a widow in the next generation.—E. Stanley Jones.

Sermon Suggestions

CHRISTIAN GROWTH.   Text: II Pet. 3:17–18. (1) The dynamic of Christian growth. (2) The direction of Christian growth. (3) The demands of Christian growth.—Stephen F. Olford.

THE TIE THAT BINDS.   Scripture: Gal. 3:-21–29. (1) A mutual background. (2) A mutual experience. (3) A mutual acceptance. (4) A mutual mission.—Charles G. Fuller.

Worship Aids

CALL TO WORSHIP.   "God hath exalted him, and given him a name which is above every name: that at the name of Jesus every knee should bow, of things in heaven, and things in earth, and things under the earth; and that every tongue should confess that Jesus Christ is Lord, to the glory of God the Father." Phil. 2:9–11.

INVOCATION.   Merciful God, forgive the halting nature of our discipleship. We confess that so little of thy love has reached others through us and that we have borne so lightly wrongs and sufferings that were not our own. We confess that we have cherished the things that divide us from others and that we have made it hard for them to live with us. And we confess that we have been thoughtless in our judgments, hasty in condemnation, and grudging in our forgiveness. Forgive us, we beseech thee.

OFFERTORY SENTENCE.   "Give unto the Lord the glory due unto his name: bring an offering, and come before him: worship the Lord in the beauty of holiness." I Chron. 16:29.

OFFERTORY PRAYER.   O Lord, upon whose constant giving we depend every day, teach us how to spend and be spent for others that we may gain the true good things of life by losing every selfish trait.

LITANY.   Almighty and everlasting God:
How good thou art to us!
By thy might are all things created and sustained, and by thy hand we are fashioned and fed. Thou hast lavishly provided for our needs and endowed us for our part in thy mission.
How good thou art to us, O God the Creator!
In thy mercy thou hast joined thyself to us in Jesus Christ. For the matchless gift of forgiveness which covers our guilt and renews our boldness in thy mission:

Accept our glad thanksgiving, O God the Savior!

And in the mystery of thy grace thou hast called us to be thy people, receiving thy gifts and investing ourselves in mission. For granting purpose to our lives and giving our days the taste of joy: *Receive our grateful praise, O God the Spirit!*

O Lord, as thou hast gathered us in a common life, nourished us in thy word, and established us in hope: *So stir and empower us in our calling.*

That our witness may further thy cause in this community and in all the world: *Bend us to thy leading and enkindle us with thine own fire.*

Because thou art worthy of the full measure of devotion, we ask for the sake of Jesus Christ: *Lord, strengthen us for mission!*—Franklin D. Fry.

EVENING SERVICE

Topic: Believe and Be Baptized
TEXTS: Mark 16:16; Acts 2:38.

I. Faith and believing describe the inner relationship of a person to God. He that believes in God and in Jesus whom he has sent has turned to him in humility, repentance, and trust for forgiveness and for salvation.

II. Faith is the important thing: the relationship of the heart to our Lord. Nothing can substitute for that. It is here where the saving experience of the Christian gospel lies. When the heart of man seeks refuge in the heart of God, accepting by faith the life and death of Christ, then the heart is reborn.

III. Baptism, as used in the scripture, means two things. (a) Its scriptural meaning of the receiving of the Holy Spirit. (See Luke 3:16.)

(b) In its material meaning baptism with water is a rite and a symbol. It is not the thing itself but a symbol of the thing.

IV. Faith and believing is the content of the Christian life; baptism is a form. Faith is the essence; baptism is a symbol. As a symbol baptism does not save. The physical water of baptism does not wash away one's sins, regardless of the quantity of water or the mode by which it is administered; it has no power to cleanse. Our sins are not where they can be touched by water, and if they were, water would be powerless to affect them.

V. Sin is a matter of the inner life, and cleansing in the heart can be achieved only by the Holy Spirit.

(a) This does not mean that the physical act of baptism cannot be a highly spiritual experience. The preparation for baptism and the catechetical classes become the plot of ground where the seeds of faith are planted. So faith is also nurtured and strengthened by the symbol of baptism.

(b) Baptism and believing are not synonymous. The water of baptism does not possess any miraculous powers, neither do we earn the grace of God by submitting to baptism. Grace is unmerited and baptism is without miracle. It is a sign on the outside of what has happened and is happening on the inside, the experience of the death and resurrection of Christ and receiving of the Holy Spirit through the response of faith.—Frank H. Epp.

SUNDAY: JANUARY TWENTY-FIRST

MORNING SERVICE

Topic: Our Unity in Christ (Week of Prayer for Christian Unity)
SCRIPTURE: I Cor. 1:10–13.

I. *The unifying and authoritative name:* "Now I beseech you, brethren, by the name of our Lord Jesus Christ."

(a) The history of religion is filled with illustrious names, but the authoritative name is that of Jesus Christ. Paul had good reason for projecting that name. (See Phil. 2:9–11.)

(b) God commanded men, with reference to Christ, "Hear ye him" (Matt. 17:-5). Jesus claimed that all authority in heaven and earth was given to him (Matt. 28:18). The apostle Peter affirmed Christ's authority in Acts 4:12.

(c) In Christianity the only savior of men

is the only authority. There is no authority in human opinions as to what saves from sin, what the church is, and how it is to be governed. Human names are divisive (I Cor. 1:12); unity is obtained in the name of Jesus Christ.

II. *Unifying speech:* "That ye all speak the same thing." (a) Christianity has a speech of its own. (See Heb. 1:1–2.) God spoke through Christ, and Christ spoke through his apostles who were inspired by the Holy Spirit to declare the message of Christianity. The speech of Christianity is the language of the New Testament.

(b) Christians all speak the same things when they speak the words of Christ with the meaning that Christ gave those words through the apostles. Men who speak the same things in matters of Christian faith work together to the glory of God, of Christ, and of the church. (See I Cor. 2:-13).

III. *Unifying organization:* "That there be no divisions among you." (a) Is it possible to have organic Christian unity? Some reply that such unity is not possible. But Paul reproves division and condemns it as of the flesh. (See I Cor. 3:3–4.) Since the inspired apostle condemned division, we must draw the conclusion that unity is a possibility in Christ.

(b) The same church that was located in Corinth was also established in Athens, Philippi, Rome, and every place where Christianity got a foothold. Furthermore, the undivided church continued for two hundred years or more. Those congregations were organized after the divinely given pattern. What was once can be again. When we built the twentieth century church according to the pattern of the first century church, we shall have organic unity.

IV. *Unifying thought:* "But that ye be perfectly joined together in the same mind."

(a) If people cannot think alike on Christianity, then Paul spoke the impossible. Jesus was the founder of Christianity. One of his apostles said, "We have the mind of Christ" (I Cor. 2:16). Paul urged the church at Philippi to possess the mind of Christ. (See Phil. 2:5.)

(b) Since Jesus was the original thinker in Christianity and since his apostles reduced to writing the thoughts of Christ and urged Christians to saturate themselves with the thinking of their Lord, it follows that Christians not only can but also should think the thoughts of Christ after him. In this way will they be of the same mind. Paul also tells us that Christ died for all. (See II Cor. 5:15.) The one atonement demands unity among Christians.

V. *Unifying judgment:* "That ye be perfectly joined together ... in the same judgment."

(a) This has to do with the exercise of the human will. The apostle called upon the Christians in Corinth to resolve to be one in Christ. An obstacle to Christian unity today is the rebellious human will. Whenever people will do strictly as Christ has commanded, the result will be a united Christendom.

(b) How tragic that some so-called followers of Christ have proved themselves to be rebellious! God's message to Israel of old in Isa. 1:2 fits a segment of the people today.

VI. *The unifying argument.* "Is Christ divided? was Paul crucified for you? or were ye baptized in the name of Paul?"

(a) The implication here offered is this: when Christians are made such by being baptized into Christ, they are immediately involved in a responsibility to unification. They belong to Christ, for he redeemed them from sin. Therefore they are under compulsion to do his will.

(b) Having been baptized into Christ, they are committed to his message, his life, and his kingdom. Men in the kingdom of Christ are not rivals, but co-workers. Since the kingdom belongs to God, those who serve within it are bound to do precisely as God directs. Those who refuse to work together under his directives prove their citizenship to be in some other kingdom.—Ard Hoven.

Illustrations

NETWORK. Church history is not the drab recital of a dull and distant past. It sketches in an exciting procession of faces and figures, lively and alert, not plaster and plastic saints. Their life stories were not always glamorous, but their lives were transparent with a kind of glory that can only be described as a gift from God. When I think of the church, I think of names like Paul, Augustine, Martin Luther, John Calvin, Jonathan Edwards, Louis Goebel, and Douglas Horton. But my church is not peopled only by the famous and the forefathers. It is a network of still living and lifting associations. It is the friendship of a former parishioner and the comradeship of a working partner. It is the sharing of a fellowship of concern with some whom I may meet infrequently, and it is the engagement in mutual ministry with those with whom I labor in close proximity. My church is the persons God has given me as fellow pilgrims, and I thank him for them.—Otto E. Sommer.

PRAYER MEETING.   When you pray you rise to meet in the air those who are praying at that very hour, and whom save in prayer you may not meet.—Kahlil Gibran.

Sermon Suggestions

PAUL'S INCOMPARABLE PRAYER.   Scripture: Eph. 3:14–21. Paul's prayer is for three things. (1) That the full "might" of the trinitarian God may be felt in every Christian's life with the result that life may be so enlarged as to contain the full measure of Christ and his life and power. (2) That by faith his readers may find their lives truly "rooted and grounded in love" (v.17) to such an extent that they may be able to "comprehend" the four-dimensional love of Christ (its "breadth and length and height and depth")—a "knowledge" that surpasses all human knowledge (v. 19). (3) That his readers may "be filled with all the fullness of God" (v. 19), obviously a "fullness" surpassing man's capacity.—John Wick Bowman.

CHURCHES LINKED IN MISSION.   Scripture: I Cor. 1:10–15. (1) To know more about each other. (2) To respect each other more. (3) To listen to each other. (4) To work together in certain areas. (5) To help each other. (6) To pray for each other. (7) To nurture each other and to

contribute to each other that which is still lacking in the body of Christ.—Frank H. Epp.

Worship Aids

CALL TO WORSHIP.   "Worthy is the Lamb that was slain to receive power, and riches, and wisdom, and strength, and honor, and glory, and blessing." Rev. 5:-12.

INVOCATION.   Our heavenly Father, who by thy love hast made us, and through thy love hast kept us, and in thy love hast kept us, and in thy love wouldst make us perfect: we humbly confess that we have not loved thee with all our heart and soul and mind and strength and that we have not loved one another as Christ hath loved us. Thy life is within our souls, but our selfishness has hindered thee. We have not lived by faith. We have resisted thy spirit. We have neglected thy inspirations. Forgive what we have been; help us to amend what we are, and in thy spirit direct what we shall be; that thou mayest come into the full glory of thy creation in us and in all men.

OFFERTORY SENTENCE.   "Lay up for yourselves treasures in heaven: for where your treasure is, there will your heart be also." Matt. 6:20–21.

OFFERTORY PRAYER.   Awaken us to the claims of thy holy will, O God, and stir us with a passion for thy kingdom, that we may respond at this time with our gifts and also with our lives.

LITANY.   *Our Father, who art in heaven:*
One god the Father Almighty, one Lord Jesus Christ, one Holy Spirit proceeding from the Father and the Son, have mercy upon us, thy children, and make us all one in thee.
Hallowed be thy name:
Thou who art one Lord have mercy upon us all who are called by thy name and make us more and more one in thee.
Thy kingdom come:
O King of righteousness and peace,

gather us more and more into thy kingdom and make us both visibly and invisibly one in thee.

Thy will be done in earth as it is in heaven:
Thou, who hast declared unto us the mystery of thy will, to "gather together in one all things in Christ, both which are in heaven and which are on earth," conform us, O Lord, to that holy will of thine and make us all one in thee.

Give us this day our daily bread:
Thou in whom we being many are one bread and one body, grant that we, being all partakers of that one bread, may day by day be more and more one in thee.

And forgive us our trespasses as we forgive those who trespass against us:
Thou who didst say, Father, forgive those who were rending thy blessed body, forgive us the many things we have done to mar the unity of thy mystical body and make us, forgiving and loving one another, to be more and more one in thee.

And lead us not into temptation:
As thou didst enable thine apostles to continue with thee in thy temptations, so enable us by thy grace to abide with thee in thy true church under all trials, visible and invisible, nor ever to cease from being one in thee.

But deliver us from evil:
From the enemy and false accuser, from envy and grudging, from an unquiet and discontented spirit, from heresay and schism, from strife and debate, from a scornful temper and reliance on our own understanding, from offence given or taken, and from whatever might disturb thy church and cause it to be less than one in thee,

Good Lord, deliver and preserve thy servants forever. —John Keble.

EVENING SERVICE

Topic: The Reach of Prayer
TEXT: I John 5:15.

The power of prayer is demonstrated by its irresistible reaches.

I. *Prayer reaches up.* (a) Prayer is communion with God; it is the soul in fellowship with its maker. Prayer is adoration. It is more than petition, more than mere asking—it is communion. It is the soul coming home to its natural habitat—God.

(b) No person truly prays who thinks only in terms of what he wants to receive. Prayer reaches up and the answering hand of God reaches down, and the two meet. If prayer can bring the soul of a person up into the presence of God, then prayer is not powerless.

II. *Prayer reaches in.* (a) The soul that finds God through prayer finds itself. No person knows himself until he has found God.

(b) When we pray we see ourselves as God sees us, for prayer is the mirror of the soul. Tell me what you pray for, and I can tell you the kind of person you are. You can discover more about yourself, your weaknesses, and your frailties through the power of prayer than by all the courses you may take in self-analysis.

III. *Prayer reaches out.* The soul first finds God, then itself, and then its neighbors. Prayer reaches its greatest privilege and joy when it becomes intercessory prayer. If you have never known the rich experience of praying for others, you have not entered the ABCs of prayer. You may have studied about prayer, but you have not prayed.

IV. *Prayer reaches through.* (a) Prayer, like Paul's great concept of love with its length, depth, breadth, and height, has four dimensions in which it travels. Have you made the personal discovery that prayer can reach through?

(b) When the soul is overwhelmed and when life like a great tidal wave has come sweeping in, then prayer coming from the heart of the person who believes makes contact with God, and back comes the answer, not always as we desire and not as we might dictate. But the inward peace that breaks upon the soul brings the consciousness that God has heard and he will answer.—Carl J. Sanders.

SUNDAY: JANUARY TWENTY-EIGHTH

MORNING SERVICE

Topic: Spiritual Weapons for Spiritual Warfare

SCRIPTURE: Eph. 6:10–24.

Paul has been expounding God's eternal purpose to create through Jesus Christ a new society or new humanity in which there are no longer any distinctions of race, rank, or sex. He has gone on to exhort his readers to live a life "worthy" of God's calling and "fitting" to their status as the people of God. It is all a beautiful dream. Now he brings us down to earth by reminding us of the opposition. He introduces us to the devil and to certain "principalities and powers" at the devil's command. Is God's plan to build a new society? Then they will do their utmost to frustrate his plan. Does God intend his people to live in harmony and purity? Then they will spread discord and evil.

I. *The enemy.* (a) If we underestimate our spiritual enemy, we shall see no need for God's armor, shall go out to the conflict unarmed with no weapons except our own puny strength, and shall be quickly and ignominiously defeated. For we are not fighting against "flesh and blood" but against cosmic forces. In a word, our enemies are not human but demonic. They have at least three characteristics.

(1) *They are powerful.* They are called "principalities and powers," which indicates the authority they wield. They are "world rulers," which shows the extent of their kingdom. And they are "spiritual hosts," which tells us that the nature of their power is spiritual rather than physical.

(2) *They are wicked.* Power itself is neutral; it can be used well or misused. But our spiritual enemies use their power destructively. They are "the world rulers of this present darkness," the "spiritual hosts of wickedness." They have no moral principles, no code of honor, and no higher feelings. They are utterly unscrupulous and ruthless in the pursuit of their malicious designs.

(3) *They are cunning.* Paul writes of "the wiles of the devil," for he seldom attacks openly. He prefers darkness to light, it is his natural habitat. So we are all the more unsuspecting and unprepared when he transforms himself into "an angel of light" (II Cor. 11:14). He is a wolf, but he enters the flock in the disguise of a sheep. He is as subtle as a serpent. We must not therefore imagine that temptation to sin is his only weapon; he also deceives people into error.

(b) Only the power of God can defend and deliver us. True, the principalities and powers are strong, but the power of God is stronger! Paul has already told us in the first two chapters that it is the power which raised Christ from the dead and exalted him to heaven, the power which raised us from the death of sin and seated us with Christ in heavenly places. So he tells us to "be strong in the Lord and in the strength of his might" and to "put on the whole armor of God."

II. *The armor.* (a) The apostle turns from the strength and power of God in general to the armor and weapons of God in particular. He was very familiar with the Roman soldier and was indeed chained to one by the wrist as he dictated his letter. Although such a bodyguard would be unlikely to wear the full armor of an infantryman on the battlefield, yet the sight of him may well have kindled the apostle's imagination.

(1) *The belt of truth.* The Christian soldier's girdle is "truth." This may mean "the truth," the revelation of God, for it is the truth which sets us free and which conquers the devil's lies. More probably, it means "truth," sincerity, or integrity. To be deceitful ourselves and to lapse into hypocrisy is to play the devil's game, and we cannot beat him at his own game. He loves darkness; it is light which causes him to flee. In spiritual health as in mental health, honesty about ourselves is indispensable. If we pretend to be other than

we are, we are asking for defeat.

(2) *The breastplate of righteousness.* The Christian soldier's breastplate is "righteousness," and in Paul's letters this word usually means justification. Certainly to have been justified by God's grace through faith, to have a righteousness which is not our own but Christ's, to stand before God not condemned but accepted. These things are an essential defense against an accusing conscience and the slanderous attacks of the devil. On the other hand, Paul has written in II Cor. 6:7 of "the armor of righteousness on the right hand and on the left," so he may here be referring to a righteous character. Just as cultivating truth overthrows the deceit of the devil, so cultivating righteousness overthrows the temptations of the devil.

(3) *The gospel shoes.* The Christian soldier's shoes are "the equipment of the gospel of peace." This may refer to our readiness to share the good news with others, for certainly we should always be ready to speak of Jesus and to give an answer to those who ask us questions, and such readiness can put the devil to flight. On the other hand, the reference may rather be to a certain readiness or firmness which is given to us by the gospel of peace. The NEB translates: "Let the shoes on your feet be the gospel of peace, to give you a firm footing." If we have received the good news and know that we have peace with God, we have a firm foothold from which to fight against our enemy. In either case the devil hates the gospel, for it is the power of God unto salvation both in us who have received it and in others to whom we make it known.

(4) *The shield of faith.* The word Paul uses denotes not the small round shield which left most of the soldier's body unprotected but a lengthy oblong shield measuring about four feet by two and a half, which covered his whole person. The Christian shield which can extinguish the fire-tipped darts of the devil is faith or trust in God. It is by faith that we lay hold of the power of God's might. Against this shield the devil's fiery darts have no chance.

(5) *The helmet of salvation.* The Roman soldier's helmet was decorative as well as protective. According to I Thess. 5:8 the Christian soldier's helmet is "the hope of salvation." But whether our helmet is salvation as already received and now experienced or the confident expectation of our full and final salvation on the last day, there can be no doubt that God's saving power is a mighty defense for us against the enemy of souls.

(6) *The sword of the Spirit.* Of the six weapons or pieces of armor listed, the sword is the only one which can be used for offense as well as defense. It is "the word of God," for when God speaks he acts. His word has power. It accomplishes his purpose. It is the weapon which the Holy Spirit uses most. Jesus used the sword against the devil when tempted in the Judean desert, and we must learn to use the same weapon.

(b) These six pieces together constitute "the armor of God." It is God's armor because he supplies it. Yet it is our responsibility to take it up, put it on, and use it against the enemy. With this provision we have no excuse for failure.—John R. W. Stott.

Illustration

LEGACY.   When Christ was about to leave this world, he made a will. His soul he committed to his Father, his body he bequeathed to Joseph to be decently interred, his clothes fell to the soldiers, his mother was left to the care of John; but what should he leave to his poor disciples? He had no silver or gold, but he left them that which was infinitely better—his peace. —Matthew Henry.

Sermon Suggestions

VIRTUES CHARACTERIZING CHRISTIANS. Text: II Pet. 1:5–7. (1) Patience gives us poise and preseverance. (2) Forbearance keeps us from flying off the handle and withholds us from pressing our advantage against weaker persons. (3) Fortitude enables us to bear our own burdens without whining. (4) Sympathy enters into the sufferings of others. (5) Humility prompts us to confess our own weakness and sin. (6)

Generosity leads us to forgive others and grant the benefit of the doubt and the boon of service.

THE LIFE OF THE SPIRIT.   Text: Gal. 5:25 (NEB). (1) The human spirit is the essence of life. (2) The life of the spirit is life lived in response to the spirit of God. (3) This life of the spirit is possible because of God's love.—Edward J. Hansen.

Worship Aids

CALL TO WORSHIP. "Oh that men would praise the Lord for his goodness, and for his wonderful works to the children of men! For he satisfieth the longing soul, and filleth the hungry soul with goodness." Ps. 107:8–9.

INVOCATION. Father God, open our eyes that we may see with an inner vision, open our hearts that we may feel with a deep conviction, and open our minds that we might know with a certain understanding. We believe that you are what we confess you to be. Help thou our unbelief! We believe that you are present to us now. Help thou our awareness! We believe that you are acting in the world. Help thou our devotion!—Richard D. Bausman.

OFFERTORY SENTENCE. "Thy prayers and thine alms are come up for a memorial before God." Acts 10:4.

OFFERTORY PRAYER. O heavenly Father, we pray that thy blessings, which are as countless as the stars, may be so used as to bring light and love to thy children everywhere.

PRAYER. Help us, O God, to come unto thy compassion with faith, even as one of old touched the border of Jesus' garment and was healed of her infirmity. Help us to come unto thee for the restoration of our bodies, for the clearing of our vision, for the cleansing of our hearts, and for the liberation of our spirits. May all that Jesus did for the people in the days of his flesh become the token of all that thou dost wait to do for our spiritual lives. Act upon us now. Answer with thy deed even the slightest flicker of our faith. May the words of Christ prove powerful in us: "Thy sins are forgiven," "Be of good cheer," and "Arise and walk." May the hand of Christ lift us up unto life more abundant and more abounding.

We feel, O God, the deep and distressing needs of the world of which we are a part. May our concern and compassion for others open the channels of our lives through which may flow thy gracious help and power. Wherever thy Spirit finds faith in the heart of man or woman or child there may thy favor rest and thy power become manifest. In returning unto thee, O God, may the world be saved, and in quietness and confidence may we become strong.

EVENING SERVICE

Topic: A Welcome to Sinners
SCRIPTURE: Luke 7:36–50.
  I. Sinners also need to be in the church (vv. 36–38). (a) Since all are sinners, all need Christ. To be in Christ is to be in the church. In the text the woman is called a "sinner," one who probably sinned in the flesh. Simon was just as much a sinner because of the sin of the spirit.

(b) The basic reason we come to Christ is for a cure of sin. Sin transcends all racial, national, cultural, and economic conditions. We join the church not as rich or poor, black or white but as sinners. Thus every sinner is a prospect. And then who is not a prospect?

II. Sinners also need forgiveness (vv. 40–43). (a) Our text points out that we need forgiveness of our debts to God. This involves the fact that moral failure is a sin against God. Nathan made David aware of his sin of murder and adultery. Then David confessed, "I have sinned against the Lord."

(b) Sin means separation from God. To be separated from God means separation from life and love. When we bring sinners to Christ, we are bringing them to experience God's mercy of forgiveness.

III. Sinners also can love Christ (vv. 44–50). (a) It may be that sinners will love

Christ more than we do because they may have been forgiven more. The woman in the gospel was forgiven not because she loved but rather she loved because Christ forgave her. The more we sin, the more we can be forgiven. The more we are for-given, the more we love.

(b) Isn't the church meant to be a fellowship of lovers of Christ? This love is the result of acknowledging we are sinners, of being forgiven, and then loving out of gratitude.—John R. Brokhoff.

SUNDAY: FEBRUARY FOURTH

MORNING SERVICE

Topic: Keeping the Faith
TEXT: II Tim. 4:7.

I. *"To keep the faith"* will mean that we have something worth keeping and upon which we put the greatest value. No doubt a great deal of what we acquire in the course of the years, we should discard. This is true of furniture, pictures, books, and clothes. They no longer are necessary. As one moves from youth to maturity there are many things of which one must say, "Now that I have become a man, I have put away childish things."

(a) Some people put faith in that category. Perhaps this should be discarded too. It has come down generation after generation and is distinctly "dated." It was very beautiful as part of our childhood, but it does not seem valuable now. It fails to fit my present need. Indeed it is true that many aspects of religious experience, biased and narrow as they are, should be discarded. Stereotyped forms of worship and of prayer fail to help as we enter into new and unforeseen experiences. Many of the things which have come with our faith we need not keep.

(b) But something must be kept, or we have thrown away our most valuable possession. It comes partly from the past, but it also comes from the fires of one's own experience. Paul is speaking of the past but also of the present as he says that he has kept the faith. It was the experience of the conversion on the Damascus Road and the allegiance which from that time he gave to the living Christ. This surged through his life with undying power.

(c) We draw upon the past and are thankful for the faith of our fathers, but we clothe that in terms we understand and we add the reality of our own experience. We have found our faith valuable, helpful; it has been tested and proved. There is something that I live by; there is belief in God in my mind, there is love for Christ in my heart, and there is desire to be of service in my will. These things keep me going. These form my faith. These must not be lost. I intend to "keep the faith."

II. *Faith needs protecting.* If one has kept the faith, it means one has protected it against its enemies. On the British coins there is stamped in Latin the slogan "Defender of the Faith" as one of the titles of the king or queen. It is a noble title. Faith always needs defense; it must ever be protected.

(a) Faith does not automatically continue after it is started. Sometimes we assume that it will and that all we need to do is to start it off.

(1) Much of educational philosophy is based on the assumption that if you get the right principles before a child or in him, you can let matters after that take care of themselves. (See Prov. 22:6.)

(2) Nothing is more evident in society today than that there are multitudes of people who have been trained in the way they should go but have drastically and decidedly departed from it.

(3) Many who have been brought up in our homes and churches have not kept the faith. Their lives have become shallow, cynical, materialistic, and useless.

(b) One's faith must be protected and defended or it will indeed be lost. This takes resolve and determination. The three parts of Paul's report on his life are filled with a sense of the struggle of the gladiatorial games: "I have fought the good fight," and one senses the struggle of the gladiatorial games; "I have finished the course," and one sees the Greek runners in the stadium at Corinth or Athens coming down the home stretch; "I have kept the faith," and one has the same feeling of effort exerted and of achievement gained. This is as difficult as the others and needs the same vigor, resolve, and will. It demands what William James called "the will to believe." One will not keep the faith unless he is determined that it will be kept.

(c) This means that I must use my faith, for I will either use it or I will lose it. I must put myself into it, making it a part of my very life.

(1) How many people fail because they do not put themselves into their work! Their lives are not fully engaged, and therefore their tasks have no power and meaning. So with faith. It is the weapon I use in the conflicts of life.

(2) I must give of my best self if it is to be strong. It is my assertion of what I believe against the forces of doubt and disorder. It is the assertion of good against evil, of God against chaos, and of Christ against selfishness and pride. Thus as I use my faith I protect it, and as I protect it I keep the faith.

III. *Christ helps us keep the faith.* He shares in its custody. Paul not only wants Timothy to keep the faith, but he also wants him to know that someone else will help him preserve it. "I know whom I have believed, and am persuaded that he is able to keep that which I have committed unto him" (II Tim. 1:12).

(a) It is a sign of man's selfishness or perhaps of his loneliness that he thinks he must do everything by himself. He has the whole task of building a good life for himself and a good society in his world. This he feels to be his burden, and he shrinks from it or revolts against it. No one can carry this great task of keeping firm the faith and of retaining and holding fast the good things of life.

(b) Man is not meant to do it all. The good in life is his to keep and to defend, but God is helping him defend it too. The whole religious experience is a partnership. When we have done all that we can, we put our achievements into God's care and keeping. He upholds what I have done that is good. He is helping me keep the faith. Have you never experienced that feeling, the sudden awareness that the tasks you thought you must carry all alone are being shared by God? Have you never felt in times when your burdens were too heavy for you that God was helping bear them too? There is no experience more reassuring than the awareness that God is with us and that he helps us keep the faith.

(c) That is what Paul means as he sums up his life. What he has achieved he has placed into the hands of God. The scars of his battle, the cup won at the end of the race, and the faith tested and tried are given to God who supports and treasures and keeps them always. I am able to keep the faith because God keeps it for me and with me. "My Savior has my treasure and he will walk with me." And I know that he will keep me even as he keeps the faith; that he will keep me firm; that he will keep me loyal and true. Thus the faith is kept as I commit it to Christ.—Phillips Packer Elliott.

Illustrations

OUTREACHING INFLUENCES.   Had we tests fine enough, we would doubtless find each man's personality the center of outreaching influences. He himself may be as utterly unconscious of this exhalation of moral forces as he is of the contagion of disease from his body. But if light is in him, he shines; if darkness rules, he shades; if his heart glows with love, he warms; if frozen with selfishness, he chills; if corrupt, he poisons; if pure hearted, he cleanses.—Newell Dwight Hillis.

WORD IN DARKNESS.   John Bunyan, author of *Pilgrim's Progress,* tells about himself when a great cloud of darkness hid from him the things of God and Christ "that it was as if I had never seen or known them in my life. After I had been in this condition some three or four days as I was sitting by the fire, suddenly I felt this word to sound in my heart, I must go to Jesus.

At this my former darkness and atheism fled away and the blessed things of heaven were set in my view."

Sermon Suggestions

THE GOSPEL IN THE RAINBOW.   Text: Gen. 9:13. (1) After the worst of storms the rainbow symbolizes the lovingkindness of our God. (2) In the worst of times the rainbow symbolizes the worthwhileness of our work. (3) Especially amid a world at strife the rainbow symbolizes the brotherhood of our race. (4) In what may seem to be the worst of all possible worlds the rainbow symbolizes the foundation of our hope.—Andrew W. Blackwood.

WHY DO WE DO WHAT WE DO IN WORSHIP? Text: Eph. 3:14. (1) We are trying to realize the presence of God. (2) When we feel his presence, we are impelled to praise. (3) We are humbled in penitence. (4) We are ready for information and illumination, the function of the sermon. (5) We enter into a fellowship. (6) We seek identification with God and dedication to him.—Ralph W. Sockman.

Worship Aids

CALL TO WORSHIP.   "Make a joyful noise unto the Lord, all ye lands. Serve the Lord with gladness: come before his presence with singing. Enter into his gates with thanksgiving, and into his courts with praise: be thankful unto him, and bless his name." Ps. 100:1-2, 4.

INVOCATION.   O Lord God, who hast left unto us thy holy word to be a lamp unto our feet and a light unto our path: give unto us all thy Holy Spirit, we humbly pray thee, that out of the same word we may learn what is thy blessed will, and frame our lives in all holy obedience to the same, to thine honor and glory and the increase of our faith.

OFFERTORY SENTENCE.   "Give unto the Lord the glory due unto his name: bring an offering, and come before him: worship the Lord in the beauty of holiness." I Chron. 16:29.

OFFERTORY PRAYER.   Help us to remember, O Lord, that a life is a more persuasive testimony that words, that deeds are more effective than argument, and that these gifts are only a portion of the loyalty thou dost require of us.

AFFIRMATION.   We believe in the discipline of the soul which results in creative Christian living.

We believe that through prayer and worship we increase the effectiveness of our faith.

We believe that we must transform the experiences of worship and prayer into a living witness for Christ.

We believe that this witness becomes meaningful when it is a shared witness in all areas of our lives.

We believe that this means a daily giving of ourselves for Christ as partial payment of the debt we owe for what he did and continues to do for us.

We believe that through the means of Christian stewardship and tithing we express our devotion to our Lord in a tangible act of love through giving.

We believe that through the shared, corporate experience of worship and fellowship in the church we discover some of the means that enable us to express these fundamental beliefs.—Chester E. Hodgson.

EVENING SERVICE

Topic: Making a Good Track Record
TEXT: Heb. 12:1.

I. *Eliminate the handicaps:* "Let us lay aside every weight, and the sin which doth so easily beset us." All encumbrances which entangle our feet should be cast aside. The greatest of all handicaps in running the race of life is related to sin. Sin always saps the strength of the runner on the roadway of life. It leaves one feeble, floundering, and flabby. It causes one to neglect the type of discipline that would bring him to the peak of his efficiency. It generates divided loyalties, mixed motives, and conflicting purposes which bring one's stamina to the nil level. It produces a guilty conscience which fractionalizes one's capacity to perform. It lowers one's resistance until he is a "pushover" when the real testing time comes.

II. *Accentuate the helps:* "Let us run the race that is set before us." The first thing that helps us is to have a sense of direction and follow through as described in the words "the race that is set before us." The Lord wants us to follow a well-marked course and not swerve to the left side or the right side, keeping a middle-of-the-road direction. We are not to be going in all directions at once but to move in a consistent stride toward a worthy goal. The second thing that helps is to master "patience" so we can be faithful in the performance of our duty.

III. *Appreciate the heroes* who have gone on before: "Seeing we also are compassed about with so great a cloud of witnesses." This glorious company of successful runners now occupy the grandstand as those who cheer us on. The faithful devotion, the inspiring example, the challenging testimony, and the glowing memories of these heroic winners make it easier for us to give our best to this noble endeavor. The supportive value of these heroes makes us more determined than ever to be true to the Lord.—Mendell Taylor.

SUNDAY: FEBRUARY ELEVENTH

MORNING SERVICE

Topic: **The Good Shepherd**
Scripture: John 10.

I. Jesus says that the good shepherd knows his sheep. (a) A close, personal relationship existed between a shepherd and his sheep. He was with them all the time. They were totally dependent on him. Consequently they were more than mere animals to him. They were his friends. They were his children. It was the custom for the shepherd to give names to each of his sheep. Verse 3 testifies to a personal, caring relationship that existed between the shepherd and the sheep.

(b) Do you know what that means? It means that you are important to Jesus. In Luke 15 the point becomes even clearer. Ninety-nine sheep are in the fold, safe and sound. Only one sheep is lost. Jesus says when that happens the shepherd leaves the ninety-nine who are safe and sound and searches everywhere until he finds that one little sheep, and when he finds him he rejoices. Every sheep is important to the shepherd, and every Christian is important to Jesus.

II. Jesus says that the good shepherd saves his sheep. In v. 9 Jesus says, "I am the door; if any one enters by me, he will be saved."

(a) The verb "saved" is in the passive voice to indicate that this salvation is something that is done for the sheep. They don't save themselves. The shepherd saves them. The verb is in the future tense to indicate that salvation is not a once for all event in the past but a progressive experience which will not be completed until some day in the future when we are ushered into the presence of God.

(b) Sheep were unaggressive animals. They were relatively defenseless. They were easily led astray. They were in constant need of care and supervision. They were constantly wandering off and getting lost like that sheep in Luke 15.

(c) The Bible says we are like those sheep. Because of that our greatest need is not to be educated, not to be made socially acceptable, not to be psychologically adjusted, and not to be financially stabilized. Our greatest need is to be saved. We need to have our sins forgiven, our lives changed, and our future secured. We need to be saved. And the good news is that Jesus the great shepherd of the sheep can save us, and he can do it this very day.

III. Jesus says the good shepherd dies for his sheep. (a) Most of what Jesus says in this chapter can be paralleled in the experience of the shepherds of that day. But this is a new thought, a distinct idea.

The shepherd had to be willing at any moment to defend his sheep against enemy attack. And on occasions a shepherd may have been overpowered by a foe and thus lose his life. But v. 18 clearly shows that what Jesus was talking about was a predetermined act on the part of the shepherd to deliberately lay down his life for his sheep. Five times in these few verses Jesus says, "I lay down my life for my sheep." The reference is to the cross.

(b) How can Jesus save us? How can this man who died two thousand years ago have an effect on our lives today? The answer is the cross. (See Col. 1:13–14, 20, TLB.)

(c) The most glorious statement in the chapter is the statement that the shepherd lovingly, freely, deliberately, purposefully, and of his own will laid down his life for his sheep. That makes possible everything else that we say.

IV. Jesus says that the good shepherd provides for his sheep. Jesus doesn't just save us and then set us up on a shelf to wait for the glories of heaven. Jesus provides everything that we need right now to experience the fulness of abundant life. That's what he says in v. 10 he came to bring.

(a) He provides *security*. He says in v. 9 that the shepherd saves the sheep and that they can go in and out. This was the Jewish way of describing a life that is absolutely secure and safe. Jesus lets us know that we are on God's side. (See Rom. 8:31.)

(b) He provides *strength*. Jesus says in v. 3 that the shepherd leads his sheep out. A shepherd would not send his sheep ahead by themselves. He would lead them and walk with them so that he could give them whatever help they needed.

(c) He provides *sustenance*. (See v. 9.) (1) What was it that the sheep needed to keep living? They needed more than security. They needed more than strength. They needed physical nourishment, and it was the shepherd who led them to the best pastures where they could get that physical sustenance they needed.

(2) That's what Jesus does for us spiritually. If you will walk with the Lord daily and drink of his wisdom daily and eat the strong meat of his word daily and feast on his spiritual pastures, he is going to give you a spiritual sustenance that will enable you to grow as you become more and more like him.

(d) He provides *safekeeping*. (See v. 28.) No wolf, no thief, no bandit, no hireling, no demon, not even the devil can pluck the sheep out of the hand of the great shepherd. And do you know why? Because he who is in us is greater than he who is in the world. (See I John 4:4.)—Brian L. Harbour.

Illustrations

WORLD RELATIONSHIPS. Most of us cannot hear what salvation is about. It is too radical for us to listen to. We keep waiting for God to speak some new word about it for our time, but he will speak no more until we have heard what he has already said. What he has said in Jesus is that the time has come—had come then and has come now—for a profound revision of the way human life is organized and perceived in the world. Every man must die to himself—to his traditions, to his insecurities, and to his property—and be born again into a new world of relationships where the other's good is preferred to his own.—John Killinger.

THE FACE. I saw myself a youth, almost a boy, in a low-pitched wooden church. There stood before me many people, all fair-haired peasant heads. All at once a man came up from behind and stood beside me. I did not turn toward him, but I felt that the man was Christ. Emotion, curiosity, awe overmastered me. I made an effort and looked at my neighbor. A face like everyone's; a face like all men's faces. "What sort of Christ is this," I thought. "Such an ordinary man. It cannot be." I turned away and suddenly my heart sank; and I came to myself. Only then I realized that just such is the face of Christ— a face like all men's face.—Ivan Turgenev.

Sermon Suggestion

SPELLBOUND. Text. Mark 12:37. (1) His was the spell of a man who knew. He always spoke with authority. (2) His was the spell of a man who was alive. Men constantly asked him about life. (3) His was the spell of a man who cared. Everybody felt the love that beat in his heart.—G. Campbell Morgan.

Worship Aids

CALL TO WORSHIP. "Now in Christ Jesus ye who sometimes were far off are made nigh by the blood of Christ. For he is of our peace, who hath made both one, and hath broken down the middle wall of partition between us. Now therefore ye are no more strangers and foreigners, but fellow citizens with the saints and of the household of God." Eph. 2:13–14, 19.

INVOCATION. Eternal God, in whom we live and move and have our being, whose face is hidden from us by our sins and whose mercy we forget in the blindness of our hearts: cleanse us, we beseech thee, from all our offenses and deliver us from proud thoughts and vain desires, that with lowliness and meekness we may draw near to thee, confessing our faults, confiding in thy grace, and finding in thee our refuge and our strength.

OFFERTORY SENTENCE. "Verily I say unto you, Inasmuch as ye have done it unto one of the least of these my brethren, ye have done it unto me." Matt. 25:40.

OFFERTORY PRAYER. Almighty God, whose loving hand hath given us all that we possess: grant us grace that we may honor thee with our substance, and remembering the account which we must one day give, may be faithful stewards of thy bounty.

LITANY. *Lord, when did we see you hungry?*
We are thankful for the bread you gave the multitudes. We are thankful for the body that was broken for us. We are grateful for the hungers that make us aware of our need of you. Make us aware that we are responsible for a hungry world.
Lord, when did we see you thirsty?
We are thankful for that water that was made wine holding out a chance for all of us. We are thankful for the water of life you bring to us. We are grateful for the thirst that brings man to you.
Lord, when did we see you a stranger?
We are grateful for your ministry to Zacchaeus and the woman at the well and Levi and Mary of Magdala. For while we were yet sinners you loved us. We are grateful for your church where we need not be strangers but fellow citizens with the saints and members of the household of God.
Lord, when did we see you naked?
We are thankful for the dignity of our faith. We thank you for the clothing you wrap around us. We thank you for the belief that all of us and each of us has a real worth. We are thankful that you take the prodigal back.
Lord, when did we see you sick?
We are thankful that in our brokenness you came as healer and that to our own ills you have come in healing love. We are thankful that the great physician is here.
Lord, when did we see you in prison?
We are thankful that while we were yet afar off you came to set us free. We rejoice that we have freedom to move and to live and to find our own uniqueness. We thank you for coming to us in our bondage and making us free.—Jack R. Van Ens.

EVENING SERVICE

Topic: Our Ministry of Reconciliation
SCRIPTURE: Rom. 15:7–33.
We have a ministry of reconciliation. Jesus had such a ministry; Paul did also; but this means little unless we are willing to accept this mission to be reconcilers. If we do accept it, we must have certain qualifications.

I. We must have *love*. David Kossoff dedicated his book, *The Book of Witnesses*, in this way: "This book is for my father, who died long ago. Once, when I was small, about eight, I was with my father, who was a loving man, in a narrow street in the East End. A huge laborer suddenly roared down at us that we had killed Jesus. My father asked him why he was so unhappy, and the fist lowered and the shouting stopped and he began to cry. We took him with us to my aunt's for tea. This book is for my father, who was a loving man."

II. To be a reconciler takes *courage.* Jesus faced the angry mob. Paul was imprisoned in Philippi, chased out of Thessalonica, smuggled out of Berea, laughed at in Athens. John Wesley also experienced this sort of thing, as have many others who have played the role of reconciler. One of the truly courageous Christians of our century in America was Clarence Jordan whose "quiet conviction and charismatic leadership" brought about the establishment of the Koinonia Farm in Americus, Georgia, in 1942. Jordan and his friends were truly reconcilers, but it took courage, as it does for all

genuine Christians.

III. The ministry of reconciliation requires a spirit of *selfless service.* As we look back to the earlier decades of this century, we remember the great Japanese Christian, Toyohiko Kagawa, who lived with the people in the slums of Kobe, Japan, some of the worst in the world at that time, that he might serve them in his Master's name. "Christ became a servant" (Rom. 15:8), and so must we.

IV. To be a reconciler we must have the desire to *share.* We must be missionaries. At this point in Paul's letter to the Romans, we find he wants to continue his ministry of reconciliation even to far away Spain (Rom. 15:22–29). We, like Paul, to use the words of a contemporary song, must "pass it on." We must share the good news.—George Wesley Jones in *Virginia Advocate.*

SUNDAY: FEBRUARY EIGHTEENTH

MORNING SERVICE

Topic: The Three Thirsts of Humanity (Brotherhood Week)
TEXT: John 19:28.

I. *A physical thirst.* (a) Who can move along the world's frontier today without hearing the physical cry of Jesus, "I thirst." I have seen and heard him in the squalid "favellas" of South America, amid the tea-pickers of Sri Lanka, from the landless Aboriginees of Australia, the oppressed blacks of South Africa, the unemployed in Western lands, and the numberless poor across the third world.

(b) We are witnessing today a momentus phenomenon. For the first time in history people facing all kinds of physical deprivation are willing to accept their lot no longer. So everywhere there are protests and uprisings which are directed at every form of physical poverty and political oppression. Through it I can hear no other than the risen Christ identified with the people, hungering and thirsting after freedom and justice.

(c) If this interpretation of the upheavals of our era be correct, what are our responsibilities as Christians? What must we do if the cry of the poor and the oppressed is the call of Christ, "I thirst"? We are committed to assuaging that thirst.

II. *An emotional thirst.* (a) Wherever there are people there is a thirst for emotional satisfaction and there can be heard the deep-throated cry for human companionship.

(b) As Jesus moved toward the end of his life he became enveloped in a deepening isolation and loneliness. As the shadow of the cross fell across his pathway the crowds thinned. To those who remained Jesus said, "Will you also go away?" Then came the garden of Gethsemane. "They all forsook him and fled." Finally even God seemed to have gone: "My God, why have you forsaken me?"

(c) Loneliness of spirit is as common today as physical hunger. Especially in the great cities of the Western world millions live in quiet desperation and loneliness. In crowded tenements, in vast antiseptic hospitals, and in huge and impersonal crowds people are physically close but separated by vast gulfs in every other way. Everybody is too busy and too encased in self-interest to reach out toward each other. So in loneliness millions live and millions die.

(d) In a lonely world how vital and relevant becomes the community of Christians called the church. Jesus developed an amazing strategy. Down in every community he planned to place a small group of people gathered around his risen presence where people could count and could say simply, "I belong."

III. *The thirst for God.* (a) On the cross Jesus cried out for God, his Father. Since that day the world has never been able to forget the awful shout of dereliction, "My God, why have you forsaken me?" We can only bear to think about it because in the end it was answered. As death came near, the love of God flooded in to surround and support Jesus: "Father, into your hands I commend my spirit."

(b) The hollowness of secular humanism and materialism is becoming obvious to millions. Many are discovering there is not enough variety and excitement in events to silence forever the needs of the spirit. There is no bottle of alcohol long enough to satisfy an eternal soul. There is not enough sex to bring peace of heart. There is not enough money to bring a soul at rest.

(c) When the pace slackens, perhaps in the middle of the night, we hear the quiet protest and yearning of the spirit within. Deep calls to deep. It is the cry of the stream for the ocean, the call of a man or a woman for a lover, the yearning of the prisoner for freedom, and the wanderer for home. It is the cry of the soul for God.

(d) There is nothing the world needs more and nothing which would add more to the sum total of human happiness than for people to come into a conscious relationship with God. To be found by the love of God, to discover the forgiveness of sin, to experience the presence of God, and to be caught up into his purposes are the ultimate in inner personal joy and satisfaction. To tell this message and to be trusted with this task is as high a privilege as can come to any one of us.—Alan Walker.

Illustrations

BREAKING THROUGH. At some points, however small, peace, love, and freedom are always breaking into affairs otherwise human; where men make peace, where human love meets human need, and where the oppressed are struggling free, at these points, however small, the kingdom of God is always breaking into the affairs of men.—American Friends Service Committee.

ALONE IN A CROWD. Lady Ottoline Morrell was one of England's great hostesses. She entertained the cream of society at her country home in Garsington during World War I. Any given weekend at that time may have included such names as Bertrand Russell, D.H. Lawrence, Aldous Huxley, Katherine Mansfield, Seigfried Sassoon, and Prime Minister Asquith. Her home rang with the voices of the great. In all of this atmosphere of conviviality she complained in her diaries of her intense loneliness. "Here I sit," she wrote, "with all these people and talk and talk, yet we remain outside each other and never really blend and live together as the flowers do. How inaccessible we all are!"—Lloyd D. Thompson.

Sermon Suggestions

MY BROTHER'S KEEPER. Text: Gen. 4:9. (1) Humanitarian concern for their secular well-being. (2) Ethical concern for their moral characters. (3) Evangelical concern for their everlasting salvation.—John Mackay.

WHEN GOD SURPRISES US. Text: Gen. 28:16. (1) God sometimes reveals himself unexpectedly in the realm of nature. (2) God sometimes reveals himself unexpectedly amid the ordinary surroundings of life. (3) God sometimes reveals himself unexpectedly in the hour of loneliness and trial. (4) God sometimes reveals himself unexpectedly in the hour of spiritual abasement.—John C. Lambert.

Worship Aids

CALL TO WORSHIP. "Having therefore, brethren, boldness to enter into the holiest by the blood of Jesus, by a new and living way, which he hath consecrated for us, let us draw near with a true heart in full assurance of faith." Heb. 10:19-20, 22.

INVOCATION. Almighty God, who of thy great mercy hast gathered us into thy visible church: grant that we may not swerve from the purity of thy worship, but may so honor thee both in spirit and in outward form that thy name may be glorified in us and that our fellowship may be with all thy saints in earth and in heaven.

OFFERTORY SENTENCE. "Whatsoever ye would that men should do to you, do ye even so to them: for this is the law and the prophets." Matt. 7:12.

OFFERTORY PRAYER. Our heavenly Father, may thy kingdom be uppermost in our minds, our hearts, and our lives. Accept our gifts and with them the rededication of all that we are and have to thy greater glory.

PRAYER. Almighty God, who hast given us this good land for our heritage: we humbly beseech thee that we may always prove ourselves a people mindful of thy favor and glad to do thy will. Bless our land with honorable industry, sound learning, and pure manners. Save us from violence, discord, and confusion, from pride and arrogancy, and from every evil way. Defend our liberties and fashion into one united people the multitudes brought hither out of many kindreds and tongues. Endue with the spirit of wisdom those to whom in thy name we entrust the authority of government that there may be justice and peace at home and that, through obedience to thy law, we may show forth thy praise among the nations of the earth. In time of prosperity, fill our hearts with thankfulness, and in the day of trouble, suffer not our trust in thee to fail.—Clifford L. Stanley.

EVENING SERVICE

Topic: From Self to Others

SCRIPTURE: Ps. 40.

Our lives swing between concern for ourselves to concern for or about others. This psalm starts off with a reference to what happened to an individual and then goes on to say how he shared his experience with others about him.

I. This man learned to wait patiently and steadfastly for the eternal Lord of life. God brought meaning to the meaningless places and forgiveness for the deep and fitting sense of guilt. God brought him out of it. He raised him, lifted him up.

II. This man found that the help of God gave him a firm footing. He was now on rock. He put his weight down, and there was God. God steadied his steps. God made his steps secure. When we know where we stand in this universe, it makes for firm, steady steps as we walk through life. No wonder the psalmist says, "He put a new song in my mouth, a song of praise to our God."

III. This note of joy came into this man's life when he (a) became aware of need, (b) acknowledged God, (c) accepted his love and faithfulness, (d) acted on the newfound life, and (e) asked for the continuance of this grace. This brought him to a sharing of this great experience of deliverance with others who believed. This is one of the functions of the church too. The church is the fellowship of the forgiven.—Paul David Sholin.

SUNDAY: FEBRUARY TWENTY-FIFTH

MORNING SERVICE

Topic: The Three Rs of the Christian Faith

SCRIPTURE: Rom. 1:16–17.

I. *Revelation* (a) The self-disclosure of God to man spans a long period of time. It has certain high points in the Old Testament such as the call of Abraham, the deliverance of Israel from bondage, giving of the commandments to Moses, the message of the prophets, but God's full revelation of himself comes in his Son. Jesus said, "He that hath seen me hath seen the Father." "We do not go beyond Jesus Christ to find something else in God—all that God is he is in Jesus Christ" (Martin Luther).

(b) Revelation has not ceased. God continues to speak to and through the hearts and minds of persons and events to make himself known. The wonder of wonders is that God makes his appeal through persons and thus reveals himself through the Christian reconciler. The church has been given the ministry of reconciliation. As she fulfills that ministry the love of God is revealed.

II. *Reconciliation* "God was in Christ reconciling the world unto himself." Reconciliation is not an achievement by man alone. Recently a member of my confirmation class told about a boy whose parents did not go to church and were not at all interested in the church. However the boy went to Sunday school and worship. He would tell his parents what he learned at church and in his childlike faith his witness for Christ made its impact upon his parents. Finally they became interested and began going with him and became Christians and members of the church. Jesus promised that "a little child shall lead them." The ministry of reconciliation continues.

III. *Resurrection* (a) The resurrection of Jesus Christ from the dead and his victory over the powers of sin and death proclaim the hope that we have in Christ. Christians do not make a yearly pilgrimage to an empty tomb. They worship the risen and living Christ. Christ is alive forevermore!

(b) Paul opens his letter to Romans with the words, "I am proud of the good news, for it is the power of God for salvation." Paul was not ashamed of his faith in Christ. He was grateful for what Christ had done for him, and he wanted to share it with others and help others to know Christ. True Christians are optimistic in their faith.

(c) God is seeking to reveal himself to every person, to reconcile everyone unto himself through his Son, and to raise everyone from the death of sin into the newness of righteousness and eternal life in Jesus Christ.—W. Aubrey Alsobrook in *Wesleyan Christian Advocate.*

Illustrations

LITTLE BOXES.   Jesus cannot be confined by any formula, theological or otherwise. He breaks out of all the little boxes in which we try to imprison him. No sooner have we defined him to our satisfaction than someone else says to us, "Wait a minute; you have forgotten something," and we discover that indeed we have.—Robert McAfee Brown.

CHRISTIAN EDUCATION.   The objective of the church as manifested through its educational ministry is that all persons be aware of and grow in their understanding of God, especially of his redeeming love as revealed in Jesus Christ, and that they respond in faith and love—to the end that they may know who they are and what their human situation means, increasingly identify themselves as sons of God and members of the Christian community, live in the spirit of God in every relationship, fulfill their common discipleship in the world, and abide in the Christian hope.

Sermon Suggestions

OUR CHRISTIAN FAITH. Text: Rom. 10:8. (1) The *foundation* of our faith consists of the self-revealing nature of God. (2) The *commandment* of our faith is capsulated by Jesus, "That you love one another." (3) The *worship* of our faith can be best demonstrated in pure praise. (4) The *doctrine* of our faith is summarized in the trinity concept. (5) The *Lord* of our faith is at once the unique and the mysterious person who lays an ultimate claim upon our soul. (6) The *reward* of our faith is the peace of God.—John W. Meister.

THE LAWS OF HAPPINESS. Text: Mark 12:30–31. (1) Surrender yourself to divine authority. (2) Practice Christlike love. (3) Respect yourself; accept the forgiveness of sins; be made whole.—Ernest R. Case.

Worship Aids

CALL TO WORSHIP. "Great is the Lord, and greatly to be praised; and his greatness is unsearchable. One generation shall praise thy works to another, and shall declare thy mighty works." Ps. 145:3–4.

INVOCATION. Eternal God our Father, who art from everlasting, thou hast made us and not we ourselves. Thou hast sent us never far from thee that we, thy children, may learn the ways of freedom and choose thee with all our hearts. Grant us now thy Holy Spirit that, confident in prayer, we may worship thee with gladness and become as little children before thee.

OFFERTORY SENTENCE. "Give unto the Lord, O ye kindreds of the people, give unto the Lord glory and strength. Give unto the Lord the glory due unto his name: bring an offering, and come into his courts." Ps. 96:7–8.

OFFERTORY PRAYER. We give thee thanks, O Father, that through our tithes and offerings thou dost give us an opportunity to illuminate the dimness of the future and to glorify our present life with the word of him who is the light of the world.

PRAYER. Our Father, giver of life, source of abundant life, and our hope of life eternal, we thank thee for every thrill and throb of life which moves our hands, stirs in our minds, and surges in our hearts. Without thy sustaining power and without the breath of thy Spirit we would be as the dust blown by the wind.

Possessors of the gift of life, we thank thee for teaching us how to live. Thou dost teach us as a good father teacheth his children. We know the way of righteousness. We see the path of truth. The road of peace lies before us. Keep our feet where they ought to go, and make us willing to follow the Christ who goeth before us.

Grant, our Father, that we may live well amid the ordinary duties and within the everyday relationships of life. May we exalt our kinships by finding in them opportunity to love. May we ennoble our friendships by accepting in them the goodwill of others and by giving even in better measure than we have received. May the casual contacts with our fellowmen be the sharing of sympathy and joy. And out beyond the bounds of daily contact and vision may we send and receive such influences as may make this world a better place in which to live.

EVENING SERVICE

Topic: How to Observe Lent (Ash Wednesday)

TEXT: Rom. 12:21.

I. *Master your mind.* Think less about the present and more about the future; think less about yourself and more about God and others; think less about the dust in your house and more about the dust on your soul; think less about the beauty or lack of it on your face and more about the ugliness of your soul. Make up your mind what you want to be: the richest body in the graveyard or the poorest soul in heaven.

II. *Master your time.* If you don't go to church at all, start going; if you go now and then, go every Sunday; if you go every

Sunday, go twice on Sunday; you can also go on, say, Wednesdays and Fridays, and of course on the holy days. Don't forget your prayers—morning, noon, and night and grace at meals. You have time. Use it. If you haven't the time, you're just the one who should take time to observe Lent.

III. *Master your body.* Stop eating so much candy, roast beef, mashed potatoes, and the like and stop drinking so much of whatever you drink too much of. When you say no to that third cup of coffee or that extra piece of pie, your stomach won't cry out, "The throat's been cut!" You'll simply be telling your stomach that the throat can indeed be cut and that you can do it. Are you so weak that your body can tell you what to do?

IV. *Master your will.* Plan to do the right thing, and then do it. Make yourself do it. Don't just think about getting up from your nice warm bed and stumbling off to church. Get up and go. You get up and go to work, don't you? Don't just think about being kind. Be kind. Don't just think about turning over a new leaf. Turn it over. If you can't do what you will to do, then maybe the goblins have got you already.

V. *Master your self.* "Of ashes thou art come, and to ashes thou shalt turne agayne." Remember that despite all the nice things people say about you or what nice things you think about yourself, you are only a tiny little speck on a second-rate planet and that you can move about and do only a few things. When you were put here, you were given power to will. You can will to serve your weaknesses or you can will to master your weaknesses and make them serve you.

VI. *Serve the master.* Whether you want to think so or not, you were put here for one purpose only, that is obviously enough, to serve God and to do his will and pleasure. Why do you think that Christ allowed himself to be mocked and tortured and nailed to a cross? Do you think that he died to make us free just to serve ourselves? He came to deliver us from ourselves so that we could serve God. Did he not mean, "Thy will can be done on earth as it is in heaven"?—*The Anglican Digest.*

SUNDAY: MARCH FOURTH

MORNING SERVICE

Topic: Love Made Visible (Lent)

TEXT: I John 3:18 (NEB).

I. When God sent his only Son to live in this world, that was love in action.

(a) There are dozens of religions that have something to say about the love of the invisible God. There is only one that says that this love became visible in the life and death of a human being who was the perfect reflection of the Father in heaven.

(b) Visible, yes, visible as Jesus walking through the streets and talking of the kingdom of God; visible as the healing of a paralytic; visible as the gesture that welcomed the children, the outcasts, the depraved, and the lost; visible as the other gesture that drove out the demons. Not a word to argue for the goodness of God but action to deliver us from evil.

(c) Then the fearful visibility of Golgotha when, as Matthew says, "sitting down they watched him there." Him—the healing, saving, strengthening, loving companion of the lonely, champion of the poor, friend of sinners, and giver of life—there on the fiendish cross where Romans killed their criminals and rebels, there with his disciples in hiding, his mother in agony, his enemies jeering, and careless soldiers gambling for his clothes.

II. There is more than the inward visibility of the crucified. Jesus broke through the cloud of words to give us something we can see, something we can touch, and something we can taste. On the night when he was betrayed he took bread and said, "This is my body," and poured out wine, saying, "This is my blood." And, looking across the centuries from the upper room in Jerusalem to us now, he added, "Keep on doing this." From that day to this, at the heart of Christian worship has been this sacrament where the love of Christ, his broken body and out-poured blood, is made visible for us all.

III. Having received the love of God in this visible, material, and concrete way, do we then go away unchanged to live for ourselves alone? Do we think it enough to celebrate the love of God in church and to assure one another that Christlike love is indeed the answer to all the problems of the world?

(a) If the love of God was made visible in Christ and is visible to us in the symbols of his broken body and poured out blood, then our love must be visible or it is just words, just talk. (See I John 4:19–21.) Our love has to be as visible as the Samaritan's donkey, as the widow's mite in the offering box, and as the bleeding hands of Jesus. John drives the message home in 3:17–18.

(b) The Bible has nothing to do with a false spirituality that avoids the plain consequences of love made visible. It doesn't shrink from telling us that the test is what we do with our possessions. And when the church is faithful to her Lord, the hard cash in the collection plate is as plain a symbol of our love as the very material bread and wine is of God's love to us.

(c) When Jesus was asked to speak about the commandment to love God and our neighbor, he told a story, not a fairytale but an incident with which everyone can identify from that day to ours. And in the center of the story we read this: "Next day he produced two silver pieces and gave them to the innkeeper, and said, 'Look after him; and if you spend any more, I will repay you on my way back.'" For Jesus love was made visible in the cash and the credit card. It was as practical and as challenging as that.—David H. C. Read.

Illustrations

THE LEPER.   St. Francis of Assisi, walking along the road, saw a leper, a man giving off a stench, a man whose bandages had not been changed for months, a man neglected, a man starving because nobody would give him a lift to the next town where he might beg. St. Francis, who had been brought up in a genteel manner, was exceedingly repulsed by this figure and

passed by. Then things began to run through his mind, including the parable that told of other people who had walked by on the other side of the road. For good or ill, St. Francis's conscience got the better of him. He went back and picked the man up and began walking down the road. As he walked he noticed that the man did not seem to weigh anything. Who was this man who weighed nothing? Finally he did what he thought he would not have the nerve to do. He decided to look at this man's face. He removed the bandages, and there was the face of Jesus.—George William Rutler.

SPIRITUAL ATTITUDE.   A member, in taking an honest look at his relationship to his church, discovered a rather interesting correlation. Said he: "I discovered that, when I am behind in my pledge one month, the choir doesn't sing as sweetly as it did before. When I am two months behind in my pledge, I begin to notice a lot more hypocrites sitting around me than I ever noticed before. If I am three months in arrears on my church pledge, I generally get suspicious of the preacher." Perhaps you had never thought of it, but keeping one's pledges up to date has a lot to do with one's spiritual attitude and one's relationship with his brethren in the church.—Gerald Kennedy.

Sermon Suggestions

COMMUNION IN THREE WORDS.   Text: Luke 22:19. (1) Commemoration of an absent Lord. (See Acts 3:20–21.) (2) Communication with a present Lord. (See Matt. 18:20.) (3) Contemplation of a coming Lord. (See I Cor. 11:26.)

WHAT IS GOODNESS?   Text: Matt. 7:12. (1) Goodness is more than opinion; it is ethical. (2) Goodness is more than a creed; it is character. (3) Goodness is more than sweetness; it is consistency. (4) Goodness is more than mental conviction; it is aggressive righteousness.—Fred R. Chenault.

Worship Aids

CALL TO WORSHIP. "They that wait upon the Lord shall renew their strength; they shall mount up with wings as eagles; they shall run, and not be weary; and they shall walk, and not faint." Isa. 40:31.

INVOCATION. O God, we thank you for leading us until this hour. Direct us in the days ahead through the difficult places of decision. When the call seems clouded and the road is in poor repair, grant the boldness to face the future in faith and to fortify ourselves in truth. Help us to be ready to recognize our own inadequacy and your sufficiency.—John M. Drescher.

OFFERTORY SENTENCE. "Of every man that giveth willingly with his heart ye shall take my offering [saith the Lord]." Exod. 25:2.

OFFERTORY PRAYER. O God, who hast given us thy Son to be an example and a help to our weakness in following the path that leadeth unto life, grant us so to be his disciples that we may walk in his footsteps.

PRAYER. Our Father and our God, from whom come all good things in us and in nature: we sensitively open our spirits to all that is holy, truthful, beautiful, and honest. In this pavillion of prayer we would more intimately find thee and be found by thee.

We have confession to make. We haven't been alert and alive to thy expressions in our lives. We have gotten sidetracked with sensual pursuits. We have been preoccupied with good times more than with good deeds. Forgive us again. Be patient with us while we learn to live beyond ourselves a bit more.

As the world is reborn every spring, grant that we may be born again in the world of the spirit. As the spring winds sweep clean the earth, may fresh breezes of the Holy Spirit refresh and clean the harmful accumulations from our lives and allow us to be free as the wind. As the brown earth warms and sends forth new life, may our lives also bring forth new life and productivity.

EVENING SERVICE

Topic: Why I Pledge

TEXT: Luke 16:2.

I. I believe in pledging. (a) I pledged my loyalty when I joined my church.

(b) I made a pledge when I was married.

(c) I made a pledge when we bought our home.

II. My pledge is my testimony. (a) The way I use my money reveals the interests in which I really believe.

(b) I'm glad to be counted as one who supports Christ's church.

III. My money is effectively used by my church. (a) Devoted workers keep overhead costs low.

(b) Funds are used to help the needy in the spirit of the good Samaritan.

(c) This investment will not fail.

IV. I want to help maintain my spiritual home. (a) Here I learn God's will for my life.

(b) Here my children learn to live as Christians.

(c) Through the church I help others to learn the good news of God's love.

V. I want my church to use good business practices. (a) A dependable income is necessary to pay for light, heat, and salaries.

(b) A trustworthy income is needed to support missionary work at home and around the world.

VI. I will pledge because it enables me to make some return to God for his goodness.

(a) All that I have is from God.

(b) It is a high privilege to answer his call to go, to teach, and to preach in a world like ours.

SUNDAY: MARCH ELEVENTH

MORNING SERVICE

Topic: Why Does God Allow It? (Lent)
TEXT: Rom. 8:18, 28 (PHILLIPS).

Jesus was asked similar questions such as why did a certain high-rise tower fall on innocent people and kill them. His questioners asked if this was due to their sins, and it would seem Jesus was also asked if the Galileans who were destroyed by Pilate as they made their sacrificial offerings to their God were worse sinners. He answered with an emphatic "No" (Luke 13:1-5). It is wise always to face the worst if we would have a growing, secure Christian faith. Lin Yutang said that peace of mind comes from facing the worst. Why does God allow the so-called natural disasters if God is good? Disasters like earthquakes, typhoons, fierce, shattering storms at sea and on land. How can roaring seas proclaim the goodness of God? What about the insensate crimes committed by mentally twisted, sick, sadistic persons—the destruction or maiming of babies and little children, helpless old men and women? What about the slaughter of potentially useful, and often innocent men, women, and children in war?

I. To these classes of evil add one which disturbs most of us most of all: the suffering, the diseases so far incurable, which men and women and children experience and who have done nothing to cause the disease. This is also evil. One of the reasons that research scientists, surgeons, physicians, nurses, and all other therapists are doing God's will is that they are fighters against the evil of sickness and death as Jesus was. Yet how often have we asked as the Lord Christ did on the cross, "My God, why?"

II. No one of us can give a complete and wholly satisfactory answer. (a) True, some human disasters and suffering are due to human perversity and the evil in us. But most of it is not. We must say that it has not been given to us to have a solution. But we do have insights.

(b) We live in a developing universe. Our faith is that the universe including man did not just happen without any purpose behind it and ahead of it and within it. While there is much in the universe that puzzles us and even depresses or distresses us, occurrences which seem cruel and callous, there are evidences of a mind at work. This mind is what Jesus spoke of when he said, "My Father has never given up working (is working still) and I am working" (John 5:17). Jesus also said, "He who has seen me has also seen the Father."

(c) If God is Christlike, he is personal and more than personal. Jesus not only argued that God is supremely good; he also demonstrated in his life and death how good God must be and how deep and unfailing and unending is God's love. This does not dispel all mystery, but it should make us unwilling to blame God for all evils.

III. Belief in God's goodness and ultimate victory over all evils grew up beside human experience of pain. Pain has its part in developing human character and personality. Sometimes the price paid for the development of patience and courage and faith seems far too high to pay. A genuine, not synthetic, pearl is the product of a concealed agony; it is the way an oyster deals with the irritating sand beneath its shell.

IV. The suffering of mankind has led men and women to provide relief. (a) Pain does serve as a means of alarm, to draw our attention to injury or disease. Then it is that wise persons seek the expert advice of physician or surgeon. Pain also helps create "that condition of voluntary immobilization of an inflamed or injured part essential to bring about a cure."

(b) Suffering, physical, mental, and emotional, has inspired what is rightly called "ultra-sophisticated research and technology to produce stockpiles of resources" to alleviate and even completely deaden pain: "pills and powders and procedures." Let no one minimize or scoff at their value. The tragedy is that while we are now helped to endure less and less hurt ourselves, we seem as a race determined to inflict more and more sufferings on others. This is true when the "others" are considered to be our enemies. We must try to get rid of over-kill in exchange for the tremendous benefits of what has been called "over-care."

(c) Would we not be living now as citizens of God's kingdom if we let our hurts turn us toward hearing and healing the hurts of others, even as dedicated medical practitioners and nurses do for those suffering from physical and mental hurts?

V. Somehow God shares our suffering—not just physical pain but the agonies of bereavement, of separation from one loved, and of our own folly and sin.

(a) A famous statesman and philosopher said that the case against the Creator was mountainous and watertight "unless one could believe in the incarnation and that God himself had thus—in Jesus Christ—come into the middle of the world to redeem it."

(b) I do not think that in this world we can hope completely to understand. We can think through to partial explanations which often do help. But this has not bothered Christians too much. They have believed that a loving God will work his purpose out. Meanwhile, Christians are to trust when we cannot see.

(c) To trust God means that we hold fast to the conviction that his purpose is wise and good. Then we have something better than a complete and final answer to the question, "Why does God allow it?" We meet the worst and find ourselves "more than conquerors through him who loves us."—David A. MacLennan.

Illustrations

GOD THE SHAKER.   Two Americans traveling in the Welsh countryside were caught in a sudden and violent thunderstorm. The only shelter in sight was a small cottage. Hurrying to it, they found an old woman living there who, when she saw their plight, quickly opened the door and gave them shelter. The lightning flashed, the thunder rolled, and the wind howled in great gusts about the little cottage. So violent did the storm become that it seemed the cottage would be blown away, and the men were quite fearful. Yet all through the storm the old woman calmly sang a hymn. "Aren't you afraid of the storm?" one of the men finally asked. "No, my lad," came the reply. "I'm just proud to serve a God who can so shake this old earth."—John W. Wade.

TURBULENT WATERS.   Sam Keen tells of swimming in the Indian River inlet as a boy. "Where the outgoing water from the bay met the incoming surge from the ocean, the currents were swift and the waves wild and irregular. Many people lost their lives in these waters. With a confidence born of folly I played with the irresistible danger and I learned something of the principles of wisdom in those waters. The outgoing currents were too swift to swim against, but if you would only yield yourself to them they would carry you to a point beyond the inlet, where it was possible to swim cross-current and come back to shore in the calm waters in the lee of the jetty that formed the south boundary of the inlet." Then Sam Keen observes, "When swimming in turbulent waters, wisdom lies in knowing when to relax and when to struggle."

Sermon Suggestions

THE MINISTRIES OF MISFORTUNE.   Text: Ps. 119:71 (MOFFATT). (1) Misfortune serves to deepen life. (2) Misfortune is often the means of releasing undreamed of powers. (3) Misfortune brings enlarged capacity to understand and help other people. (4) Misfortune can make real and vital one's relationship to God.—William M. Elliott.

AN ANGEL IN THE SUN.   Text: Rev. 19:-17. (1) The symbol of an angel standing in the sun suggests that we should always try to see the spiritual in the material. (2) This symbol suggests that we look for the divine in the human. (3) This symbol suggests that we should look for the constructive elements in every destructive experience.—Harold Cooke Phillips.

GRACE ABOUNDING.   Text: Rom. 5:20. (1) Sovereign grace. (See Heb. 4:16.) (2) Saving grace. (See Eph. 2:8–9.) (3) Schooling grace. (See Tit. 2:11–13.) (4) Sufficient grace. (See II Cor. 12:9.) (5) Sustaining grace. (See II Tim. 1:9.) (6) Supplying grace. (See II Cor. 9:8.) (7) Surpassing grace. (See Eph. 2:7.)—Jimmy Johnson.

Worship Aids

CALL TO WORSHIP.   "Blessed is the man that trusteth in the Lord, and whose hope the Lord is." Jer. 17:7.

INVOCATION.   We turn our minds unto thee, O God, that thou wilt give us deeper insight into the meanings of the life of thy Son, our Lord. We turn our hearts unto thee that thy love may flow through them. We turn our wills unto thee that thou mayst guide us in all that we do and in all that we say.

OFFERTORY SENTENCE.   "If ye then, being evil, know how to give good gifts unto your children: how much more shall your heavenly Father give the Holy Spirit to them that ask him?" Luke 11:13.

OFFERTORY PRAYER.   Dear Father, may we ever give thee a definite, consistent, and heartfelt service.

PRAYER.   O God, overlook our words and hear our thoughts this morning. In these moments of pondering, in this search for significance, we bow our heads but we raise our hopes to thee, O God.

We do not always recognize the riches that we receive—a body that functions without pain and a mind that moves out beyond time and space. We have enjoyed advantages that we did not work for and advances that we did not make—the warmth of the sunshine and the nourishment of the rain, the music of creative Christians and the wonder drugs that heal bodies.

We are puzzled by human nature, our nature, because we have such potential for creating life, yet we seem bent on destroying it. We are blessed with ever-increasing knowledge, yet we do not know how to live at peace either with ourselves or with each other.

Maybe that is the reason we are here today, O God. We need forgiveness for doing what we knew was wrong, and we need forgiveness for not doing what we honestly believed was right. Guilt is a heavy load, and we need a reprieve. We need to be moved and motivated by thy Spirit, O God, because the facts of division and distrust, of hate and hostility, have been quite plain to us and we still did not move into action.

Sometimes, O God, we cannot even recognize a truth. Our antenna for ideas seems disconnected. May this new week not be identified by our weakness but by our strength, and may our strength, like that of Jesus Christ, bless life and not curse it.—Earl F. Lindsay.

EVENING SERVICE

Topic: The Benediction of Beauty
TEXT: Gal. 6:9.

The RSV hyphenates two Greek words, one of which it translates "well" and the other "doing." But listen to commentator Herman Ridderbos: "*Kalos* (the Greek for 'well') really means the beautiful. "What we arrive at is a translation that is itself beautiful: "Let us not grow weary in beautiful action," or alternatively, "acting beautifully." Paul does three things in this hauntingly charming sentence.

I. *The appeal.* "And let us not grow weary in beautiful doing." (a) Beautiful doing, we may ask, as compared with what? Paul has already given his reply in the preceding chapter: "immorality, impurity, licentiousness, idolatry, sorcery, enmity, strife, jealousy, anger, selfishness, dissension, party spirit, envy, drunkenness, carousing" (Gal. 5:19–21.) The whole kit and caboodle is there, and it's all ugly. So ugly that not all the cosmetics in the Revlon line can hide it from ourselves or from God.

(b) By contrast the beautiful doing for which Paul pleads is described in these words: "love, joy, peace, patience, kindness, goodness, faithfulness, gentleness, self-control" (Gal 5:22). Don't grow weary of practicing love, expressing joy, evidencing peace, demonstrating patience, showing kindness, revealing goodness, proving faithfulness, displaying gentleness, and exemplifying self-control.

(c) Because tired goodness is neither contagious nor convincing, God offers us the limitless energies of his Holy Spirit to prevent our growing weary in this business of being Christlike.

II. *The assurance.* "In due season we shall reap." (a) This is farmer talk. It is instructively earthy. Paul is arguing that in life there is a choice to be made: "He who sows to his own flesh" or "he who sows to the Spirit." Each kind of sowing has its appropriate harvest: from the flesh, a harvest of "corruption"; from the Spirit, a harvest of "eternal life."

(b) Neither real ugliness nor authentic beauty is the cause. Each is an effect. Beauty, let's remember, is the engraving that God puts upon virtue.

(c) Thomas Carlyle told about a Paris mob that swept down the street, looting and killing. But at one point they were stopped by an old, white-haired man who cried out to the mob and its leader: "Citizens, I am De la Eure. Sixty years of pure living are about to address you!" They listened, quieted by the ineffable glow on the old man's face.

III. *The admonition.* "If we do not lose heart." (a) Be warned against weariness. If the heart falters, the beauty will fade.

(b) Don't lose heart in the beautiful business of caring for children—your own and others. Don't lose heart in the beautiful business of helping the poor to help themselves. Don't lose heart in the beautiful business of giving all of God's human creatures an opportunity to respond to his redeeming love in Jesus Christ, the Savior and Lord.

(c) For that beauty is fairer and finer than the beauty which at evening lies on purple hills or the beauty of the bud which in the dew-drenched morning crowns with its resplendence the rosebush that bears it.—Paul S. Rees in *World Vision.*

SUNDAY: MARCH EIGHTEENTH

MORNING SERVICE

Topic: **Living with Death (Lent)**
Scripture: Luke 24:1–12.

What are some guideposts for living with death?

I. Jesus faced the reality of death realistically. When he told his disciples he was going to Jerusalem to die, he was facing his death, not seeking it but facing it squarely.

(a) Our living is transformed when we have honestly come to grips with the fact that we will die. Our efforts to avoid that confrontation are truly pathetic. We seldom think of our own death. When we think about and consider death, it is usually in terms of another, probably a loved one. But this is just one subtle way we keep death at arm's length from ourselves.

(b) Instinctively we rebel against the finality of death, for the whole universe and all of life is brutal nonsense unless death has some larger reason and more ultimate hope. The capacity of death to influence our living is one of the marks that separates us from other creatures. There is sharp contrast between dying and having to die and knowing it.

(c) The religion which grew up around the teachings of Jesus suggests that he was ruthless in facing the reality of death. For Christianity has declared clearly, "The last enemy is death." Jesus understood that. In facing the finality and reality of death, he lived differently.

(d) When Jesus told his disciples, "The Son of Man must die," he had first told himself, "I am going to die," To say simply, "Well, I know that," is not really to face it, and unless the reality of death is faced, life will always be distorted by the deception.

II. Jesus lived with death with the same capacity of grief and sorrow that we share.

(a) We certainly hope there were more than the little children and the disciples, but the scripture tells us of only a very few friends of Jesus. One of these was Lazarus, and when Lazarus died Jesus stood at his grave and wept. Whatever victories Jesus achieved, whatever confidence he possessed, and whatever calm he displayed, it was not because he was untouched by the same hurts we experience.

(b) Jesus was not immune to the hurt of the separation death brings. Jesus could say, "He who lives and believes in me shall never die and if he dies, yet shall he live." He could affirm the continuation of life beyond the experience of death, but that did not cancel for our Lord the finality of the earthly separation from our loved ones. His knowledge of immortality, whatever it may have been, did not leave our Lord immune to the ravages of grief that we can know when a voice will never be heard again, when a lingering touch is the last, and when a smile must be only a memory. Jesus cried. He was, as the scriptures declare, "touched with the feeling of our infirmities, he was a man acquainted with grief." He was strong enough to acknowledge the emotion of sorrow without worrying about it being a sign of weakness.

(c) The Bible says of Christians, "We do not grieve as the pagans do." Of course that is profoundly so. But we do grieve, and our Master wept at the grave of a friend and is touched with and understands our sorrows. I believe that this man, who could sympathize with us, stands with an arm around us in our moments of sorrow.

III. Jesus lived this life fully because he understood that the next life would be different.

(a) We would see each child's smile, each bud on every bush or tree, and each experience of love and friendship differently if we really believed the words of that poem, "I'll not pass this way again." This knowledge heightened the appreciation of Jesus for the potentials and dimensions of this life.

(b) There is no question that Jesus believed in a resurrection, not just for himself but for all of God's children. But in the same passage in Luke where he affirms the resurrection, he makes it clear that life after death is different. Paul says, "There is a natural body and a spiritual body." He reminds us that flesh and blood cannot enter the kingdom of heaven. Jesus is willing simply to affirm the difference of immortality.

(c) Jesus lived with death by cutting through all speculation and affirming all we can know. Life beyond death is on terms we cannot conceive from our own experience. "There is no marriage there," he said. "They cannot die anymore." It is all different. But while Jesus would draw no blueprints of heaven, he was crystal clear on this central fact: God is a God of the living, and he will not be content with death as the cancelation of life.

(d) A living God means care and love and life here and hereafter. It is not a long journey from that faith to the quiet confidence, "In my Father's house are many mansions." Those who live with Jesus have been able to share the breathless affirmation of Paul, "For I am persuaded that neither death nor life . . . shall be able to separate us from the love of God in Christ Jesus."

IV. His commitment in death was one with his commitment in life. (a) With almost his last breath he said, "Father, into thy hands I commit my spirit." But that final commitment to God is all part of that twelve-year-old boy saying to his parents in amazement, "Didn't you know I had to be about my Father's business?"

(b) The commitment to God in facing death was the same as his commitment in living life. The fact that Jesus made that kind of a total trust in God makes a tremendous difference to us if we hear it because it would result in a life that would hear our Savior say, "Because I live, you shall live also."

(c) There is a world of comfort in the faith that these dear dead ones are not lost, angel faces that are just hidden for awhile. But it is always more personal, it cuts deeper, and it is as near as your next breath, "Because I live, you shall live."

(d) The quality of that commitment of Jesus, consistent with his living and his death, sets at variance so much of what we do in his name. For so much of religion and what we've made of Christianity has nothing to do with the total commitment in Christ. So much of what we're about is our way of evading that confrontation of eyes that fix upon us and words that would change us, "Because I live, you shall live." —Harry N. Peelor.

Illustrations

ON BEING READY. When I was about twelve years of age, an itinerant peddler in our neighborhood was delivering tracts from door to door, and as he passed me on the street, he handed me one. It bore the scare headline: "THE END OF THE WORLD WILL COME THIS YEAR." The tract went on to say that Christ would return and gather his own unto himself and the whole world would be destroyed by fire before that year would come to a close. Greatly agitated and not a little frightened, I brought the tract to my mother and asked her if she thought this were true. Never shall I forget her wise and reassuring words. "Son," she said, "the man who wrote that tract doesn't know one thing more about the end of the world than you do—and that's nothing at all. Just go about your business and pay no attention to all this." Then as I turned to go, she added: "But remember this, that while you don't know when the end of the world will come, the end of *your* world may come any time. So live that you may always be ready."—John Sutherland Bonnell.

CONVERSION. By faith and that alone can man convert the tragedy of human life, full of disappointments, disillusionments, and with so-called death ever looming ahead into the most glorious field of honor, worthy of the dignity of a son of God.—Wilfred T. Grenfell.

Sermon Suggestions

CHRIST AND THE CHRISTIAN'S LIFE. Text: Phil. 1:21. (1) We must have some interpretation of life. Christ supplies the clue to its meaning. (2) We must have some inspiration for life. Christ supplies the necessary drive. (3) We must have integration of life. Christ is the cord that holds it together.—Robert Ferguson.

THINKING RESPONSIBLY. Text. Acts 24.* 25. (1) Often when we say, "I'll think about it," all that we really mean is that we don't want to decide. (2) When we say, "I'll think about it," we are often simply postponing something that we ought to do. (3) It is all too true that often, if we go on saying, "I'll think about it," the thing will so often not be done at all.—William Barclay.

Worship Aids

CALL TO WORSHIP. "They that wait upon the Lord shall renew their strength; they shall mount up with wings as eagles; they shall run, and not be weary; and they shall walk, and not faint." Isa. 40:31.

INVOCATION. Almighty and everlasting God, whom the heaven of heavens cannot contain, much less the temples which our hands have built, but who art ever nigh unto the humble and the contrite: grant thy Holy Spirit, we beseech thee, to us who are here assembled; that cleansed and illumined by thy grace, we may worthily show forth thy praise, meekly learn thy word, render due thanks for thy mercies, and obtain a gracious answer to our prayers.

OFFERTORY SENTENCE. "As we have therefore opportunity, let us do good unto all men, especially unto them who are of the household of faith." Gal. 6:10.

OFFERTORY PRAYER. Help us, dear Father, to be cheerful givers of our time, means, talents, and self to the Master that he may use us in the upbuilding of his kingdom.

PRAYER. Most gracious God, our Father, who giveth us life and through Jesus Christ giveth it more abundantly, we rejoice today in thy lovingkindness. We are convinced of thy great love toward us by the life and death and resurrection of our Lord. He fulfills his promise to be with us. Thy Spirit guides us, comforts us, and reveals unto us the things which pertain to Christ.

Increase our faith, O God, that we may enter more fully into the blessings thou dost provide that we may acquire a nobler stature and render unto thee a greater obedience. Help us to be responsible persons, using our blessings for the good of others and becoming channels of grace in the world.

We pray for great changes to come in the world: the end of wars, surcease from poverty, and the restraint of crime. Bless those who teach by word and life the gospel of Christ that its influence may reconcile men to thee and heal the divisions which separate them in ill will from one another. We long for a better day, and we believe that through the power of Jesus Christ and in his name the better day will come.

EVENING SERVICE

Topic: Christ in Five Dimensions
Text: Phil. 3:10.   –

I. Matthew presents the first dimension: *Christ the king.* He presents the genealogy of the kingly line, the wise men's acclamation of Christ as king, the law of Christ's kingdom, the miraculous works of the king, the promise of the king's ultimate world-wide rule, and the triumph of the king on the cross.

II. Mark adds the second dimension to the portrait: *Christ the commander.* A commander is one who leads his subordinates in fulfilling his superior's orders. Christ was a commander par excellence. He humbled himself to become the servant of the Lord. He came to do his Father's will. Daily, step by step, he did what he was told, even when all forsook him, until his task was fulfilled.

III. Luke presents the third dimension: *Christ the companion.* Here we behold him as the one who lovingly and patiently walks beside us to comfort, cheer, and challenge us. In this book he is the Son of Man. He took upon himself flesh and blood so that he could be "touched with the feeling of our infirmities" and to be "in all points tempted like as we are" (Heb. 4:15).

IV. The fourth dimension of this portrait is presented by John: *Christ the creator.* In each book he progressively comes closer to us until here he actually comes to dwell within us.

(a) Twice in his opening verses John states that Christ created all things. He is the creator of life and all that sustains life. His greatest creation, as John clearly illustrates, is the new birth or spiritual life.

(b) This creation takes place when we receive Christ the creator into our lives. (See John 1:12.) When we receive him he enters our lives and becomes the inner source of the "well of water springing up into everlasting life" (John 4:14). As he possesses and controls us, that well of water within us will issue forth in "rivers of living water" (John 7:38). This is life more abundant.

(c) John goes on to say that we cannot produce this by our own efforts. We must abide in him and he in us, before this abundant fruit can be created. (See John 15:5.)

V. In the book of Acts Luke puts the final touches on the portrait with the fifth dimension: *Christ the churchbuilder.* Once we know him as our king above us, our commander before us, our companion beside us, and the creator within us, he can begin to build his church through us. In other words his work through us can only come after his work on and in us. He must have vessels that are "meet for the master's use, and prepared unto every good work" (II Tim. 2:21).—Lud Golz.

SUNDAY: MARCH TWENTY-FIFTH

MORNING SERVICE

Topic: Religion that Counts (Lent)

TEXT: Jas. 1:27 (NEB).

There are different kinds of religion, but only one kind, as James puts it, "which is without stain or fault in the sight of God our Father." There are the false kinds, and there is the true kind. And we do well to ask ourselves the question, "What kind of religion is mine?" Certainly if we take seriously the words of James, there can be little doubt in our minds.

I. He first approaches it from a negative point of view. (a) The first mark of false religion is that it is *hypocritical*. Even his choice of words is important. He doesn't say, "If a man is religious," but rather, "If a man *seems* to be religious or *thinks* himself to be religious." Is not this the essence of hypocrisy? A hypocrite is one who feigns to be something he is not; he is someone who tries to appear pious and and holy in the eyes of others, when in actuality he is just like other men. His religion is altogether an outward show. Our Lord condemned such behavior when he said, "This people pay me lip service but their heart is far from me."

(b) A second mark is *self-deception*. James says, "The man whose religion is false deceives himself." It's bad enough to go through life seeking to fool others, but what fools we are when we fool ourselves. Yet our churches are full of so-called religious people who have duped themselves with their church membership and regular attendance and good deeds yet know little of the meaning of true Christianity. The rich young ruler was such a man. So good was he in his own mind that he could say to Jesus, "I have kept all of the commandments from my youth up."

(c) The final mark of false religion is that it is *futile* and *worthless*. It is empty. It is useless, devoid of value and substance when the chips are down. Many people wear their religion like a wig. It has the appearance of being the real thing, but it is lifeless. It can be put on or taken off at will. It's an outward show. It's not really a part of themselves. They've never experienced the cleansing flow of God's grace. They know nothing of his pardon. And when trials and sorrow come, there is no help or comfort. In the face of death all hope vanishes.

II. What is the religion that God takes note of? James gives three positive suggestions.

(a) True religion is demonstrated by a *controlled tongue*. (1) Elsewhere James tells us to "be quick to listen and slow to speak." We are mindful that God gave us two ears and two eyes but only one tongue. There may well be a lesson for us in that. Perhaps he meant for us to hear twice as much as we speak.

(2) How easy it is to fly off the handle, to cuss someone out, to say an unkind, careless, even untrue word. But when we do, what is the difference between us and the man who has no religion? The psalmist prayed: "Set a guard, O Lord, over my mouth. Keep watch at the door of my lips." Even he recognized the difficulty of controlling his own tongue. Only someone who has truly yielded his life to God and is led and controlled by his Spirit can show this first mark of true religion.

(b) True religion is demonstrated by a *compassionate heart*. (1) God takes note of the hand that reaches out in the name of Christ with a cup of cold water or a tender touch or a smile. He sees that visit to the sick and that gift to the poor. Jesus said, "Anything you did for one of my brothers here, however humble, you did for me."

(2) True religion is far more than a ritual or ceremony or even regular attendance at worship services. True religion responds to the cries and needs of those about us with a compassionate heart. There's no such thing as religion by proxy. We can't give so that others will do it for us. It's no credit to us if someone else visits the hospital, or feeds a hungry man, or provides a listening ear.

(3) That's not to say that salvation is earned by our good works nor is it to say that the gospel is only concerned with man's physical needs. But it is to say that if our faith is genuine and if our religion is true, it will find expression in compassionate concern for the need of others.

(c) True religion is demonstrated by a *consecrated life.* (1) The religion that pleases God is a religion that seeks after godliness. It is a way of life that seeks to keep one's self untarnished by the world, and that is no easy task. When James mentions this side of our religion, however, he rescues his definition from being purely practical; this is the holy side of the Christian life. It should not be interpreted as a call to some kind of monastic asceticism or puritanical austerity; God expects us to remain in contact with the world.

(2) God expects that our contact with the world will change it, not us. He calls each of us to labor in such a way that "others may see our good works and glorify our Father who is in heaven." We are to combat the corrupting influences of the world and change them by God's redemptive power. The religion that our Lord gave us is a religion that can and must be lived in the marketplace.—Fred H. Boehmer.

Illustrations

THE NARROW WAY. Jesus was never narrow-minded for the sake of narrowness but for the sake of God, of truth, and of our own souls. Jesus calls us to a narrow way because all others are false. God is not whatever we think him to be; he is God. Truth is not whatever we choose; it is truth.—Leighton Ford.

CHOOSING SIDES. During the War between the States an advance column of the Confederate Army was proceeding along a country road in southern Pennsylvania. An irate old lady, "Aunt Hettie," stood firmly in the middle of the road, threateningly brandishing a stove poker. The troop of calvary brushed her aside, fortunately without harming her. Later, as she would recount the story, friends would gently tease her and say, "Well now, Aunt Hettie, you didn't really think you could stop those soldiers, did you?" "No, perhaps not," she would reply, "but I sure let 'em know what side I was on!"—Keith E. Duehn.

Sermon Suggestions

THE ETERNAL REFUGE. Text: Deut. 33:-27. (1) The eternal God is the refuge from the insoluble mysteries of life. (2) The eternal God is the refuge from all the illusions of life. (3) The eternal God is the refuge from all human limitations and the sense of insignificance. (4) The eternal God is the refuge from the sense of sin and loneliness. (5) The eternal God is the refuge in the last great adventure into the future life.—Thomas W. Davidson.

GIVE YOUR HEART TO THE HEAVENLY. Scripture: Col. 3:1–17. (1) The exalted life. (2) The encompassed life. (3) The exchanged life.—William McLeister II.

LIVING THROUGH A TIME OF CRISIS. Text: Rom. 8:19. (1) Look for a man holding a hope. (2) Look for a man seeking understanding of another. (3) Look for a man under orders to love.—Gene E. Bartlett.

Worship Aids

CALL TO WORSHIP. "He that dwelleth in the secret place of the most High shall abide under the shadow of the Almighty. I will say of the Lord, He is my refuge and my fortress: my God; in him will I trust." Ps. 91:1–2.

INVOCATION. Almighty God, regard, we beseech thee, thy church, set amid the perplexities of a changing order and face to face with new tasks. Fill us afresh with thy spirit that we may bear witness boldly to the coming of thy kingdom and hasten the time when the knowledge of thyself shall encircle the earth as the waters cover the sea.

OFFERTORY SENTENCE. "If there be first a willing mind, it is accepted according to that which a man hath, and not according to that which he hath not." II Cor. 8:12.

OFFERTORY PRAYER. Our Father, help us to love thee so well that we shall have all thy kingdom interests and all thy children at heart.

LENTEN CONFESSION. O God of mercy and judgment, we acknowledge that we have fallen short of our own standards and that we have debased our standards from the best that we know. We have deceived ourselves and others that we might be excused. We confess that we have not felt the need to confess because we have measured our merit by those around us. We have closed our eyes to the needs of others. We have judged them severely and ourselves easily. We have called our sin by kinder names, and we have chosen the wrong when we knew the right. Create in us a clean heart, O God, and renew a right spirit within us.—Chester E. Hodgson.

EVENING SERVICE

Topic: Living by the Spirit
SCRIPTURE: Gal. 5:16–26.
Paul contrasted the "works (plural) of the flesh" with the "fruit (singular) of the Spirit." The works of the flesh are separate acts performed by an individual, but the nine-fold fruit is the creation of the Holy Spirit. When the Holy Spirit comes into one's life, he begins to bear fruit. There cannot be any fruit apart from him. The nine virtues which constitute "the fruit of the Spirit" fall into three groups.

I. Those related primarily to God. (a) *Love.* The Holy Spirit produces in the heart of the believer a deepening sense of God's love and the disposition to love him in return.

(b) *Joy.* Real joy dwells in the heart of true love. Without the proper relationship to God and love for him there cannot be any real joy.

(c) *Peace.* Peace is not derived from circumstances but is the product of the Spirit. It is enjoyed when one realizes God's presence in life's circumstances whether painful or pleasant.

II. Those related primarily to others. (a) *Long-suffering.* This is a patient endurance under injuries inflicted by others, and this quality is unnatural to man.

(b) *Gentleness* is that ability given by the Holy Spirit to hold all turbulent feelings in check.

(c) *Goodness.* Godliness always finds expression in deeds.

III. Those related primarily to ourselves. (a) *Faith.* Genuine faith in God will cause one to be faithful in the discharge of his duties.

(b) *Meekness.* The very opposite of conceit, pride, and self-assertiveness, meekness is an evidence of real strength.

(c) *Self-control* is not the result of the energy of the flesh but is the fruit of the Spirit.—H. C. Chiles.

SUNDAY: APRIL FIRST

MORNING SERVICE

Topic: The Truth that Confronted an Empire (Passion Sunday)
TEXT: John 18:37–38.
I. *Truth is a person who confronts us with God.* As Jesus stood before Pilate, he declared himself to be king of truth. Truth is a person and not a mere abstract proposition. (See John 1:14, 17; 14:6.)

(a) When Jesus said that he came "to bear witness to the truth," he was affirming that he came to bear witness to God.

(1) In the Old Testament the word for truth is *emeth,* a very important word occurring some 126 times and denoting reality which is regarded as firm, solid, or sure. Truth is a quality which most properly belongs to God. He revealed himself as the "true and living God" (Jer. 10:10). God is a firm, sure, and abiding reality on whom you can depend and on whom you can confidently build your life. (See Ps. 31:1, 3, 5.)

(2) God is absolute, dependable, and unchangeable. Paul Tillich thought of God as ultimate reality and ultimate truth. In answer to the question "What is God?" the framers of the Shorter Catechism answered, "God is a Spirit, infinite, eternal, and unchangeable in his being, wisdom, power, holiness, justice, goodness, and truth."

(3) Another translation of *emeth* is "faithfulness." (See Lam. 3:22–23). Just as God is faithful to his promise of blessing, he is faithful to his promise of judgment. The conditions were clearly spelled out in Deut. 28:1–2, 15. History records Israel's disobedience in Deut. 28:47–48. Israel was conquered by her enemies, Assyria and Babylon, and was carried away into captivity. God is reliable in his goodness and in his severity.

(4) In the New Testament the word for "truth" is *aletheia*, meaning the real or actual as contrasted with myth, rumor, or false report. To the philosopher truth was that which really exists as opposed to what only appears to exist. Thinking leads to truth, and truth leads to right action. Wrong doing is a result of ignorance. Plato taught that truth could be found by disciplined thinking. New Testament Christianity however teaches that truth comes by a faith response to revelation.

(b) "What is truth?" asked Pilate. Jesus tells him in effect, "If you had a disposition to know the truth, you would recognize truth in me," but Pilate did not recognize the truth though Jesus, the living, ultimate, and incarnate truth, stood bound before him. Here was the truth that could have transformed his life for time and eternity, but he turned his back and walked away.

(c) For two thousand years the church has asserted that the truth of human life is attainable only in a personal relation to Jesus Christ. He is the true life of God for the true life of man. Truth is not the mastery of theories nor the massing of intellectual data. It is the true and living God become a human being in the person of Jesus Christ. It is by building your life on him that you come to the knowledge of the truth. No error was found in him. Every person who is redeemed by his cross and made alive through his resurrection is liberated from the bondage of past failure into the full life of reality. Jesus is the truth who makes us free. (See John 8:32, 36.)

II. *Truth is a person who confronts us for action.* We are made free that we might live the truth. Truth is something to be done. The Christian must be careful to stand clearly for truth both in doctrine and practice, even when it is costly. To be a Christian is to be committed to the truth wherever it is found.

(a) Pilate's question "What is truth?" is as contemporary as the kid who cheats on his school exam, the millions in America who live by the standard of modified honesty and morality, and those who scoff at the suggestion that there are objective standards of right and wrong. Many of our youth are living without categories and without the possibility of saying that this is right and this is wrong. When they say "We are caught," we need to weep for them because they are not wrong; they are right. Many are lacking parental example, and even more are missing exposure to Christian teachings in Sunday school and church.

(b) The whole structure of a free and responsible society is based upon the principle that truth between man and man is essential. When the majority of our citizens no longer feel the obligation to live the truth and to tell the truth in his family, with his neighbor, and in his place of work, then we shall experience the decline and fall which we will so justly deserve. (See John 3:20–21.)

III. *Truth is a person who confronts us for decision.* Jesus stood in Pilate's hall, and truth confronted the official representative of the emperor for a decision. It becomes clear that it is not Jesus who is on trial but Pilate. It was the moment for decision. What was Pilate to do with Jesus?

(a) Pilate tried to evade the responsibility of making a decision. (1) Twice he attempted to place the decision concerning Jesus on someone else. When he heard that he was from Galilee, he sent Jesus to Herod. Galilee was Herod's jurisdiction. Let Herod pass judgment on him. The Jews clamored, "We have a law and by that law he ought to die!" "Take him, then," said Pilate, "judge him according to your laws." Let the Jewish leaders pass judgment on him.

(2) Pilate tried to avoid responsibility for decision by resorting to the custom of releasing a prisoner at Passover time. "Will you have me release for you the king of the Jews?" Let's dodge the issue by manipulating the situation.

(3) Pilate tried to evade responsibility for a decision by compromise. It occurred to him that scourging might satisfy or or at least blunt the edge of the hostility of the Jewish leaders. He felt he might possibly avoid having to give the verdict of the cross by giving the verdict of scourging. Let's compromise. I'll permit scourging; you take the pressure off me.

(4) Pilate tried to avoid a decision by resorting to an emotional appeal. He led Jesus, broken and bleeding after the beating, to the people. "Shall I crucify your king?"

(b) His attempts were all to no avail. It was Pilate's responsibility to make his own decision. The temple authorities had made their decision: he ought to die. The crowd had made its decision: "Crucify him!" The disciples had made their decision: they all forsook him and fled.

(c) It rested now with Pilate. They needed his verdict before the execution could be carried out. When confronted with the truth of Jesus, the roar of the crowd, the insistence of the leaders, and the possibility of being accused of disloyalty to the emperor, he did not have the courage to take his stand for Christ.

(d) Jesus Christ confronts us today as he confronted Pilate. A decision has to be made. (See John 14:6.) Most of you have made the decision to receive Jesus as Son of God and as savior and lord. But what will you do with the truth in each day's situations where you live?—Walter L. Dosch.

Illustration

THE STRANGER'S CROSS. Aleksandr Solzhenitsyn said that only once during his long imprisonment in a Soviet Union labor camp did he become so discouraged that he contemplated suicide.

He was outdoors on a work detail, and he had reached the point where he didn't care whether or not the guards killed him. When he had a break, he sat down, and a stranger sat beside him—someone he had never seen before and never saw again. For no explainable reason this stranger took a stick and drew a cross on the ground. Solzhenitsyn sat and stared at that cross and then said, "I realize therein lies man's freedom." At that point he received new courage and a will to live and work.—Billy Graham.

Sermon Suggestions

THE WAY OF THE CROSS. Text: John 19:-30. (1) Christ saw his passion and death as a cup to be drunk. (See Matt. 26:39.) (2) Christ saw his passion as a road to be traveled. (See Mark 14:21.) (3) Christ saw his passion as a price to be paid. (See Matt. 20:28.)—A. M. Hunter.

THREE CROSSES. Text: Luke 23:33. The three crosses of Calvary represent the crosses of humanity. On one of these three crosses every man is crucified. (1) The cross of selfishness. (2) The cross of self-surrender. (3) The cross of self-sacrifice. —B. G. Newton.

Worship Aids

CALL TO WORSHIP. "The Lord is great in Zion; and he is high above all the people. Exalt the Lord our God, and worship at his holy hill; for the Lord our God is holy." Ps. 99:2, 9.

INVOCATION. O God our Father, creator of the universe and giver of all good things: we thank thee for our home on earth and for the joy of living. We praise thee for thy love in Jesus Christ who came to set things right, who died rejected on the cross, and who rose triumphant from the dead. Because he lives, we live to praise thee, Father, Son, and Holy Spirit, our God forever.

OFFERTORY SENTENCE. "What shall I render unto the Lord for all his benefits toward me? I will pay my vows unto the Lord now in the presence of all his people." Ps. 116:12–14.

OFFERTORY PRAYER. O Father of our Lord Jesus Christ, we dedicate these offerings to the fellowship of him, whom to know aright is life eternal.

PRAYER. Let us pray for the company of all faithful people and followers of the way of the cross: for those who are asking honest questions, lest they lose the way; for those who know all the answers, lest they become proud; for those who withdraw from all fellow-travelers, lest they become arrogant; for those who are disappointed and discouraged, lest they give up in despair; for those who will not accept changes, lest they become inflexible; for those who change with every passing fad and fancy, lest they lose their direction; for those who have the spirit but neither the will nor the power, for those who have the will but not the imagination, and for those who have the faith but not the love; for all these, hear our prayer, O Lord, and let our cry come unto thee.

For those who can withstand everything that life can do to them and be neither downcast nor bitter; for those who follow the way even though they see it only dimly; for those who shine like stars in a dark world; for those who stagger not at the uneven motion of the world or censure their journey by the weather they meet or turn aside from anything that befalls them; for those who by their steadiness keep us in the way when we are tempted to drop out, we are thankful, O Lord.—Theodore P. Ferris.

EVENING SERVICE

Topic: The Risk of Discipleship
TEXT: Luke 14:27 (PHILLIPS).
There is no possible way we can meet and fulfill the demands of Christian discipleship without risk. Anyone who is unwilling to pay the high cost of living the Christian faith will never find himself or herself in the endless line of splendor which is the Christian heritage. It costs to be Christian! Jesus left no doubt as to the demands of Christian discipleship.

I. *Calculate the risk.* (a) Jesus wanted no misunderstanding among potential disciples. There is risk in discipleship. There is no guarantee of earthly joy and a life of ease, plenty, and riches. Discipleship may lead to misunderstanding, conflict, condemnation, poverty, and even a criminal death. The experience of Jesus is a graphic illustration of what this risk means.

(b) Discipleship brings the calculated risk of involvement. No longer can we be indifferent to the needs of humankind. There can be no such person as an innocent Christian bystander. We must reach out even to those who spurn our efforts.

II. *Count the cost.* Jesus rejected any jaunty discipleship or impulsive loyalty that was merely a quick response to the inspiration of the moment. He was not unaware of the fringe fellowship who hung on at the edge of the crowd and "followed Jesus from afar off." Perhaps they were convinced that Jesus had something, but they had not become certain that it was all Jesus was saying it was. One wanted to follow Jesus, but he didn't want to remove the dollar sign from the altar of his heart. Another wanted to bury his father. Jesus suggested that he let "the dead bury the dead." Jesus wanted full-hearted devotion without any "if" clauses in the contract. Primary loyalty must be to God or one could not enter the circle of discipleship. And there could be no returning. "No man who puts his hand to the plough and looks back is fit for the kingdom."

III. *Carry the cross.* Jesus knew there can be no Christianity without a cross. In how many ways we have tried to get the cross out of the picture. We may remove its symbol from the altar in the sanctuary, but we cannot remove it from the altar of our hearts and remain followers of Jesus. We honor the cross because it symbolizes for us the love of God made real in the sacrifice of Christ. We sing hymns to its glory. We offer prayers of gratitude for its gift of redemptive love and Christian life. But carrying the cross ourselves is something else.—Hoover Rupert.

SUNDAY: APRIL SEVENTH

MORNING SERVICE

Topic: What Were They Looking For?
(Palm Sunday)
SCRIPTURE: John 12:12–26.

The triumphant entry of Jesus on Palm Sunday stirs our hearts not because he was greeted with joy and acceptance but because the drama reflects simple, humble, serving love, riding into a crowd of ill-aligned and indecisive people. It is not the kingly crown that symbolizes this day but the lowly donkey. Here is the pleading, never pushing love of God, evident in all its simplicity and beauty and yet missed by the festival-minded curiosity seekers of the world. In the crowds who were around Jesus as he entered Jerusalem you find an assortment of reasons for their interest.

I. *There were those who were looking for profit.*
(a) Their spirits were not totally misguided. They felt they were good lieutenants, and any good soldier deserved a promotion. John and James were bold enough to say, "Master, when you come into your kingdom, may we sit on your right and left hand?" Judas may not have asked the question, but he knew that once the Romans were militarily defeated Jesus could ask anything and it would be granted.

(b) The profit angle has always been part of religion. Sometimes it enters the revivalist who rationalizes that his profit is nothing more than expressions of love and gratitude from the people. Sometimes pride and profit encircle the church when it builds lavishly only to become a hollow monument to prestigious-minded people and preachers. Sometimes it seeps into the person in the pew who is convinced that he has an "in" with God and looks with disdain at God's "lesser children."

II. *There were some who followed Jesus for miracles.* (a) Nothing is wrong in seeking God's help through the miraculous, but when this is the only interest in Jesus we lose sight of his meaning. The Bible describes some who greeted Jesus on Palm Sunday: "The reason the crowd went to meet him was they heard he had done this sign" (John 12:18). The "sign" was the raising of Lazarus.

(b) The miracle seekers believe only if the leader can do the tricks. The Pharisees said: "What sign can you give us? Our forefathers found bread in the desert. Can you top that, Jesus?" But Jesus quickly reminded them that it was not Moses who brought the bread but God. It was not the act that was important but the one who caused it to happen.

(c) The gospel of John considers miracles to be signs that point to a greater truth. Jesus never demanded that a person believe in miracles in order to believe in him. He condemned such faith in Matt. 12:39. Miracles may come out of faith, but faith that is enduring and strong does not come just from miracles. Jesus knew that, and he worked constantly to bind his followers to a deeper, more lasting faith.

III. *There were those who were looking for a political victory.* (a) In Jesus they saw an ally for their cause. The crowd standing by the road shouted "Hosanna." Some have interpreted this to mean: "Save us now. The Roman yoke is heavy. Save us from it, Jesus. Bring in a new political power. Be our leader, one of us!"

(b) Many civilizations since Jesus' death have tried to use him as a political ally. Constantine conquered, murdered, and plundered in the name of Christianity. The Crusaders set fires to cities, burned, and pillaged in the name of the cross. There have been times when we have assumed Americanism and Christianity to be undeniably the same.

(c) Jesus Christ will always be the guide, the leader, and the inspiration for political empires, but we cannot identify him with our political cause and use him as a tool for accomplishing it. If Christ did not die for every person alive, for the communist world as well as the free world, for the black as well as white, for the African as well as the Australian, then he did not die for any.

(d) Nations are not alone guilty of making Jesus Christ a partner in selfish alliances. It happens in churches and denominations. If you don't belong to our church, to our group, or to our club, then you have taken the wrong path. Some there were in Jerusalem who looked for one to support their fraternity of thought, not one who remolded and reshaped their thought.

IV. *There were those who looked for self-preservation.* (a) The Pharisees, watching the crowds as they follow Jesus, said: "We've lost. Look! The whole world has gone after him!" (John 12:19, TLB). Those words came from people who saw themselves in competition with any revelation they did not originate. How stuffy and unmoving tradition can become! How threatened are some with the unfamiliar, and how convinced they are that God has poured milk only in their ecclesiastical bowl!

(b) People like this remind us of one who has been shipwrecked and swims desperately to a small island in the distant horizon. After many grueling hours he reaches it. There is no food on the island. There is no fresh water. There is not another living human being. But he refuses to be rescued because he so fears the water from which he has escaped. There are people who live in their own traditions, whether it be in the church or out, who are dying because they will not leave an island meant only to be a resting place, not a residence. We cannot preserve ourselves as we are and refuse to let God change us and remold us. The Pharisees were not open to God's new word of life. They were looking for self-preservation.

V. *What am I looking for?* What kind of messiah does my life need? How have I responded to the man on the donkey?

(a) The people in the scripture reading missed the meaning of that drama on Palm Sunday because they missed seeing the greatest need of their lives. Deep in everyone of us is a basic yearning, a crying, and a hunger that can never be satisfied by any of their expectations. With unerring insight Jesus tried to clear all the props away and show how God met that hunger to be brought back to God again, to be reconciled (as Paul described it), to be made whole (as John described it), to be of the kingdom of God (as Jesus described it).

(b) The separation that caused this yearning is not an overnight affair. Sin is so much a part of us that we often do not recognize it, and when we try to stick to God, it never lets the glue dry. Jesus showed how a loving father sought us out, seeking always to restore us to himself. He told of a lost coin and the lost sheep. He told of a father who gives good gifts to his children. He told of a father who counted the hairs on our head, who cared for the lilies of the field and even more for his children. He told of the prodigal son whose loving father was eager to forgive and ran out to meet him. But it became increasingly apparent to Jesus that such forgiving, reconciling love must be demonstrated. So he took the role of a suffering servant, dying on the cross in order to forever plant the heart of God in the heart of men.

(c) When I stand in the crowd on Palm Sunday, I am looking for one who so totally understands who I am that he totally brings a way, a message, an act that makes the forgiving love of God real in my life. Palm Sunday is about Jesus Christ unlocking the gates of our needs not with the keys of profit, miracles, political victory, or self-preservation but with the simple, humble, forgiving act of love, riding on a donkey.

VI. *What is God looking for?* (a) He is looking for your decision to accept that suffering love. You may do it in the privacy of your bedroom. You may do it in the service of worship. You may do it a hundred times a day. But until you do it you are always going to be trapped by the bars of your own making.

(b) Soon it will be time to put down the palm branch and pick up the cross. It is a little heavier, but when you decide to take the cross it changes from a burden to a gift of freedom in your hands.—Joe A. Wilson.

Illustrations

ON KINGS WHO DIE. On May 20, 1910, at 9:30 in the morning, cannons were fired, the bagpipes wailed, and the body of Edward VII, son of Victoria, father of George V, rolled through the streets of London to Westminster Abbey. Lined along the way were 28,000 troops: Royal

Hussars, Bengal Lancers, Territorials, soldiers from all corners of the Empire, helmets, swords, plumes, nine kings and forty-four princes. They came from Norway and Persia, from Spain and China. At the head of the procession was the coffin of the king with an empty crown rattling on top. It was the same crown that he had worn in the Abbey at his coronation. The people sang Elgar's new tune, "Pomp and Circumstance": "Land of hope and glory, mother of the free, how shall we extol thee, who are born of thee?" The crown and the king rattled through the streets. In the midst of the procession was the king's white terrier with an engraved silver collar that read: "My name is Caesar. I belong to the king." They said it was the end of an age.—George William Rutler.

SYMBOL OF VICTORY.   There are over 100 species of palm trees, but the one found in Palestine is the date palm. It rises gracefully to a height of from fifty to ninety feet. The female tree bears a cluster which may contain 200 dates. And it may continue to bear for two hundred years. The dates are half sugar and in times of drought may become the main energy-producing food in Arabia and North Africa. The palm tree because of its nourishing fruit, its beauty, and its shade was an emblem of the righteous in their prosperity. Its form was carved on the walls and the doors of the temple, and its leaves were borne as symbols of rejoicing at the Feast of Tabernacles. This tall, firm, and unbending tree was emblematic of moral qualities—rectitude, constancy, gracefulness, and usefulness—such as are the constituents of success. The palm tree came to be regarded as a symbol of victory and triumph. The carrying of palm leaves at the triumphal entry of Jesus into Jerusalem signified that the people looked on this as an event heralding a victory.—Solomon F. Walter.

Sermon Suggestions

DAY OF CONTRASTS.   Text: Matt. 21:5. (1) There is the contrast between a sorrowing Christ and a rejoicing crowd. (2) There is the contrast between a steadfast Christ and a fickle crowd. (3) There is the contrast between a Christ going toward his crown and a crowd going toward a crime.—W. Mackintosh Mackay.

REMOVING THE VEILS.   Text: Matt. 27:-51. (1) The incarnation takes away our ignorance of God. (2) The atonement takes away the barrier of sin. (3) The gift of grace removes our helplessness. (4) The gift of immortality removes the evanescence of humanity.—John Oman.

Worship Aids

CALL TO WORSHIP.   "Let all those that put their trust in thee rejoice: let them ever shout for joy because thou defendest them: let them also that love thy name be joyful in thee." Ps. 5:11.

INVOCATION.   Our Father, thou who wast received amid the shouts of an earlier day, open our hearts and journey into our inward parts. Help us to lay aside all prejudices, forsake all sins, and overcome all biddings that might bar thy entrance. Let thy entrance into our hearts be triumphant. Conquer our fears, silence our unbelief, and quicken our faith. Lead us through thy Spirit to spiritual victory and conquest.

OFFERTORY SENTENCE.   "If any man will come after me [saith Jesus], let him deny himself, and take up his cross daily, and follow me." Luke 9:23.

OFFERTORY PRAYER.   As thy faithful disciples blessed thy coming, O Christ, and spread their garments in the way, covering it with palm branches, may we be ready to lay at thy feet all that we have and are, and to bless thee, O thou who comest in the name of the Lord.

PRAYER.   O God, take us beyond the pagentry and palm branches and give us eyes to see this one who enters the city this week. Let us ask who will greet him at the gates, who will hear his words in the marketplace, and who will shout "Crucify him!" before the week is out. He is eternal, but he is also our contemporary. We have him on our hands as did Pilate. What will we do with him?

Help us to recognize him and not to be shocked by the company he keeps nor impatient with his kingdom if it does not fit our designs. When he entered the city of his fathers, he did not fit the expectations of the religious. He may not fit ours. But if he is who we say he is, we had better make sure we recognize him.

Let us hear what he is saying. His words are familiar, yet strange and comforting and disturbing. Yet they are the words of life and all we need to know about life. At least for this week let us put down our newspapers, our novels, and our television programs and read what he has to say about what we are and what we can become.

Give us courage to follow him all the way through Gethsemane to Calvary and beyond. For in his suffering and triumph we can learn how to live our own lives. It will be a greater adventure than we imagined, for he can give us purpose, the knowledge of right and wrong, and the grace to live with ourselves and with others. He brings to us the ability to rise above our doubts and our failures and the wisdom to handle success. If he is who we say he is, then he can do this and much more.—George M. Mann, Jr.

EVENING SERVICE

Topic: The Night Jesus Sang (Maundy Thursday)

TEXT: Matt. 26:30.

I. Singing is nearly as important as praying. If Jesus prayed, he surely sang also. We have heard about the prayers of Jesus, about his tears and his sighs, but seldom about his singing. We know Jesus wept, but did he sing? Of course he did. He joined with the disciples in singing a hymn on the night he was betrayed.

(a) A hymn is usually a confession of faith that has become lyrical. When the people of God have a great experience, they sing about it. Laughter and singing! These are closely related in religion. In our songs we have inherited the faith of the hilarious saints. We should never be afraid of expressing our joy openly; it is a part of our Christian witness.

(b) What did this little company sing that night in the upper room? They sang from the Hebrew hymnbook which is our book of Psalms. They sang the hymns before the Passover, which are Psalms 113 and 118: "Praise ye the Lord" and "It is better to trust in the Lord than to put confidence in man." They are songs of joy, thanksgiving, and an affirmation of faith in God's goodness and his ultimate victory.

II. Although this was the last time the disciples would sing with their Lord before his cruel death, their songs were full of gladness and confidence.

(a) Jesus was about to leave them. Could you sing at all? Would we whine and whimper, or would we express ourselves in song. Jesus was on his way to death, yet they sang. Ever since that time Christians have taken him as their example and have been able to sing in desperate straits. When the early Christians were thrown into the arena to face hungry lions, they sang praises to God. Nothing mystified those hard, cruel, and prosaic Romans more than this.

(b) It was a strange night on which to sing, an ominous night, but his was a song before a sacrifice. Indeed some of the finest songs are those connected with sorrow and with sacrifices. Our Lord saw the cross looming ahead of him, but he sang. He was about to pour forth his life-blood in a great act of self-sacrifice, and the air around him was vibrant with music. It is what one might expect. Love is always full of music.

III. Although Jesus saw the darkening night of sorrow and of tragedy before him, he was not without hope. The song he sang was full of hope.

(a) Beyond the darkness and the sorrow Jesus saw the light. In spite of the utter darkness through which he had to pass he saw the gleaming of the resurrection morning as he sang in that upper room. He was so close to his heavenly Father that his song was one of praise and of thanksgiving in spite of the sufferings which were so near. Some of the world's greatest songs have been sung because of sorrow shot through and through with hope.

(b) Jesus sang a song of earth, but it had a deeper and higher meaning and the promise of heavenly joy and glory in it. When Jesus sang his hymns with the disciples, the meaning and the significance were beyond the mere words which were sung, and the souls of the little band were lifted up so that they caught a glimpse of eternal realities. Jesus as he sang must have felt himself to be one with all the hosts of heaven. Eternity itself came into the upper room that night when Jesus sang.—Ernest Edward Smith.

SUNDAY: APRIL FIFTEENTH

MORNING SERVICE

Topic: An Easter Faith in a Good Friday World (Easter)
TEXTS: I Cor. 15:14, 20.

I. If it is true that we come to all our Easters by way of our Good Fridays, then what an exciting, hope-filled time to be alive! Our world today is definitely a Good Friday world.

(a) A Good Friday world in which nations reel and stagger from one crisis to another, whether it be an energy crisis, an economic crisis, or a political, racial, or military crisis.

(b) A Good Friday world anguished with the tensions and violence of an old era dying while a new world with new lifestyles, new priorities, new goals, new urgencies, new value systems struggles to be born.

(c) A Good Friday world in which whole areas are erupting, while others are so volitile that a miscalculation in Washington or Moscow or Jerusalem or Cairo or Peking would cause our planet to burst into flame.

(d) A Good Friday world in which the tinderbox of ancient hatreds is filled to overflowing with all humanity nervously knowing as on that first Good Friday in Jerusalem that an incendiary word or act would ignite not merely a city or a nation but an entire world.

II. In a world like ours, what difference does Easter make? What good is an Easter faith in a Good Friday world?

(a) An Easter faith means the Christian faith, for no other religion can point to an empty tomb. Resurrection is written all over Christianity, and it is Christianity alone that is an Easter faith.

(1) The external evidence of an empty tomb and the presence of a living Christ is overwhelming. So is the internal evidence of personal experience. Millions in countries around the world will sing today: "You ask me how I know he lives? He lives within my heart!"

(2) Easter is about a risen Christ who was crucified on a cross and buried in a borrowed tomb on Friday but who arose on Sunday, triumphant over death, hell, and the grave. (See I Cor. 15:14.)

(3) The great apostle and the other early Christians didn't have time to debate the fact of the resurrection; they were too busy declaring it. They didn't argue about it; they affirmed it. As far as they were concerned, the risen Lord was his own best argument.

(b) There he was in their midst. That was a fact they could see and feel, and they knew that you don't argue with a fact; you examine it. And examine it they did, and announce it they did, and proclaim it they did. And his followers are still proclaiming it. For a risen Christ is self-authenticating in any age.

(c) In a Good Friday world shaken by so much violence, deceits, cover-ups, and revolutionary change the resurrection of Christ remains the unshakable reality.

III. For many the supreme question is not whether the resurrection is real but whether it is relevant. After all, what difference does Easter really make in a world like ours?

(a) If all that Easter means is springtime, flowers, bunnies, eggs, new clothes, and a semiannual trip to church, then Easter doesn't make too much difference in a world on the brink of catastrophe. It is then only a beautiful but irrelevant interlude in life's urgent concerns.

(b) If Easter means that when life is lived according to God's plan to the accomplishment of God's purpose, even if that plan and purpose include a cross, and that kind of life can never be finally defeated and can never suffer permanent disaster, then that makes a terrific difference in a world where right seems so often on a cross.

(c) If Easter means that God really cares what happens in this world and will personally see to it that Good Friday is always followed by Easter Sunday to those who are obedient to his will, then that makes a tremendous difference.

(d) If Easter means that one day all the violence, hatred, bigotry, and cruelty of Good Friday will be swallowed up in the victory, joy, peace, and exaltation of Resurrection Day, then a world torn by strife and defiled by sin should not only hear that good news but should glory in it.

(e) As we witness at this Easter time the awful agonies of a Good Friday world that is dying and the anguish and labor pains of a new world being born, if Easter means that very soon there will be the dawning of a new day with a resurgence of hope, faith, joy, and peace, then that is a difference that we can shout about and praise God about and tell our children and neighbors and friends about.—C. William Fisher.

Illustrations

EASTER AT LARGE.   Easter is not something you can program for a time and place and be sure it will happen then and there or something you can limit to a day and know you are thereby done with it. The fact is, you never know when, suddenly, it will be Easter.—Kenneth L. Wilson.

IRRESISTIBLE AUTHORITY.   Easter morning declares the irresistibility of the authority let loose among men in Jesus of Nazareth. Paul, writing out of his experience, said, "God was in Christ, reconciling the world to himself"—not in Buddha, not

in Muhammad, but in Christ. Not in authoritarianism, religious or otherwise, but in Christ. And if that's true, then comparing religions may simply waste my time. One thing matters. God did something in Jesus. He openly declared his authority by reconciling black and white, rich and poor, ambitious and lazy, intelligent and stupid, hopeful and hopeless, sinner and saint to himself. The authority of God came to life in a manger, hung on a cross, broke loose from death, and lives for all men. That marked the beginning of a new way of life in which I'm invited to share.—Arthur Fay Sueltz.

Sermon Suggestions

THE CHALLENGE OF THE RESURRECTION. Scripture: I Cor. 15:50–58. (1) The challenge of the mystery of the resurrection (v. 51). (2) The challenge of the majesty of the resurrection (v. 57). (3) The challenge of the ministry of the resurrection (v. 58).—Stephen F. Olford.

EASTER DISCOVERIES.   Text: Acts 1:3. The friends of Jesus made at least three discoveries. (1) They discovered that Christ is alive. (2) They discovered Christ on the highway. (3) They discovered Christ within their own hearts.—Carl J. Sanders.

Worship Aids

CALL TO WORSHIP.   "Blessed be the God and Father of our Lord Jesus Christ, which according to his abundant mercy hath begotten us again unto a lively hope by the resurrection of Jesus Christ from the dead, to an inheritance incorruptible, and undefiled, and that fadeth not away, reserved in heaven for you." I Pet. 1:3–4.

INVOCATION.   O God, we thank you this Easter morning for the eternal beauty and everlasting power of the resurrection of Jesus. We pray that these days shall see our Christ emerging from the tomb in which our generation has placed him—a tomb which we have closed with the stone of our selfishness and sealed with our hardness of mind and heart. Fill us this day with the spirit of reverence and humility because we are permitted to sing your praise. Help us to remember that we are your children living in your divine presence in our human lives. Make us faithful to duty and worthy of your love, through Jesus Christ our risen Lord.

OFFERTORY SENTENCE. "For ye know the grace of our Lord Jesus Christ, that though he was rich, yet for your sakes he became poor, that ye through his poverty might be rich." II Cor. 8:9.

OFFERTORY PRAYER. O living Christ, help us to know the ecstasy of thine everlasting lordship that we may more perfectly become cheerful givers.

PRAYER. O God, Lord of all worlds, seen and unseen, transient and eternal, we worship thee. Soul of the universe, Creator of our bodies, Father of our spirits, to thee we turn for strength and peace. We are children of a day; our sun has its rising and its setting; yet deep within our hearts is the instinct of immortality and the reach of our souls is beyond the grasp of our hands.

O thou, who has so mysteriously made us that, living in the midst of the temporal, we still think thoughts that lay hold upon eternity, we trust in thee. Thy promises are written in our hearts. We will believe them. What eye hath not seen, nor ear heard, and what hath not entered into the heart of man, thou hast laid up for them that love thee. Give us eyes today to see the open road ahead, and touch our spirits with the radiant hope of life eternal.

Thanks be to thee for Christ our Lord, for the beauty and strength of his life, the truth of his teaching, his powerful influence upon the world, the nobility of his sacrificial death, and for his victory. Thanks be to thee for his life, continued in the house not made with hands, and in those who welcome his spirit in their souls. On Calvary death slew life, and yet life was conqueror; hatred slew love and love triumphed; evil slew goodness and goodness proved the stronger. Fill our hearts today with the joy of his victory.— Harry Emerson Fosdick.

EVENING SERVICE

Topic: The Emmaus Road Incident
TEXT: Luke 24:34–35.

Mary and her husband Clopas made their despairing way back to their little cottage in Emmaus. They hadn't been able to face up to the anointing of the body with the other women. All she wanted was to get away with her husband and get home and shut the door on their grief. Secretly she was thankful that at least her own dear Clopas was safe.

I. *Revelation.* From the harrowing experience of the cross and from the new knowledge of the final defeat of despair and doubt in the resurrection, the Lord spoke to them: "Beginning with Moses and all the prophets he interpreted to them from the scriptures the things concerning himself." Their situation, so full of terror, was put in perspective. God is in command in his world, and even the darkest situation must be viewed in this light. As this great truth was revealed to Clopas and Mary so the darkness did indeed lift, and despair and doubt retreated in the light of Jesus Christ.

II. *Response.* The hearts of the couple responded to the words of Jesus. They no longer withdrew into themselves, but they were freed for living once again. No longer trapped in the prison of their despair, they were able to offer themselves and their home in service to others, and they invited this stranger to stay overnight with them. Once more they were open to caring and all the hurt which comes from that caring, and in their very openness they found the life which had such a short while before seemed torn away from them.

III. *Recognition.* Again as always a real response to others and to the real needs of others was the prelude to their recognition of the Lord. For we find that Jesus is with us in our responsiveness. As Clopas and Mary sat down to their supper and offered the loaf to the stranger, something about the characteristic way in which he broke it perhaps led to the sudden recognition of Jesus with them as he had always been with them. Only then did they realize the full significance of that glow which had filled their hearts and dispersed the darkness on the desert road. They had seen the Lord.

IV. *Rejoicing.* Now a new element had entered their lives. Mary's secret worries about the safety of her husband were no longer important, for here was a message to be taken to others, regardless of the inconvenience and danger. They rushed back along the Emmaus road, but this time with joy burning in their hearts. There was no thought of danger now. For had they not a great truth to impart, a great message of joy and hope and comfort for all their friends? What should stand in the way of the delivery of such a message as this?—Philip Nash.

SUNDAY: APRIL TWENTY-SECOND

MORNING SERVICE

Topic: Yet He Lives On

TEXT: John 20:11.

Have you wondered why Christ appeared to Mary, and why he appeared to her before appearing to anyone else? As far as Mary was concerned, Jesus was dead. Her best friend and reason for living had been snatched away from her, and he had been buried in that garden tomb some two days before. But in a flash of joy and glory, she discovered that, although Christ were dead and buried, yet he lives on!

I. Jesus appeared to Mary in the early hours of that Sunday morning, before he went to anyone else, because she needed him so much.

(a) Before she knew Jesus, Mary was possessed by seven devils. We're not quite sure just what this implies. Some have thought that she was a woman in sin. Others believe that the seven devils were in fact the seven deadly sins, usually given as pride, envy, wrath, sloth, covetousness, gluttony, and lust. We are closer to the truth when we think of this devil possession as a condition which affected the core of Mary's personality. She may have been under the power of evil spirits, or she may have been in a situation of severe mental unbalance. In any case the affliction struck at the very center of her personality and left her in a pitiable condition. Mary had made her bed in hell and had gone down to unfathomable depths. Her will was sapped, her character was gone, she was a slave in hell, and she knew it. And then in some never-to-be-forgotten hour the eyes of Christ had found her, and she saw the angels smile.

(b) Not one of the apostles had such an experience, for they were for the most part reputable men. Only Jesus did what someone had to do; he reached out and took Mary away from the grip of her tormented soul. I don't believe that even Peter felt such a need for Christ. After that life of hers, Mary could not rely totally on her own strength; she needed Christ! Only in his companionship and only when she knew he was near did Mary feel herself strong enough to keep the spirit she had been privileged to gain. She would not leave him for a moment, so she stood by the cross and kept her silent vigil at the tomb. She remembered her past and all the horror of it, and the same devils were whispering to her still. And just because she needed him so much to establish and reinforce herself, he appeared to her on that resurrection morning.

II. Jesus appeared to Mary first because she grieved for him so much.

(a) It was the immediate coming of the comforter to a grief that was too bitter for delay. Of course the death of Jesus upset all his followers. To lose a friend is always tragic, and they had lost a friend who had never faltered in his support, had shown them all that life might be, and had changed their whole outlook on life. Now he was gone and with him went the sun. Darkness had settled in upon their world. They were like Rachel mourning for her children and in her sorrow refusing to be comforted. As poignant as their grief was, perhaps more poignant was the grief of Mary.

(b) Mary's grief was so bitter that it filled her with the desire to be alone. Alone we find her on that dark and chilly morning watching, waiting, and weeping in the garden. For a brief time she is with other women, bearing the spices to sprinkle on the shroud. For a brief time, hurrying to the grave, she is in the company of Peter and the disciple whom Jesus loved. And then the other women disappear and Peter and John turn for home, and Mary is by the sepulchre alone. She could not endure company just then. She could not bear the sound of human voices. She did not want even a kind word of sympathy. One overwhelming desire possessed her and made her oblivious of every danger. It was the deep desire to be alone. That is always a mark of the most poignant grief.

(c) We may learn how bitter her grief was when we remember that it made her blind, for that same morning Christ himself drew near to her, and she did not know him. Of course there are several reasons for this which come to mind. There was the dimness of the morning light. There was the change in the nature and appearance of Jesus after his resurrection. But the deepest cause is not to be found in Christ; the deepest cause is to be found in Mary whose heavy, breaking heart had made her blind. All great passions have a blinding power. They throw a veil before our eyes.

III. Christ came to Mary first because Mary loved him so much. (a) To her all the evil of hell had been forgiven, and so with all the love of heaven she loved him. No matter what her sin or what her scandal or what her trouble, Jesus had saved her from degradation infinite, so that every day she lived Mary would say, "I love him because he first loved me." Think of the misery of seven devils. Think of her anguish. And then if you want to know her love for Christ, think of all that he had done for her in setting the diadem upon her head again.

(b) With the coming of the morning Mary stands apart from all the others. It was she alone who refused to believe her Lord was lost. "The disciples went away

again unto their own home." There was nothing more to be done. The grave was empty. They had examined the tomb and seen the napkin there, and nothing was to be gained by senseless waiting. But Mary, though she knew what they had seen and had not a ray of hope they did not share, could not tear herself away. There is a kind of love which faces facts, and it is a noble and courageous love. It opens the eyes wide to dark realities, and bowing the head it says, "I must accept them." But there is an agony of love that defies hope and beats against all evidence.

(c) Perhaps it is only a woman who can love like that, and it was a love like that which filled the heart of Mary. No one will ever doubt John's love for Jesus. No one will ever doubt the love of Peter. "Simon, son of Jonah, lovest thou me?" "Yea, Lord, thou knowest that I love thee." Yet the fact remains that on that first Easter morning Peter and John went to their homes again, and only a woman lingered by the grave.—Andrew W. Parmelee.

Illustrations

CONSEQUENCE. Something happened to turn the disciples from the broken followers of a dead leader and a lost cause into the confident proclaimers of good news. Something happened to turn the ghastly ignominy of a death by crucifixion into being itself divine good news. Something happened to account for the subsequent history of the apostolic age.—Michael Ramsey.

ON BLESSING GOD. Let us bless God before we pray, while we pray, and when we have done praying, for he always deserves it of us. If we cannot understand him, we will not distrust him. When his ways are beyond our judgment, we will not be so foolish as to judge; yet we shall do so if we consider his dealings to be unkind or unfaithful. He is, he must be, he shall be, forever, our blessed God. Amen and amen. All our hearts say so. So be it, Lord, we wish it over and over again. Be thou blessed evermore.—Charles H. Spurgeon.

Sermon Suggestion

CHRIST UPLIFTED AND UPLIFTING.   Text:
John 12:32 (RSV). (1) Christ uplifted on the
cross. (2) The cross uplifting Christ. (3)
Christ uplifting the cross. (4) The uplifted
Christ through the uplifted cross uplifting
humanity.—B. G. Newton.

Worship Aids

CALL TO WORSHIP.   "I will bless the
Lord at all times: his praise shall continually be in my mouth. O magnify the Lord
with me, and let us exalt his name together." Ps. 34:1, 3.

INVOCATION.   O thou who art the light
of the minds that know thee, the life of the
souls that love thee, and the strength of
the wills that serve thee, help us so to
know thee that we may truly love thee and
so to love thee that we may fully serve
thee, whom to serve is perfect freedom.

OFFERTORY SENTENCE.   "Take heed
what ye hear: with what measure ye mete,
it shall be measured to you: and unto you
that hear shall more be given." Mark 4:24.

OFFERTORY PRAYER.   O Lord, who hast
given us the privilege of life, help us to
magnify eternal values and to show forth
by our lives and our tithes the Christ,
whom to know aright is life eternal.

PRAYER.   O God, who forever uphold-
est all things by the word of thy power and
without whom we, the creatures of a day,
are helpless, we have sinned against thee
and done evil in thy sight. But thou hast
revealed thyself to us as the God of love,
and we beseech thee to forgive us for
Jesus' sake. Let the Savior stand over our
life where we may hear his "Peace, be still"
above the frightening roar of modern history. Thou knowest the dangers that
threaten us and all the trials that will yet
come over us. We have faith; Lord, make
it strong. Let us be courageous in the
knowledge that thy helping hand is constantly stretched out to us, so that we need
but take it to be assured of triumphing

over every enemy. Deliver us from every
fear of death because as Christ has conquered death it can no longer separate us
from thee.—Armin C. Oldsen.

EVENING SERVICE

Topic: Resurrection Witnesses
SCRIPTURE: I Cor. 15:5–8.
  The bodily resurrection of Jesus was not
a myth but a verifiable fact. Paul cites important witnesses to that fact.
  I. "He was seen of Cephas" (v. 5). (a)
"Was seen" in all these verses means to
see with the natural eye. These appearances were not hypnotic visions brought
on by grief as some claim. These people
could testify from personal experience. In
all Jesus made ten post-resurrection appearances. Paul mentions only six. He selected the more prominent ones.
  (b) "Cephas" is the Aramaic name for
Simon Peter (John 1:42). Peter had denied
Jesus which probably explains this special
personal appearance. He did not believe
in Jesus' resurrection until he saw him
alive (John 20:2–8).
  II. "The twelve" was a technical name
for the apostles. Paul called them this,
even though Judas was dead. This probably refers to Jesus' appearance on Sunday
night (resurrection day) when Thomas
was absent (John 20:19–25). "All the apostles" (I Cor. 15:7) evidently refers to his
appearance the next Sunday when
Thomas was present (John 20:26–29).
  III. The "above five hundred" probably
is the same appearance recorded in Matt.
28:18–20. Those who insist that these appearances were hypnotic visions brought
on by grief must reckon with this appearance. It is highly unlikely that this many
would have such a vision "at once" (I Cor.
15:6). Paul adds that most of these were
still living and could testify to the fact if
anyone cared to check it out.
  IV. James was Jesus' half-brother who
did not believe in him as the Christ until
after this appearance. He most likely witnessed to this fact to his other brothers
who then believed (Acts 1:14). Judas
(Jude) later wrote the book of Jude. James
became the pastor of the Jerusalem church

(Acts 15; Gal. 2) and wrote the book of James. He was later martyred by being thrown from the southeast corner of the wall of the temple area into the valley far below.

V. Jesus appeared to Paul on the Damascus road (Acts 9). "Born out of due time" means that the appearance came to him after Jesus had ascended to heaven. This appearance changed Paul from a persecuting rabbi into a persecuted apostle. He certainly had no hypnotic vision brought on by grief. One of the strongest arguments for the bodily resurrection of Jesus is the change wrought in his followers by it.—Herschel H. Hobbs.

SUNDAY: APRIL TWENTY-NINTH

MORNING SERVICE

Topic: God Above and Within

TEXT: Isa. 57:15 (NEB).

I. God is so high and exalted that we cannot worthily describe him. He is altogether holy and dwells in a light of glory that sinful men cannot approach. The eternity of his being no man can comprehend; the depths of his wisdom no man can fathom.

(a) It is sufficient for us to know that he is righteous, just, and merciful and that he can be trusted to make sure that in the end right will triumph over wrong, good over evil, and love over hate, and that he has made us for himself so that our hearts are restless until they rest in him. For he has created us in his own image that we may have fellowship with him. It has been truly said, "The chief end of man is to glorify God and enjoy him forever."

(b) He is all-loving and we must love him too; his commandments are just and we must obey him. He will make all things work together for good to those who love him; we can trust his goodness absolutely, for shall not the judge of all the earth do right? His strength will always uphold us, so that amidst all life's sorrows and tribulations our hearts can be at perfect peace because they are stayed on him. Underneath us are his everlasting arms of love and mercy.

II. So great is God's love toward us that, though he is so high and exalted, yet he humbles himself to dwell in the heart of every sinner who is lowly, trusting, and penitent. There are four ways in which the humility of God in his dealings with men manifests itself.

(a) He is the friend of all men including the poor and weak and unlearned.

(b) He gives might to those who have no strength, wisdom to the unlearned, and pardon and righteousness to the penitent and trusting sinner. He inspired the lowly tinker John Bunyan to write *Pilgrim's Progress* and *Grace Abounding* and the humble cobbler William Carey to become the pioneer of modern missionary work and a great linguistic scholar and translator.

(c) God's humility is seen in his patience with those who rebel against him. He seeks obstinate, ungrateful, proud, arrogant, and unfriendly men and women not once only but again and again. The closed door of the hardest heart does not turn him away. Still he patiently waits and says, "Behold, I stand at the door and knock." He goes on seeking till he finds and saves.

(d) God shows his humility in the minute care he bestows in perfecting his every work. He lavishes his skill not only on his more striking works such as the creation of the mighty universe and of human personality and intellect, the gorgeous rainbow, the sun, moon, stars, mountains, valleys, and trees but also in his making of the tiniest flower, the smallest bird, and our very fingertips in the fashioning of which in their unnumbered millions he never repeats himself. Such detailed precision in the lowliest work and such painstaking devotion in bringing even his tiniest work to perfection are beyond our understanding.

III. God's double dwelling-place is the key to our salvation. He whose power is heavenly and eternal and infinite dwells in every humble and contrite heart, not just to sympathize, comfort, and strengthen but to cleanse, redeem, save, and endow with eternal life. His advent today to the believing soul is an extension of the great event of the incarnation when his beloved Son came to earth to minister to man's needs and to give his life as a ransom for all. The Lord Jesus Christ and the Holy Spirit who continues his gracious ministry on earth form the link between the heavenly home and the human personality which, as Paul tells us, God designed to be the temple of the Holy Spirit. (See I Cor. 3:16.)

(a) It is in this double dwelling-place that the supreme revelation of God's holiness and love in Jesus Christ, his only-begotten Son, is perpetuated. When the prophet Ezekiel wanted to prove his love for his own people in their trials and tribulations and the wretchedness of exile, he simply went and "sat where they sat" (Ezek. 3:15). His loving concern was not expressed in a letter sent from a distance. He went to where the sinful sufferers were, identified himself with them, and shared their hardship, homesickness, and sense of captivity.

(b) Ezekiel's divinely inspired act was a dim foreshadowing of what God himself does in Jesus Christ and his Holy Spirit in the supreme revelation given to us in the events of the New Testament and the daily experience of every believing, penitent, trusting, and loving Christian to this day. God does not speak to us from afar. Though immeasurably beyond us in holiness, purity, glory, wisdom, and power, he is "God with us" because of the great love with which he loves us, and he is "God within us" because in the person of his Holy Spirit he has made our hearts his dwelling-place.—A. W. Argyle.

Illustrations

ACCEPTANCE. Nothing is demanded of you—no idea of God and no goodness in yourselves, not your being religious, not your being Christian, not your being wise, and not your being moral. But what is demanded is only your being open and willing to accept what is given to you—the being of love and justice and truth as it is manifest in him whose yoke is easy and whose burden is light.—Paul Tillich.

ROOTAGE. It is normal for the believer to want to grow up in the Lord Jesus and to become more like him. But the believer does not at first realize how much his upward development depends upon a deep and solid root system. This the Spirit accomplishes by making us aware of the fleshly life within and the sin of our alliance with it. By such negative means he brings us to the place of humility. Thus we learn the necessity of complete dependence upon the Spirit of God, the Son of God, the word of God, and our heavenly Father, who is the husbandman. We are being rooted and grounded for growth.—Miles J. Stanford.

Sermon Suggestion

GOD'S REST. Scripture: Heb. 4:1–11. (1) The *promise* of rest. (See vv. 1, 3.) (2) The *peril* of failing to rest. (See v. 1.) (3) The *pursuit* of rest. (See v. 11.) (4) The *pathway* to rest. (See vv. 3, 6–7.)

Worship Aids

CALL TO WORSHIP. "The Lord is exalted; for he dwelleth on high: he hath filled Zion with judgment and righteousness. And wisdom and knowledge shall be the stability of thy times, and strength of salvation: the fear of the Lord is his treasure." Isa. 33:5–6.

INVOCATION. Almighty God, who in thy providence hath made all ages a preparation for the kingdom of thy Son: we beseech thee to make ready our hearts for the brightness of thy glory and the fulness of thy blessing.

OFFERTORY SENTENCE. "Prepare ye the way of the Lord, make straight in the desert a highway for our God." Isa. 40:3.

OFFERTORY PRAYER. O eternal God, may these gifts represent an inner commitment to love thee above all else and to love our brethren in need because they are loved by thee.

A CALL TO PRAYER.   Let us gratefully remember all of God's dealings with us which manifest his great love for us and for those also in which love is hidden from our eyes: for friendship and duty, for good hopes and precious memories, and for the joys that cheer us and the trials that teach us to trust in him.

Let us gratefully remember all the tokens of his mercy: his protection round about us and his guiding hand upon us.

Let us gratefully remember his unbounded favor unto our land: his gifts of liberty and order, unity and peace, and peaceful times and fruitful seasons.

Let us gratefully remember that in his inestimable love he redeemed the world by our Lord Jesus Christ and gave to all mankind the means of grace and the hope of glory.

Let us therefore, as we give thanks unto almighty God for all his benefits toward us, also beseech him to give us such a due sense of all his mercies that our hearts may be unfeignedly thankful and that we may show forth our praise not only with our lips but also in our lives.

May he grant unto us, along with his continued gifts and magnanimous mercies, hearts to love him and wills to serve our fellowmen. And may we delight in all things to do his blessed will and seek to walk before him in holiness and and righteousness all our days.—Herman L. Turner.

EVENING SERVICE

Topic: Did Jesus Tithe?
TEXT: Lev. 27:32.
I. Jesus was reared in a pious Jewish home. The pious Jews tithed.

II. The Old Testament was the Bible in that day. Jesus loved and quoted this Bible. He believed it was God's word and revealed will. The presumption therefore is that Jesus tithed.

III. Jesus said he had not come to destroy the law of the prophets but to fulfill. (See Matt. 5:17.) Tithing is taught in both the law and prophets.

IV. Jesus said, "Except your righteousness shall exceed the righteousness of the scribes and Pharisees ye shall in no case enter the kingdom of heaven" (Matt. 5:20). The scribes and Pharisees were tithers.

V. Jesus rebuked the scribes and Pharisees for inadequate tithing. (See Matt. 23:23; Luke 11:42.)

VI. Jesus taught that his followers should go the "second mile," that is, go beyond the things required. One cannot go the second mile until he has gone the first. Jesus certainly taught that one should go beyond the tithe.

VII. Jesus never lowered moral standards but always raised them. Read again what he said in the sermon on the mount on the subject of murder, adultery, oaths, etc., then ask if you think Jesus would be satisfied with a lower standard of Christian giving than the tithe.

VIII. The enemies of Jesus tried to convict him of breaking the law, for example, in regard to Sabbath observance. Isn't it strange they never accused him of the tithe if he did not observe it?

IX. Jesus observed and commended other requirements of the law. (See Matt. 8:4; Luke 17:17; Matt. 23:23.) The evidence seems to be ample and conclusive that Jesus not only taught and practiced giving of a tithe but also went far beyond it.

SUNDAY: MAY SIXTH

MORNING SERVICE

Topic: The Handwriting on the Wall
SCRIPTURE: Dan. 5:1-8.
Belshazzar was guilty of several trans-

gressions which come perilously close to us. His relationship to God, whatever there was, was strained and filled with warnings. His grandfather had at one time actually worshiped the God of the

Jews, so Belshazzar was aware of our God. Why was he found wanting and why was he without excuse?

I. *He had an adequate standard of right and wrong which he ignored.* (a) Whenever men or nations fall we are tempted to ask the questions: "Did they know better?" or "Was judgment too severe?" I know that arguments can be waged on almost every side on the subject, but when men willfully sin against God most of them do it not out of ignorance but out of lack or regard for the truth.

(b) Daniel reminded Belshazzar that he had had the example of his grandfather's sin in his earlier years but that he did not learn a thing from it. We have all seen this happen. The sins of one generation don't seem to serve as a deterrent to sins in later generations. Somehow the sins of the fathers continue to become the dominant characteristics of the children. Why this is so we cannot say. We can only say with positive assurance that it need not be so. Some men do profit from wayward fathers and some girls do profit from poor examples of mothers. With all the talk about shades of gray and no black and white, right or wrong situations, anyone who wants to find the true balance of the scales can find it.

II. *He broke three immutable laws of God.* (a) He practiced idolatry even though he knew better.

(1) His setting up of the idols was a venting of his own wrath against God. In this sense there is a tendency within many men to strike back at God. Moses when he thundered, "You shall have no other Gods before me," was speaking the mind of the Lord God.

(2) Man's heart is made for God, and when man's affections are placed on anything less his entire life is out of focus. This is the answer to some of the blighted ways of men and their misery. Jesus taught of the singular purpose of consciously serving God. He did not promise to make us rich or healthy, but his care was promised in Matt. 6:33.

(b) He desecrated holy things. He brought in the golden and silver vessels of the Lord and profaned them. This was his way of showing his disgust for spiritual things. Men have strange ways of showing utter disregard for the finer things of life, even their own reputations. Our bodies are the temples of God's spirit, we are told by Paul.

(c) He made a mockery of the consequences of sin. There are those moments when it does seem as if men can shake their very fists in the face of God, and there are those moments when men seem to be able to master the situation, no matter how evil it is. But is there another side to the story? This foolish young fool thought he could beat the game, but he sowed the wind and reaped the whirlwind. And the results were not all in the realm of the spiritual. He had been derelict in his duty as a civil ruler, and his kingdom fell at the same time his soul was destroyed. This is the way it happens with us as well. A wasted life seldom touches only one area.

III. *Belshazzar's days of grace were coming to an end much sooner than he had thought.*

(a) I cannot help thinking of the fragile nature of life. In a small town where I spent several years I can count no less than eight of my classmates who never made it past twenty years of age. Not that they were punished for any wrong doing. I am only pointing to the thin thread which holds our last breath in balance.

(b) In Belshazzar's case his sin was already at work to destroy him. His lack of a good military defense and the immorality of his leaders of state had corrupted the nation to the breaking point. The enemy troops were inside the walls. It is true with most men, if not with all, that their downfall starts from the inside.—Merle Allison Johnson.

Illustrations

TEST.   Bruce Larson tells of a retreat for a senior class at a theological seminary and of an interesting test which they took. Each was to list the sins in his life and raise his hand when he had finished. In fifteen seconds most of the class was finished. Then they were asked to list the good things about themselves. The time it took them was more than double what it took to list their sins. It was proof that they were more conscious of their sins than their good points.—C. Neil Strait.

MORAL BATTLEGROUND. It grows daily more obvious that the real battleground for the moral life of America is the family. We may multiply our inventions and raise to its pinnacle the highly articulated, mechanized miracle of a civilization which we have started here; we may increase our industries and accumulate wealth; we may even build great temples dedicated to public worship and great schools dedicated to public education; but after all, what this country amounts to in the end depends upon what happens in its homes. There is no substitute for parents.—Harry Emerson Fosdick.

Sermon Suggestions

FOUR BASIC QUESTIONS. Text: Matt. 5:-47. (1) What do you *see* more than others? (2) What do you *hear* more than others? (3) What do you *know* more than others? (4) What do you *do* more than others?

HOW TO OVERCOME JEALOUSY. Text: I. Cor. 13:4 (NEB). (1) Admit it. (2) Analyze it. (3) Attack it. (4) Abandon it.

Worship Aids

CALL TO WORSHIP. "Hereby perceive we the love of God, because he laid down his life for us: and we ought to lay down our lives for the brethren. Let us not love in word, neither in tongue; but in deed and in truth." I John 3:16, 18.

INVOCATION. Teach us, good Lord, in our days of rest to put our worship and prayer first, and may we never let the services of the church be crowded out of our lives. Keep before us the vision of thy dear Son Jesus Christ, who in his boyhood days worshiped with his family, and may that vision inspire us and all men to unite as members of the church universal in witness, in worship, and in love.

OFFERTORY SENTENCE. "As every man hath received the gift, even so minister the same one to another, as good stewards of the manifold grace of God." I Pet. 4:10.

OFFERTORY PRAYER. O Christ, may we walk constantly in thy way and work fervently for those causes which are dear to thee.

PRAYER. O God, help us find thee. Help us find thee through the wonders of the world: through skies that color, heavens that tremble, hills that rise, mountains that soar, canyons that descend, mesas that spread, plains that extend, machines that produce, structures that tower, and engines that fly.

Help us find thee through nature: through a drop of water, the seven seas, massive mountains, high hills, pointed peaks, a blade of grass, the flight of birds, the harmony of flowers, the rhythm of growth, and through the pulse beat of life.

Help us find thee through the arts: through the conflict of drama, the grandeur of a contata, the cheer of a carol, the joy of a hymn, the color of a painting, the rhythm of a dance, the flow of words, and the lines of a temple.

Help us find thee through the lives of people: through the laugh of a child, the winsomeness of a lad, the glow of youth, the vigor of manhood, the understanding of womanhood, and the wisdom of age.

Help us find thee through scripture: through the vision of Abraham, the wrestling of Jacob, the purity of Joseph, the strength of Deborah, the conscience of Amos, the faith of a centurion, the vigor of Peter, the humility of Mary, and the forgiveness of Stephen.

Help us, O God, to find thee most through the life of the Man of Galilee who walked the highways of the Holy Land leaving behind pictures of thee, our Father.—Fred E. Luchs.

EVENING SERVICE

Topic: Church and Home as Allies

SCRIPTURE: Deut. 6:4–7; Mark 10:13–16.

I. The church and the home are allies in combating the tide of secularism. They are not to be competitors or rivals for the time and energy of parents and children. The church is to strengthen the home and to give it direction and purpose.

II. The church can put the home in touch with God and give it a spiritual foundation and roots. St. Augustine saw the disintegration of the Roman Empire in his lifetime. He said Rome fell "for want of order in the soul." It is this order in the soul which the church helps the family to know. The church proclaims the gospel, calls us to faith, and introduces us to the Master. This is what we mean by "evangelism."

III. The church teaches the biblical ideals of marriage and family. Henlee Barnette says, "Be it ever so jumbled, there's no place like home." The church through its Bible study and preaching ministries helps us to deal with the "jumble." As an example, the Bible teaches that sex is sacred—related to love, commitment, and faithfulness. The biblical ideal is one man and one woman, committed to each other for life. The purposes of marriage include companionship, parenthood, mutual nurture, and affection.

IV. The church ministers to the family in terms of marriage enrichment and in the crisis of failure. Divorce represents a failure as do anger, hatred, and murder. Divorce is not an unpardonable sin nor is it some kind of social and spiritual leprosy. The church reaches out to all the hurting members of a broken family saying, "God loves you, and so do we." It takes three partners to achieve the marriage ideal: a husband, a wife, and Christ.

V. The church nurtures the Christian home. It teaches loyalty, faithfulness, and freedom with responsibility. It applies the gospel principle in family life, social life, economic life, and political life. Marriage is not merely a contract but a commitment "in the presence of God." It is not merely a private matter but a public one under the lordship of Jesus Christ.—Alton H. McEachern.

SUNDAY: MAY THIRTEENTH

MORNING SERVICE

Topic: **The Motherhood of God** (Mother's Day)

Text: Isa. 66:13.

I. The prophet, after presenting vivid pictures of disaster and judgment, presents also a contrasting picture of the ultimate consummation of history in the Holy City, the New Jerusalem, redeemed, transformed, purified, and now at last open to the entire world as a place where all can come without distinction to worship God. "As one whom his mother comforteth," says God to his people, "so I will comfort you." They are beautiful words.

(a) In the ancient world it was quite natural to employ the father image in connection with deity. In a patriarchal society, like that in which the Bible was written, the father had all authority and power. It was he who was able to accomplish what he set out to do, and we still believe that this is true of God.

(b) But the Bible contains mother imagery when it speaks about God. One thinks of the words in Hosea 11:1, 3–4, 8–9. Jesus in one of the most unforgettable of his parables compares God to a woman who loses a coin and then sweeps house incessantly until she finds it again. Moses is reported as saying to the Hebrew people, "You were unmindful of the Rock that bore you, and you forgot the God who gave you birth" (Deut. 32:18).

(c) Just as the word "father," accustomed as we are to it, does not do complete justice to the biblical idea of God, neither does the word "brother" exhaust the meaning of Christian fellowship. (See Gal. 3:28.)

II. The language we use really is important. (a) We should be thinking of God as a combination of father and mother much more often than we do. Does he not really include the best and highest of each?

(b) The masculine image usually indicates strength, power, and authority—and also, at times, the tyrant, the destroyer, and the scourge of one's enemies. This picture needs to be supplemented with the feminine gender: mercy, love, self-sacrifice, forgiveness, readiness to welcome back, and continually to love the "miserable sinners" and disobedient children we so often seem to have become.

(c) The picture of "the man upstairs" with his long white beard and hurling his thunderbolts never was an authentic picture of the loving, graceful God of the gospel of Jesus Christ. "As one whom his mother conforteth, so I will comfort you," saith the Lord.

III. I haven't yet reached the place where I can read Ps. 23, "The Lord is my shepherdess," but on the other hand I don't want to call God "It," as if God were some formula or merely an impersonal force that neither thinks nor knows enough even to care about you and me.

(a) The "personhood" of God inevitably includes both male and female images. God may well be more than either man or woman, but he is not less than a person. The stream cannot rise higher than the source nor can the creature be greater than the creator of all that is.

(b) If, as the New Testament insists, love isn't just "something" that God "feels" but rather the very essence of the divine being, then motherhood must be affirmed along with fatherhood. We have that kind of God. There is no other way.

(c) Today we honor all worthy mothers, and this is appropriate. Our mothers were our first teachers about God and, even more important, our first imparters of the forgiving, healing, understanding, yet challenging and demanding love that we later learned to identify as the love whereby you and I are loved by God: One does not have to be male or a father to teach or to embody the qualities which are central in our Christian understanding of the mysterious, unfathomable divine reality that is found at the heart of each person's life experience and yet encompasses and sustains the apparently limitless and infinitely expanding world in which we find ourselves today.—Edward C. Dahl.

Illustrations

INDISPENSABLE.   Home is the place where you don't need to be brave. Home is the place where they know us at our worst and still love us. I believe in home, I believe in marriage, and I believe in the family, for I could not have lived without them.—William Barclay.

THE HAPPINESS MACHINE.   Leo Aufmann in Ray Bradbury's book, *Dandelion Wine*, is obsessed with creating a "happiness machine." In it the temperature will always be perfect, a beautiful sunset will last forever, and the air will always smell good. Finally he achieves his dream. The happiness machine becomes a reality. Leo tries it out on his wife; but when she emerges from the machine, her eyes are not glowing but are weeping. She says, "Leo, the mistake you made is you forgot some hour, some day we all got to climb out of that thing and go back to dirty dishes and the beds not made." Leo is saddened. He has devoted his life to the happiness machine, blind to all else. And it does not work. He walks until it is dark. Then, coming up the front walk, his eyes are opened. His wife is working at the stove in the kitchen. One of the children is setting the table. Another is reading a book, while the others play a game. "Ah, there it is," he breathes, "the happiness machine!"—John Robert McFarland.

Sermon Suggestion

CHRIST AND THE GENERATION GAP. Text: Ps. 148:12-13. (1) For the young, he has the gospel of living; for the old, the gospel of dying. (2) For the young, he has the gospel of inspiration; for the old, the gospel of consolation. (3) For the young, he has the gospel of giving; for the old, the gospel of receiving.—James Stalker.

Worship Aids

CALL TO WORSHIP.   "Lord, who shall abide in thy tabernacle? Who shall dwell in thy holy hill? He that walketh uprightly, and worketh righteousness, and speaketh the truth in his heart." Ps. 15:1-2.

INVOCATION.   Out of our darkness we are come to thee for light; out of our sorrows we are come to thee for joy; out of our doubts we are come to thee for certainty; out of our anxieties we are come to thee for peace; out of our sinning we are come to thee for thy forgiving love. Open thou thine hand this day and satisfy our every need. This we ask for thy love's sake.

OFFERTORY SENTENCE. "Every man shall give as he is able, according to the blessing of the Lord thy God which he hath given thee." Deut. 16:17.

OFFERTORY PRAYER. Our Father, forgive our indifference and neglect and help us to hear thy call to partnership with thee in making a new heaven and new earth.

PRAYER. Most gracious God, our Father, who watcheth over thy children to direct their ways, to correct their faults, and to fulfill thy purposes in them and through them, we come into thy presence with desire to worship thee in spirit and in truth.

Our hearts are thankful for thy fatherly love and care. Thy providence has brought unto us an abundance of material things, and thy lovingkindness has given us spiritual blessings without number. Most deeply do we thank thee for our world. Grant that we may learn more about him, and more surely may we know him in the intimacy of his saviorhood and friendship.

Help us, our Father, to render unto thee a greater obedience. May we be quick to know thy will and eager to do it.

Bless us, we pray, in all the relationships of life that through these we may find deep joy and render service to one another. May we bring deep satisfaction to our parents, a brotherly spirit to our friends, and a good example to children and youths. Bound up in the bundle of life with one another in our homes, may these be the abiding places of love, peace, and joy.

Grant, our Father, that we may serve thee well in the stewardship of our talents, time, and wealth.

Continue to bless this land in which we live, and may it prove more worthy of thy blessing.

May thy kingdom come throughout the whole wide world. Bring peace and goodwill in our time, O Lord.

EVENING SERVICE

Topic: A Place for God
TEXT: II Kings 4:10.

Elisha was going to Shunem, and a very grand lady offered him the customary hospitality of the East. After that first meeting the prophet stopped there whenever he had to go that way. So one day the lady and her husband decided to build and furnish a room on the roof of their home for him to have as a place to stay whenever he was in the vicinity.

I. It was because they had found him to be a man of God that they did it. For them it was making a place for God in their home and family. Their relationship with God was more than custom or polite courtesy. In modern terms we might call them more than "Sunday-go-to-meeting Christians." Too many people are seen in church or worship only on special occasions. They "tip their hats" to God because it is the going thing. They want to be known as "respectable folk" who maintain all the customs of the "best society," much as the lady of Shunem when she first offered the hospitality of her house and bread to the traveler she came to know as Elisha. But there came a day when she and her husband realized that their home must have more than a superficial relationship with God. They felt they should provide a special place for God so that he would not be just a passerby but a member of the family.

II. Homes that have a place for God have a better basis for being. The place may take the form of a family altar where the whole family joins in moments of worship and sharing, or it may be the presence of pictures or other symbols of faith. At any rate it will find expression in the value system and lifestyle. I guess that's why I like the idea of the room for the prophet on the roof. It seems to say God's place towers over every other interest. It reminds me that the place of meeting with the Eternal is always the "upper room."

III. It was because of the prophet's

chamber the lady of Shunem received the promise of her heart's desire—a son. A place for God is the best place to find the assurance of one's hope. Has your home its unfulfilled promises? Do your plans for it now seem to be hopeless? Maybe it is because you did not make a top place for God. Well can I understand the lady's plea to the prophet. Don't, she begged, raise my hopes again. What we have wanted is not and cannot be ours. But it did happen, even though they had given up and all be-cause they had given God first place.

IV. A place for God is a matter of proper priorities, of fulfilled promises, and of certain help in the crises of life. No home or family, Christian or otherwise, escapes the crises of life. They are as inevitable as rain. They often leave wounds or tragedies, as much as we try to avoid them. But the home or family that has a place for God has a place of healing and help.—T. E. Martin.

SUNDAY: MAY TWENTIETH

MORNING SERVICE

Topic: Loving Ourselves Properly
Text: Rom. 12:3 (rsv).
If we really loved ourselves in the biblical sense, both our lives and the world around us would be considerably different. It was with deep awareness of this truth that Jesus, when asked what is the greatest commandment, included in his reply not only love of God but love of self as the criterion for love of neighbor.

I. Much of what goes by the name of self-love is really false self-love. There are two kinds of self-love.

(a) There is the kind that glorifies self, blows up our talents and charms and general desirability all out of proportion to reality. That is false self-love with its origin in the depths of hell.

(b) There is self-love of a kind that God intends all of us to have. And it is that self-love which Jesus commanded because he knew it to be the basis of both love of God and love of neighbor.

II. What is this authentic self-love really like? (a) In the text the apostle Paul was concerned, as he was with the Corinthian church, that persons who had certain gifts were looking "down their noses" at other persons who had different gifts. From the twelve Greek verbs that convey various shades of meaning in the field of thinking, reasoning, and so on, the Holy Spirit has chosen one of these verbs, *phroneō,* and uses it four times in this verse. The word has a shade of meaning that was used in the ancient world to describe a man who was in his right mind.

(b) When we relate this to a proper self-love, it implies that we must understand ourselves and accept ourselves. Each of these exercises is to be undertaken in faith.

(c) If I were to ask you what are your strengths and weaknesses and what are your unique gifts and talents, would your answer indicate you were thinking of yourself "with sober judgment"?

(d) And understanding yourself, do you accept yourself? To know what our gifts and talents are is one thing, but to accept them is often something else. Most people have an inadequate view of their abilities, especially when they compare themselves with others. But God does not require us or even want us to compare ourselves with others. He wants us to be the unique selves he created us to be.

(e) The clue lies in accepting ourselves for what we are and in faith that God has something to accomplish through our being willing to grow and develop in the abilities and talents with which he has blessed us.

III. Paul says, "Having gifts that differ according to the grace given to us, let us use them."

(a) What is your gift? Don't say that you have no gift because that is a denial of the God who has given each of us at least one unique talent which can be used to help others.

(b) Maybe your gift is the gift of prayer

or of making friends or of organizing or of supplying funds for missions or of visiting the sick or of teaching the young or the old. But somewhere you have a gift all your own. And God wants it, and loving yourself properly depends on your offering it willingly in the service of others.

(c) Learning to love ourselves properly, as Christ commanded us to do, means looking at ourselves "with sober judgment, according to the measure of faith which God has assigned us," acknowledging the talents we have as a gift from God and then using them to build up the body of Christ which is the church. We are able to love ourselves properly—to understand ourselves and to accept ourselves—because of our assurance that we are loved and accepted by another. It is virtually impossible for a person to accept himself until someone else has accepted him for what he is.

(d) All of these accepting persons and fellowships are only pale reflections of the greatest acceptance of all—the acceptance of our Father God whom we experience most vividly in our Lord and Savior Jesus Christ. Nothing can be more deep or more real or more healing or more ultimately satisfying than that, and nothing is more likely to create in us a genuine self-love.

(e) We do not feel worthy, yet he sees us as possessing supreme worth. We cannot love ourselves properly, yet he declares that we are loved with "an everlasting love." And we are able to love because he first loved us. There must be something truly wonderful about us if he can love us and accept us so readily. What he loves about us is that image of himself which he has planted deep within, and he wants to restore that image until it shines with the reflected glory of a thousand suns. He wants that light to shine in our hearts to give to others the light of the knowledge of the glory of God, even as that light is reflected in the face of Jesus Christ.—Henry S. Date.

Illustrations

BEFRIENDED. When Mt. Everest was climbed for the first time, a newspaper headline read, "Hillary Conquers Everest." Huston Smith tells of the response of an Oriental who said, "Everest has not been conquered but befriended." This is the important difference in attitudes toward our environment. It is to think of nature and all of her contents as something with whom we live and move and have our being rather than as something over which we have an obligation to rule. The world about us is our partner in life, and we need to hear her, talk with her, and cooperate with her. Our environment is made up not only of the things of nature but also of things that people create in cooperation with nature. Important aspects in our life are flowers, trees, dogs, sun, rain, stars, and other living things that God has made. But houses, buildings, streets, cars, table cloths, church buildings, newspapers, and clothes are also living things which have been made in cooperation with nature. These are not lifeless. The things we make come alive and we do not just move them, but they move us. This is when we learn that in God's world we are not to be conquerors but friends.—C. Ray Dobbins.

SIDE BY SIDE. Love is not so much a man and a woman looking into each other's eyes as standing side by side and looking in the same direction.—Albert D. Hagler.

Sermon Suggestions

CARING ENOUGH. Scripture: Gal. 6:2. (1) Care enough to be aware. (2) Care enough to individualize. (3) Care enough to give.—George W. Davis.

LEARNING TO LIVE WITH OURSELVES. Text: Rom. 12:3. (1) Know yourself. (2) Respect yourself. (3) Enjoy yourself. (4) Invest yourself. (5) Entrust yourself.

Worship Aids

CALL TO WORSHIP. "It is good for me to draw near to God: I have put my trust in the Lord God. . . . God is the strength of my heart, and my portion for ever." Ps. 73:28,26.

INVOCATION. Most holy and gracious God, who turnest the shadow of night into morning: satisfy us early with thy mercy that we may rejoice and be glad all the day. Lift the light of thy countenance upon us, calm every troubled thought, and guide our feet into the way of peace. Perfect thy strength in our weakness and help us to worship thee in the spirit of Jesus Christ our Lord.

OFFERTORY SENTENCE. "Give unto the Lord the glory due unto his name: bring an offering, and come before him." I Chron. 16:29.

OFFERTORY PRAYER. Almighty God, may we trust more and more in thy kind providence, and may our submission to thy will be revealed in the deep devotion expressed through these gifts we offer in Christ's name.

AN AFFIRMATION. I believe in God the Father and that he created all things to be good.

I believe that he loves all his children equally and that he intends for the abundance of his creation to be used for the joy and welfare of all his family.

I believe in Jesus Christ, the Son of God, the way, and the life.

I believe that in both his preaching and his ministry he has clearly laid before us the challenge of being faithful stewards of that portion of the world's wealth for which we are responsible. I believe that much is expected from those to whom much is given.

I believe in the Holy Spirit and that it quickens the trained and compassionate Christian conscience.

I believe that the activity of the Holy Spirit is exemplified in the life of Jesus Christ, who consistently cast his lot with the needs of the poor and the powerless.

I believe in the church of Jesus Christ and that it is given the happy opportunity of bringing together the human needs that exist in God's world and the resources he has provided to meet those needs.

I believe that those persons who are responsible stewards of their material blessings and share generously as they receive know the joy of being full partners with God here on earth and prepare themselves for the judgments of eternity.

I believe in man, created in the image of God and capable of establishing his kingdom on earth.

I believe that man can by yielding to the guidance of God create on earth a social order which will allow all persons to live out their God-given gifts and to share alike in the abundant life Jesus promised.—Melvin E. West.

EVENING SERVICE

Topic: I Can't Get Over It!
TEXT: Mark 5:42 (NEB).

I. If a person cannot get over something, one option is a return to the past. He can regress.

II. If a person cannot get over something, another option is to stand transfixed before it. Here we can speak of frozenness. We could even call it extended shock.

III. If a person cannot get over something, a third option is to circumvent it. This is a form of denial in which we simply decide not to acknowledge the roadblock and instead go around it. Such a maneuver though does not change the fact of the roadblock. Here we are very much captive of that which we cannot get over.

IV. If there is something you cannot get over you can go through it. That is the option of the gospel.

(a) "A man is the slave of whatever has mastered him" (I Pet. 2:19, NEB), and any option other than going directly through that which we for the moment can't get over means that we are a slave of what we cannot get over. The gospel of Jesus Christ says that if we go through what it is that troubles us we will be free of it, and the freeing of men and women is the goal of the gospel. Churchmen are called to be liberators and how great the need for liberators.

(b) The courage to go through something is rewarded by the deep and abiding satisfaction that we have grown. Beneficial fruits arise from spiritual suffering. Each experience of suffering can carry us further in our trek for a fuller and richer human life.

(c) To go through that which we have not been able to get over is to experience the meaning of salvation inasmuch as we are saved from the mocking forces of personality that would have us think that we are more resourceless than we really are, that would have us think we are more plastic than we are, and that would have us think we are more despicable than we are.

(d) We are in the biblical company of a great number of persons who got over difficult circumstances. Joseph got over the fact that his brothers sold him, Ruth got over the early death of her husband, Job got over his trials, Hosea got over Gomar's unfaithfulness, Paul got over his Damascus Road revelation, Peter got over his cowardice, and Jesus got over the cross. It has happened, and it can happen to us.

(e) Jesus reminds us that "the gate is narrow and the way is hard, that leads to life, and those who find it are few." Sometimes that narrow gate and that hard way is the disciplined willingness on the part of persons to walk through that which heretofore they have not been able to face.—Robert A. Noblett.

SUNDAY: MAY TWENTY-SEVENTH

MORNING SERVICE

Topic: Words Fitly Spoken

The Christian message has from the first been known as "news," good news at that. The word "gospel" means "good news." If in this day of space races and international explosions the Christian message seems "old hat" instead of "good news," perhaps we need to pause again to hear just what's at stake.

I. *Pardon is God's good news.* (a) The Christian news is that man has pardon. The word of pardon which the Bible speaks is that men are enjoined to confess their sins, but they are not condemned to bear them.

(1) Dietrich Bonhoeffer said, "He who is alone with his sin is utterly alone." Bonhoeffer pled for a new understanding of confession. Few backs are strong enough to bear the weight of sin when unconfessed. Martin Luther spoke often of the freedom of the Christian man. His phrase described the promises of God, one of which is that the weight of sin need not be borne. Pardon will relieve that load.

(2) Pardon follows only upon confession. This is more than saying we are sorry; we must be sorry enough to rise and sin no more. Sin must be admitted before almighty God and loathed and finished with. Pardon bestowed without this kind of feeling would demoralize us in the long run. But with frank confession and the resolve to quit the sin, God acts to lift our load. Strange it is that confession comes so hard. Most of us would let our backs be broken by our sin than ever to admit we have done wrong. Yet God requires confession of us and our deep contrition.

(b) Is this too much to ask? Someone has said, "If ever we think thy demands too great upon us, God, remind us how hard it was for Christ to hang upon a cross." What God requires is only a trifle when compared to what he has done. Here again we fail to see all of this as true because our sin both weighs us down and casts our eyes upon the ground; instead we ought to see the heavens for there is pardon there.

(c) "The Bible is a gloomy book," a casual reader was heard to say, "because it talks so much of sin." But that reader had it wrong! Life with no good news of pardon is the gloomy thing; the crush of unconfessed and thus unforgiven sin is the dismal expectation. (See I John 1:9.)

II. *Hope is God's good news.* (a) The second word of Christian news follows close along: man has hope. The simplest thing that can be said about this news is that hope means hanging on. If we cherish hope, we then are hanging on. Hope's firm grasp is not the product of stubbornness but rather of purpose. Christian hope clings to the promise that God has something better yet in store.

(b) It was hope like this that sustained the early Christians. Society was against them; numbers were against them; few things seemed to be on their side. Injustices were common, and persecution was the order of the day. In the face of all this the majority of believers still held on. How stubborn can you be? their accusers heckled. But little did the accusers understand. These Christians saw that God yet ruled and that he had something better just ahead both for them and for their world. Not stubbornness but purpose defined their action. And this was nothing less than hope, for hope means hanging on.

(c) It is hope like this that leads and in the past has led many Christians through the valley of the shadow of sickness and even death. Their firm expectation is that darkness endures but for a time and joy will come with the morning dawn. Here is why the resurrection means so much: it symbolizes the promise that God has something better yet in store. This is no cheap escape and no wishful thinking. The highest, holiest member of the human race died in misery, shame, and loneliness upon a cross, proving that God's promises were sure. Each of us can take new courage from him and from what he suffered there. He faced the starkest tragedy with a heart of hope, and so can we, for hope means hanging on.

III. *Faith is God's good news.* (a) Thank God for hope, and thank him too for faith, for faith is one more headline of our gospel news. I like Wilfred T. Grenfell's definition of faith. Faith, he said, is reason grown courageous. Think of that for a moment. Reason is the tool by which we organize and advance the information we have about life and the world around us. Reason can stop with this job of organization or it can become venturesome and creative. The breakthroughs of modern science and the developments in literature and the arts represent reason at the growing edge. And reason grown courageous is simply the further step which marks out faith.

(b) Faith, like hope and pardon, is a gift of God. He asks us to trust in him, and he gives us the means for doing it. He asks us to accept his promises as true, and he stirs our minds to seek them. God gives us both our reason and our courage; together these become the gift of faith. Reason grown courageous is fervent in its zeal and adventuresome in its action. Make no apology for the life of faith unless of course you wish to apologize for thinking any thought at all. Faith is the mind's best thought, the soul's best stance, and life's best venture.

(c) Biblical faith is person-centered. That is to say, individual persons turn in the direction of that supreme person, Christ himself. Their courageous reason tells them that here is God's own Son. Their faith enables them to count on him. —John H. Townsend.

Illustrations

WATCHWORD. Every new idea that has ever burst upon the world has had a watchword. Always there has been some word or phrase in which the very genius of the thing has been concentrated and focused, some word or phrase to blazon on its banners when it went marching out into the world. Islam had a watchword: "God is God, and Mohammed is his prophet." The French Revolution had a watchword: "Liberty, equality, fraternity." The democratic idea had a watchword: "Government of the people, by the people, for the people." Every new idea that has stirred the hearts of men has created its own watchword, something to wave like a flag, to rally the ranks and win recruits. —James S. Stewart.

MEMORIES. After a call to the United Nations building, I stepped for a few moments into a room that has been set aside for prayer and meditation. The room is noted for its simplicity. At the front is a wooden pedestal on which is an arrangement of white flowers. The only other object, except for a few rows of chairs, is the blue and white banner of the United Nations. I was impressed at first by the uncluttered directness of the room. But after a few moments I found myself vaguely troubled. Something was lacking. A few days later I realized what it was. This time I was participating in the dedication of a building. It was another place of prayer and meditation. It was a newly completed church. This structure also was unpretentious, built in the plain style of the New England meetinghouse. But it had something which the UN chapel lacked. It had memories. For all its newness, it spoke of remembered things. The objects and symbols were not many, but each of them was rich with powers of recall.—Truman B. Douglass.

Sermon Suggestion

BEHOLD, A SOWER.   Text: Matt. 13:3. (1) The beaten path shows the hearer who does not hear. The seed never enters the soil. (2) The rocky soil shows the hearer who does not think. The thin layer of soil over a substratum of rock. (3) The thorny soil shows the hearer who does not heed. The best of soil infested with thorns. (4) The good ground shows the hearer who really hears. The bountiful return from all the seed.—Andrew W. Blackwood.

Worship Aids

CALL TO WORSHIP.   "Ho, every one that thirstest, come ye to the waters. Incline your ear, and come unto me: hear, and your soul shall live; and I will make an everlasting covenant with you, even the sure mercies of David." Isa. 55:1, 3.

INVOCATION.   O God, in glory exalted and in mercy ever blessed, we magnify thee, we praise thee, we give thanks unto thee for thy bountiful providence, for all the blessings of this present life, and all the hopes of a better life to come. Let the memory of thy goodness, we beseech thee, fill our hearts with joy and thankfulness.

OFFERTORY SENTENCE.   "Verily, verily, I say unto you, he that believeth on me, the works that I do shall he do also; and

greater works than these shall he do. And whatsoever ye shall ask in my name, that will I do, that the Father may be glorified in the Son." John 14:12–13.

OFFERTORY PRAYER.   God of our fathers, dearly do we cherish the blessings which thy church brings to us and dearly do we covet the privilege of sharing through these gifts the proclaiming of thy word until all of the earth shall praise thee.

PRAYER.   O thou creating God, by whose laws the universe is sustained, by whose art thy handiwork shows beauty, and by whose will man is created to hold dominion in the earth, we bow in awe before thy wisdom and power.

We worship thee in thy goodness. We praise thee for the image of thyself given to thy children in powers of thought and feeling and will. We thank thee for thy leniency with our mistakes and for the grace of Christ unto the forgiveness of our sins.

We come in this our day as perplexed children come to a wise and loving Father. We live in changing times when old things are passing away. In many places the work of our hands is no longer needed. Many of our brothers find no labor by which to earn their daily bread. Leisure becomes less than a blessing; we have little wisdom in the use of it. We need wisdom, O God. We need thy Holy Spirit to guide us. Grant unto our nation and our world wise men and good men to lead the people into a future of blessing and not of doom. Grant unto the hearts of the people a sense of responsibility, not only for their own welfare but also for the good of others. Help us to be good Samaritans. Grant unto us high vision, creative faith, long patience, and unsullied motives as we go about our daily living.

Whatsoever our hands and minds find to do, O Lord, may we do it unto thy glory, always responsive to thy will. With a heart of compassion may we travel our several roads, ever ready to serve a stricken neighbor.

EVENING SERVICE

Topic: What Price Peace? (Memorial Day)

TEXT: Acts 10:36.

Man must have peace in his heart or perish is the teaching of the gospel. Mankind must have peace on earth or perish is the warning of history. Peace ranks among the major themes of the Bible, the Hebrew word for it, *shalom,* occurring more than two hundred times and the Greek word, *eirene,* almost a hundred.

I. Biblical peace has a dimension of depth. It is God's response to man's hunger and thirst after righteousness. And righteousness is the consequence of bringing man's will into conformity with God's will. No peace without righteousness, declares the Bible. "Righteousness shall yield peace and its fruits be quietness and confidence for ever," says Isaiah the prophet. Peace and righteousness are indivisible.

II. Biblical peace is positive, by which I mean that it is infinitely more than the mere absence of war or of tribulation, which is often the significance of *eirene* in classical Greek. Biblical peace has been described as "a positive experience of the fulness of righteous living wherein the human person is enabled to develop to his fullest stretch"—the life in all its fulness, which our Lord came on purpose to give us.

III. Biblical peace is first inward. The realism of the Bible does not distinguish between inward and outward peace, the former being a condition of the latter and the latter a sign and symptom of the former. As man is, so is his world. When man is reconciled to his God he is reconciled to his brother also. "He has reconciled us men to himself through Christ, and he has enlisted us in this service of reconciliation (or has made us agents of this reconciliation)." The miracle must happen in us before it can happen in our world.

IV. Peace in the fulness and richness of its biblical significance can be assured only by the rule and reign of Christ. And the acceptance of his rule is costly. Everything that is worth having has a price. We must be prepared to sacrifice voluntarily for peace as much as we have to sacrifice compulsorily for war. Just as when you plane a piece of wood against the grain you get nothing but splinters, so we never shall have peace on earth while we live against the grain of the universe. And it was the Prince of peace who put the grain in the universe. For "through him all things came to be; no single thing was created without him."—T. Glyn Thomas.

SUNDAY: JUNE THIRD

MORNING SERVICE

Topic: Why I Love and Cherish This Church (Pentecost)

TEXT: Ps. 84:1–2.

I. I love and cherish this church because it is a part of the mystical body of Christ in this world, provided by the Son of the living God to help us on our pilgrimage back to him. It is not man's creation but God's.

II. I love and cherish this church because in it is to be found the whole faith, all that there is—the catholic faith of the ages but the catholic faith genuinely reformed and genuinely scriptural.

III. I love and cherish this church because it is honest enough to admit the utterly obvious truth that it is not perfect and that it is filled with anomalies and sin and imperfections.

IV. I love and cherish this church because it clearly distinguished between the word of God, the book about Jesus Christ, our Lord and Savior, and the incarnate word which is Christ himself. It clearly teaches that the Christian religion is not chiefly about a book but chiefly about a person, our blessed Lord Jesus Christ.

V. I love and cherish this church because in it the worship of God is paramount. Despite our frailties in this area, we know that the worship of God is the first reason for the existence of the church. And that worship is objective and solemn and beautiful and joyous.

VI. I love and cherish this church because her sacraments from holy baptism onward—the beginning of our life in Christ and all through this earthly pilgrimage—are objective and true means of grace. The holy sacraments feed our immortal souls.

VII. I love and cherish this church because it teaches without qualification that Jesus Christ is God in human flesh and that he alone can save us for all eternity.

VIII. I love and cherish this church because it resists every attempt to be fanatical about matters. My intelligence is never insulted by the demands of the faith. I am expected in faith to honor God's gift of reason. And so I share the apostolic faith with a St. Thomas Aquinas, a C. S. Lewis, on one hand, and countless simple souls, on the other, and in between those extremes. All of us can find our spiritual homes here, however brilliant or however pedestrian we are.

IX. I love and cherish this church because of its continuity. It is part of that which for nearly twenty centuries has survived the worst and the best the world could do to it. It is Christ's church, and not even "the gates of hell can destroy it."

X. I love and cherish this church because it does not "play games" with me.

(a) In its authentic teaching it tells me plainly that I am a child of God by adoption and grace but a sinful child. But it also provides for me a medicine to cure and heal my sins against God and neighbor. It teaches me that he who died on the cross of Calvary for the sins of all mankind also applies that forgiveness to me in particular when I am penitent or when I make my sacramental confession.

(b) I am grateful that the church does not "play games" with me about this life or the one to come. I know that there is death, judgment, heaven or hell yet to undergo, but I also know who it is who can guide me through it all, back to himself, if I but hold on to him.

XI. I love and cherish this church in its wild mixture of holiness, transparent honesty, utter simplicity, and great sophistication, in its ability to laugh at our foibles, and in its enjoyment to the full of our blessed freedom under authority. I have no illusions about the "warts" and sins of this church, but there are "warts" and sins in every part of the body of Christ.—William C. R. Sheridan.

Illustrations

TRANSFORMING FORCE. With all its benighted antiquities, its stock of shopworn and second-hand goods, and its large proportion of timorous members and leaders, the church nevertheless is the most august and spiritually effective body of persons on this planet. It has been in every century of its history, including the present one, an extraordinarily creative and transforming force. There are more saints in the world today than in any other century in history. There are more happy Christian homes than ever before.—Rufus M. Jones.

LIFTING POWER. Here is a huge ship moving into the spacious Davis Lock at Sault Sainte Marie. This lock is eighty feet wide and more than thirteen hundred feet long. The immense gates are closed. One sees the ship far down the lock. Only the superstructure of it is on the level with Lake Superior. The ship waits and the lake waits. The ship cannot rise above its present level nor can the lake help the ship until an engineer appears high up on a bridge and turns a wheel which opens the sluice gates. Instantly the water far down in the lock begins to boil and seethe and churn, and the level of it creeps up on the sides of the lock. Quietly, effortlessly, and gently that giant ship is lifted by waters that have behind them all the resistless power of Lake Superior. Soon the ship rides on the level of the lake. The upper gates are open, and it sails forth on a higher plane. But the power did not come from the lock. It did not come from the canal. It did not come from the engineer who opened the sluice gates. It came from the inestimable lifting power of that vast lake thousands of square miles in area. The one central abiding need of our church and of all other churches is an infusion of God's Holy Spirit lifting us to

higher levels of spiritual achievement.—
John Sutherland Bonnell.

Sermon Suggestions

INGREDIENTS IN THE APOSTOLIC PREACHING.
Scripture: Acts 10:34–43. (1) The promise
in the Old Testament. (2) The fulfillment
in Christ. (3) The presence of eyewit-
nesses among us. (4) The warning of judgment to come. (5) The preparation
through repentance and faith.—C. H.
Dodd.

WHY THE EARLY CHURCH GREW.   Text:
Acts 14:27. (1) Christians had a sense of
destiny at a time when most people were
afflicted with anxiety and self-doubt. (2)
They looked to the future and had a joyous optimism of God's triumph. (3) They
were not afraid of death and often longed
for it with anticipation. (4) They exhibited
a radiance and a love which were lacking
in a sophisticated and weary society. (5)
They had a quality of fellowship among
themselves which the world could not du-
plicate. This gave their critics second
thoughts.

Worship Aids

CALL TO WORSHIP.   "The kingdoms of
this world are become the kingdom of our
Lord, and of his Christ; and he shall reign
for ever and ever." Rev. 11:15.

INVOCATION.   Almighty God, our heavenly Father, who reignest over all things in
thy wisdom, power, and love: we adore
thee for thy glory and majesty, and we
praise thee for thy grace and truth to us in
thy Son our Savior. Grant us the help of
thy Holy Spirit, we beseech thee, that we
may worship thee in spirit and in truth.

OFFERTORY SENTENCE.   "If thou draw
out thy soul to the hungry, and satisfy the
afflicted soul; then shall thy light rise in
obscurity, and thy darkness be as the
noonday." Isa. 58:10.

OFFERTORY PRAYER.   O God, thou
giver of all good gifts, in gratitude we

bring our gifts on this day of joyous
worship. Refine them, we pray thee, in
the mint of thy divine purpose and use
them to the end that thy kingdom may
come and thy will be done on earth as it
is in heaven.

PRAYER.   O God, we thank thee that thy
Holy Spirit moves in our minds and hearts
to teach us truth, to set us free, and to
make us righteous. Help us to open our
lives to thy Spirit's influence so that we
may see more clearly, choose more wisely,
and act according to thy will.

Amid the complexities of this world we
need the mind of Christ. Our own
thoughts and opinions too often betray us.
Our prejudices lead us astray. May thy
Spirit keep the words of Jesus before our
minds, interpret their meaning for the
present time, and give us grace to heed
them.

May the compassion of Christ abound in
our hearts. May our love for him overflow
in love for our neighbor. In the wisdom of
the mind of Christ and with the warmth of
the love of Christ may we serve in our
place and time.

By the power of thy Spirit may we grow.
In the power of the Spirit may we aspire
and do far beyond that which we could do
alone. By the acts of Spirit-filled people
may the evils of the world be uprooted,
righteousness established in the earth,
and thy kingdom come.

EVENING SERVICE

Topic: The Spirit and Our Witness
SCRIPTURE: Acts 2:1–21.

I. *Why say it* (vv. 1–4). We have the pros-
pects for membership: add the church's
inactive members to the 40 percent of the
American population outside the church
and you have an estimated 106 million
people, or three out of every four adults,
needing to be won for Christ.

II. *Something to say* (v. 11). What is the
sense of contacting the unchurched if you
have nothing to say? On Pentecost the
Spirit gave the apostles content for their
witness: "the mighty works of God." Jesus
proclaimed that the Holy Spirit would

guide us to the truth. It is the gospel, the good news of what God has done in Jesus. It is something the unsaved are dying to hear, for to them it can mean life and peace and joy.

III. *The way to say it* (v. 6). The miracle of Pentecost was that each foreigner heard the gospel in his own language, in a tongue he could understand. There were no "unknown tongues" in this experience. When we go to visit the unchurched, we need to put the gospel in the prospect's language—simple, plain, ordinary language which makes sense to him or her. The Spirit enlightens and makes plain. He throws light on the subject as well as the language. The witness does not speak his own language but the language of the prospect. The Spirit makes the witness sensitive to this need and helps him or her find the proper words.

IV. *The power to say it* (vv. 4, 18). The Spirit is a fire which came upon the apostles as cloven tongues of fire. Fire generates heat and produces energy. Jesus began preaching after "the Spirit of the Lord is upon me." At Pentecost "the Spirit gave them utterance." Prior to that they were dumb and had not a word to say about the gospel. Joel promised, "I will pour out my spirit, and they shall prophesy." After the disciples on the way to Emmaus said, "Did not our hearts burn within us?" they rushed back to tell about the resurrection. Jeremiah had to preach because there was a fire in his bones.—John R. Brokhoff.

SUNDAY: JUNE TENTH

MORNING SERVICE

Topic: The Ministry of the Holy Spirit (Trinity Sunday)

SCRIPTURE: John 16:7–14.

I. The Holy Spirit establishes our relationship with God. (a) The Bible clearly states that man without Christ is separated from God. (See Isa. 59:2.) Our sins create a wall that rises up around our lives and separates us from the one by whom and for whom we were made.

(b) Salvation is that experience in which we are brought back together. Our sins are removed. The barriers are broken down, the obstacles are swept away, and we are reconciled to him. The word "reconciled" means that two things which were separated have been brought back together.

(c) The death of Christ makes this reconciliation possible. (See II Cor. 5:19.)

(d) How do we appropriate this new life? How is this new life imparted to us? How do we enter into this new relationship? That is the work of the Holy Spirit. (See Tit. 3:5; I Cor. 6:11; Eph. 4:30.) What does the Holy Spirit do in the life of the believer? He appropriates into our lives the atoning affect of the cross of Jesus Christ, he ushers us into the presence of God, he establishes us in a new relationship with him, and he puts God's stamp of approval on our lives.

II. The Holy Spirit enriches our lives. (a) The Holy Spirit enriches our lives by giving us gifts. (See I Cor. 12:7.)

(1) The Holy Spirit endows every Christian with some gifts. He imparts to every believer the ability to do certain things well. He equips every child of God to fulfill that purpose for which we are created.

(2) God not only has a wonderful plan for your life, but he also equips you and enables you to fulfill that plan and experience the fulness of that life by the gifts which the Holy Spirit plants within you. As we discover these gifts and develop these gifts and dedicate them to the Lord, our lives will be enriched.

(b) The Holy Spirit enriches our lives by producing certain fruit within us. (See Gal. 5:22–23.) When you allow the Holy Spirit to fill, control, and dominate your life, you will enjoy this fruit.

(c) The Holy Spirit enriches us by developing us toward Christlikeness.

(1) When you become a Christian, when you are saved, your old nature is not destroyed. Rather you are given a new nature side by side with the old nature. And as Paul states it in Rom. 7, there is a con-

stant struggle between these two natures. The Holy Spirit helps your new nature to win the battle.

(2) The Holy Spirit draws on the death of Christ to make your old nature powerless. He then administers the life of Christ to make our new nature productive. He deadens and subdues the old nature and quickens and develops the new nature. The result is we become more and more like Jesus Christ. It is the Holy Spirit working in our lives that makes it happen.

(3) Jesus came that we might have life. (See John 10:10.) By giving gifts, producing fruit, and developing our new nature within us, the Holy Spirit helps us to experience that life to the fullest.

III. The Holy Spirit enlightens our minds. (a) Jesus said in John 16:12 that there were many things which at that time the disciples could not yet understand, but when the Holy Spirit comes, Jesus said, he would guide them into all truth. One of the most marvelous ministries of the Holy Spirit in the life of the believer is his teaching ministry.

(1) When you face a difficult situation in life, it is encouraging to know that the Holy Spirit is there in your life to guide you to the proper decision.

(2) When you are on your knees in prayer and the words do not come, it is thrilling to know that the Holy Spirit is there in your life to voice your prayer for you in words that cannot be uttered. (See Rom. 8:26–27.)

(3) When you pour over the sometimes perplexing passages of God's word, it is comforting to know that the Holy Spirit is there in your life to translate the truth of scripture and make it real and living to us in our own experience.

(b) What a remarkable thought to realize that ultimate truth is not to be sought in a set of timeless facts which can be mastered in a moment and then filed away, but it is to be found in companionship with the Spirit of truth whom we follow on a pilgrimage of discovery.

(c) Every believer has a master teacher —the Spirit of truth—who goes with us everywhere we go, who faces every experience with us, who confronts every decision that we confront, and who shows us the way to go. He guides us into all truth.

IV. The Holy Spirit encourages our hearts. (a) The word *Paraclete,* which Jesus is using here to refer to the Holy Spirit, is translated comforter in the KJV and helper in the NASB. It is the word *parakalein* which actually means "one called alongside to help."

(b) Life gets tough sometimes. Depression and discouragement are realities in the life of every person. But here is a promise you can take with you. Whenever you are down or discouraged or depressed or defeated, the Holy Spirit is there to console you, to fill you with courage, to cheer you on, and to keep you going.

V. The Holy Spirit empowers our spirit. (a) Jesus predicted it in Acts 1:8, the early church portrayed it in Acts 4:31, Paul proclaimed it in Eph. 3:16, and all of history has proved it. Power comes from the Spirit of God.

(b) You discover in the history of the church that whenever lives were changed, whenever churches were started, whenever the lost were saved, whenever Christians were used, and whenever power was experienced it was always because of the mighty movement of the Holy Spirit of God.

(c) You evaluate your own life and you will find it to be true as well. Those moments of real power in your life came when you waited upon, yielded to, and were controlled by the Holy Spirit. For the Holy Spirit empowers us with supernatural strength and enables us to put into practice the things that Jesus taught.— Brian L. Harbour.

Illustrations

THE TORN PAGE. A young mother finally got her three children to bed one night and wearily came down into the den when an awful sight met her eyes. An encyclopedia lay open on the floor. A page had been ripped out and torn into little pieces. As she gathered up the mess and reached for the scotch tape, this experience seemed to symbolize the hectic futility of her life. She heaved a sigh. As she repaired the torn page she realized it was the face of a child, and when she turned it over she found on the back a map of the world. And it suddenly struck her that her vocation was not useless. For as she patiently gave herself to putting together the life of a child, she was really giving shape to both the world of tomorrow and reality itself.—James L. Pleitz.

RENASCENCE.   The good news is that there is resident in each of us the creative energy of rebirth. It is latent, seemingly dead, but the power of renascence is there to be awakened and released by the Spirit. It is not a matter of what becomes of us but who we become. It is a death-resurrection matter. So the question is, What's dying in us? The answer will give us the clue as to what is being born in us.—Robert A. Raines.

Sermon Suggestion

THE WAYS OF THE SPIRIT.   Scripture: Acts 2:1–4. (1) He works spontaneously: "And suddenly there came a sound from heaven" (v. 2). (2) He works sovereignly: "A rushing mighty wind" (v. 2). (3) He works significantly: "Tongues like as of fire" (v. 3).—Stephen F. Olford.

Worship Aids

CALL TO WORSHIP.   "O send out thy light and thy truth: let them lead me; let them bring me unto thy holy hill, and to the tabernacles." Ps. 43:3.

INVOCATION.   O Lord Jesus Christ, who art the truth incarnate and the teacher of the faithful: let thy Spirit overshadow us as we meditate on thy word and conform our thoughts to thy revelation that, learning of thee with honest hearts, we may be rooted and built up in thee, who livest and reignest with the Father and the Holy Spirit, ever one God, world without end.—William Bright.

OFFERTORY SENTENCE.   "Bring ye all the tithes into the storehouse, saith the Lord, [and I will] open the windows of heaven, and pour you out a blessing." Mal. 3:10.

OFFERTORY PRAYER.   Eternal God, give us a vision of thy glory that no sacrifice may seem too great, and strengthen us in every step we take from selfishness to generosity.

A BACCALAUREATE PRAYER.   Eternal God, before whose face the generations rise and pass away: age after age of the living seek thee and find that of thy faithfulness there is no end. Thou art the inspirer of every true prayer, the giver of all wisdom, the source of all truth, the beginning of all human freedom, and the end of all human responsibility.

Look, O God, upon this community of learning. Let it ever remain faithful to thee and to the truth as we come to know it in thee and in thy son Jesus Christ. Keep us ever from surrendering truth or giving over freedom to those who in fear or faithlessness tell us we must fight evil with the tools of evil, falsehood with lies, or tyranny with the ways of tyrants. Let this school be a light of truth in a world of darkness and a witness to freedom in a world where many are enslaved to idols and to ideologies, a place where men shall come to know the good and to know thee, the wellspring of all good.

We pray for her graduates, those present, those who have gone before, and those who are yet to come, that in the midst of timid uncertainty they may boldly stand for something, in the midst of aimlessness they may have a goal, in the midst of false prophets for panaceas they may look to thy kingdom in Christ as the hope of the world, and that in the midst of careless ease they may mount up with wings as eagles, may run and not be weary, and may walk and not faint. Hear our prayer as in praise and thanksgiving for all that we now have and hold we pray in the name of Christ our Lord.—Robert B. Moore.

EVENING SERVICE

Topic: Christian Discipleship
TEXTS: Luke 6:46; 14:27.
What does it mean to be a Christian disciple today? Even though our world has changed drastically since the days of Jesus, the purpose and meaning of disci-

pleship have not changed one iota.

I. A Christian disciple will have perception. He will have the capacity to see where others are blind. A Christian will not be either morally blind or spiritually inert. It was perception which helped to make the prophets spiritual giants. They perceived that service to God consisted of more than performing rituals and offering sacrifices. It was perception which caused Jesus to point out that it took more than offering the tithe of mint and anise to make one pious. Christian discipleship requires a heart that is quick to discern and a hand that is ready to reach out.

II. To be a Christian disciple means to have a willingness to live with a sense of dedication.

(a) It demands consecration, sometimes even in the nature of heroism. It is something we reach for because we want it. We know how much it costs, but we come with the purchase price in our hands. Some-times it demands sacrifice. At other times it means privation and foregoing pleasure. Jesus demanded denial, and no one ever accomplishes much in life who does not practice this.

(b) A man ought to be able to point to his days with some satisfaction and say: "I do this better than I did yesterday. I forgive more readily; I understand more easily; I live more genuinely; I see God more clearly."

III. We must be able to measure up to the test laid down by Jesus. What was that test? Jesus said, "If ye continue in my word, then are ye my disciples" (John 8:-31) There is no variableness in a man's intention to be a Christian. Here is a vow a man does not and cannot break. It is now and tomorrow and always. There are no holidays from Christian living. There is no recess from a commitment to Christ. It means living in his words; it means living by his words.—A. Ray Adams.

SUNDAY: JUNE SEVENTEENTH

MORNING SERVICE

Topic: The New Covenant
Texts: Jer. 31:31; Heb. 8:6.

I. Behind the religious quest in every age lie three elemental needs of the human spirit.

(a) A moral imperative: some authoritative guideline for character and conduct, a standard to deal with our innate awareness of responsibility and obligation.

(b) A divine fellowship: the longing for a living presence in the unseen, a transcendent reality beyond this transient material world.

(c) An inward cleansing: the chance to make a new beginning when sin has corrupted the standard and broken the fellowship and left an angel with a flaming sword barring the road back to paradise.

II. God's first covenant with Israel had three basic factors, corresponding closely to these perennial demands.

(a) The covenant met the demand for a standard with the law. "Here is your norm," it said to Israel. "By rendering obedience here, you will settle the question of responsibility, and peace and prosperity will follow."

(b) It met the demand for a divine fellowship with the priesthood. For the function of the priest was precisely to be a link between the human and the divine. He would penetrate behind the veil and bring back news from the beyond, and thus the fellowship between God and man would be established and preserved forever.

(c) It met the demand for cleansing with the system of sacrifices which reached their zenith in the Day of Atonement, the great Yom Kippur. By perpetual repetition right on to the end of time, perpetual pardon would be secured and the shadows accumulating around the conscience dissipated like mists before the dawn.

III. Is this remote from twentieth-century man's concern? Not in the least. In fact, would it not be true to say that there is something in all of us which is more at home with the old covenant than with its fulfillment in the gospel?

(a) There is a certain satisfactoriness about having a code to keep and a dictated standard to observe especially in these days when so many inherited standards have been dissolved by the acids of modernity.

(b) The priesthood. There is a considerable relief in the thought of being able to deal with God in some other way than by personal encounter. Religion by proxy is so much less disturbing than direct confrontation.

(c) The Day of Atonement. It can be comforting to confide in the apparatus of religious ordinances and observances, if indeed these can somehow help to secure the divine favor and thus lift life's burdens and heal its wounds.

IV. But even in Israel awkward questions kept arising. (a) The law was indeed the gift of God and the norm for the people's life. But was the law itself perhaps just a symbol of man's fallen estate and therefore impotent to redeem?

(b) How could the priest, a mortal man and a sinner like all the rest, bridge the gulf and bring men to God?

(c) Could the Day of Atonement, constantly requiring to be repeated, really salve a guilty conscience? How could its slain beasts and altars splashed with blood save the sinner from his sin?

V. All this fermenting dissatisfaction came to a head with Jeremiah. "Days are coming," he heard a voice from heaven say, "when I will make a new covenant with Israel." A new move was impending from the side of God and a new strategy to revolutionize history and to reveal the cosmic patience of the Almighty. Three points the oracle stresses.

(a) Over against the externalism of law, the inwardness of the divine word: "I will put my law in their inward parts, and write it in their hearts." Here is the assertion that the world cannot be redeemed by statutes nor evil eradicated with a decalogue. The constant and desperate struggle to observe the prescribed conditions of obedience could only minister to self-righteousness, thus riveting the shackles of sin more surely on the soul. But now God's delivering grace is going to penetrate to the hidden seat of human frustration and capture the last bastion of pride and corruption.

(b) Over against the derived and mediated character of priestly religion, the immediacy of the divine fellowship: "They shall teach no more every man his neighbor, saying, 'Know the Lord': for they shall all know me, from the least of them unto the greatest." No more second-hand dealing with God through imperfect intermediaries. There can be no verve nor lustre in a faith shining with a borrowed light. That must give way to the directness of touch and the sureness of vision which come when heaven and earth authentically meet and heart can speak with heart.

(c) Over against the inefficacy of cultic sacrifice the initiative of the divine forgiveness: "I will forgive their iniquity, and I will remember their sin no more." For the perpetually repeated sacrifices with their crassly material symbolism could never break into the doomed and vicious circle which sin's self-propagating power inexorably creates. But one day God would take the initiative and make obsolete all such vain oblations by one eternal offering. This would be the all-sufficient amnesty for sin through the everlasting mercy of the Lord. "The day is coming," said Jeremiah.

VI. "The day has come," declares the writer to the Hebrews, quoting the Jeremiah oracle in full. Christ in his own person is the new covenant. See how the vision came true.

(a) The inwardness of the divine word is made actual in Christ. For what Jesus does is to de-externalize the norm for life and character and inscribe it on the heart. He does this by himself becoming the norm, so that those who are united to him by faith and interpenetrated by his Spirit are lifted into a realm of devotion where life ceases to be regarded in legal terms at all. Law has been transmuted into love.

(b) The immediacy of the divine fellowship is made actual in Christ. For here is a high priest, untouched by sin, eternal, who not only stands on the side of men in complete and utter self-identification, representing them to God, but also stands absolutely on the side of God to bring him to men. Thus the veil is rent in twain from the top to the bottom. The unbridgeable gulf is bridged once and for all.

(c) The initiative of the divine forgiveness is made actual in Christ. For now—and this is what makes Christianity such a miracle to crown all miracles—the oblation is not man's but God's. It is God who makes the offering in the person of his Son. The cross is the one true altar, the defeat of the devil, and the atonement of the world. And the resurrection seals the act of reconciliation.—James S. Stewart.

Illustrations

THE LIGHTED WAY.   Christopher Fry has written a play with the intriguing title *The Dark Is Light Enough.* The play rebukes our tendency to take refuge in the idea that moral and ethical values are relative and that, since we are confused, we are excused of responsibility. Fry depicts a heroine who moves "undemandingly" among morally confused persons so that they are backed up "against eternity." The light of a strong, compassionate woman's life is enough to show others the way, so that lives are made whole "in her neighborhood." The play suggests that in questions that matter most we have the light we need for acting responsibly.—Woodrow A. Geier.

FELLOWSHIP AND SOLITUDE.   Only in the fellowship do we learn to be rightly alone and only in aloneness do we learn to live rightly in the fellowship. It is not as though the one preceded the other; both begin at the same time, namely, with the call of Jesus Christ. Each by itself has profound pitfalls and perils. One who wants fellowship without solitude plunges into the void of words and feelings, and one who seeks solitude without fellowship perishes in the abyss of vanity, self-infatuation, and despair. Let him who cannot be alone beware of community. Let him who is not in community beware of being alone.—Dietrich Bonhoeffer.

Sermon Suggestions

THE EVERLASTING ARMS.   Text: Deut. 33:27. (1) Underneath the cosmos there is something everlasting. (2) Underneath nature there is something everlasting. (3) Underneath history there is something everlasting. (4) Underneath human personality there is something everlasting.—Edward L. R. Elson.

TO HAVE THE MIND OF CHRIST.   Text: Phil. 2:5. (1) To think his thoughts with him and after him. (2) To live like him with trust and faith in God's eternal presence and constant availability. (3) To face life and death with the assurance of an infinite companionship. (4) To embody and express his love and concern for others and his willingness to give unceasingly of himself. (5) To know and affirm that nothing is impossible to the almighty Creator in whom we live and move and have our being. (6) To pray at the time of testing and decision, "Thy will, not mine, be done."—Edward C. Dahl.

Worship Aids

CALL TO WORSHIP.   "I will lift up mine eyes unto the hills, from whence cometh my help. My help cometh from the Lord, which made heaven and earth." Ps. 121:1-2.

INVOCATION.   God of all life, we have come here today alone as persons, together in families, all joined in the community of Christian faith. Though we seek your face in the world of life we ask your blessing in these moments of withdrawal. Take us not from the world, but prepare us for life in the world. Let us not imagine special privilege for ourselves, but let us encourage common opportunity for all. Give us not love for ourselves alone, but make us instruments of your love in the midst of every human place.—Richard D. Bausman.

OFFERTORY SENTENCE.   "Therefore, my beloved brethren, be ye steadfast, unmoveable, always abounding in the work of the Lord, forasmuch as ye know that your labour is not in vain in the Lord." I Cor. 15:58.

OFFERTORY PRAYER. As we bring our offering today we thank thee, O God, for the happiness of our earthly life, for peaceful homes and healthful days, for our powers of mind and body, for faithful friends, and for the joy of loving and being loved. We pray that these blessings may come to abound throughout all the world and to all people.

LITANY. We thank you, God, for your blessings. For all your blessings in creation, for the beauty of the earth and sea and sky, for your manifold works, and for the wisdom with which you have made them all.
We thank you, O God.
For the joy of our earthly life, for peaceful homes and healthful days, for our powers of mind and body, for faithful friends, and for the joy of loving and being loved.
We thank you, O God.
For the revelation of your love and for newness of life in our Savior, Jesus Christ, for the blessings brought to us by your holy church, and for our fellowship with you in Christ.
We thank you, O God.

EVENING SERVICE

Topic: Partners in the Gospel
SCRIPTURE: Phil. 1:3–11 (RSV).
The scripture lesson contains a fourfold illustration of the principle of "partnership in the gospel" (v. 5). Translated by the KJV as "fellowship," the Greek word for "partnership" literally means "participation."
I. Christians are partners in "work" (v. 6), which Paul subsequently (v. 7) gives a double definition. Such work involves the "defense" of the faith against outside attacks from the enemies of the gospel. It

also requires "confirmation," which means the additional strengthening of fellow-Christians. Consequently a church is more than a religious kindergarten in which the preacher exhorts and the people listen, more than a religious theater in which worshipers are spectators enjoying a performance, and more than a religious club that exists for the benefit of its members. "The laity are not the helpers of the clergy so that the clergy can do their job, but the clergy are helpers of the whole people of God so that the laity can be the church." In other words, the clergy are the church within the church, while the laity are the church out in the world.
II. Christians are partners in "grace" (v. 7) drawn together by a common sense of unpayable debt to the sheer goodness of God in Christ. Accordingly Paul insists not that he has apprehended but that he was apprehended (3:12–13).
III. Christians are partners in pain. Paul's reference to "imprisonment" (v. 7) serves as a reminder that first the Jew and then the Gentile harrassed the Christians from place to place, so that the church was hardly born before it began to form its list of martyrs. Indeed its central symbol is a cross. Each Christian however should find strength through the realization that he does not suffer alone but belongs to a great fellowship of sacrificial service.
IV. Christians are partners in love or "the affection of Christ Jesus (v. 8), who said sublimely, "He who loses his life for my sake will find it" (Matt. 10:39). Christians enjoy a far richer life simply because they are unselfish. An appropriate epitaph for every true member of Christ's body is one written of a former governor-general of Canada: "He lit so many fires in cold rooms."—N. Keith Polk, Jr.

SUNDAY: JUNE TWENTY-FOURTH

MORNING SERVICE

Topic: Doubt: Doorway to Belief
TEXT: John 20:25.
Thomas, the most misunderstood and maligned of the disciples, has set the pat-

tern by which all our beliefs ought to be tested, for doubt and belief are linked inseparably in the quest for truth. Doubt is the doorway to belief. I speak for Thomas. May his tribe increase!
I. The process of doubting has made

possible the remarkable progress of the race. The right to doubt is one of our most cherished possessions. Doubt is as native to man as the air he breathes; it is the golden key by which he has unlocked and continues to unlock doors of mystery. The world is greatly indebted to those courageous men and women who have insisted upon the right and the duty to question the most fundamental laws projected by man.

II. We readily concede that the process of doubting is essential to the progress of science. However when we come to religion we seem to have a suspicion of the inquiring mind.

(a) We find it difficult to associate doubt with religious belief. Where does this notion that it is improper, even irreligious, to ask questions about the great things of the soul come from? Certainly not from the Bible or from the biographies of great men and women.

(b) I sometimes think that the Bible is primarily a book about man and his doubts. Surely the great worthies of the Bible were not afraid of the interrogation point.

(1) Of all the writing prophets none lays siege to our hearts so surely as does Jeremiah. He was a man of deep emotions, and one reads his messages with warm tears welling up behind the eyes. He identifies with his people until his great heart breaks over their suffering. He is torn by the dreadful paradoxes of doubt and certainty. Like Job he was not afraid to talk to God about his doubts.

(2) Job was not afraid to interrogate God. He doubted the then popular view that only the wicked suffer and the righteous prosper. He told God that the wicked prosper like a green bay tree. He called the conventional notion of prosperity and suffering into court for questioning. He wanted to see the evidence. He was not afraid to present his case before God.

(3) Walk with Jesus over the hills of Palestine, and you will have fellowship with one of God's great doubters. And how much he doubted! He doubted the small ideas of God; he doubted the wisdom of men praying in the marketplace to be heard of men; he doubted the right of the Pharisees to prohibit his healing of a sick man on the sabbath. He doubted ancient traditions which demeaned life. He had his doubts too about God. Nailed to a criminal's cross, forsaken by most of his friends, scorned and ridiculed, there was a moment when he asked, quite frankly: "My God, my God, why hast thou forsaken me? Why art thou so far from helping me?" Our Lord's life is the world's supreme hosanna, yet it passed "through great whirlwinds of doubt."

III. In religion, as in the kingdom of science, the doubting mind is a healthy mind. I believe that it is an unarguable fact that the great believers have been and are the great doubters. We need not pretend that faith in God, in our individual worth, in the kingdom of heaven, or in immortality is easily arrived at. When I hear a person talking glibly about his faith, condemning those who doubt, I am always suspicious. They talk too much. Their doubts and insecurities are protruding everywhere.

(a) In our religious life most of our thinking about God has come as the result of man's capacity to doubt. There was a time when it was believed that God demanded human sacrifice. Then some ancient man doubted that idea of God; he believed that God would be satisfied with the sacrifice of a ram. In later years men doubted even this idea and came to believe that God would be satisfied with sacrifices of grain and libations of oil. Then the great ethical prophets appeared on the scene—Amos, Hosea, Jeremiah, and Isaiah—in whom the whole system of idolatry and sacrifice was held up to question.

(b) What we question is not God in this instance but the ideas that we have of God. It is not easy to believe in God as the mystery behind all existence and as that which gives meaning to our pilgrimage, but it is immeasurably more difficult not to believe in this God. For if God is not at the heart of the universe, forever bringing order out of chaos and light out of darkness, then our world is nothing but a cruel slave mill in which we are destined for ultimate extinction.

(c) We need to doubt the current pessimism concerning man. The modern pessimist sees him plunging headlong toward ultimate extinction. Jesus knew what was in man. He knew that he had demonic capacities, but he also realized that he had within him Godlike qualities. He believed that if these qualities were cultivated man could eventually overthrow evil and establish righteousness on the throne.

(d) There is much in our modern world that we need to doubt. Moreover our faith in the great things of the soul will not be easily held. But if we have the capacity to keep on doubting—by which I mean the process of seeking new light and new truth about ourselves and the meaning of our world—we will at last be able to say with Thomas, "My Lord and my God!" It is forever true that doubting is the doorway to belief. Yet man's vision is limited and he can never know all there is to know about God. But if he gives himself up to that power that binds him, loves it, trusts it, and prays to it, he can say, even as Jesus did, "Father, into thy hands I commend my spirit."—Charles F. Jacobs.

Illustrations

HEART AND HEAD.   Christ wants a child's heart but a grown-up's head. He wants us to be simple, single-minded, affectionate, and teachable, as good children are; but he also wants every bit of intelligence we have to be alert at its job and in first-class fighting trim.—C. S. Lewis.

ACCOUNTABILITY.   So long as men and women believed themselves to be responsible beings, called to choose and accountable to God for their choices, life might be tragic, but it was not trivial.—Sydney Cave.

Sermon Suggestions

GOOD NEWS AND BAD.   Scripture: I John 1:7-10. (1) The bad news is that every person is a sinner: "If we say that we have not sinned, we make him a liar" (v. 10). (2) The good news is that every

person can be forgiven: "If we confess our sins, he is faithful and just to forgive us our sins" (v. 9). (3) The bad news is that every person has inherited sin: "If we say that we have no sin, we deceive ourselves, and the truth is not in us" (v. 8). (4) The good news is that every person can be freed from inherited sin: "If we walk in the light, as he is in the light . . . the blood of Jesus Christ his Son cleanseth us from all sin" (v. 7).—Mendell Taylor.

CHRIST THE DOOR.   Text: John 14:6. (1) Christ is the door to salvation. (2) Christ is the door to security. (3) Christ is the door to satisfaction.—H. C. Chiles.

Worship Aids

CALL TO WORSHIP.   "Sing unto the Lord, sing psalms unto him. Glory ye in his holy name: let the heart of them rejoice that seek the Lord." Ps. 105:2-3.

INVOCATION.   Eternal and ever-blessed God, grant this day light to the minds that hunger for the truth and peace to the hearts which yearn for rest. Grant strength to those who have hard tasks to do and power to those who have sore temptations to face. Grant unto us within this place to find the secret of thy presence and to go forth from it in the strength of the Lord.

OFFERTORY   SENTENCE.   "And they came, every one whose heart stirred him up, and every one whom his spirit made willing, and they brought the Lord's offering to the work of the tabernacle of the congregation, and for all his service." Exod. 35:21.

OFFERTORY PRAYER.   O God, help us so to practice by our gifts and our lives the divine principle of goodwill that in our homes, our communities, and among all the nations of the earth men may enjoy the boon of peace.

PRAYER.   Almighty God, we thank thee for the love wherewith thou dost follow us all the days of our life. We thank thee that thou dost inform our minds with thy divine truth and undergird our wills with thy divine grace. We thank thee for every evidence of thy Spirit's leading and for all those little happenings which, though seeming at the time no more than chance, yet afterward appear to us as part of thy gracious plan for the education for our souls. Let us not refuse the leading or quench the light which thou hast kindled within us, but rather let us daily grow in grace and in the knowledge of Jesus Christ our Lord and Master.—John Baillie.

EVENING SERVICE

Topic: His Finest Hour

TEXT: Dan. 6:10.

Darius held over his subjects the power of life and death. At a word from him Daniel knew that he could be destroyed either by fire or by the sword or by ferocious beasts. And yet Daniel is prepared to forfeit even life itself rather than be unfaithful to his God. It was his finest hour!

I. No man comes empty handed to such an hour as that. And Daniel is no exception. To that hour he brought three things which go a long way toward explaining his conduct.

(a) He brought a great conviction. A conviction is not so much something that we hold on to as something that holds on to us, and Daniel was sustained by a great conviction. He came to that hour believing in a God who stood over all the kings of the earth. He believed that God was in the place of ultimate control, not Darius, nor the presidents, nor the satraps but God alone. He believed that God had a plan both for his servant's life and for the world. Daniel was convinced that nothing could happen to him which God did not allow, and he was persuaded that even if death came he would not drift beyond God's love and care.

(b) He brought a deep commitment. Long before when he was first brought to Babylon "he resolved that he would not defile himself with the king's rich food or with the wine which he drank" (Dan. 1:8). This was not a commitment to physical fitness. Daniel had nothing against good food and good wine. It was religious commitment. He was afraid that the food might have been offered to idols and that it would be ceremonially unclean. To us that may seem a trivial thing, but to Daniel it was part of the deep commitment which he had made to God. He had put his hand to the plow, and he was not prepared to turn back.

(c) He brought a long-established custom. "He got down upon his knees three times a day and prayed and gave thanks before his God, as he had done previously" or "as was his wont" (Dan. 6:10). By that custom he was spiritually sustained.

II. The hour of testing is at hand and it can either be our finest hour or it will be the hour of our shame. If it is to be our finest hour there are some things which we must bring to it just as Daniel did.

(a) There must be a clear understanding of the faith. If Daniel had yielded, the Jewish faith might have disappeared and been lost. That suggests the need for a clear understanding of the Christian faith today, and that means honest effort and sincere Bible study. Suffice it to say that you can't get great saints with a skimmed theology.

(b) There must be a sincere love for Jesus Christ. We must realize afresh who he is and what he has done for us, and there must be a willingness on our part to suffer and sacrifice for him. We need to recognize that there is a cost to being a Christian. Jesus made that quite clear. (See Matt. 16:24.)

(c) We must begin now to make use of the means of grace. Worship and participation in the work of the church produce vital Christianity. These things produce convictions and attitudes which help to hold men steady when they face the storm. And it is through worship and devotion and involvement that we give God a chance to strengthen and sustain us. Certainly no one can deny that the man or woman who uses the means of grace which God has provided is more likely to stand, and having done all to stand, than the individual who simply depends upon his own strength.—S. Robert Weaver.

SUNDAY: JULY FIRST

MORNING SERVICE

Topic: The Good News of Freedom (Independence Sunday)
TEXT: Gal. 5:13–14.

I. Drawing upon his own experiences Paul wrestled with the issue of freedom. He affirmed the good news that Christian freedom is not only from something but is also for something.

(a) Paul and Barnabas had traveled through Asia Minor. Other teachers came among the people later, questioned Paul's authority as an apostle, and precipitated a conflict. Reactionary Jews insisted that in order to become a Christian a gentile first had to become a Jew by circumcision and then had to adhere to a dietary regulations. Paul had lived as a strict Jew; he had felt the pressures of the law. A religion of rules usually encourages persons to break them or to be broken themselves in trying to fulfill the regulations.

(b) By contrast freedom is internal and supplies the power to achieve what love seeks. Love here is defined as wholesome self-esteem and genuine concern for the needs of others. Christian freedom is the ability to consider external factors and internal convictions and then to decide what love does. Freedom and responsibility go together.

(c) Paul, irritated by the accusations of the troublemakers and unable to make a personal trip to Asia Minor, wrote his "manifesto of freedom."

(1) Passionately defending his independence of the church's conservative leaders in Jerusalem, he declared that it is more important to have the faith of Abraham than to be physically descended from the patriarch.

(2) He affirmed that a faithful response to what God has done in Jesus Christ is more important than following the law given on Mount Sinai.

(3) He related his apostolic authority to his encounter with Christ on the Damascus Road. Paul and the more liberal elements of the early church knew that faith in Jesus Christ develops Christian freedom.

II. Paul warns against using freedom to do as persons please. (a) He suggests that love rather than law is the best safeguard of freedom. Freedom is recognizing our obligations to all persons and the effect of our decisions. To appeal to rules, however noble they may seem, is to be a slave. We are free to the extent that we let love determine our decisions.

(b) As a nation we have often acted as though we could do whatever we want to do without concern for the rest of the world. Today we can no longer use more than our fair share of earth's resources and produce more than our proportion of the earth's garbage without creating anger and resentment among underdeveloped nations. Shortages of wheat, corn, and other grains and the energy crisis are reminders that one nation's freedom ends where another's begins. We cannot live independently of each other. Our futures are intertwined. We need one another in ways that we are only beginning to glimpse. Hopefully we will learn that whatever any nation does has global consequences.

III. Jesus Christ's life, teachings, death, and resurrection communicate the good news of freedom. Jesus forgave opponents, loved the unlovable, served those who could or would not return his kindness, and chose death on a cross. He is the model of Christian freedom.

(a) Christ began his ministry by referring to the metaphor from Isa. 61 regarding what God was about to do in releasing the people from Babylon. He presented himself as the liberator and pointed to the deliverance wrought by his coming. (See Luke 4:16–21.)

(b) Jesus's example is a reminder that freedom means choices, and choices bring consequences. Responsible freedom is real, not imagined. We often choose and then try to avoid the consequences. Followers of Jesus choose to act responsibly toward themselves and others. Christian freedom is a conscious decision to obligate ourselves to all of history.

(c) Jesus Christ, the model for a lifestyle of Christian freedom, empowers us to be instruments of liberation to others. The good news of freedom is that our past, however horrible, has been accepted through God's act in Jesus Christ. Our present has been approved as "good." Our future is open to new possibilities. What better news could anyone desire?

(d) God calls us to continue the ministry of Christ in a world plagued with ignorance and torn by prejudice. This sounds idealistic, perhaps impossible. The highwater marks of moral leadership in history have been left by persons disciplined to risk their lives for the conviction that Christian freedom is the best way to make sense out of life. They have learned to say yes to life.—William H. Likins.

Illustrations

CHURCH AND SOCIETY.   William Temple said the method of the church's impact on society must be twofold. It must first announce Christian principles and point out where the existing social order is in conflict with them at any given time. It must then pass on to Christian citizens in their civic capacity the task of reshaping the existing order in closer conformity to those principles. To proclaim the truth so that society can understand it and then to motivate the people of God to apply it in their lives and in the world around them is the minimum responsibility of the church in politics. After all, Jesus was not teaching his disciples just a pretty ritual when he taught them to pray: "Thy kingdom come. Thy will be done on earth as it is in heaven." He was actually teaching them something very near to the heart of the gospel and something very important for the affairs of daily life in general and citizenship in particular.—Foy Valentine.

THE NATION AND THE BIBLE.   Suppose a nation should take the Bible for their only lawbook and every member should regulate his conduct by the precepts there exhibited. Every member would be obliged in conscience to temperance and industry, to justice and kindness and charity toward his fellowmen, to love purity and reverence toward almighty God. In the commonwealth no man would steal or lie or in any way defraud his neighbor but would live in peace and goodwill with all men. No man would blaspheme his maker or profane his worship, but national and manly and sincere and unaffected piety would reign in all hearts.—John Adams.

ON LOVING AMERICA.   I love my country. To say that is like saying I love my family. I did not choose my country any more than I chose my parents, but I am her daughter as truly as I am the child of my mother and father. What I am my country has made me. She has fostered the spirit which made my education possible. Neither Greece nor Rome, nor all China nor Germany nor Great Britain has surrounded a deaf-blind child with the devotion and skill and resources which have been mine in America.

But my love for America is not blind. Perhaps I am more conscious of her faults because I love her so deeply. Nor am I blind to my own faults. It is not easy to hold a steady course in a changing world.

It need not discourage us if we are full of doubts about America. Healthy questions keep faith dynamic. In fact unless we start with doubts we cannot have a deep-rooted faith. One who believes lightly and unthinkingly has not much of a belief. He who has a faith which is not to be shaken has won it through blood and tears and has worked his way from doubt to truth as one who reaches a clearing through a thicket of brambles and thorns.—Helen Keller.

Sermon Suggestion

TOLERATION AND LIBERTY.   Text: Ps. 33:12. There is a vast difference between toleration and liberty. (1) Toleration is a concession; liberty is a right. (2) Toleration is a matter of expediency; liberty is a matter of principle. (3) Toleration is a

grant of man; liberty is a gift of God.—
George W. Truett.

Worship Aids

CALL TO WORSHIP. "Know therefore
that the Lord thy God, he is God, the faithful God, which keepeth covenant and
mercy with them that love him and keep
his commandments to a thousand generations." Deut. 7:9.

INVOCATION. Almighty God, the giver
and lord of life: we bless and praise thee
for thy merciful keeping and gracious
care, for all the gifts of thy providence and
grace, and for all the blessings which manifest thy fatherhood. We thank thee for the
faith which sustains us, the hopes which
inspire us, and the light by which we daily
walk. We thank thee for Jesus Christ, who,
by the life he lived, the temptations he
conquered, the gospel he taught, and the
cross he bore, has brought us nigh to thee
and closer to one another.

OFFERTORY SERVICE. "And whatsoever
ye do in word and deed, do all in the name
of the Lord Jesus, giving thanks to God
and the Father by him." Col. 3:17.

OFFERTORY PRAYER. We thank thee, O
God, for another anniversary of our nation's independence and pray that this rich
gift may be an opportunity to serve one
another in love.

PRAYER. Almighty God, who hast given
us this good land for our heritage: we
humbly beseech thee that we may always
prove ourselves a people mindful of thy
favor and glad to do thy will. Bless our
land with honorable industry, sound
learning, and pure manners. Save us from
violence, discord, and confusion; from
pride and arrogancy; and from every evil
way. Defend our liberties, and fashion into
one happy people the multitudes brought
hither out of many kindreds and tongues.
Endue with the spirit of wisdom those to
whom in thy name we entrust the authority of government, that there may be justice and peace at home and that, through
obedience to thy law, we may show forth
thy praise among the nations of the earth.

In the time of prosperity fill our hearts
with thankfulness, and in the day of trouble suffer not our trust in thee to fail.—
Henry van Dyke.

EVENING SERVICE

**Topic: Christian Conscience and Civic
Duty**

SCRIPTURE: Rom. 13:1–10.

Paul gives three reasons why Christians
should submit to the governing authorities, pagan or Christian.

I. His first reason is that "there is no
authority but by act of God and the existing authorities are instituted by him;
consequently anyone who rebels against
authority is resisting a divine institution." Perhaps Paul means that civil
order is not only a desirable thing but
divinely appointed; it is the will of God
for man to live to the best advantage
only in an ordered society. The Christian must obey all laws because the authority of the state, regardless, of the
use made of it by those in temporary
possession of it, is in accordance with
the divine will.

II. The second reason Paul gives for this
duty is a corollary of the first and appeals
more directly to our own self-interest:
"Anyone who rebels against authority is
resisting a divine institution and those
who so resist have themselves to thank for
the punishment they will receive" (NEB).

III. There is a third reason given by Paul
for the faithful performance of this duty.
Conscience itself bids one to support the
state which functions—on the whole, we
might add—for the promotion of the good
and the suppression of evil. (See vv. 3–5.)
In other words conscience itself will compel one to support the state, which in spite
of minor defects, is yet on the whole a
necessary arrangement for the preservation of decency and order. Paul may well
have had in mind the certain truth that to
disobey the law in one particular weakens
respect for the law in general and therefore weakens that universal law enforcement which is so necessary for human welfare.—Ernest Trice Thompson.

SUNDAY: JULY EIGHTH

MORNING SERVICE

Topic: The Experience of Joy
TEXT. John 15:10–11.

The gospel is both a message of joy and an invitation to begin living a life of joy. Notice some characteristics of this all too rare fruit, the experience of joy.

I. Consider the source of genuine joy. (a) God, Paul declares, is the blessed and only potentate (I Tim. 6:15). Since blessed means happy, Paul is here speaking of the happy God. If all truth and beauty and goodness are rooted in the very nature of our creator, so too is all joy.

(b) God is not a grim and emotionless tyrant, the unmoved mover of Aristotle, a kind of cosmic icicle of eternally congealed solemnity. The Old Testament says this about him: "He will rejoice over thee with joy . . . He will joy over thee with singing" (Zeph. 3:17). Our Lord Jesus reveals that "there is joy in the presence of the angels of God over one sinner that repenteth" (Luke 15:10). God himself is the source of all genuine joy.

II. Notice that genuine joy, reflecting the beatitude of God's own being, is not the same as pleasure.

(a) Pleasure is the feeling of delight we derive from the stimulation of our senses. It too is good, provided it is traced back to God, the giver of all good gifts, and serves as a stimulus to gratitude. A misguided hyperspirituality must not motivate us to belittle the pleasure that our God-given sensory equipment makes possible.

(b) Yet pleasure regrettably is short-lived. And it can easily degenerate into self-centered indulgence, an all-absorbing sensual quest that overrides morality, reason, and love.

(c) Joy differs from happiness, that very positive state which comes through human relationships. Happiness, like joy, is one of God's choicest blessings. Yet even the best of human beings are limited in their power to understand and meet our needs. And sooner or later they die. Happiness, the inner glow we experience in and through our human relationships, is changing and fleeting.

(d) Joy is that abiding beatitude, that deep-down exuberance which comes from God through his Spirit by faith in his Son. Joy is thus supernatural in its source and essence, a foretaste of the face-to-face communion with God that will be rapture forever.

III. Notice that joy, according to the apostle Paul, is a fruit of the Spirit. It is one of that gracious cluster of Christlike characteristics enumerated by the apostle. (See Gal. 5:22–23.)

(a) An orange tree cannot bear fruit in total independence. Sunshine, rain, and soil must play a part if oranges are to be brought forth. So it is with ourselves and joy. We may crave joy and fiercely will to be joyful. But as psychologist Abraham Maslow put it: "You cannot seek ecstatic moments directly; you must be surprised by joy." And in saying that Maslow is endorsing Paul's teaching that joy is a fruit. We cannot directly produce it.

(b) We can cooperate with the fruit-producing forces, and at the same time we can eliminate anything that might blight productivity. An orange-grower prunes his trees, fertilizes and waters them, fights insects by spraying, and sometimes, when frost threatens, puts out smudge-pots. Having done his human best, he waits for forces outside of himself to produce the desired fruit.

(c) Does this help us better understand how we may foster the fruit of joy?

(1) What about pruning our lives by spiritual discipline?

(2) What about enriching them through the word of God?

(3) What about combating carnal blight by prayer?

(4) What about warding off chilling frost by the warmth of Christian fellowship?

(5) What about taking seriously the condition that our Savior in John 15:10–11 lays down before he makes the promise of joy to his disciples?

(6) What about adjusting our schedules in order to spend time with God? (See Ps. 16:11.)

(7) What about asking specifically that a great prophetic declaration may come to pass in our own lives: "The Spirit of the Lord God is upon me; because the Lord hath annointed me . . . to appoint unto them that mourn in Zion, to give unto them beauty for ashes, the oil of joy for mourning, the garment of praise for the spirit of heaviness" (Isa. 61:1, 3)?—Vernon C. Grounds.

Illustrations

GRACE AND GRATITUDE.   Grace always demands the answer of gratitude. Grace and gratitude belong together like heaven and earth. Grace evokes gratitude like the voice an echo. Gratitude follows grace like thunder follows lightning.—Karl Barth.

FULLY ALIVE.   The soul leaps to newness of life when the selfish self begins to respond to the concerns of others. Joy is the exhilarating sense of being fully alive, and that cannot come to narrow minds absorbed by selfish concerns.—Frederick Brown Harris.

Sermon Suggestions

THE EXPERIENCE OF WORSHIP.   Scripture: Isa. 6:1–8. (1) The first step in the experience of worship is a vision of God. We need to be able to say, "I saw the Lord!" (2) In despair Isaiah asks, "What hope is there for me?" Having seen God, we see and confess our humanness. (3) The third step is the assurance of being forgiven. For Isaiah it took the form of the cleansing action of fire being applied to his lips, which were the agent of his sins. (4) The fourth step is to hear God's call. For Isaiah, God's call is expressed succinctly: "Whom shall I send? Who will be our messenger?" (5) The final step is our answer to God. Isaiah's was again brief and to the point: "I will go! Send me!"—Lewis R. Rogers.

WHY CHRISTIANS REJOICE.   Text: Matt. 5:12. (1) We may rejoice because our behavior is not born of expediency, selfishness, or purposelessness but derives from the noblest and most unfailing of motives: for the Master's sake. (2) We may rejoice in the heavenly reward that may be ours not sometime in the future after we are dead and gone but here and now. (3) We may rejoice because of the royal company of sublime moral heroes we are in—the immortal "saving remnant," "the persecuted prophets before us." (4) We must rejoice that we may thereby reveal the "rightness" of our spirit, its freedom from any trace of rebellion or bitterness, resentment or revenge, its suffusion with the light of that radiant and inextinguishable goodwill of the Master who prayed "that they might have my joy fulfilled in themselves."—Henry Hitt Crane.

Worship Aids

CALL TO WORSHIP.   "Thou wilt keep him in perfect peace, whose mind is stayed on thee: because he trusteth in thee. Trust ye in the Lord for ever: for in the Lord Jehovah is everlasting strength." Isa. 26:-3–4.

INVOCATION.   O Lord of light, in this hour of worship in thy house make pure our hearts, and we shall see thee; reveal thyself to us, and we shall love thee. Strengthen our wills, and we shall choose the good from the evil, and day by day manifest in the world the glory and power of thy blessed gospel, which thou hast made known to us through thy Son Jesus Christ.

OFFERTORY SENTENCE.   "Remember the words of the Lord Jesus, how he said, It is more blessed to give than to receive." Acts 20:35.

OFFERTORY PRAYER.   Accept, O Lord, these offerings thy people make unto thee and grant that the cause to which they are devoted may prosper under thy guidance, to the glory of thy name.

PRAYER.   O, God, before whose judgment seat we shall all someday stand together, we frankly confess that we have broken thy law and penitently, yet confidently, plead for thy forgiveness in Christ the Savior. We thank thee for having planted deep within our being the voice of conscience. May it always be in harmony with thy will. Keep it strong and healthy. Let it make us uncomfortable when we deliberately disobey it and thy commands. Give our nation and every nation more men and women who in their innermost hearts are true to thee and honest in all their professions. When we sin against thee and our conscience hurts, may we always turn to thee in faith and be assured of thy forgiveness so that our conscience may again be clean. When we shall all stand together before thy judgment throne, may each of us hear the thrilling verdict, "Not guilty."—Armin C. Oldsen.

EVENING SERVICE

Topic: Up Against It
TEXT: Gen. 42:36.

We can easily understand the plight of the patriarch and sympathize with him. We often find ourselves in the same cruel net and repeat the same complaining cry, "All these things are against me." What can we say in such circumstances to reassure ourselves?

I. We must beware of self-pity. To it we must never give way. We are apt to brood upon our troubles and to magnify them until we can think of nothing else. Others seem to get through life so much more easily. They haven't the struggle or the heartbreak that we have.

II. We should remind ourselves that however baffling and strange our experiences may be and however we may wish to escape them, they have their place in the moulding of our character. That may be cheap comfort and difficult to accept at the time, and yet it is true. A life that has never been tested is apt to be shallow and self-centered. It doesn't know its own strength or weakness. It simply floats along with the current. But we have often to swim against the current, to take our stand, and to endure hardship as good soldiers. If there was no conflict, there could be no victory. If we were never tested, we could never achieve.

III. We must learn not only that adversity has its uses but that it is also often a blessing in disguise. Many things that seem to be against us are working for us. So it was with Jacob. Everything seemed to be going against him. One after another the lights that had cheered him had been extinguished. We would have thought and felt as he did. Yet Jacob was wrong. In a wonderful way events were working not against him but for him. He was on the eve of finding his long lost Joseph. He was about to enter a period of peace and prosperity such as he had never known.

IV. Lest we despair too hastily or give up too readily, we must have faith in our God. It is that which makes all the difference to our interpretation of life. If there be no God, we may well be filled with dismay as we meet the mystery and tragedy of life. But we believe in the God whom Christ has revealed to us, the God whom he himself trusted. In his life many things came against him. What hatred and hostility and suffering he had to endure! Yet he believed in his Father's working and guidance. In his darkest hour in Gethsemane, we hear him declare this heroic confidence: "The cup which the Father hath given me, shall I not drink of it?" In this he has left us an example that we should follow in his steps.—Alexander Gemmell.

SUNDAY: JULY FIFTEENTH

MORNING SERVICE

Topic: The Worst Is Yet to Be.
TEXTS: Dan. 12:1; Mark 13:19 (RSV).

I. Neither Daniel nor Jesus had in mind just natural disasters, disease, and personal difficulty. Their warnings that trouble lies ahead grew out of the conviction that the kingdom of God comes into being only amid struggle and anguish. There is a persistent idea in scripture that the inauguration of God's kingdom is like the birth of a child, a cause for great rejoicing in the midst of much pain. In talking about the tribulation Daniel and Jesus are describing the birth-pangs of God's righteous kingdom.

(a) It is a viewpoint which is utterly honest. Justice and righteousness have never had an easy time of it. The world is filled with selfishness, greed, and oppression. God's ways are not readily adopted. The central symbol of the Christian faith is a cross. We may gild it, decorate it, and even try to disguise it. But that cross still proclaims that a righteous servant of God suffered persecution and death at the hands of us sinners.

(b) Those who follow Christ share in his agonizing struggle to bring peace where there is war, to promote brotherhood where there is conflict among races or classes of people, and to bring healing and honesty and courage.

(c) The powers against which the church struggles in the world are not paper tigers. They are real predators with claws and fangs and muscles strong enough to do us in. This is the point to all that unpleasant biblical language about wars in heaven and suffering such as has never been known before.

(d) We should not be kidded into thinking that we can snap our fingers and suddenly correct every wrong. Nor should we suppose that the whole world will readily agree to observe God's law. The persecution of the church is less common today, but the demands of the gospel are no more popular. Only the form of the rejection of righteousness has changed. God's kingdom comes amid anguish. Those who do not understand this are ill-prepared to engage in the conflict.

II. While the Bible declares that the worst is yet to be, it never ends the story there. When an angel warns Daniel about a great tribulation, he also says, "But at that time your people shall be delivered." Jesus concludes his description of future ordeals by promising that God will see his people through. The days of suffering will not be longer than we can withstand. For God is faithful; he joins with us in the struggle.

(a) Too often we think of God as a dis-

tant monarch who sits serenely upon a golden throne, detached from all problems and difficulties on earth. But the God made known in Jesus Christ is in the midst of us, strengthening those who wrestle in his cause. A faith which has a cross at its center has to be about a God who is involved and not detached, enters into conflict, and turns crucifixion into resurrection.

(b) The conflict between good and evil may be violent, but God is bound to win. Evil cannot contend with God and prevail, for the Almighty is truly Lord over all things. (See Rom. 8:31–37.)

III. The worst is yet to be, and the best is yet to be. The Bible begins with a story of the God who struggles against the chaos of darkness; from it he calls forth light. And the Bible ends with a vision of the God who creates a new heaven and a new earth out of great tribulation and resistance.

(a) The faith we embrace as Christians does not give in to despair. We are a realistic people. But we are also a people of hope. Whatever may come in our personal lives or in the witness of the Christian church as a community of faith, God is with us. He is worthy of our trust. (See Ps. 46:1–2.)

(b) When the worst that we can imagine comes upon us, God is in our midst, revealing his faithful love. He is our refuge and strength.—Laurence H. Stookey.

Illustrations

EVERMORE CREATING. A man went up from Fort Collins, Colorado, to view the Poudre Canyon with a geologist friend. He saw how a mighty force had heaved the rock to mountain height. He saw a torrent of water pouring down the mountain in leaps and falls. He was stirred by the fantastic colors and shapes and by the trees which grew in stately beauty. "My," he said to the geologist, "I wish I could have been here to see this take place." The geologist quietly answered, "You are." The same forces are still at work. The power that lifted up the mountain and caused the waterfall and planted the forest is still there, working quietly and constantly.—William Jackson Jarman.

TRADITION.   *Fiddler on the Roof* is set in a Russian Jewish village, Anatevka. The prologue begins with a word from Tevye, the leading character and father of five daughters: "A fiddler on the roof. Sounds crazy, no? But in our little village of Anatevka you might say everyone of us is a fiddler on the roof, trying to scratch out a pleasant simple tune without breaking his neck. It isn't easy. You may ask, why do we stay up here if it is so dangerous? We stay because Anatevka is our home. And how do we keep our balance? That I can tell you in a word—tradition!" The prologue ends with Tevye's observation: "Without our tradition, our lives would be as shaky as . . . as a fiddler on the roof."

Sermon Suggestions

THE MINISTRY OF INTERRUPTION.   Text: Job 26:12. (1) By the ministry of interruption God wakens us to the value of time. (2) By the ministry of interruption God checks the force of evil in the world. (3) By the ministry of interruption God imparts a certain charm to life. (4) By the ministry of interruption God shows us there are larger plans than ours.—George H. Morrison.

LIVING AMID SHADOWS.   Text: Acts 5:-15. (1) Shadows are created by light. (2) Shadows enhance beauty. (3) Shadows give strength to life. (4) We can use shadows for the service of others.—Ralph W. Sockman.

Worship Aids

CALL TO WORSHIP.   "Bless the Lord, O my soul: and all that is with me, bless his holy name." Ps. 103:1.

INVOCATION.   Heavenly Father, we are grateful for this beautiful world thou hast created for us; for the singing birds, the radiant flowers, the blue sky, the soft breeze; for the dark night which gives way to a bright dawn; for the good earth which, when tilled by the plow, shoots forth the wheat, the corn, the beans that our hungry bodies may be fed; for the trees which will fruit and a thousand gifts which come from thy bountiful hand. Help us to share this wealth, this treasure, with all who are in need.

OFFERTORY SENTENCE.   "Let the beauty of the Lord our God be upon us: and establish thou the work of our hands upon us; yea, the work of our hands establish thou it." Ps. 90:17.

OFFERTORY PRAYER.   Our Father, open our eyes, we pray, to the glorious opportunities of sharing with others our blessed experiences of fellowship with one another and with thee.

PRAYER.   Thy thoughts, O God, are higher than our thoughts and thy ways than our ways. Our thoughts are often inadequate and without understanding. Grant us the inspiration of thy Holy Spirit that our perceptions may be enlightened, our hearts more sensitive and compassionate, and our wills more effective in serving thee in the world.

Grant unto thy people, O God, clearer understanding of thy purposes. May they meet with wisdom the problems which need to be solved. May they learn to overcome evil with good. May their lives become redemptive. May they become channels of thy grace, bringing thy truth and thy love into the lives of men.

Use us, O Lord, to cast down the great evils which persist in the earth. Cause wars to cease. Between races and nations may peace and goodwill prevail. Help us to find relief from poverty. Teach us how to deal with crime and the criminal. In all our ways enable us not to add to the hurt of the world but to seek its welfare. We pray in the name of him who went about doing good, who gave his life that our lives may be lived abundantly.—Merlo K. W. Heicher.

EVENING SERVICE

Topic: Our Search for Understanding

SCRIPTURE: John 1:43–51.

I. The great effort of all our lives, if it had to be stated in one word, is spent in search of understanding.

(a) Understanding is the vital link in the chain of living that ties us to others. This tie helps us to link our thoughts, feelings, and aspirations with the human race. Without understanding we are locked into our own mental selves with no give and take and no true picture of how we measure up against others.

(b) To have someone share our cares, our hopes, our feelings, and our thoughts gives the most bouyant feeling. On the other hand nothing is so depressing as living alone, especially if it means we are not merely away from someone who cares but truly without such a person.

(c) Most of us walk, work, and live among a good many people. We may even say "good morning" or "good evening" or pass the time with people yet feel that there is no real care or concern and that nobody really cares or takes the time to sense how we feel. No wonder there are so many people around us who are crying out in word and deed for genuine human feeling. Some are driven to the most outrageous deeds; others are motivated to the warmest feelings and to great understanding.

II. Nathaniel had been a lonely man. He seems to have kept pretty much to himself. We don't really know a great deal about him except that he was from Cana in Galilee and that Philip, a disciple of Jesus for only one day, had told Nathaniel about his new Lord and persuaded him to come and see Jesus for himself.

(a) Jesus first caught sight of Nathaniel under a tree across the way, so when he came close enough for Philip to introduce him to Jesus, the master paid him a great compliment, "Behold, an Israelite in whom there is no guile."

(b) When Jesus looked into Nathaniel's face he found the man to have no deceitfulness, no secret schemes, no disguise, and no phoniness. He came as he was, expressing his feelings, "Can any good thing come out of Nazareth?" But before Nathaniel could finish asking his question, he knew the answer. It perhaps sounded strange that he had come here with no great expectation of Jesus, yet when Jesus had spoken to him, he sensed that Jesus understood him. Jesus could somehow see into his heart and know his real devotion, his secret longings, and his hopes. He had dared present himself just as he was, without pretense or dissimilation, and had been understood for the first time.

III. It was a great moment for Nathaniel as it is for anyone who experiences the joy of a heart warmed by the love of Christ. Nathaniel did not have to wait any longer. His great moment of acceptance had come.

(a) Yet in spite of the great joy of the love of God it is like a love affair of one night if we do not go all the way with Jesus. How many people under the inspiration of a great service have come forth to accept Christ but gone on their way without finding a church or engaging themselves in any ministry of the gospel?

(b) Jesus told Nathaniel about Jacob's dream of a ladder reaching from earth to heaven with the implication that Nathaniel had not completely understood the fulness of what a meeting with Jesus can mean. Jesus is the link between heaven and earth and between man in mortality and man in eternity. Nathaniel became a disciple immediately, although like us he may never have understood discipleship completely.—George W. Davis.

SUNDAY: JULY TWENTY-SECOND

MORNING SERVICE

Topic: Why I Am a Christian
Text. Jas. 2.7.
I. *I want to be a Christian because I want to get the best that life has to offer.*
(a) I want to get all the enjoyment and satisfaction that I can. I want to enjoy life to the fullest extent. No one ought to be satisfied with anything less than the best.
(b) Many claiming to be Christians find life dull, uninviting, and joyless. This is not because Christianity has failed them but rather because they have failed Christianity. Jesus said, "I am come that they might have life and that they might have it more abundantly." He gives the good life here as well as hereafter but only when life is brought into the proper relationship with him. Only thus can life become truly songful.
(c) Many bemoan the fact that being a real Christian denies them many things that they once considered important. But now in Christ we find that those things are not important after all. We want to give them up because they hinder the enjoyment of the full life. We find that his commandments, instead of being galling or irksome or burdensome are a blessing and a thing of joy: "His commandments are not grievous."
(d) Someone has said that there is too much of the world in us to enjoy the church and too much of the church in us to enjoy the world. People in that condition truly find life miserable. Jesus put it well when he said you cannot serve two masters. Someone else has said: "If you are not happier because you are a Christian, then there is some doubt as to whether you actually are a Christian. Christianity not only tells me about the sweet bye and bye, but it also enables me to endure and to enjoy the nasty now and now."
II. *I want to be a Christian because I need outside help.*
(a) Christ can help us only when we realize our need of his help and allow him to give it. "Blessed are the poor in spirit"—those who realize their own insufficiency—for only such can receive the blessings of the kingdom.
(b) When I am weary and heavy laden, with him I find rest for my soul. When sorely tempted, I have his assurance that he will not allow me to be tempted above that which I am able to bear. With each temptation he will provide a way of escape. In my anxieties I find release, knowing that not even a sparrow can fall to the ground without his notice. How much more concern he has for me, created in his image! I have this assurance that the eternal God is my refuge and that underneath are the everlasting arms to uphold and to sustain. And I know that if I cast all my care upon him he will care for me.
(c) I know that he is able to do exceeding abundantly above all that I can ask or think if only I will allow his power to work in and through me. All the spiritual resources of heaven are back of me because he has given assurance that "he that is in us is greater than he that is in the world." I know that "unless there is within us that which is above us, we will soon succumb to that which is about us." (See Ps. 40:2–3.)
III. *I want to be a Christian because I have sinned and need forgiveness.* All have sinned. Those in our day who study mental health tell us that the main reason for many of our emotional problems is a guilt complex. Sin leaves man with a guilt complex. God pity the man who can continue to live in sin without a feeling of guilt. But thanks be to God, "there is a fountain filled with blood drawn from Emmanuel's veins, and sinners plunged beneath that flood lose all their guilty stains." (See I John 1:7.)
IV. *I want to be a Christian because I appreciate the goodness of God.* "In him we live, and move, and have our being." He not only created but also sustains our lives. (See Ps. 103:1–5.) "The goodness of God leadeth thee to repentance" (Rom. 2:4). His goodness constrains me to surrender to him.

V. *I want to be a Christian because of the good I can do for others.* I am as a light penetrating the gloom of darkness. I am as salt preserving that which is good. I am blessed with the privilege of bringing comfort where there is sorrow, truth where there is ignorance, peace where there is discord, love where there is hatred, right where there is wrong, strength where there is weakness, hope where there is despair, and words of salvation where there is sin.

VI. *I want to be a Christian because I want to be ready for death.* (a) I have a divine appointment with death, as "it is appointed unto man once to die." I may make big plans for tomorrow, expecting to buy and sell and get great gain, but I have no certainty of tomorrow. Tomorrow is as uncertain as the morning mist. My whole life is as a wisp of vapor that is visible for a little while and then is gone. (See Jas. 4:13–14.)

(b) With the same assurance of hope that sustained the sweet singer of Israel, I can approach the vale of death knowing that I have no need to fear. Why? Because I have my divine companion to guide me safely through.

VI. *I want to be a Christian because I want to go to heaven.* I know there is a heaven because Jesus said so, and his bodily resurrection guarantees my resurrection. "Because I live, ye shall live also." However, I must not be deceived into believing that I will go to heaven just because I desire to go there. Jesus is the way. No one can hope to be with him in heaven without following him here on earth. I am fearful for those who claim to be Christians and yet cannot enjoy spiritual things here and now. How are they going to be able to enjoy heaven?—Paul Berthold.

Illustrations

LAST WORDS. After long months of excruciating suffering, George W. Truett spoke for the last time to his people of the First Baptist Church, Dallas, Texas. It was made possible by a telephone line run into loudspeakers in the church auditorium. On a Sunday morning to a packed house he spoke from his bed. Not one murmur of complaint was heard. Nothing was said about himself. But the climax of his message, uttered in triumphant voice, was "Be true to Christ! Be true to Christ!"—Herschel H. Hobbs.

AT PRAYER. One day a student came upon Pierre Curie bending over his microscope and thought he had discovered the professor in prayer. He was about to tiptoe out of the room when Curie raised his head and turned. "Excuse me, sir," stammered the student, "I thought you were praying." "I was, son," said the professor, returning to his work. "All science, research, and study is a prayer that God will reveal his eternal secrets to us, for God does have secrets, and he reveals them only when man searches reverently for them. Yes, son, I was praying."—Homer J. R. Elford.

Sermon Suggestions

SEEKING LIFE'S HIGHEST GOAL. Text: Matt. 6:33. (1) We are to seek his kingdom in person: "Seek ye." (2) We are to seek his kingdom with primacy: "Seek ye first." (3) We are to seek the kingdom with purpose: "The kingdom of God, and his righteousness." (4) We are to seek his kingdom to gain the richest profit: "And all these things shall be added unto you."—Mendell Taylor.

I LOVE THAT CHURCH BACK HOME. Text: Eph. 4:17–19 (RSV). (1) I love that church back home because it speaks loudly of things eternal. (2) I love that church back home because it is the workshop of the Holy Spirit in bringing God's life to me. (3) I love that church back home because it has been the stabilizing factor in my life. (4) I love that church back home because it lifts my sights. (5) I love that church back home because it challenges me to respond to Christ's highest expectation.—Carl W. Segerhammar.

Worship Aids

CALL TO WORSHIP. "And we declare unto you glad tidings, how that the promise which was made unto the fathers, God hath fulfilled the same unto us their children." Acts 13:32–33.

INVOCATION.   O Lord, who hast taught us that the love of money is the root of all evil, teach us to care for what money can buy—not security but opportunity, not withdrawal from the world but a full participation within it, and not prestige but use. Help us to handle all the goods of life in the spirit of thy Son who out of his poverty made many rich.

OFFERTORY SENTENCE.   "Unto whomsoever much is given, of him shall be much required: and to whom men have committed much, of him they will ask the more." Luke 12:48.

OFFERTORY PRAYER.   Our heavenly Father, help us to remember that though Christ does offer his companionship, yet to us belongs the decision as to whether or not we will follow him. May we through these gifts and our witness share with all the world the blessedness that comes to us through thy grace.

PRAYER.   Our Father who art in heaven, thy Spirit bears witness to our spirits that we are thy children. The source of our lives is in thy being. The salvation of our lives from sin and death is by thy grace. The hope of our lives rests in thee. In thee we live and move and have our being.

The mystery of life and of our own lives is far beyond our understanding. Thy thoughts are higher than our thoughts, O God. Grant unto us growth in understanding, ability to live as thy children, and a deepening love for thee.

We desire to live in this world as thy daughters and sons. Increase our perceptions that we may be aware even as we pursue the everyday activities of life and that we may move in thy love and care. Help us to relate all that we do to the coming of thy rule in the hearts of men. May this give a quality to life that is enriching, fulfilling, and effective.

Hear our prayer, O God, for the world of which we are a part. Help us to be agents of righteousness and peace in the world. May we witness to Christ the world's Savior, and may we receive an abundant measure of his grace that we may fully pass it on to the world's healing.

EVENING SERVICE

Topic: Staying Power
TEXT: Heb. 11:27.
Why do many persons fail? Studies show that often the cause is lack of staying power and ability to persist in spite of discouragement and failure. What is the secret of persistence?

I. From the career of Moses we can learn much, for of him it is written, "He endured." In his first effort to help his oppressed people, he succeeded only in making their burden heavier. When pharaoh's army pursued them, the people held Moses responsible for their new plight. In the wilderness they complained about the monotony of a diet of manna. Moses turned to God and asked why he must be nurse-maid to such ungrateful people. What gave him staying power? The New Testament writer tells us.

II. "He endured as seeing." We need to see something beyond our present situation. Perseverance, as the experience of Moses shows, is the result of being captured by a cause greater than one's self that will not let us relax effort. Moses' cause was the liberation of the Hebrew people from bondage in Egypt. For a young person today it will be the goal to be achieved by study. For the church school teacher it will be the ceaseless work of passing on Christian heritage.

III. "He endured as seeing him." This additional word "him" may stand for the person or the group to be helped by our persistence. Perseverance is stimulated and sustained by concern for others. The devotion of Moses to the people God told him to lead out of bondage is one of the most impressive things about him. The desire to support his family has given many a man the staying power he would otherwise have lacked. For the sake of others Robert Louis Stevenson kept cheerful despite physical suffering.

IV. The word "him" also reminds us of the encouragement to persistence that comes from the sight of other persons persevering, despite obstacles. God introduced himself to Moses as "the God of Abraham, the God of Isaac, and the God of Jacob." Moses could take courage from what God had enabled them to do.

V. "He endured as seeing him who is invisible" is the complete statement about Moses. It points to his awareness of God as the chief stimulation of his perseverance. In all situations he knew that God was with him, giving him wide horizons, long outlooks, steady hopes, and firm purposes. Often through our unyielding faith in God a disappointment in what we are trying to do can be turned into a new opportunity for service. Perhaps God is trying to show us something by our set-back. We may be knocking at the wrong door. Ask him and see.—J. Francis F. Peak.

SUNDAY: JULY TWENTY-NINTH

MORNING SERVICE

Topic: Secure in God's Love
SCRIPTURE: Rom. 8:28–39.

I. *God's inconquerable sovereignty.* (See vv. 28–30.) God's sovereignty over history and the universe is maintained throughout the Bible. It is one thing to affirm God's sovereignty; it is another thing to understand it. Several considerations about God in v. 28 should assist us in doing the latter.

(a) God is active: "in everything God works." Contrary to a popular translation (KJV), it is not that "all things work together." Things do not work; God works. Things, if left to themselves, would become hopelessly bungled. It is not that God causes all things to happen that do happen. Many things happen contrary to his will—some by human carelessness or disobedience, some by natural law, and some by sheer chance. But nothing can possibly happen that can defeat God's purposes. If compared to a checker game, God does not move the checkers of the opposing forces of evil as well as his own. Yet there is no move that the evil one can make that God cannot counter by salvaging good from it.

(b) God is benevolent: "God works for good." God is not a God of sheer power. He is a God of love, and his power is ever subdued and directed by his love. He is irrevocably pro-people, and despite all of his power he must always be true to himself.

(c) God is cooperative: "with those who love him." God not only works for people; he works with them. He not only operates; he cooperates. He not only acts; he interacts. He gathers up our sympathetic efforts and incorporates them into his doings. One of the greatest wonders is that we can be his coworkers.

(d) God is personal: "who are called." It is a personal God who calls us and awaits our response. Although he wills the good of all men, this good can be activated and assured only where God's call is issued and where a response has been made in terms of love. This personal "call" is mentioned again in v. 30 as the third of five words which indicate our place of assured standing with God. This call can be better understood if we view it in relation to the other four words.

(1) What leads to our call? We are called because we are predestined. Our predestination is to be conformed to the image of his Son, an original image marred by our sin but which through Christ is being restored. This predestination is not simply God's arbitrary choice of certain people. It is the biblical way of stating God's undefeatable determination to complete what he has begun in us. God predestines us because he foreknew us. This is perhaps intended to show how God's elective purposes can be reconciled with human freedom. God chose because he knew in advance.

(2) What does our call lead to? It leads to our justification and through that to our glorification. As we are progressively conformed to Christ's image, the ultimate outcome will be the reflecting of and sharing in that glory which is God's.

(e) God is purposeful: "called according

to this purpose." Two ideas are present here.

(1) God's purpose involved his inclusion of us in his call.

(2) We are called to be a part of that task force for furthering God's purpose in the world. Because God has a purpose that cannot be defeated and we are a part of that purpose, then we cannot be defeated either. This is the basis for our assurance.

II. *Man's inseparable security.* (See vv. 31–39.) God's benevolent and purposeful sovereignty provides for God's people a security which nothing can take away. Although there are many questions contained in this scripture portion, there are three that are basic and provide the structure for the passage.

(a) "What then shall we say to this?" (vv. 31–32). The New Berkeley Version renders this question: "Then what conclusion do we draw?" The assurance that he is for us disarms all opposition and leaves it powerless. The fact that he has already made the supreme gift of his Son has to mean that he will not withhold any lesser gift that we may need but will generously give it along with that supreme gift.

(b) "Who shall bring any charge against God's elect?" (vv. 33–34). God's justification or acquittal of us silences all voices and makes our condemnation or conviction impossible. Not only is there now no condemnation (v. 1), but we can never again be brought into condemnation (John 5:24). Christ's death, his resurrection, his enthronement, and his intercession are all cited as proof that he who is our attorney (intercessor) certainly is not going to press charges against us. The case is permanently closed!

(c) "Who shall separate us from the love of Christ?" (vv. 35–39). A common charge in the courtroom is that of "alienation of affection." Nothing can alienate us from God's affection; nothing can make him stop loving us or render his love ineffective. Two lists of potential "alienators of affection" are made, and their weakness is observed in both instances. There are interesting contrasts in these lists.

(1) The first list is a part of a question (v. 35), while the second is a confident statement (vv. 38–39). Although the first list is a question, it is given a bold answer in v. 37. The surplus or extra margin of assurance is seen in that we are "more than conquerors."

(2) It is the "love of Christ" that is in question in the first instance and the "love of God in Christ Jesus our Lord" in the second instance.

(3) In the first list we encounter a whole range of human experiences to which the Christian is certainly no stranger. This is attested to in the lives of many great Christians including Paul. The second list has to do not with contingent human experiences but with cosmic powers and forces. The reverberating assurance is that none of these things shall be able to defeat us ultimately.

(d) Although our assurance is complete, it is not a cause for complacency. The secure are not complacent, and it is not the complacent who are secure.—W. Clyde Tilley.

Illustrations

LIVING GRACE.   Someone asked Dwight L. Moody, "Have you enough grace to be burned at the stake?" "No" was the reply. "Do you not wish you had?" "No, for I don't need it. What I need now is grace to live in Milwaukee three days and hold a mission."—*The Preachers Magazine.*

SISTERS.   Love and suffering are sisters. Their purpose in life is neither to make us miserable nor make us happy; rather they are to ennoble our characters. They make us capable of suffering without whining. They make us capable of loving without possessing. As such they become the inexhaustible sources of spiritual beauty.—John Biegeleisen.

HIS HAND ON OURS.   God puts a little of his love into us, and that is how we love one another. When you teach a child writing, you hold its hand while it forms the letters; that is, it forms the letters because you are forming them. We love and reason because God loves and reasons and holds our hand while we do it.—C. S. Lewis.

Sermon Suggestions

GOD'S LOVE.   Text: Jer. 31:3. (1) The fact of his love: I John 4:16. (2) The worldwide character of his love: John 3:16. (3) The individuality of God's love to us: Gal. 2:20. (4) The freeness of God's love: Deut. 7:8; I John 4:10; Rom. 8:38. (5) The measure of God's love: Eph. 3:17, 19. (6) The strength of God's love: Jer. 31:3; John 13:1. (7) God's love not contradicted by afflictions: Heb. 12:6; II Cor. 5:14–15. (8) The working of God's love: II Cor. 5:14. (9) The benefit of God's love: I John 1. (10) The counsel of God's love: Jude 21. —G. F. Pentecost.

HOW THE CHURCH CAN HELP YOU.   Text: Heb. 10:25. (1) Come regularly. (2) Come prepared. (3) Come expectantly. (4) Come obediently.

Worship Aids

CALL TO WORSHIP.   "Be strong and of a good courage, fear not: for the Lord thy God, he it is that doth go with thee; he will not fail thee, nor forsake thee." Deut. 31:6.

INVOCATION.   O God of mercy, in this hour in thy house have mercy upon us. O God of light, shine into our hearts. O thou eternal goodness, deliver us from evil. O God of power, be thou our refuge and our strength. O God of love, let love flow through us. O God of life, live within us, now and forevermore.

OFFERTORY SENTENCE.   "The end of the commandment is charity out of a pure heart." I Tim. 1:5.

OFFERTORY PRAYER.   O God, in whose sight a contrite heart is more than whole burnt offerings: help us with these our gifts to dedicate ourselves, body, soul, and spirit, unto thee, which is our reasonable service.

PRAYER.   O God, creator of all beauty and loveliness, we are ever grateful for all the beauty and loveliness that are a part of our lives. Keep us sensitive to them. For the beauty of form and sound, of voice and instrument, and of nature and human nature, we give you thanks. For the gift of expression and the power to create which you have planted in us, we express our debt. Help us to use these gifts for the edification and inspiration of your children and for your glory. Help us to recognize that in praise and worship we put them to their highest and noblest use. Grateful for our gifts and the willingness to share them, keep us, O Lord, from using them for personal ends or gain. May those who have greatly received greatly give. May those who give and those who receive be abundantly blessed, that everyone will be enriched from the abundant storehouse of your gifts.—Chester E. Hodgson.

EVENING SERVICE

Topic: Danger! Keep Out!
TEXT: Eph. 5:27.

Some workmen busy on a building site put up a large notice warning people not to come too near because of the danger of falling bricks. As work proceeded the notice had to be moved because it was in the way. Someone pushed it carelessly further along the pavement. But the building next to the site was a church, and passersby were amused to see at the entrance to the church a big notice: "Danger! Keep out!" We don't usually think of a church as a dangerous place. But it can be.

I. It is dangerous to enter church if we are harboring evil thoughts in our minds, for there we may well hear about God's purity and goodness and be reminded that he expects the same from us.

II. It is dangerous to enter church if we are selfish people, for in church we may hear about Jesus. His life was utterly free from selfishness, and he asks us to give up selfish ways.

III. It is dangerous to enter church if we are unforgiving toward other people, for in church we will say the Lord's Prayer in which we ask God to forgive us our trespasses as we forgive those who trespass against us.

IV. In church we open our lives to God's presence, and that spells danger for all those things which God cannot approve. But those things—evil thoughts, selfishness, angry resentment, etc.—are things which God longs to remove from our lives because they are things which spoil and damage our lives. God's church threatens danger to those evil things which we and the whole world are better without.—C. R. Thomas.

SUNDAY: AUGUST FIFTH

MORNING SERVICE

Topic: Come Down from the Mountain (The Transfiguration)

SCRIPTURE: Luke 9:28, 31, 33 (RSV).

I. In the gospel lesson we see Jesus in a rare moment of eternal splendor. We are given a glimpse, a beatific vision of Jesus in transfigured glory. Suddenly he becomes the cosmic Lord who transcends time and space and is seen in company with Moses and Elijah who have already entered the larger life. There is brightness and beauty and incredible, awesome peace. Peter, James, and John behold this immortal moment, and they do not want to leave. They want to enshrine their experience in brick and mortar. They want to hold onto that vision as one might hold onto a piece of colored glass.

(a) Did you ever ask: "If such a thing could happen to Peter and John and James, why couldn't it happen to me? If visions were granted to certain people in history, why not me? If those sparkling moments of God's presence manifested themselves through a voice from heaven and a burning bush, then why couldn't it come into my life?"

(b) Those questions might have remained unanswered if the story of the transfiguration had ended on the mountaintop. But it did not. Reading on in St. Luke we find that the next day Jesus and his companions went down from the mountain and returned to the city, and Jesus' first act there was to heal an afflicted child. The transfigured glory of Jesus is now to be seen in the transfigured lives of people whom he touches. The true dwelling place of God is with his people. The glory of God is not only to be seen in the firmament but also in the faces of men and women in whom he lives.

II. Like Peter, James, and John we are called by Jesus to walk with him, to open our eyes to the glory, and to let the glory transform and transfigure our lives.

(a) Our activities in the church offer many opportunities. There is the breaking of bread. Each time we draw close to the altar and lift an imploring hand upward, he comes. He comes literally in transfigured splendor, assuring us that we are holding time in our hands and eternity in our hearts.

(b) He comes into our lives as we read together and reflect on the scriptures. The Bible is the cradle where the word of life is first revealed. And as we gain new insights into the eternal events told in this mighty book, we become more open to the illumination of Jesus in our lives and to the grace and glory of his truth.

(c) He comes in glory when we interact together in the fellowship of his body, the church, and when we share and witness our life and experience in him. Each time we open our lives in trust to each other, he comes, lifting us up out of despair and discouragement, instilling love where we no longer can love, creating among us a community of people who honestly care about people.

III. Like Peter, James, and John, we are reminded that the infinite glory of God cannot be domesticated and put on a leash. Just as the apostles wanted to preserve their experience by remaining on the mountain and building shiny arks of covenants to enshrine the glory of the Lord, so we too often want to cherish and preserve our comfortable pew and prayer group among ourselves. But the Lord, the almighty Lord who rules the whole universe, will not let us. The earth is the

Lord's and all that therein is, and he cannot be content with smallness.

(a) So while many of us are experiencing a new awakening to the glorious presence of Christ in our lives, we must be careful not to turn our energies to the building of tabernacles. We dare not try to contain Jesus in our own little prayer group or Bible class. For he will not be contained. His presence blows from all points of the eternal compass. And like Peter, James, and John, he sends us out into the world to encounter him in new ways.

(b) Sometimes the new ways are painful, sometimes they are hard, and sometimes they bring struggle. But then the cross and not the dove remains the indelible sign on our forehead.

(1) Whenever there is the reawakening in us of the personal, whenever in our daily encounter we know that we are more than just a chemical episode of life, whenever at the very depth of our being there pulses the desire to know, to love, and to forgive, and whenever there is the willingness to suffer for others, there breaks forth the transfigured beauty of our Lord, shining in all its glory, his face changed and his clothes dazzling white.

(2) Whenever we begin to understand that giving is better than receiving, whenever we feel the urge to serve rather than wanting to be served, and whenever we go out of our way to show our love rather than waiting to receive the love of others, then we feel the grandeur and majesty of God fill our being and transform us.—Frank S. Cerveny.

Illustrations

RESURRECTION SOCIETY. After the American Civil War many organizations arose to help former slaves deal with the problems of their new freedom. One of these was called the "I Will Arise Society." The church too could be described as an "I Will Arise Society." The church is the society of repentance, forgiveness, and the new start. This society, created by the resurrection, helps us to arise from our dead selves to new freedom.—Woodrow A. Geier.

LITTLE BY LITTLE. The greatest things ever done on earth have been done by little and little—little agents, little persons, and little things—by everyone doing his own work, filling his own sphere, holding his own post, and saying, "Lord, what wilt thou have me to do?"—Thomas Guthrie.

Sermon Suggestions

CHRIST'S CROWNS. Text: Heb. 2:9. (1) When we look backward, we see Jesus crowned on the cross. (2) When we look upward, we see Jesus crowned in heaven. (3) When we look onward, we see Jesus crowned on the earth. (4) When we look inward, we see Jesus crowned in our hearts.—Geoffrey R. King.

THE CHURCH IN AN AGE OF CRISIS. Text: Rev. 2:7. (1) It must be doctrinally sound to reclaim truth. (2) It must be evangelistically passionate to proclaim truth. (3) It must be efficiently organized and get to work. (4) It must be liturgically inspiring to worship meaningfully. (5) It must be an adequate fellowship to which all belong. (6) It must be socially concerned facing problems frankly. (7) It must be spiritually effective planting the seeds of sainthood and reaping the harvest of righteousness.—William Frederick Dunkle, Jr.

Worship Aids

CALL TO WORSHIP. "Let us search and try our ways, and turn again to the Lord. Let us lift up our heart with our hands unto God in the heavens." Lam. 3:40–41.

INVOCATION. Our Father, we give thanks for Jesus Christ our Savior. Help us to receive the fulness of thy salvation. Grant us grace to live joyful, obedient, and triumphant lives as thy children in this thy world. May the spirit of peace reign within our hearts and invade the nations of the world.

OFFERTORY SENTENCE. "Go, and sell that thou hast, and give to the poor, and thou shalt have treasure in heaven: and come and follow me." Matt. 19:21.

OFFERTORY PRAYER. Our Father, take us with all of our failures and develop us after thine own heart. Give us more of the mind of the Master, more of his spirit of compassion, and more of his sacrificial and loving heart.

PRAYER. Grant, almighty God, that as thou hast given us once for all thine only begotten Son to rule us and hast by thy good pleasure consecrated him a king over us, that we may be perpetually safe and secure under his hand against all the attempts of the devil and of the whole world. O grant that we may suffer ourselves to be ruled by his authority and so conduct ourselves that he himself may ever continue to watch for our safety; and as thou hast committed us to him that he may be the guardian of our salvation, so also suffer us neither to turn aside nor fall, but preserve us ever in his service until we at length be gathered into that blessed and everlasting kingdom, which has been procured for us by the blood of thine only Son.—John Calvin.

EVENING SERVICE

Topic: Christ Above All
SCRIPTURE: Col. 1:15–19.
This magnificent passage from Colossians makes four bold claims on behalf of Christ.

I. *Christ reveals the true nature of God.* He is "the image of the invisible God" (v. 15). Our situation as Christians is not that we know what God is like and reason from him to Christ, but we know what Christ is like and reason from him to God. We believe that God is like Christ; we believe in a Christlike God.

II. *Christ's supremacy is extended to the heavenly regions.* In him everything was created "in heaven and on earth" (v. 16). The "thrones, dominions, principalities, and authorities" mentioned in v. 16 do not refer to earthly beings or entities but to various ranks of angels in heaven. This is particularly significant in view of the heresy at Colossae which involved the worship of angels.

III. *All things are created for Christ.* The universe is not only created by Christ but for him. Everything finds its fulfillment in Christ. Teilhard de Chardin in *The Phenomenon of Man* asserts that all mankind is evolving toward the Omega Point when man's true nature, which is like that of Christ, will be revealed.

IV. *Christ holds together the universe.* He is the spiritual force of gravity since "in him all things hold together" (v. 17). This passage points to Christ's role as the sustainer of creation. It also points to his role as the reconcilor of those who are alienated. We have to admit that things are not "holding together" in our nation and in our world. This points to our need to turn to the one in whom all things hold together.—Willie A. Chappell.

SUNDAY: AUGUST TWELFTH

MORNING SERVICE

Topic: All by Myself
TEXT: Num. 11:14.
I. It is not surprising that Moses should be not only angry but deeply discouraged as well.
(a) He had not wanted leadership in the first place. He had been comfortable in Midian with his wife and her family. He had tried to beg off when God called him to go back to Egypt, pleading his inadequacy for the task; but he could not escape the gnawing summons to set his people free. Now he felt trapped and helpless with people weeping and complaining all around him.
(b) We all have burdens of one sort or another, and at times we wish we could run away from it all. The trouble is, as Moses knew, we cannot run far enough to escape from ourselves and the responsibilities we know are ours. If we run, we wish we hadn't. We know down deep in-

side that we belong precisely where our responsibilities are focused. We can make all manner of excuses for being elsewhere and rationalize our running, but when all is said and done we can't make our self-deceptions stick.

II. Too often we have a way of magnifying our burdens. There are some who seem to thrive on making other people feel sorry for them.

(a) Throughout the centuries there has been a long succession of wailing choirs. The people of Israel provided a number of them. As they looked, after nearly forty years in the wilderness, toward the promised land, they turned back because they saw their enemies to the north as giants, while as the scriptures note, "they were as grasshoppers in their own sight." It seemed to them that the burden of their venture was more than they should be asked to bear. They made it impossible by seeing the obstacles before them in giant-like proportions.

(b) Roger Price notes that the chief malady of our time is what he calls "copelessness" or the inability to cope. It should be added that often our "copelessness" comes from our disposition to magnify our burdens and to see ourselves as "grasshoppers" trying to cope with problems of giant stature. Of course we cannot cope with life and with our necessary loads if we magnify our problems as we often do.

(c) Granted, Moses had a problem of major proportions on his hands with his people complaining bitterly and quite unwilling to go on with their venture into the promised land. His burden was a heavy one, but history witnesses to the fact he was more than able to bear it.

III. Moses overlooked two things most of us are inclined to forget when we confront burdens that seem too heavy for us. In the first place there were seventy elders among the people who would share his burden. In the second place Moses was not alone. He simply had failed to count God in. Indeed in his despair Moses had left God out of his calculations.

(a) It is sometimes amazing the way sharing, not complaining, gives us a new lease on life. When Moses got over thinking of himself as alone and began to share his burden with the seventy, he discovered he could cope with his load. There are men who find their wives a priceless resource when they face their business problems. They do not simply retreat into themselves. On the contrary they share their frustrations and their disappointments and find both bearable.

(b) Strangely enough, like Moses, we often fail to count God in when we are "weary and heavy laden." We resent the fact that things have so piled up that we are tortured by the feeling we cannot cope with life, and our very resentment shuts the door on God.

(c) There are resources of the Spirit that can put us on our feet again when we escape our own self-imprisonment and seek the will of God for us. When we protest in frustration, we keep God out; when we relax in trust, we let him in.

IV. We often find strength and courage to bear our own burdens when we increase them by accepting the burden of another. Without concern for other lives there is no faith in God, and without faith in God there is little concern for other lives. So it is that as we "bear one another's burdens" we "fulfill the law of Christ" and at the same time find the grace of God that enables us to bear our own burdens with courage and steadfastness. We never really come to the time when we can say with Moses, "I am not able to carry all this . . . alone, the burden is too heavy for me." The truth is, as we "bear one another's burdens," we never are alone.—Harold Blake Walker.

Illustrations

TRUE SECURITY.   The man who desires to believe in God must know that he has nothing at his own disposal on which to build this faith, that he is, so to speak, in a vacuum. He who abandons every form of security shall find the true security. Man before God has always empty hands. He who gives up, he who loses security, shall find security.—Rudolph Bultmann.

FULFILLMENT. I have always been bewildered by three of God's creatures: the worm that becomes a butterfly, the flying fish that leaps out of the water in an effort to transcend its nature, and the silkworm that turns its entrails into silk, for I always imagined them the symbol symbolizing the root of my soul for me. The grub's yearning to become a butterfly always stood as its and man's most imperative, and at the same time, most legitimate duty. God makes us grubs, and we by our own efforts must become butterflies.—Nikos Kazantzakis in *Report to Greco.*

WHOLLY EMPLOYED. Therefore as every person is wholly God's own portion by the title of creation, so all our labors and care, all our powers and faculties must be wholly employed in the service of God, and even all the days of our life, that this life being ended, we may live with him forever.—Jeremy Taylor.

Sermon Suggestions

THE WELL IS DEEP. Scripture: John 4:-5–15. (1) The well of Christian imagination. (2) The well of inner peace. (3) The deep well of God's eternity.—Winfield S. Haycock.

WHAT PRAYER DOES FOR US. Text: Luke 18:1. (1) Prayer helps us to know God better and to have fellowship with him. (2) Prayer enables God to work more effectively through us. (3) Prayer helps to bring us into line with God's will so that he can accomplish his purpose in us and through us.—A. W. Fortune.

Worship Aids

CALL TO WORSHIP. "O come, let us sing unto the Lord: let us make a joyful noise to the rock of our salvation. Let us come before his presence with thanksgiving, and make a joyful noise unto him with psalms." Ps. 95:1–2.

INVOCATION. Heavenly Father, we come before thee in trembling because we are conscious of our many sins and yet boldly because we know that thou dost love us. Forgive us our sins, and help us to become more worthy of thy goodness and love. May we gain that strength from communion with thee which will enable us to walk humbly and righteously before thee and uprightly before the world, manifesting in life's every experience that faith and courage which befit thy children.

OFFERTORY SENTENCE. "Greater love hath no man than this, that a man lay down his life for his friends." John 15:13.

OFFERTORY PRAYER. Dear Lord, as we travel the highways of life give us a generous and sympathetic spirit for all people in all circumstances of life.

PRAYER. Almighty Lord, who hast commanded that no man should be idle, uphold us in the duties of that state of life to which thou hast been pleased to call us and let thy blessing be upon our persons, our labors, and upon all that belongs to us. Enable us to resist our temptations; to follow the motions of thy good Spirit; to be watchful over our thoughts, words, and actions, diligent in our business, and temperate in all things. Give us grace that we may improve the talents which thou hast committed to our trust and that no worldly business and no worldly pleasures may ever divert us from our preparation for the life to come.—Thomas Lee.

EVENING SERVICE

Topic: Questions for Those Listening to Sermons

TEXT: II Cor. 4:5.

I. *What is the idea, issue, or problem to which the sermon addresses itself?* That central idea or issue should be clearly stated, and your preacher should let you in on his intent early in the sermon.

II. *What does the Bible say about this idea or issue?* Every sermon must rest firmly on the authority of biblical teaching. The preacher must clearly indicate that biblical foundation. If you keep your Bible open before you, you may encourage yourself and your preacher to look for that biblical word.

III. *How does this biblical teaching apply to my life?* The Bible is God's word addressed to our human condition. It deals with real and vital issues of human existence. However some of its ideas may appear to us like distant and hazy horizons. An important part of your preacher's task is to bring that biblical truth up close and into clear focus. It should do what the zoom lens on a television camera does to the distant horizon, bringing it so close you feel you can touch it.

IV. *How should this biblical truth change my life?* What difference does it make to me? Does it give me comfort, reassurance, or new strength? Does it bring me under conviction, lead me to repent, or turn the direction of my life? At the close of each sermon each of us should ask ourselves: How can this truth make me a better person? How does it contribute to the effectiveness of my ministry as one who is called to share the good news?—Garret Wilterdink.

SUNDAY: AUGUST NINETEENTH

MORNING SERVICE

Topic: On Finding Faith on Earth
TEXT: Luke 18:8.

It was recognition of man's impatience with God, impatience prompted by the inscrutability of God's ways and by his seeming heedlessness to men's prayers, that led Jesus to put this question.

I. Our Lord's question is a rhetorical question. (a) Jesus posed it; he did not attempt to answer it. Perhaps he could not answer it. Perhaps it was in wisdom that he left it unanswered. If he could not answer it, certainly we cannot. We do not know the hearts of men, and we cannot say with any certainty where faith is found and where it is not. Church statistics are no reliable guide. The church is both larger and smaller than its statistics suggest. And we cannot even guess at the measure of God's patience with mankind.

(b) Is the answering of the question important for us? Should it be our concern? If we love men, then inevitably it is our concern, and in times as somber as the present we may well believe that, if the world is to survive, whether men are men of faith or not is a matter of huge importance for all. But as touching the establishment of our own personal faith, how many or how few share our beliefs should not greatly concern us. In the sphere of politics, what the majority thinks is critically important, but in the sphere of religious faith, what the majority believes is of no great account, and certainly no absolute authority may rightly be accorded to it. What matters is the individual's dealing with the truth, what the individual believes, and what he does with God's word in Jesus Christ.

(c) In awareness of God and in response to his word, no man can be proxy for another. No man can be religious in another's stead. In matters of faith we can help one another, and we can hinder one another. But no man can believe for another. A man's believing is his own intensely personal, private affair and responsibility, even though the importance of its impact on society cannot be overestimated. And a man's believing is a man's religion.

II. Our Lord's question reflects uncertainty. (a) When the Son of Man cometh, when history is fulfilled, will men be found believing or apostate? Jesus was not sure. He saw that in every age men are free to accept and to reject God's witness to himself. Such freedom belongs to man as a creature made in the image of God. And Jesus never sought to override that freedom. But he was uncertain how men would exercise it.

(1) Perhaps he foresaw that many at first would respond avidly to his word and also that some of those would ultimately desert him when they found that religious faith, far from immunizing believers from the ills of life, makes them more vulnerable and sensitive to those ills and sometimes

leads them, as it led him, to a cross.

(2) Perhaps he saw that many, at first believing, would change when they found that belief in God makes God no man's servant to do his bidding, to satisfy all his desires, and to answer all his prayers.

(3) Perhaps he saw that a day would come when many would not know what to believe in face of their own and the world's enigmatic story. Maybe they would note that, by and large, it is worldliness that wins the day and that despite many generations of Christian teaching, war and injustice continue unabated. In a word, that Christ is always being crucified afresh. And noting these things they would decide that they must be on the winning side in this world's life. Thus Jesus "wondered." He was uncertain.

(b) That faith is not widespread on earth and that a few embrace it is reason for sorrow but not for doubt and not for our falling away. Truth is truth though the whole world deny it. Christ is Christ though all men despise and reject him. Belief that all men will believe is no article of the Christian creed.

III. Our Lord's question reflects certainty about God. (a) He has doubts about man, but he has no doubts about God. "The Son of Man cometh"—that is certain. God's purpose moves on to fulfillment; the king whose rule will justify history's travail and life's pain comes. God, God's purposes, and God's reign are independent of us. We may believe and we may not; we may worship God and strive to obey his word in Jesus Christ, or we may become athiests or idolators. But whatever we do and whatever we are, God exists. He does not "live" by reason of men's believing, and he does not "die" when men cease to believe. The Son of Man cometh, and God's purpose unfolds!

(b) We do well to remember this certainty of Jesus. On it he built his life; from it all his teaching proceeds; in it he went to his death. At no time was it in doubt. Even his cry of derelliction from the cross was a cry of questioning faith *to* God.

(c) His experience of life was essentially the same as ours. (1) He was sheltered from none of those things that repeatedly challenge and often shatter our beliefs— the arbitrary incidence of natural calamity, suffering and disease, utterly unrelated to men's deserving and without redemptive power.

(2) He knew men's fear of death and their sense of bitterest outrage as it disrupts the life and world of the bereaved. Nevertheless, despite it all, his certainty stood firm.

(d) The certainty of Jesus demands our attention if only because we so rarely share it. We must heed it, ponder it, accept it, and rest in it. It is integral to the gospel. Indeed without it there is no gospel, no gospel of God and no good news for man. —Kenneth H. Tyson.

Illustration

TRIVIALIZATION.   The true meaning of the church has given way to the manipulations of the organization. In place of the sacraments, we have the committee meeting; in place of confession, the bazaar; in place of pilgrimage, the dull drive to hear the deadly speaker; in place of community, a collection of functions. This trivialization of religious life has made the middle-class search for religious meaning even more desperate. Every church activity seems to lead further into a maze of superficiality.—Gibson Winter.

Sermon Suggestions

MAKING PRAYER REAL.   Text: Luke 11:1. (1) In prayer there should be sharing. (2) Prayer can be a time of cleansing. (3) Prayer allows us to get our proper focus on life. (4) In prayer we can receive counsel from God. (5) In prayer we can have a wonderful fellowship with God.—Bill Duncan.

A PEOPLE SHALL BE CREATED.   Text: Ps. 102:18 (ARV). (1) In the Christian revelation the goal of creation is the emergence of a people in whom God is redemptively expressed. (2) The emergence of a people is through the redemptive activity of God. (3) The result of the creation of a people shall be the praise of God. (4) The emergence of a people created by God through his redemptive activity brings the challenge to all of us to permit God to work this renewing in our own lives.—John S. Stamm.

Worship Aids

CALL TO WORSHIP. "Lift up your heads in the sanctuary, and bless the Lord. The Lord that made heaven and earth bless thee out of Zion." Ps. 134:2–3.

INVOCATION. Father God, you are known to us through loving persons who affirm the faith. May we be loving too. Father God, you are known to us through trusting acts which proclaim the truth. May we be trusting too. Father God, you are known to us through the joyous story which celebrates your Son. May we be joyous too. For we are here to affirm, to proclaim, and to celebrate. We believe! Help thou our unbelief! Amen!

OFFERTORY SERVICE. "We then that are strong ought to bear the infirmities of the weak, and not to please ourselves." Rom. 15:1.

OFFERTORY PRAYER. Our Father, we thank thee that thou art so generous to us. All that we have is a gift from thee. Help us to serve one another so that we may reflect thy spirit and goodness.

PRAYER. Eternal God, our Father, who sent into this busy, needy world thy Son and who thyself workest even until now, give us, we beseech thee, that rare and subtle gift, a sense of due proportion in our lives. Save us, we beseech thee, from a depressing sense of life's fluidity. Give us instead a glowing faith in its ever-changing opportunity. Lay thou thy life against our lives; breathe into us the breath of thine abundant spirit; in the early morning call us; in the heat of noon refresh us; walk with us in the evening cool. Save us from frittering our days away in silly or unlovely uses. Give us the high wisdom to create in all our days beauty for ourselves or others.—*The Altar of Stewardship.*

EVENING SERVICE

Topic: Paul Prays for the Ephesians
SCRIPTURE: Eph. 3:14–21.

Possessed by the love of God, nurtured by the working of the Holy Spirit, and yielded to the lordship of Christ, Paul prayed this majestic and meaningful prayer for the Ephesians, revealing God's longings for all of his children. Paul asked for four things in particular.

I. That believers might have spiritual power (v. 16). Paul did not ask for physical or intellectual strength to be given to believers but that they might receive the inward strength of the Holy Spirit.

II. That Christ might dwell in the hearts of believers by faith (v. 17).

(a) As used in the scriptures, the heart is the seat of the intellect, the emotions, and the will. The heart is the region of affection and desire, the place where thoughts spring up and purposes are formed, and the area in which future actions have their birth.

(b) Paul prayed that Christ might become a permanent occupant in the hearts of believers rather than an occasional visitor. When he is a permanent resident there, Christ liberates the heart from the power of Satan, weans it from other things, satisfies it, strengthens it, and fills it with the hope of glory.

III. That believers might understand the love of Christ (vv. 18–19). Paul prayed that believers might be able to comprehend the love of Christ in its four dimensions and that they might have an experiential knowledge of it.

IV. That believers might be filled with the fulness of God (v. 19). Before Christians can have this delightful experience they must be emptied of self. There must be an implicit faith in God and not in self. Paul declared God's infinite power far exceeded all that we can ask or think.—H. C. Chiles.

SUNDAY: AUGUST TWENTY-SIXTH

MORNING SERVICE

Topic: The Name of Jesus (A Dialogue)
TEXT: Phil. 2:9.

I. *Prophet.* (a) A first-century Christian might have put it like this: "It's been a long time between prophets! From the days of Moses on God has always raised up men who could speak for God to us. Moses promised that God would always do this, that after Moses' death another prophet would come and another and another. And so they did—leaders like Joshua and great prophets like Isaiah and Jeremiah. But then Malachi seemed to be the last one. For centuries we've been looking for a new Elijah. We'd almost given up hope. A few men came who claimed to be prophets, but they turned out to be fools or liars. The best we had were rabbis who could quote what ancient teachers had said. And then came Jesus. He didn't quote older teachers. He didn't even say, "Thus saith the Lord." But when he spoke, my heart knew who was speaking. These were words right from God. And it wasn't just what he said either. It was who he was. He didn't tell us about God, like the old prophets. When we were with him we knew God was there."

(b) Perhaps a twentieth-century Christian would phrase it this way: "I've been all mixed up about God. What do you mean by God? How do you even know there is a God anyway? You can't see him. Maybe we just imagine him. I can't even imagine him; really I don't go for this old man on a cloud idea. And then I got to studying about Jesus. I didn't have the answer to all my questions. I can still get pretty full of doubts. But every time I get back to Jesus I know that here is something real. Something I can count on. Following him is what really matters. My questions just don't bother me as they used to. Maybe following Jesus is all I really have to know, the ultimate concern of life. Anyway, it's given—or he's given—me a new start."

II. *Priest.* (a) A first-century disciple might have put it like this: "God is holy, and I am unclean. I cannot enter the holy place of the temple, for my hands are covered with guilt. Once a year the high priest goes in for me. A sacrifice is offered. In symbol the lamb takes my guilt and punishment, and I am cleansed. The priest bridges the gap between me and God. But that is all symbols. When I was with Jesus I knew God loved me. Even when I ran away and let Jesus be crucified, he forgave me. He sacrificed himself for me. But he could go right to God like a son to his father. And with Christ, in his Spirit, I know that I am now made a child of God, living in God's love."

(b) A twentieth-century Christian might say it this way: "Most of the time I try to boast or make excuses or convince myself that I'm really all right. But deep down I know I keep making a mess of everything. I try to dress up or buy a new car or cover up some other way the fact that I'm what I am. But it's no use. And then I remember Jesus, I remember that in him God loves me and accepts me just as I am. I don't have to cover up or make excuses. Even though I'm a sinner it's still all right. God forgives me and loves me just as I love my boy. And remembering that, I don't have to fight back the world. I can love too."

III. *King.* (a) A first-century disciple: "My country used to be strong and free. Our greatest king, David, ruled an empire that made men proud to be Jews. Now we are slaves of Rome. We've dreamed of a new David, but none ever came to free us. And then came Jesus. He had no army, but he even conquered death. When he spoke, his word was my command. I don't take orders even from Roman soldiers. But I have to do what he says. He commanded me to try to free those enslaved by poverty and sickness and sin. And as I obey I find the freedom and victory of the kingdom of God."

(b) Or a twentieth-century Christian: "I'm too scared to watch the news on TV. And sometimes I think my family is falling apart. And then I think about Jesus. If he really rose from the dead, then God is still in charge. When it's all said and done, I know who's going to win. And when I read what Jesus said and did, I know what I've got to do. When I think about Jesus and try to follow him, I'm not scared and I'm not mixed up. I know who's in charge of the world and of me too."—William M. Ramsay.

Illustrations

HIS VIEWPOINT AND OURS. Jesus calls into question our perception of things. No matter how we look at the world, he challenges our viewpoint. If we believe that the world is an evil place, we are confronted by the fact that he embodied love within it in such a way as to suggest that love is at the very heart of things. If we believe that the world is a beautiful place, we are confronted by the fact that when Jesus gave expression to that beauty the world could not fit him in and very quickly did away with him. There is no stance we can take about ourselves or our world that is not challenged when we confront Christ. He shows us the gap between how he looks at the world and the way the world really is, and he enables us to enter vicariously into his own experience and discover that the way we see things is not the way things really are.—Robert McAfee Brown.

IN HIS PRESENCE. Salvation is not an idea; it is a person. It is Jesus himself, God himself, who yields himself up. In his presence all the interminable debates which arouse within us the feeling of guilt and all moralistic hairsplitting and our defenses against the judgments of others fall away. We see it happening in the story of Zacchaeus who enriched himself, so popular report had it, at the expense of the people. He tried to justify himself and to demonstrate his good conscience, but Jesus cut him short with the words, "Today salvation has come to this house." Salvation is no longer some remote ideal of perfection, forever inaccessible; it is a person, Jesus Christ, who comes to us and comes

to be with us in our homes and in our hearts. Remorse is silenced by his absolution. He substitutes for it one other single question, the one he put to the apostle Peter, "Do you love me?" We must answer that question and find in our personal attachment to Jesus Christ peace for our souls.—Paul Tournier.

Sermon Suggestion

GUESTS OF GOD. Text: Rev. 19:9. (1) We are in this world as guests of God. (2) We are to use but not abuse his hospitality. (3) We are to add to the enjoyment of the other guests. (4) We are to have fellowship not only with our fellow guests but also with our Host himself.—Ralph W. Sockman.

Worship Aids

CALL TO WORSHIP. "If a man love me, saith Jesus, he will keep my words: and my Father will love him, and we will come unto him, and make our abode with him." John 14:23.

INVOCATION. Almighty and everlasting God, in whom we live and move and have our being, who hast created us for thyself so that we can find rest only in thee: grant unto us purity of heart and strength of purpose so that no selfish passion may hinder us from knowing thy will and no weakness sway us from doing it and that in thy light we may see light clearly and in thy service find perfect freedom.

OFFERTORY SENTENCE. "Every one of us shall give account of himself to God." Rom. 14:12.

OFFERTORY PRAYER. Our Father, help us this day to remember that we do not live in our own strength but that thou art our help and that from thee cometh even these gifts which we consecrate in Christ's name.

PRAYER. All-knowing and all-loving God, who created man and redeemed his life from destruction, according to thy purposes grant unto us an understanding mind, a desire to respond to thy love, and a will to serve thee.

Clarify our sense of values that we may distinguish between the trivial and the important, the mediocre and the excellent, and the ephemeral and the eternal. Deliver us from a covetous and greedy spirit Help us to hold in stewardship all life, all time and talent, and all possessions. Daily recall to our minds that every good gift cometh from thee and that we are held responsible for their use.

Increase our sensitivity, O God, to human need. Erase from our minds all prejudices that inhibit our sympathy with our fellow men. May love dwell in our hearts and move our hands to loving service.

We are grateful, our Father, for thy continual care over our lives and especially for him whom we know as Savior and Lord.

EVENING SERVICE

Topic: Guidelines for Christian Criticism

TEXT: Isa. 11:3.

I. To be of value it must be open and face-to-face. If we indulge in nagging criticism of another but never make it to him directly, we can only expect to poison personal relationships and sap the confidence and effectiveness of the one criticized.

II. Criticism to be effective must issue from a loving concern, not from a desire to hurt and humiliate. Often if we look into our hearts when we criticize others, it is not that we want to help them to a better course of life but because we ourselves feel slighted or threatened and want to hurt them in return. It is hard to think how any good can result from such tainted motives.

III. We must learn to direct our criticisms not to the person as such but to the specific factors in his words and actions which we find unsatisfactory.

IV. Before we criticize another we ought to ask ourselves the question, "Can I take it as well as give it?"

V. God has the final word and issues the final judgment. He is not a harsh, retributive, and inflexible judge but a loving Father. He accepts us not because we are perfect but because he is love. If this awareness permeated all our dealings with others, even our criticism will bear the same mark.—Selwyn Dawson.

SUNDAY: SEPTEMBER SECOND

MORNING SERVICE

Topic: Daily Work and the Christian (Labor Sunday)

TEXT: I Cor. 3:9.

In a day in which our working lives are lived out in smaller and smaller niches in larger and larger organizations, many people have come to experience work as drudgery. Labor Day for these has ceased to be a celebration and has become merely a welcome day off in which the goal is to forget about labor. Yet for Christians who are "labourers together with God" it should be different. Labor Day is an opportunity to celebrate and to contemplate the meaning of the work which so dominates our waking hours.

I. Work is a means by which we can love our neighbors as ourselves.

(a) No matter how trivial our tasks may seem, any worthwhile work helps to sustain other people. In growing food, building buildings, assembling cars, healing sick people, keeping house, and typing letters we engage in activities which enhance the lives of others. Through any respectable work we show ourselves to be responsible members of society. This is the idea which underlies Paul's instructions, "If any one will not work, let him not eat" (II Thess. 3:10, RSV). We should not eat food produced by the labor of others if we have refused in our turn to labor for them.

(b) Paul did not say, "If any one cannot work, let him not eat." There are many who, either through infirmity or lack of opportunity, cannot work. It is not those who have been denied the privilege of God-ordained work who are condemned by Paul; rather it is those who are irresponsible to God and to their fellow men in their refusal to work.

II. Work is a means by which we can be responsible to ourselves as God has created us.

(a) We normally see work as a means of obtaining material possessions. Indeed work often does make it possible for us to acquire material essentials and sometimes luxuries. But work has personal benefits other than earning money. Leisure, for example, when experienced as relief from our labor, becomes a time to celebrate with God the goodness of life and to experience the joy of rest as he did on the first Sabbath.

(b) Meaningful work, whether paid or voluntary, gives us the opportunity for self-development as we learn with our minds and strengthen our bodies. Working for the self is part of God's plan and is good. Working only for the self, whether it be for self-development, for material reward, or for personal praise, is an evil to be avoided at all costs.

III. Work allows us to participate with God in his activity. (a) When the Bible speaks of persons as "labourers together with God," it means that the Christian can never be satisfied with work which is just a means to eat or just a means to serve one's neighbor. The Christian can only be content when his or her work is an arena where God's call to discipleship is lived out. The word "vocation" was originally a religious word which meant "calling." In all kinds of vocations, people are still living out God's call to subdue the earth and to have dominion over it as responsible stewards.

(b) The greatest commandment is to love God, and the second greatest commandment is to love our neighbors as ourselves. Work is one way in which we can fulfill both commandments as we serve both God and neighbor in our labor.—W. David Sapp.

Illustrations

DISHWASHING AT IONA.   John Murray spent a short time in the Iona Community on the sacred island of Iona off the coast of Scotland. Historians claim that this was the first place in the British Isles to receive Christian missionaries. He had gone there with others to rebuild the ruins of the monastery that surround the abbey. He was eager to share in the work. Imagine his disgust when, after the others in the party had been assigned their jobs of mixing cement, carting bricks, and hauling timbers, he was told, "You will help with washing the dishes after each meal." All he could think of were fishy tins and plates coated with porridge. Yet it slowly dawned on him, as the week went by, that the walls could not be built unless someone did the cooking and the dishwashing for those who were capable of doing the building. The one job made possible the other, and the dishwashers could help rebuild Iona no less than the stonemasons and the carpenters.—Homer J. R. Elford.

NEW PERSPECTIVE.   An executive of a steel company in Cleveland resigned his position and applied for work at the gates of a steel mill in another city. He became a day laborer. Some friends thought this action rather bizarre; others regarded it as merely a "stunt." But he knew exactly what he was after. Having worked side by side for half a year with other employees, he gained a perspective of the workers' problems from a new and entirely different viewpoint. He became a recognized authority on management-labor relations. He was really fulfilling Paul's injunction that we "should learn to see things from other people's point of view" (Phil. 2:4, PHILLIPS).—John Sutherland Bonnell.

Sermon Suggestions

LIVING TEMPLES.   Text: I Cor. 6:19. (1) Every true Christian is a house of worship. A temple is a place where God's presence is felt. (2) Every true Christian is a house of wisdom. In the ancient temple the scribes were teachers. (3) Every true Christian is a house of witness. The very existence of a temple is a public reminder of the reality of God. (4) Every true Christian is a house of welcome. All were invited. Trumpets rang out a welcome. Loud voices from its pinnacles bade people come to the house of God.—David Burns.

BUILDING HIGHER HABITS.   Text: Prov. 3:6. (1) By dedicating ourselves to God. (2) By acknowledging him and believing that he is directing our paths. (3) By living faithfully the teachings of Jesus. (4) By practicing those attitudes toward God, life, and people which make old lives new. —Roy A. Burkhart.

Worship Aids

CALL TO WORSHIP.   "We are laborers together with God: ye are God's husbandry, ye are God's building. Let every man take heed how he buildeth. For other foundation can no man lay than that is laid, which is Jesus Christ." I Cor. 3:9–11.

INVOCATION.   Our heavenly Father, we thy humble children invoke thy blessing upon us in this hour of worship. We adore thee, whose nature is compassion, whose presence is joy, whose word is truth, whose spirit is goodness, whose holiness is beauty, whose will is peace, whose service is perfect freedom, and in knowledge of whom standeth our eternal life. Unto thee be all honor and all glory.

OFFERTORY SENTENCE.   "Offer unto God thanksgiving; and pay thy vows unto the most High." Ps. 50:14.

OFFERTORY PRAYER.   Our Father, enable all Christians to know that their lives may be lived with Christ in God and that their gifts are means by which thy love in Christ may reach into the lives of wayward and needy persons everywhere.

PRAYER.   O God, most merciful, we beseech thee for all our brothers of this nation, of the great cities and quiet country places, high and low, rich and poor together, that thou wouldst prosper agriculture, manufacture, commerce, and every lawful industry, and that thou wouldst fill our hearts with thy love and our homes with thy peace.

And for all the nations of the human race that thou in thy providence wouldst make an end of war and grant to every land the blessings of peace and order, justice and spiritual knowledge.

We beseech thee for the church universal throughout the world in all its branches and in all its ministries that the word of God may be in its utterance and the spirit of charity in all of its good works.

Do thou give rest to the weary backs of tired men, give patience to those who suffer, wipe the tears of those who weep, be companion to the lonely, and at the end of the day bring us all home to our Father's house.—Clifford L. Stanley.

EVENING SERVICE

Topic: Did Jesus Praise a Crook?
SCRIPTURE: Luke 16:1–8.
Did Jesus really praise a crook, or if not what did he mean his followers to learn from this parable of shameless rascality?

I. This parable is a challenge to face squarely the facts, however black and forbidding they may be.

(a) This man had been discovered engaged in his blameworthy practices. He realized that he would be fired and would not be able to get such lucrative employment again. He did not live in a fool's paradise, which someone has described as the anteroom to a fool's hell.

(b) This quality of willingness to look at the facts is one which Christians would do well to cultivate and apply.

II. This story is a challenge to look ahead and to exercise foresight.

(a) This rascally manager had the wisdom to think ahead, to project himself into the future, and to picture to himself the homelessness, poverty, and unemployment into which he would soon be plunged, and he sought to make the best provision he could for that bleak future which he faced.

(b) This quality of foresight has never been in large supply, but it is a quality which Christians are bound to cultivate and apply if they are to fulfill their calling in a manner well-pleasing to God. For Christians believe that their life here in this world is only a preparation for life in eternity and that this present life must be ordered in the light of their eternal destiny. This means that, looking ahead, they will order their earthly lives in such a fashion that they make it clear that they believe that "the things which are seen are temporal, but the things which are unseen are eternal."

III. This parable is a challenge to Christ's followers to use their minds, their God-given intelligence, as an integral part of their commitment to God in Christ.

(a) This rascally manager not only faced up to the uncomfortable facts of his situation and looked ahead, but he also used his brains in order to make secure through ample provision for the bleak future which he had to face.

(b) When Jesus was asked on one occasion the question, "Which is the greatest commandment of the law?" he replied by quoting Deut. 6:5. But he added a highly significant clause not found in Deuteronomy, namely, "And with all thy mind." What he meant was surely that for full Christian commitment it is necessary not only to dedicate oneself to the doing of the will of God in Christ but also to think out the most effective way in which God's will can be carried out in practice.— Norman V. Hope.

SUNDAY: SEPTEMBER NINTH

MORNING SERVICE

Topic: The Church and the Gospel
TEXT: Eph. 3:10.

I. The gospel is not our invention. It is the gift of God. Far too many of us are prone to make the grave mistake of thinking that the good news of Jesus Christ is at worst a human illusion and at best a human discovery.

(a) How clever we were to think that God cares for men and is ready to act on their behalf! Or how stupid we were to believe for a moment that God could care thus for men and act on their behalf! The Christian proclamation is taken to be either a pretty dream with no basis in reality or a remarkable discovery which we owe to people of deep spiritual insight and discernment.

(b) There can be no doubt that human thinking has had much to do with working out the implications of the gospel and its application to human existence. But the gospel is not based on such human thinking.

(1) It is based on a fact ploughed into history; it is all about a man who actually lived and taught and acted and suffered and died and was raised again to be with his people to the end of the world.

(2) That fact is not only a notable human fact; it is a supreme and decisive divine act. To us men and women in our need God has come in his deed which was "determined, dared, and done" (Christopher Smart) with the initiative on

God's side, not on ours.

(c) This is the way the New Testament talks; this is the way the Christian ages have spoken; this is the only conceivable interpretation of the meaning of the gospel if we are to remain men and women of faith and not succumb to the blandishments of a this-worldly, all-too-human pride in our own inventive capacity.

II. The gospel has to do with God in his gracious concern for human wholeness.

(a) It does not begin with man in a mess and look around for some remedy for the messiness. It is not primarily about the old Adam, our unregenerate selves "in whom we die" but about the new Adam, the Christ to be formed in us so that we may live. The gospel cannot adequately be stated in what somebody has called "a desperation theology," for its origin is in the love of God.

(b) Surely it does answer human need. Its answering that need however comes from its being a disclosure of what is everlastingly true of God. He is always what the fact of Christ tells us he is; that same giving of life to men is what he is up to, world without end.

(c) This is why the proclamation of the gospel has an extroverting character. It turns us from ourselves with our miseries and inadequacies and sins and failures toward God who is unfailingly faithful and ceaselessly concerned about his human children.

(d) We know ourselves to be sinners not just because we feel inadequate and miserable and lonely and lost but because to be so much loved by the great cosmic Lover is to see ourselves for just what we are. In comparison with him we are but as beasts, as Ps. 73 so properly and realistically reminds us.

(e) Yet in the light of our awareness of the divine love we know that God holds us by his right hand, that we are always with him because he is always with us, and that although heart and strength may and do fail, "God is the strength of my heart and my portion forever." We look at God, not at ourselves, and we are saved from self-absorption, self-worry, self-defeat, and self-despair.

III. The gospel is so astounding a proclamation, telling as it does of an illimitable love that will never let us go, that we cannot fail to turn to praise and thanksgiving. We are moved to live to God's greater glory. And if we live that way, we wish to vocalize our sense of gratitude and thanksgiving and praise. Hence this church and this service of worship, the intention of which is to give God the glory precisely because we have heard and, please God, have welcomed and received the gospel proclaimed to us.—Norman Pittenger.

Illustrations

FALSE DOCTRINE. An old farmer who had resisted the gospel invitation for many years finally accepted Christ and was baptized. Some days later a neighbor, passing his farm, saw the old man at work on the roof of his barn. "What are you doing up there?" he shouted. "I'm tearing down the weather vane!" came the reply. "Was it broken?" "Nope," replied the old farmer, "but it had on it the points of the compass —north, south, east, and west. Just last week we sang a song, 'In Christ there is no east nor west.' I sure don't want my weather vane teaching false doctrine to the whole community, and so down it comes!"—John W. Wade.

RENEWAL. The church will only be renewed as we, her members, are renewed. The church will know new life only as we, her members, experience new life. The church will care about people and

be on mission to the world only as our care deepens.

MEANING AND DOING. A great divinity school had several outstanding theologians on its faculty. Some of these men were much more "orthodox" than others. In particular one teacher was extremely well-versed in the New Testament and devoutly confessed the creeds of the church. Just across the hall from this professor's office was the study of another theologian. This second man had ideas of his own, some of them considered heretical by the students and faculty. Nevertheless the unorthodox teacher was kind and generous; he was helpful and concerned about his students far beyond any teacher's call of duty. And over the years a saying arose among the students of this school, "If you want to know what Jesus Christ means, go ask the orthodox theologian; but if you want to know what Jesus Christ does, go watch the unorthodox one."—John C. Cooper.

Sermon Suggestions

A TIMELESS BOOK FOR OUR TIMELY NEED. Text: Ps. 119:165. (1) The Bible is the sourcebook of our religious faith. (2) It is the textbook about God revealing the God in whom we live, move, and have our being. (3) It is the guidebook for Christian living. (4) It is the sourcebook for the life of Christ.—Frank A. Court.

WHAT GOD HATH JOINED. Text: Matt. 19:6. (1) God has united truth and love. (2) God has united privilege and responsibility. (3) God has united belief and conduct. (4) God has united submission and freedom. (5) God has united sin and punishment. (6) God has united faithfulness and reward. (7) God has united character and destiny.—W. Graham Scroggie.

Worship Aids

CALL TO WORSHIP. "Come unto me, all ye that labor and are heavy laden, and I will give you rest. Take my yoke upon you, and learn of me; for I am meek and lowly in heart: and ye shall find rest unto your souls." Matt. 11:28–29.

INVOCATION.   O God our Father, who dost dwell in the high and holy place, with him also that is of a humble and contrite heart: grant that, through this time of worship in thy presence, we may be made the more sure that our true home is with thee in the realm of spiritual things and that thou art ever with us in the midst of our common walk and daily duties so that the vision of the eternal may ever give meaning and beauty to this earthly and outward life.

OFFERTORY SENTENCE.   "Seeing ye have purified your souls in obeying the truth through the Spirit unto unfeigned love of the brethren, see that ye love one another with a pure heart fervently." I Pet. 1:22.

OFFERTORY PRAYER.   Open our eyes that we may see thy goodness, O Father; our hearts that we may be grateful for thy mercies; our lips that we may show forth thy praise; and our hands that we may give these offerings according to thy wish and desire.

PRAYER FOR CHURCH LEADERS.   O thou who makest the clouds thy chariots, yet workest with man in his labors; who coverest thyself with honor and majesty as with a garment, yet forgettest not thy children: lay thy hand upon these thy servants who, having been called, now go out to lead thy people.

Thou hast placed in their hands power; now clothe them mightily with wisdom of mind and love of heart. Grant them patience for the days when their followers move too slowly; grant them love to sustain them when men will mock, provide them faith in themselves when failure stalks their paths, and give them strength when temptation would lure them into the easy way.

Use them as instruments to further thy ways of pleasantness, of peace, of justice, and of brotherhood. Where they find discord, may they bring unity; where they see despair, may they set up hope; where they encounter bitterness, may they sow love; where they meet the darkness of night, may they bring the light of a morning star. —Fred E. Luchs.

EVENING SERVICE

Topic: A Mind Set on the Spirit

TEXT: Rom. 8:6 (RSV).

I. To have one's mind set on the Spirit means that one's attention is riveted on that which God has done for us in the Lord Jesus Christ.

(a) Obviously we cannot direct our attention to the Spirit in the same way a person who is dominated by fleshly things can set his mind on fleshly things. Fleshly things are in the nature of the case visible and touchable. If a person is dominated by material possessions, he can buy them, use them, display them, and do whatever he wants with them. But when we focus our attention on the Spirit, there is nothing there, nothing in the usual sense, for the Spirit is invisible.

(b) Our attention must be focused on what God has accomplished through his Holy Spirit. When we read of the Lord Jesus Christ in the Bible, we learn that he did what he did in the power of the Holy Spirit. Heb. 9:14 speaks of a Christ who offered himself through the eternal Spirit as a sacrifice without blemish.

II. This means that we focus our attention on the Spirit when we make the book that tells us about God's great work of salvation the center of our interest. The mind that is set on the Spirit is a mind being formed by the book which the Spirit wrote.

(a) We need not be vague and unspecific when we talk about the works of the Spirit of God. God through his Spirit sent his Son and gave him the power to be the Savior.

(b) God through his Spirit wrote a book. There is a work of the Spirit of God that is actually visible before our eyes. That is the Bible, the book that is the product of God's working with men by the power of his Holy Spirit.

III. Those who have the Spirit of God and whose minds are focused on the Spirit are people who fight against the works of the flesh.

(a) The deeds of the body are all those appetites, things, and religious ideas that reflect the will of man and not the will of God. (See Rom. 8:13.) To fight against such things is a serious and lifelong struggle. But it is a struggle finally crowned with victory.

(b) According to the Bible, the state of a person's mind is the most important thing about him. The seriousness of this is expressed in Rom. 8 where the point is made more than once that the question of one's mind is a question of life and death. If you are a person whose mind is enslaved by the things of this world and you think about them alone, you are in grave danger. What you need is the change that comes to a person when he believes in the Lord Jesus Christ and receives his Holy Spirit.—Joel Nederhood.

SUNDAY: SEPTEMBER SIXTEENTH

MORNING SERVICE

Topic: Where Service Begins
Scripture: John 13:1–17.

What is happening in this interchange between Peter and Jesus? Peter is learning what it takes to be a person like Jesus. Jesus' whole style of life had been that of serving other people. This was what Jesus expected of persons who would follow him. Yet, only hours away from death, Jesus saw little of this quality exhibited in the lives of those closest to him. Here, even in the intimacy of a fellowship meal, no one had stooped to wash another's feet as they sat down. Not willing to serve one another whom they knew, how would they ever go out to serve those in need whom they did not know? They needed to grasp where service begins.

I. Service begins with a humility that is not condescending. The amazing thing to Peter was that his Lord and Master would humbly wash his feet. It was not fitting for Jesus to act that way toward him. Yet Jesus insisted in a way that was not condescending but natural. Jesus was not lording it over them. He was not saying that since nobody else would stoop so low as to get the feet washed he would do it. He was not taking pride in his humility. Jesus' washing of the disciples' feet was done in loving identification with those he served.

II. Service begins not with giving but with receiving. When Jesus kneels before Peter to wash his feet, Peter tells him, "I will never let you wash my feet." Jesus sharply replies, "If I do not wash you, you are not in fellowship with me." Jesus is telling Peter that if he is too proud to receive help from Jesus he cannot be a part of his fellowship. We do not know how to offer help until we have learned to receive help.

(a) We don't like to be helped any more than did Peter. This is also true of those whom we would serve. They will not receive our service unless they sense we are one of them through the common bonds of need.

(b) Jesus knew Peter could never serve in his fellowship if he did not see himself as one who is in need of help. Peter particularly needed to submit himself to the ministrations of Jesus. He needed to know that, apart from that divine kind of love shown to him by Jesus' washing his feet, he would be nothing. It is only through humbly accepting the love of God into your own life that you can possibly be equipped for service.

(c) One of the hardest lessons we have to learn from Christ is that "our most important need is not to love and to forgive but to be loved and to be forgiven." We need to recognize we live in dependence upon God's graciousness toward us. Our pride needs to be broken upon the love of God as seen in Christ's dying on a cross for us. Humbled by God's undeserved love for us, we are readied to share that love unpretentiously with others.

III. Service begins with us. (a) I think it is essential for us to grasp the import of Peter's response to Jesus' insistence that he wash Peter's feet or Peter could not fellowship with him. Peter overreacts. He says if he must let Jesus be his servant then he will let him do it all. "Take over, Jesus," he says. Jesus refuses.

(b) Relying on God's love does not demean us into irresponsibility. He humbles us not to humiliate us but to equip us to be of worthy service to others. We need to feel dependent upon a loving power greater than ourselves who gives us a sense of awesome security in the midst of all life's uncertainties. This is God whom we call Father. But as children of the Father we have our own dignity which shares responsibility with him. We need to keep that shared responsibility in focus.—Culbert S. Cartwright.

Illustrations

CHOICES MAKE US. Every time you make a choice you are turning the central part of you, the part that chooses, into something a little different from what it was before. And taking your life as a whole, with all your innumerable choices, you are slowly turning this central thing either into a heavenly creature or into a hellish creature and either into a creature that is in harmony with God or else into one that is in a state of war with God.—C. S. Lewis.

WHAT AN ACTRESS WROTE. When I was 17, I came to the theater on the eve of the opening and saw my name being posted in big letters. I then had the very strange experience of becoming paralyzed. I suddenly grew aware that I was expected to be very, very good. I became like the centipede with the fly in the old German story. The fly says to the centipede: "I have six legs and know how to walk. You have 100 legs. How can you walk?" And the centipede starts to think about it and then becomes paralyzed and can't walk. I became so afraid on opening night I had a temperature and told my mother that I wanted to stay home in bed, but my mother made me get up and go to the theater. She told me something that I will never forget. She said, "If you cannot be

good, then you must have the courage to be bad."—Maria Schell.

Sermon Suggestions

THE CHURCH WELCOMES ALL. Text: Eph. 2:19. (1) Welcome to the weary. (2) Welcome to the mourners. (3) Welcome to the lonely. (4) Welcome to all who pray. (5) Welcome to all who sin.

TRANSLATING BIBLICAL EXPERIENCE. Scripture: Acts 8:26–39. (1) Divine directive translated into human ministry (v. 26). (2) Divine providence translated into human opportunity (v. 27). (3) Divine testimony translated into human understanding (v. 30). (4) Divine command translated into human obedience (v. 36).—Ard Hoven.

Worship Aids

CALL TO WORSHIP. "How beautiful upon the mountains are the feet of him that bringeth good tidings, that publisheth peace; that publisheth salvation; that saith unto Zion, thy God reigneth!" Isa. 52:7.

INVOCATION. O God, whose name is great, whose goodness is inexhaustible, who art worshiped and served by all the hosts of heaven: touch our hearts, search out our consciences, and cast out of us every evil thought and base desire; all envy, wrath, and remembrance of injuries; and every motion of flesh and spirit that is contrary to thy holy will.

OFFERTORY SENTENCE. "It is God who is at work within you, giving you the will and the power to achieve his purpose." Phil. 2:13 (PHILLIPS).

OFFERTORY PRAYER. O thou who art the Father of all, may we live as thy children and brothers of all whom thou hast made to dwell upon the face of the earth that thy kindness may be born in our hearts.

PRAYER. Almighty God, we know thee in so many ways. Thou art the steady light before the pilgrim's eyes. Thou art the fountain of renewing water in the wasteland experiences of life. Thou art the cool breeze upon the warm brow of all who labor and are heavy laden. Thou art the conciliator between hostile camps. Thou art the reviving hope breaking through the bleak nightmares of sorrow and despair. Thou art the comfort of home, the security of love, the warmth of acceptance, and the glow of self-affirmation.

At the same time we know thee to be the question which sometimes disturbs our answers, the explosion which disrupts our walls of prejudice, the flame of judgment that consumes our evil and selfishness, and the whirlwind that uproots our complacency and self-satisfaction.

We express gratitude to thee for all evidences of thy love and of thy correcting discipline. We express gratitude to thee for those who have invested so much time and love in our growth, for children who bring so much joy and pleasure, for health and healing, and for all the agents of science that serve our needs.

We remember those who don't feel remembered. We pray for them and would seek to know them. We pray for the confused and alienated and hard-pressed. May those who have lost their place in the marketplace because of injury, age, or lack of skill or education be known to us in their need and accepted for whom they are.

May the fellowship we feel together here extend through us to all who are touched by our lives as we go forth in thy name.—Richard Brand.

EVENING SERVICE

Topic: **The Successful Congregation**
TEXT: Col. 3:16.

The successful congregation too frequently is determined by numbers, the size and quality of its building, the kinds of people who attend, dollars given, or the popularity of the minister. But a church is successful and is really fulfilling its calling when the following are in evidence.

I. What happens on Sunday has relevance to what happens from Monday morning through Saturday evening.

II. There is a consistent effort to comfort the afflicted (those who hurt in one way or another) and to afflict the comfortable (those who resist change, growth, or any kind of involvement that is demanding).

III. There is evidence that people are seeking to discover their needs and the way God has acted to meet those needs.

IV. There is a strong concern for alleviating the hurt and pain in the world through various expressions of love and justice.

V. People in the church enjoy being together and express regular interest in growing as sons and daughters of God and as brothers and sisters.

VI. The truly successful church reflects a quality of life that is rooted in God's loving action and his expectations and urgings for our lives. It is a quality that enriches our own lives and compels us to want to share it with others through our attitudes, resources, and commitment.—James W. Dyson.

SUNDAY: SEPTEMBER TWENTY-THIRD

MORNING SERVICE

Topic: **The Last Generation (Christian Education Sunday)**
TEXT: Isa. 53:11 (RSV).

I. Why doesn't the church get with it? Why doesn't it shed what some would call the unnecessary baggage of the past? Why does it persist in its peculiar sense of history? Why does it insist that church school children become familiar with the story of ancient Israel or the mores of a bygone religious movement?

(a) Perhaps the answer lies quite simply in the fact that the church, as a community with a long history, also has a longer memory than any single generation of human beings. The church is a community that remembers.

(b) Its faith is not a set of abstract principles or vague ideals which humans make up afresh each morning or in every new generation. Its faith is a recital of deeds actually recorded in the real world of history. God did something! In the history of Israel and in the subsequent life of the Christian church—the new Israel—God proved himself to be the creator and savior of human life and destiny, the only force in life worth loving with all one's heart and soul and mind.

(c) The Bible is an old book, but its story covers many hundreds of years. One of its early heroes looked back as he spoke to the people of Israel and reminded them of their heritage. "Remember who you are!" Moses said in effect, "You are a people with a name, a history, a meaningful present existence, a sense of purpose, an undying hope, and a destiny. Why? Because the Lord rescued you from slavery to the Egyptians and led you into freedom so that you could remember and be the rememberer for all humankind. You were saved in order to remind the people of all nations that in their experience and in their need they have a divine helper, a deliverer, and a savior. What God has done in the past gives us a true understanding of who and what we are in the present.

II. One of the basic purposes of any program of Christian education in the church is to prod our collective memories and to remind us of what God has done so we may sense where it is we are going. The modern world desperately needs this old-fashioned recital which the church embodies in her history, for our culture knows much about the mechanics of life on this planet but little about its final purpose and meaning.

(a) "The fear of the Lord is the beginning of wisdom; fools despise wisdom and instruction" (Prov. 1:7). By "fear" is meant not terror or fright but the healthy sense of awe and respect by which a person acknowledges that God has a plan and a purpose for human life which we neglect only at our own peril. The central purpose of the whole teaching venture within the church is to remind men and women and children of their destiny, to ensure them

that they are the sons and daughters of God, and to lift them to a better life by virtue of their having been created in the image of the eternal God.

(b) That kind of knowledge of who we are, that kind of recital, and that kind of education cannot be carried out in a vacuum or in a neutral environment. It is more than a transmittal of facts; it is a sharing of knowledge. But neutral people cannot share this knowledge; it can only be transmitted by caught-up people, by committed people, and by enthusiastic on-fire-with-the-good-news people.

(c) This type of education cannot be limited to a classroom. It flourishes in a faith community which literally grounds its every word and thought and deed in the memory of what God has meant in the past. We cannot expect our culture to instill in our children this biblical sense of the sacredness of life; our culture is too secularized and too caught up with the material aspects of existence.

III. The great religious faiths by which mankind is inspired and lives are composed not of abstract thoughts of peace and goodness. They are associated with events and persons to be remembered. This is a superb definition of Christian education.

(a) It is up to us to seek and cherish that education. Men and women, if they really love the Lord God with all their heart and all their soul and all their mind, will want to bring their children to know him and to value him. Yet both by neglecting to take seriously the program of church education and even by outright rejection of it there are many parents who seem to be saying: "I'm not going to force my child. I don't believe in indoctrination. I don't believe in influencing so young a mind with any particular religious opinion until it is able to choose its own brand of religion."

(b) We must impart the knowledge of the past. We must show forth the good news of the gospel in our lives. All of us who belong to the Christian community share the responsibility. If we dwell and worship in a place where the spirit and the joy of our faith can be felt, a place where love and acceptance are contagious, a place where God is obviously loved with heart and soul and mind, and a place where "first things" are first, then the sense of divine destiny which shapes us will be caught by each new generation.

(c) Someone has suggested that every child is a first-generation Christian; he must receive the faith within the context of family and church or he will not receive it at all. By the same token we might say that every generation is potentially the last generation of the Christian faith unless it realizes anew its responsibility to give this eternal inheritance to the children of the next generation.—Otto E. Sommer.

Illustrations

QUESTION. The question for all of us is not whether man is basically good or evil but how best to bring out the good and cope with the evil.—Norman Cousins.

SINGULAR. It is the wonderful property of the Bible, though the authorship is spread over a long list of centuries, that it never withdraws any truth once advanced and never adds new without giving fresh force to the old.—Andrew Melville.

Sermon Suggestions

CHRISTIAN GUIDANCE. Text: Ps. 32:8–9. (1) A divine way that we must go. (2) A divine will that we must know. (3) A divine wisdom that we must show.—Stephen F. Olford.

GOD'S WORD IN HUMAN EXPERIENCE. Scripture: Acts 8:26–39. (1) Reading God's word (vv. 8:27–28, 32–33). (2) Understanding God's word (vv. 8:29–31, 34–35). (3) Obeying God's word (vv. 8:36–38).—W. Clyde Tilley.

Worship Aids

CALL TO WORSHIP. "Delight thyself also in the Lord; and he shall give thee the desires of thine heart. Commit thy way unto the Lord; trust also in him; and he shall bring it to pass." Ps. 37:4–5.

INVOCATION. Almighty God, who hast given us minds to know thee, hearts to love thee, and voices to show forth thy praise, we would not know thee if thou hadst not already found us. Help us to know thee with pure minds and to praise thee with a clear voice.

OFFERTORY SENTENCE. "Every good gift and every perfect gift is from above, and cometh down from the Father of lights." Jas. 1:17.

OFFERTORY PRAYER. We pray thee, O God, to give us sight to see the Christ, the insight to choose him, the steadfastness to follow him, and the stewardship of loyalty represented in these gifts offered in his name.

LITANY. Father, we thank thee for the fact that thou art unchangeable, the one secure foundation in an insecure world:
Father, we thank thee.
For the prophets, apostles, priests, martyrs, and all those who have revealed thee to us in thy dazzling completeness:
Father, we thank thee.
For the artists, musicians, writers, scientists, and doctors who have been used by thee to unlock for us the secrets of beauty, health, wisdom, and justice:
Father, we thank thee.
For the courage our Lord gives us when he shows us how to live and how to die:
Father, we thank thee.
For the knowledge that we are not alone and that we have a divine companion who has walked the road before us and though unseen walks the road beside us:
Father, we thank thee.
For the sure faith that amidst all the troubles of life we can be more than conquerors through Christ who loves us:
Father, we thank thee.
For thy grace and strength given to us through thy holy sacraments:
Father, we thank thee.
For the gift of our redemption through Jesus Christ who brings us into the fellowship of thy love:
Father, we thank thee.

EVENING SERVICE

Topic: Discovering Your Gifts
Scripture: I Cor. 12.

If the Spirit has endowed each of us with a gift and if our gift is vital to the healthy working of the body of Christ, then it is extremely important that everyone discovers what his gift is. There are several steps that will help us to discover our spiritual gifts.

I. *Acceptance.* There are many people who never discover their gift because they do not believe they have one. They never look for it. The Bible says that every Christian has at least one gift. Acceptance of the fact is the beginning point in discovering what your gift is.

II. *Awareness.* The list of gifts in I Cor. 12, Rom. 12, Eph. 4, and I Pet. 4 are not exhaustive, but they are exemplary. Study the texts. Examine the gifts. Analyze ways in which God has gifted people in the past. You might not have the gift to teach, but you might have the gift of helps. You might not have the gift to preach, but you might have the gift of craftsmanship. Expand your mind with the possible gifts with which God endows an individual Christian. Become aware of what the gifts are.

III. *Appeal.* What do you enjoy doing? What are you good at? God reveals his will to us sometimes in the very normal, common sense experiences of life through the things that appeal to us.

IV. *Asking.* Prayer needs to be a key part of discovering your gift. "You have not because you ask not" (Jas. 4:2). Prayer is our tool for discovering the will and purpose of God, and it is vital in discovering our gift. Ask God to show you what your gifts are.

V. *Association.* One of the most marvelous results of Christian fellowship is that someone else often sees something in us that we do not see ourselves. Rufus Jones called this "finding the life cue." Others often will find the life cue in our lives and draw it out and in so doing help us to find our gift.

VI. *Action.* Many people get so caught up in discovering their gift that they never do anything for God. They spend all their time analyzing themselves. We don't have to discover our specific gift before we act. As we act in Christian love and as we minister to other members of the body of Christ, our gift or gifts will become increasingly clear to us and to others as we act. And as we look back at our past ministries in Christ's name, we will say, "Oh, that is the gift that God has given me to use."—Brian L. Harbour.

SUNDAY: SEPTEMBER THIRTIETH

MORNING SERVICE

Topic: The Way of the Few
Text: Matt. 7:13–14.

We think of ourselves as unique; we are obsessed by our uniqueness. This obsession with our uniqueness is exemplified by a cliché, "We live in a rapidly changing world." Never before, we like to think, have people had to cope with living in a time of such rapid change. I would like to submit to you the proposition that nothing has changed, that our time, far from being unique, is in all important respects no different from any other in history and not more complex or confusing and not more difficult or demanding.

I. The fact is that it has always been costly and lonely to be honest and to dare to care. Things are no more complex and no more difficult now than they were then.

(a) When the prophet Amos came into the city of Samaria 2500 years ago, he deplored that society's degeneracy and called for a return to the old values of honesty, respect, compassion, and self-sacrifice. The affluent of Samaria would hear none of it. Those old values, they said, had no meaning in the modern world. They were irrelevant to contemporary life. When Amos refused to buy the argument that these values were irrelevant, when he refused to shut up, and when he challenged the complacent self-indulgence of his listeners, he was driven out of the city. "Get out of here, you troublemaker," they cried.

(b) Socrates in ancient Athens was sentenced to death for challenging the self-satisfied Athenians. When a group of well-intentioned friends tried to persuade him to let them sneak him out of town, Socrates refused. His friends were indignant; they didn't really believe that one should suffer for one's convictions. Victimized by his fellow townsmen and unsupported by his friends, Socrates remained in Athens to die for what he thought was right.

(c) When Jesus of Nazareth challenged by the sincerity and commitment of his life the smug complacency of the scribes and Pharisees and when he challenged their materialism, their dishonesty, their sophisticated self-indulgence, and their keeping-up-with-the-Joneses morality, he was first threatened and then put to death.

(d) It is difficult and costly in every generation for the few to stand for honesty, compassion, and sincere commitment to others. The few will be laughed at and ridiculed, and if they persist and won't go away, then they will often be silenced. The prophets of Israel were stoned, Socrates was sentenced to death, Jesus of Nazareth was crucified, and Martin Luther King was assassinated.

II. We are faced with exactly the same choice people have always been faced with. Will we be on the side of the many or the few? Will we choose the easy way or the hard? Will we rationalize our way to sophisticated self-indulgence, or will we dare to choose the hard and often the lonely way of sacrifice, honesty, sincerity, and commitment to others?

(a) The quality of life in each generation is determined by the few individuals who dare to care. Jesus said to the tiny band of people who followed him, "You are the salt of the earth." We know from our own experience that a few tiny grains of salt can transform the taste of a whole meal. So, Jesus said, a tiny number of apparently insignificant individuals-who-care can transform society.

(b) It has never been easy to be the "salt of the earth" and to be individuals-who-

care. Jesus never said it would be easy. Unlike the modern politician, Jesus never promised a rose-garden to those who followed him. His was not the appeal of the relentless television commercial: do this and enjoyment and ease will follow. False prophets with cheap promises abound in every generation.

III. Real Christianity is going the last mile and then some.

(a) Try as we can to rationalize away the commands of Jesus, we cannot alter their demanding imperative, "Go, sell what you have—your talents and your abilities—and give to the poor—to those whom you meet every day who are impoverished of love, of values, and of meaning—and come and follow me." The young man to whom Jesus said these words, a man who had apparently much to give the world, went away sorrowful when he heard Jesus' words. They were too hard. He wanted something easier.

(b) There is another way. Those who choose it have always been a small minority, sometimes seemingly a minority of one. This other way is harder, more costly, and more lonely; it is even heartbreaking at times. It is the way of the few who try to follow Jesus. It is the way of the few who dare to try to care all the way.

(c) Whatever else this way is, it is not dull. In the end it is not only more interesting and a lot more fun. It is the only way to real happiness. That must be why Jesus can say in his divinely mysterious way to those from whom he asks so much: "Come unto me. My yoke is easy, my burden is light."—F. Washington Jarvis.

Illustrations

LOOKING HIGH. Earl Marlatt once was a private in the U. S. Army. Like many another young man, he had many things to learn about army discipline and routine. One of his greatest problems was to learn how to march straight. After many reprimands from his sergeant, he went to his brother who was soldiering in the same outfit and said: "I can't be a soldier, I can't even march straight." His brother replied: "Sure, you can. All you have to do is to pick out something high against the sky, such as a flag or a tree or a church spire, and walk straight for it. You'll march straight if you look high enough."—Homer J. R. Elford.

ANSWERED PRAYER. In his early years Winston Churchill served as a war correspondent in South Africa, writing for the London *Morning Post.* Churchill often was in danger, and he prayed for protection, never neglecting to express gratitude when danger was past. Describing an escape from Pretoria on one occasion he wrote, "I realize with awful force that no exercise of my own feeble wit and strength could save me from my enemies and that without the assistance of the high power which interferes in the eternal sequence of causes and effects more often than we are always prone to admit, I could never succeed. I prayed long and earnestly for help and guidance. My prayer, as it seems to me, was swiftly and wonderfully answered."—John H. Townsend.

Sermon Suggestions

ONE THING. (1) The reply of Jesus to the rich young ruler was "One thing thou lackest" (See Mark 10:21.) (2) When Martha criticized her sister, Jesus said to her, "One thing is needful" (See Luke 10:42.) (3) The man who received sight at the hands of Jesus said, "One thing I know" (See John 9:25.) (4) The psalmist said: "One thing have I desired of the Lord, that will I seek after" (See Ps. 27:-4.)

THE MIND OF CHRIST. Text: Phil. 2:5. (1) An awareness of God as reality nearer than breathing and closer than hands and feet. (2) An awareness of human need as offering the best opportunity to serve God. (3) A dependence upon forgiveness received and given as the essence of life. (4) An acceptance of the peace of Christ as our legacy from our Lord. (5) A compulsion to witness to truth by word and deed. (6) An ability to live at once in both time and eternity.—John W. Meister.

Worship Aids

CALL TO WORSHIP. "O come, let us sing unto the Lord: let us make a joyful noise to the rock of our salvation. Let us come before his presence with thanksgiving, and make a joyful noise unto him with psalms." Ps. 95:1-2.

INVOCATION. Almighty God, fountain of all good, kindle in us insight and aspiration, that this hour of prayer may be a moment of time lived in eternity. Open our ears that we may hear. Soften our hearts that we may receive thy truth. Reveal thyself to us here that we may learn to find thee everywhere.

OFFERTORY SENTENCE. "Give, and it shall be given unto you; good measure, pressed down, and shaken together, and running over." Luke 6:38.

OFFERTORY PRAYER. Our Father, may we who have seen thy providential hand in all the experiences of our lives seek to possess such greatness of mind and spirit that we shall be enabled to offer these gifts with an unselfish joyfulness.

PRAYER. O God, who speaketh in the language of love to the hearts of men, we rejoice in thy word spoken to us through our Lord Jesus Christ. Help us with open minds and responsive wills to receive him, full of grace and full of truth.

In the name of Christ we come unto thee, O God, that we may hear thy word of forgiveness. We bow before thee with repentant hearts; we have departed from thy ways and failed to love thee and our fellow men; we have hurt the world in which we live. Grant unto us thy word of forgiveness, and may we be quick to hear it and to give it heed.

How often, O God, we have received thy word of grace! Added strength has been given to us to meet the duties of the day. Our Master has spoken, and we have taken up our beds and walked. Through Christ, O God, thou hast spoken peace and confidence and joy unto our hearts. Accept, we pray, our thanksgiving for all thy lovingkindness. As we have freely received, help us, O Lord, freely to give. May our lips speak truth and grace. May our lives carry messages of loving concern to all whom we meet. May they witness to the grace and truth which came through Jesus Christ.

EVENING SERVICE

Topic: The New Covenant
SCRIPTURE: Jer. 31:31–34.
Jeremiah speaks of this new covenant or relationship with God. It is one of the mountain peaks in the Bible, and when you read it you feel you are being lifted to new heights. There are some vital characteristics of this new covenant.

I. The new covenant, like the old one made at Sinai, is centered in the initiative of God. He makes the offer, and the people are invited to respond. It is not between equals. We need to remember that God is "down-front" in the Bible and mightily at work in the arena of history. He is the protagonist.

II. Working through the new covenant, God will write his law in the hearts of his people. God will speak to us not on tablets of stone, but he will come through to the very inner center of our being. We can make a highly personal response to God. We see that inwardness especially in the sermon on the mount.

III. The new covenant will bring about a new community. "I will be their God, and they shall be my people" is essential to the covenant. Western Christianity easily picks up on the one-to-one relationship with God, but Jeremiah would stress the community of the faithful as well. Are you not only loyal to God but loyal also to the people who are loyal to God?

IV. The knowledge of God is not so much knowledge about God but a personal fellowship with God. More than securing information about God, the people are called to know God as one friend knows another in close trust and loving relationship. And forgiveness is basic in this relationship. God not only comes through in judgment, pulling down the idols and destroying the pride of people, but now he also graciously forgives them. It is good to know that when we are vulnerable to God he enters us as gracious reality.—Robert C. Brubaker.

SUNDAY: OCTOBER SEVENTH

MORNING SERVICE

Topic: More than Bread (World Communion Sunday)
TEXT: John 6:35, 51.
I. Throughout the Bible bread served as a great symbol. As early as the book of Exodus we find reference made to "the bread of the presence." It was called "shew bread" because it showed or witnessed to the presence of God. It consisted of an offering of twelve loaves of bread which signified the twelve tribes of Israel. These were always to be in front of the ark of the covenant or the holy of holies which contained the ten commandments and symbolized the presence of God. Fresh loaves were set out each week, and the old loaves were eaten by the priests of the temple. Those who ate of it were to be ceremonially clean.

II. When David returned with his hungry soldiers from a fierce battle and could find no other food for them, he demanded the "shew bread" from the altar to feed them. It was given to him only after he assured the priests that his soldiers were ceremonially clean. Jesus was later to recall this incident when the Pharisees were arguing with him about keeping the sabbath. His hungry disciples had plucked some corn along the way and eaten it. (See Matt. 12:1–4.)

III. Like David before him, Jesus was emphasizing the fact that the needs of people are to be considered of far greater importance than ceremonial rules and rituals. That was why Jesus said, "The sabbath was made for man, not man for the sabbath." It was not that Jesus did not have a high and holy respect for the sacred symbols. Rather it was because he had a much higher and infinitely more holy regard for people. He was seeking to show that he shared with the highly respected David the conviction that such symbols as the "shew bread" or "the bread of the presence" was meant to signify and make available to people the continuing, strengthening, and life-saving power of God.

IV. Against that background and understanding of the deeply significant symbolism of bread as used in services of worship, after having eaten the Passover meal, Jesus took bread, and when he had given thanks, he broke it, saying, "Take eat, this is my body which is broken for you." Earlier he had said of himself, "I am the bread of life" and thereby identified himself with God, whose incarnation he was. As the manna provided the Israelites in the wilderness sustained life for them and made it possible for them to fulfill their hopes and expectations of reaching the promised land, so Jesus is giving assurance that he will sustain the lives of all who believe in him. If they take him to themselves and allow him to nourish their inmost beings, he will enable them to fulfill their hopes and expectations of attaining a quality of life which is worthy of living forever.

V. Do you wonder that Christians look upon the bread they receive at the altar as something infinitely more than bread? It is for them a symbol of the very presence of God as he revealed himself in Christ. We truly believe Christ is present at this service and in the bread, even as we believe he is always and everywhere present in all things made by his heavenly Father and our Father. The fragments of bread remind us, as the fragments of bread in the Passover reminded the disciples and as they remind the Jews today, that we can never experience more than a part of the life of God in our own little lives. He is too great, too wonderful, too powerful, too high, and too holy for mortal man to comprehend or fully to experience. But as we receive even this small symbol of his divine presence, we are renewed in the inner man.

VI. It is because all of us, "what'er our name or sign," have found in the bread of the sacrament something far more than bread that we have obeyed our Lord's command and do this in remembrance of him. People in a wide variety of worshipful situations are today approaching the altar and taking this holy sacrament to their comfort. We know that in the Bible the term "comfort" is a near-relative to the word "strength," so we take Christ's strength to ourselves that we may go forth to serve him more effectively.

VII. Today he offers us more than bread as we gather before and around his table. He offers us life. He offers us strength. He offers us himself. Why? That we may receive power from on high to go forth and help him meet the great needs of the world's people. Let us not fail to dedicate ourselves, our souls and bodies to be a reasonable, holy, and lively sacrifice unto him that he may use us as instruments of his peace and his work of reconciliation and redemption.— Homer J. R. Elford.

Illustrations

TWO WORLDS.   We used to think of our world as being divided into East and West. We are now starting to think of it as divided into North and South with the dividing line drawn at about the 38th parallel of latitude. North of the 38th parallel are most of the developed and industrialized nations. South of that parallel are most of the world's people who live in what is known as the "third world" or "developing world." The two worlds are very different. One is rich and one poor, one literate and one largely illiterate, one overfed and overweight and one malnourished and hungry, and one affluent and one poverty-stricken. North of the 38th parallel life expectancy is seventy years; south of it the average life expectancy is thirty-seven. North of the 38th parallel is the United States of America, where six percent of the world's people live, use thirty percent of the world's energy, and own fifty percent of the world's wealth. The gap between the "haves" and the "have-nots" is widening. Growing inequities and the rising expectations of those in the "developing world" threaten to cause violence.

INCREASE OF LOVE. The reality of our communion with Christ and in him with one another is the increase of love in our hearts. If a man goes out from his communion to love and serve men better he has received the real presence. If he feels every thrill and tremor of devotion but goes out as selfish as before, he has not received it. It was offered, but he did not receive it.—William Temple.

Sermon Suggestions

A SERVANT CHURCH. Text: Matt. 20:28. (1) A servant church has open doors. (2) A servant church helps people. (3) A servant church is a pilgrim church. (4) A servant church sets priorities on its ministries. (5) A servant church serves love and justice without fear for its own safety. (6) A servant church has a ministry to the whole world. (7) A servant church is comprehensive in its ministries, taking the New Testament church as a model.

WHAT COMMUNION MEANS. Text: Exod. 12:26. (1) It means commemoration. (2) It means communion. (3) It means commitment. (4) It means consecration.—Murdo Ewen Macdonald.

Worship Aids

CALL TO WORSHIP. "The cup of blessing which we bless, is it not the communion of the blood of Christ? The bread which we break, is it not the communion of the body of Christ? For we being many are one bread, and one body: for we are all partakers of that one bread." I Cor. 10:-16–17.

INVOCATION. Most gracious Father, who withholdest no good thing from thy children and in thy providence hast brought us to this day of rest and of the renewal of the soul: we give thee humble and hearty thanks for the world which thou hast prepared and furnished for our dwelling place, for the steadfast righteousness which suffers no evil thing to gain the mastery, for the lives and examples of those who were strangers and pilgrims and found a better inheritance in peace of soul and joy in the Holy Spirit, and above all for the life, teaching, and sacrifice of thy Son our Savior Jesus Christ.

OFFERTORY SENTENCE. "Walk in love, as Christ also hath loved us, and hath given himself for us as an offering and sacrifice to God." Eph. 5:2.

OFFERTORY PRAYER. Cleanse and accept these our gifts, O God, and may they be used according to thy will to redeem, restore, and renew the ministries within thy kingdom.

PRAYER. Out of our need, our frailty, and our human insufficiency we turn to thee, our God, in prayer. Thou hast been very good to us in our lives, surrounding us with blessings in greater abundance than we can deserve or understand. Never hast thou required that we manage life alone, but always in our times of need thou hast been beside us, ministering to us even in ways that we did not recognize. Thy power has undergirded us in our weakness, thy light has guided us in our perplexities, and thy protection has encompassed us in danger.

In confidence of thy goodness and great mercy we lift up to thee the inmost desires of our hearts, trusting thee to satisfy them according to thy will. Thou knowest what is good for us better than we know ourselves. We lay before thee our most intimate concerns: the responsibilities of our daily work, the care of those who depend upon us, our duties as parents and providers, the health of our bodies and minds, and the secret agonies and anxieties that we cannot share even with our closest friends. O minister to us from the fulness of thy mercy, and grant that even in this moment of holy converse with thee we shall feel the indwelling of spiritual resources that will make us adequate to life's demands.

Not for ourselves only do we pray but for all thy children who stand in need of a power beyond their own, those whom we can name before thee and those known only to thyself. Come close this day to discouraged souls whose spirit has been broken on the wheel of living and save them from their despair in the faith that thou dost cooperate in all things for good with those who love thee. Take the sorrowful into thy comforting arms, soothe the bodies of those who are racked by pain, quiet the turbulent minds of all who are obsessed by worry, and ease the burdens of all who struggle under privation and hardship.

We beseech thee for our wider relationships. Earnestly we pray for a renewal of high purpose in the hearts of all our people that we shall not be intimidated by the loss of any material prestige but may grow stronger in spirit and may give to the world those deep, abiding values which belong to our best heritage.—Leonard Griffith.

EVENING SERVICE

Topic: The Church in Our Kind of World
TEXT: I Tim. 3:15.

I. The Christian knows by faith that no structure of society and no system of human power and security is perfectly just, and that every system falls under the judgment of God insofar as it is unable to reform itself in response to the call of justice of those who are under its power. The Christian is therefore called to speak a radical "no"—and to act accordingly—to structures of power which perpetuate and strengthen the status quo at the cost of justice to those who are its victims.

II. The Christian lives in the world by the hope of the final victory of Christ over the powers of this age. He therefore sees the struggle for justice and true humanity in our time under the signs of this hope. But because Christ has risen from the death to which perverted human power put him, Christians are called to work to transform human society at every point in the hope that God will use their work for good whether they succeed or fail.

III. The church is called in the world to be that part of the world which responds to God's love for all men and to become therefore the community in which God's relation to man is known and realized. The church is in one sense the center and fulfillment of the world. In another it is the servant of the world and the witness to it of the hope of the future. It is called to be the community in which the world can discover itself as it may become in the future. When it does not fulfill this mission and reflects the prejudices of the world, as is often the case, it is not faithful to its calling.—World Conference on Church and Society.

SUNDAY: OCTOBER FOURTEENTH

MORNING SERVICE

Topic: Advertising Christ (Laity Sunday)
TEXT: Matt. 5:16.

By the commission of our Lord we who bear his name are in the advertising business. "Ye shall be witnesses unto me," he says. While it is the business of business to sell goods, it is your business as Christians to sell that particular brand of goodness found in Christ. It is possible that our failure to sell him more effectively lies in faulty methods of advertising. Put together the failure of Christians in selling goodness and the success of business in selling goods, and what it comes to is the opportunity of Christians to learn from business how better to advertise Christ. So consider the principles of advertising to see what light they can throw upon our text.

I. The first requisite of a good advertisement is that it must be seen. Signs are placed on buildings to get hold of your attention. Lights flicker on and off because a moving object gets your attention more quickly than does a stationary one. Yellow is the dominant color in most advertisements because yellow gets attention more quickly than does any other color. An effective advertisement must be seen. So Jesus says, "Let your light so shine before men that they may see. . . ."

(a) There are two ways by which you can hide the light that is in you.

(1) The first is by denial in deed of the truth you profess to believe. When our Lord was being tried before the high priest, Simon Peter sat in the courtyard outside. A maid came up and said to him, "You were with the Galilean too." But Peter denied it before them all. "I do not know what you mean," he said. You might call Peter the original white-feathered Christian, but he was not the last one. The consciences of all of us plague us with memories of times when we might have taken a stand for Christ and did not.

(2) A second way you can keep the light from being seen is by failing to seem as Christian as you are. There is a certain modesty which distrusts pretension in religion. You do not want to be seen wearing your heart religiously on your sleeve. And in trying to stand up straight and not seem better than you are, you fall over backward and fail to seem as good as you are.

(3) You know well what Jesus thought of those hypocrites who seemed better than they were. "Whited sepulchres," he called them, "which outwardly appear beautiful but inwardly are full of dead men's bones." But that is not the only kind of hypocrites he knew. He talked about those people who failed to seem as good as they were. (See Matt. 5:15.) To have light and keep it dark, to have some faith in Christ in you and hide it and to refuse to set it out where it can be seen—that is hypocrisy too.

(b) It could be that there are certain secret Christians listening now. You have faith but you consider it is no one's business but your own, and so you say nothing about it and hide it. There is a double danger that you face. Cover up a light and it will go out, and so you may lose your faith; and secondly, you will be held accountable in the day of judgment for those who took their cue from you and remained in the dark.

II. Commercial advertising says that to be effective an advertisement must be read. There must be about it a certain something that will awaken sufficient interest in the person who sees it to make him read further.

(a) You have to take off your hat to the ingenious creations of these propagandists of commerce. Sit down to read a magazine and before you know it you are so fascinated by the advertisements that you have little time left for the articles. These advertising men know that they must not only get your attention but hold it; and with colors, with pictures, and with bits of verse here and narrative there they achieve an attractiveness which holds your attention until you have read what they have to tell you.

(b) There is a notion that there is nothing interesting about being a Christian. In the verses which lead up to the text our Lord speaks of his followers as not only the light of the world but also as the salt of the earth. In the climate of Palestine salt was an item of value; a bag of salt was as precious as a man's life. There are two qualities possessed by salt: it gives taste to food and it preserves it from spoiling.

(c) There are many people for whom life has either lost its taste or has taken on a bad taste. And the number is even larger of those for whom life not only tastes bad but is bad. It has spoiled, gone rotten, and is fast decaying. And whenever in an office or a business organization you find a man who is like salt, whose faith puts meaning into life and adds zest to living, and in whom there is a power which keeps his marriage on an even keel, which saves him from the ravages of liquor, and which gives him peace of mind and the ability to rise above disappointment, there will be those who turn to him in time of need. It is the method of salt that it works quietly. The point is that it works. And people are looking for something that will work.

(d) There is not a home where you will not find salt in the kitchen. It is there because it is needed. Fortunate is that business organization in whose personnel there are Christians whose lives are like salt. They are written epistles which will not only be seen but read with absorbing interest.

III. Your advertising friend will tell you that to be effective an advertisement must be believed. Not only must it be seen and read but it must also possess a genuineness which will make it believed. Any dishonesty in advertising is suicidal.

(a) In the same way does our Lord lose out when his followers display in their show windows values which they do not carry in stock. (See John 1:14.) Jesus' religion was a seven-day-in-the-week affair. Had there been any discrepancy between what he professed and what he practiced, you and I would know nothing about him today because he would not have lasted this long.

(b) There is no more damaging thing that can be said about a product than that its advertising is dishonest. In the home or at the office, anyone who names the name of Christ but who cancels his creed by his conduct is a liability to his church and to its Lord. The early Christians won their victory over a pagan world because they lived their faith, and it will not be otherwise in our time.

IV. A good advertisement must secure decision and get action. Even if an advertisement is seen and read and believed, it is worthless to the advertiser unless it gets action. The advertisements that you see and hear never leave you without urging you the next time you go to the store to try a can of soup or a bar of soap.

(a) You know people in whom you see nothing that makes you want to be different; they leave you just as they found you. You know others who seem to possess a quality of life which you have never experienced, and they leave you with a hunger for that something which you seem to be missing. Then and there you make your decision not to stop short of possessing it.

(b) Jesus possessed that power of advertising the good life in a way that made men want it. Nicodemus came at night seeking it. Peter and John looked him up in the crowd and said, "Rabbi, we want to go home with you." The Greeks said to the disciples, "Sirs, we would see Jesus." And all along the way you find those who do the same thing. In Cambridge they had a way of saying that every time Phillips Brooks walked across Harvard Yard another student decided for the Christian ministry. Someone asked a Scottish student why he was a Christian, and he said, "It was the way Henry Drummond put his hand on my shoulder and looked me in the face that led me to Christ."

(c) It would be much easier if we could let our life speak for us and never have to say anything to anybody about being a Christian. And yet if we are going to get action, the time will come when we must go to see a man and sit down and talk with him and invite him to join our circle of the friends of Jesus.

(d) Several years ago the elders and deacons were asked to find one man each and introduce him to Christ. I know one deacon who took his job seriously and, although it took him two years, he finally landed his man. And I am sure that is one of the deepest satisfactions he knows.

(e) I want to put that proposition to you men. You want to know what you can do in the work of the church. Here is something you can do which is the primary task of the church. If each man who is a member of this church found one other man who is not a Christian—just one—and introduced him to Christ, think what it would mean for the life of our city. One thousand more men playing on Christ's team! And think what it would mean to your church. And think what it would mean to you. I have no doubt it is the thing of which you will be proudest when the time comes to look your Lord in the face. —John A. Redhead.

Illustrations

AN OLD TALE.   During the dark of the night two British vessels approached each other on the high seas. One fearing the other to be an enemy fired upon her. She returned the fire. They battled on through the night. When came the dawn, can you imagine the horror of their seeing tattered British flags flying from the staff of both ships? When dawn comes, we may be horribly embarrassed to discover we have been doing war with our allies, not our enemies.—T. V. Warnick.

COLUMBUS DAY MEMO. Columbus discovered America by accident while seeking to prove that one could reach India by sailing west from Europe as well as east. Too often we act as if the American nation could be brought to fruition in an incidental manner by concentrating first on personal and group goals, then attending to the nation's concerns. Many individuals do this. Much of big business does this. Numerous institutions do the same. These say our profits and position and prestige first, then the nation's matters will come out all right. Columbus Day is an excellent time for us to discover that sailing in this direction will never lead us to the land that America is meant to be. We will reach this destination only if our own ships and the ship of state are turned in the direction of the interests of the whole people.—Herschel T. Hamner.

Sermon Suggestions

UNDERSTANDING THE LORD. Text: II Pet. 3:18. (1) He animates every Christian impulse. (2) He guides every Christian strategy. (3) He illuminates every perplexity and eases every anxiety.—Robert S. Bilheimer.

DISCIPLES WITH RESERVATIONS. Scripture: Luke 9:57–62. (1) The first man said in effect, "Lord, I will follow you but not to the point of self-denying devotion." (2) The second man said in effect, "Lord, I will follow you but not to the point of giving you absolute priority." (3) The third man said in effect, "Lord, I will follow you but not to the point of giving you my exclusive attention."—Leonard Griffith.

Worship Aids

CALL TO WORSHIP. "Thy word is a lamp unto my feet, and a light unto my path. I have sworn, and I will perform it, that I will keep thy righteous judgments. Quicken me, O Lord, according unto thy word." Ps. 119:105–107.

INVOCATION. Lord God Almighty, holy and eternal Father, who dwellest in the high and lofty place, with him also that is of a humble and contrite spirit: we come before thee, beseeching thee to cleanse us by the grace of thy Holy Spirit, that we may give praise to thee, now and forever.

OFFERTORY SENTENCE. "Every man according as he purposeth in his heart, so let him give; not grudgingly, or of necessity: for God loveth a cheerful giver." II Cor. 9:7.

OFFERTORY PRAYER. Dear Lord and Savior of us all, may we become obedient to thy will both in the dedication of our tithes and of our talents.

PRAYER. O God, our heavenly Father, we thank thee for the life thou hast given us. We thank thee for the privilege of citizenship in this our native land. Help us each to have a part in making it a land of righteousness and of justice for all. May we realize that it was no choice of ours that gave us the citizenship, and so may we cherish it as a gift to be honored and used wisely and justly.

Yet may we remember, O Lord, that our citizenship in our country is but for a few years, and then we shall find our home in eternity. For this reason we praise thy name for the everlasting kingdom of our Lord and Savior to whose citizenship thou hast called us. Help us to cherish this privilege above all else and to earnestly strive to share it with all the peoples of the earth, for thou dost love them all.—*The Lookout.*

EVENING SERVICE

Topic: Paul's Advice to Church Members

SCRIPTURE: Rom. 12:9–13.

This is Paul's advice to those who are part of the Christian community. It is not addressed to a general audience but to those who belong to the church. The things he mentions and urges here are those things that ought to characterize the lives of dedicated Christians.

I. *Love one another.* (a) Paul's emphasis is that love is the guiding principle of Christian conduct. The Christian, like Christ himself, ought to be known by his loving concern for others.

(b) This ought to be true on more than an individual basis. The Christian church should be known as a group of people who truly love and care about each other. In a world that often exhibits hatred and intolerance, the Christian church ought to be an example for others to follow. The way in which Christians deal with each other says more to the world at large than all the programs and special activities the church can plan. If the church truly wants to influence the world, let its members "love one another with brotherly affection."

(c) How does our church compare with this standard? Paul's world was impressed by the church because it was moved to say, "See how these Christians love one another." Is this said of our church? The world will pay little heed to the church if it sees division and lack of love within it.

II. *Rejoice in your hope.* (a) "Hope" is often a misunderstood word. To many it means a naive kind of wishful thinking. We live in a pessimistic world. Those who express any real hope for a better society, a better church, and a peaceful world are usually looked on as being childish and unrealistic.

(b) Paul was no stranger to the pessimism and hopelessness of the world. This is why he urged his readers to rejoice in their hope; they had a hope. This word is for us too. Those who are Christians do not have to give in to futility and hopelessness. The Christian's hope is not mere wishful thinking; it is an assurance. Those who believe in God know that he is with them, that Christ has opened a wider life to them, and that the world is moving toward the fulfillment of God's purposes.

(c) Hopelessness is for those who have not heard the gospel. For those who are known by Christ's name, there is a hope that is realistic. Whatever may come now or in the future, we know that God is there, and that is enough to sustain our lives. We cannot know everything the future holds. But what we do know is enough to keep us from despair.

III. *Let love regulate your relationships with all men.* (a) Paul has clearly said that love ought to be a characteristic of the Christian community as members deal with each other. In the next few verses he goes further to say that Christians ought also to treat in love all people, whether Christians or not and whether sympathetic to the gospel or not.

(b) Paul says, "If possible, so far as it depends upon you, live peaceably with all." He is giving a profound truth that we need to grasp. Most of the time we assume our relationship to others depends on them. If others treat us decently, we will treat them decently. If others love us, we will love them. But this is not what Paul says. In words that sound like the sermon on the mount, he says to repay no one evil for evil, never avenge yourselves, and bless those who persecute you.

(c) Paul is talking about our attitude toward others. We cannot be sure how others will treat us, but we can be sure of how we treat them. If there is provocation and strife, let us be sure as Christians that it does not come from us. Let us manifest the spirit of Christ in our dealings with all men and especially toward those who are a part of the household of faith.—John Rutland, Jr.

SUNDAY: OCTOBER TWENTY-FIRST

MORNING SERVICE

Topic: Faith at Work

SCRIPTURE: Luke 19:1–9.

I. At the opening of our story we find Zacchaeus a rich but lonely person. He is filled with anxiety, guilt, and brokenness, and experiences with his fellows have maimed him deeply. Without Christ he finds himself unhappy and unfulfilled. All along he believed that money could purchase peace, contentment, and satisfaction. Money he has, but the aching void in his life only intensifies with the passing years.

II. Zacchaeus had heard about Jesus.

Now he sought him out for himself. The watchword of seeking faith is "Sir, we would see Jesus" (John 12:21). Surely every time you come to church you should come expectantly. You should be communicating to your pastor just one message, "Sir, we would see Jesus." At the turn of the century there were two famous preachers in London. When people came away from hearing one, they were saying, "What a wonderful preacher!" When they came away from the other, they were saying, "What a wonderful Lord!"

III. A first reading of this story seems to suggest that Zacchaeus is the seeker. But then you find that the real seeker is none other than Christ the Lord. He came to Jericho, and passing through he was seeking Zacchaeus. Then beyond Jericho to Jerusalem he came to the cross seeking you and seeking me. "The Son of man has come to seek and to save the lost" (Luke 19:10). Ever since the first sin in the human race, God's persistent question has been, "Adam, where art thou?" (Gen. 3:-9).

IV. When Jesus came to the foot of the tree, he looked up, and there was Zacchaeus. He said, "Zacchaeus, make haste and come down; for I must stay at your house today."

(a) The primary emphasis in any encounter with Christ in the gospel records shows that there must be both the word of truth and the word of grace. You might put it like this, "There you are, and I love you." "There you are" is a word of judgment, not in a sense of condemnation, but in the sense of realistic evaluation. It is an evaluation that is painful but necessary.

(b) In this evaluation he calls us to repentance. He says, "There you are in your brokenness and in your need of me, but I love you," and that changes the word of judgment into a word of forgiveness. It is not destructive but creative, assuring, and redemptive. "There you are, and I love you" is the same as saying, "Make haste, and come down; for I must stay at your house today." (See Rev. 3:20.)

V. Zacchaeus came down and received him joyfully. He opened the door to his house, but the real opening was the openness of restored relationship. Zacchaeus came out of hiding. He dropped his mask, and there was a real openness to Christ. Their fellowship and openness to each other was signified by eating together. It was about the table that the healing occurred.

VI. Always in the Bible a change in behavior derives from a change of heart. Today we call it a new life-style. Good works result from reconciliation; they do not produce it. Here was Zacchaeus making available his resources to meet the needs of the poor.

(a) Social compassion will never save a person, but a person who is truly saved will have social compassion. It is simply a matter of making our deeds fit our words and making our conduct match our profession.

(b) Those who are genuine in the faith are longing to give themselves to people in the world through evangelism and social action. The church should always afford an opportunity for people to show their concern in these ways. In a word, when we feel sorry for someone, we should not be satisfied until we have done something to help.

VII. There is personal authenticity in Zacchaeus' commitment, "If I have defrauded anything I restore it fourfold." Was there ever a time that needed this attitude more than today? People are demanding moral integrity. The youth are crying out, "God, show us authenticity!" Christ has called us to be human, but Christian humanness marches to the beat of a different drum. Zacchaeus marched by that beat.—Walter L. Dosch.

Illustrations

FAITH AND WORKS.   Two men were earnestly disputing the relative importance of faith and works when they came to a ferry over a river. As they started across they asked the ferryman his opinion on the subject. Was it faith by itself or works by themselves that was the Christian duty and the Christian hope? For answer the ferryman pointed to his two oars. "One," he said, "I will call 'faith' and the other 'works.' If I pull only on the right oar, I get nowhere but go round in a circle. Just so if I pull only on the left oar. But when I pull on both oars, then the ferry moves across the river."—Clarence E. Macartney.

LOST ADVANTAGE.   We manufacture everything but men. We blanch cotton, we refine sugar, we strengthen steel, and we shape pottery, but to strengthen or to refine or to shape a single human soul does not enter into our estimate of advantages.—John Ruskin.

TWO COLUMNS.   Horace Bushnell, one-time tutor at Yale, was immensely popular, being first in athletics and first in scholarship. But he was "all at sea" religiously. He wasn't sure what he believed or whether he believed anything. In the winter of 1831 a powerful religious revival swept over Yale, and scores of her ablest men were caught up in the movement. Bushnell held aloof, and a crowd of his young admirers stood with him. These students almost worshiped him. Being a responsible individual, his conscience began to trouble him. He realized that his example was holding back some of these students from a religious experience which might bring great blessing to their lives. He resolved to come to grips with his inner life and his thinking. He would set down a list of negatives and another column of positives. On the negative side he wrote: "(1) I believe that Jesus of Nazareth was nothing more than a shrewd Jewish peasant. (2) I believe that the Bible is a collection of Jewish tales and Chaldean folklore. (3) I see no reason why I should believe in a God at all." Turning to the positive side, after prolonged thought, he was able to write only this: "I do believe that there exists in the essential nature of things an eternal distinction between right and wrong." That was not much, but he resolved to follow the right at whatever cost and it brought him to the feet of Jesus Christ. The result was the commitment of his life to the Christian ministry in which he rendered unique service. The name of Horace Bushnell is most frequently mentioned with that of Phillips Brooks as two spiritual giants of the nineteenth century in America.—John Sutherland Bonnell.

COMPREHENSION. The only direct statement of Jesus which is simple enough for me to comprehend when my heart is breaking or when I'm discouraged or scared is "Follow me." I cannot understand life because life is not understandable. But I can grasp "Follow me."—Eugenia Price.

Sermon Suggestions

HOW ARE WE JUSTIFIED?   Text: Job 9:2. (1) We are justified by God. (See Rom. 8:33.) (2) We are justified by grace. (See Rom. 3:24; Tit. 3:7.) We are justified by blood. (See Rom. 5:9.) (4) We are justified by resurrection. (See Rom. 4:25.) (5) We are justified by life. (See Rom. 5:18.) (6) We are justified by faith. (See Acts 13:39; Rom. 5:1.) (7) We are justified by works. (See Rom. 4:5; Jas. 2:24.) —R. S. Beal.

WHEN FAITH DOESN'T WORK.   Text: Matt. 19:20. (1) Have I faithfully counted the cost? (2) What is God seeking to teach me in this failure? (3) Have I really surrendered my life to let God work his way in me?

Worship Aids

CALL TO WORSHIP.   "I will praise thee with my whole heart. I will worship toward thy holy temple, and praise thy name for thy lovingkindness." Ps. 138:1–2.

INVOCATION.   Father God, we come to this place to ask for a new vision of your presence and a resurrected spirit of life within history and beyond history. We come as humble pilgrims, none of us possessing all faith and knowledge but all of us seeking your truth as it lives in our midst. Be with us now, we pray, that we may be aware of you in a special way and being thus aware that as we live in the world we may be aflame with your joy.— Richard D. Bausman.

OFFERTORY SENTENCE. "He that hath a bountiful eye shall be blessed; for he giveth of his bread to the poor." Prov. 22:9.

OFFERTORY PRAYER. O thou source of all light, open our blind eyes to see the beauty of the world as thy gift, and grant us the will and wisdom to do our part in bringing thy light into dark places.

PRAYER. Bring forth strong persons in the world, O God. Raise up men of wisdom and integrity to govern the nations. Give those who communicate knowledge to the people deep insight into truth. Deliver from their abject condition the millions who suffer from hunger and disease because of ignorance and superstition. As new discoveries and inventions are made, may they be applied only to human welfare and never to human hurt. May those who do the work of the world be given broad vision, deep understanding, and high motives that they may relate their labors to the common good. May it be said of all, "They helped everyone his neighbor; and everyone said to his brother, 'Be of good courage.' "

As we worship today may we rejoice in thy love and in the blessings wrought out for us by Jesus our Savior and Lord. May thy Holy Spirit energize our lives and guide us in our living. Use us individually and collectively to bring about that for which we pray. Help us to do justly, to love kindness, and to walk humbly with thee.—Merlo K. W. Heicher.

EVENING SERVICE

Topic: Four Lies

SCRIPTURE: I John 1:6–10; 2:4, 9.

I don't think anyone likes to be called a liar, especially if it concerns his religious beliefs. After all, how can anyone possibly know what is in the heart of another person? Yet John in his first epistle four times refers to certain kinds of professing Christians as "liars." He uses the word twice, and twice it is clearly implied. Although he doesn't pin the label on anyone in particular, in effect he is saying to every Christian,

"If the shoe fits, wear it."

I. *The first lie.* (See 1:6.) The first liar is the man who says he has fellowship with God but continues to "walk in darkness." The Gnostics in John's day claimed that their spiritual knowledge of God had nothing to do with their behavior. John says to them and to us that no matter how strongly one says he is in the right relationship with God, his words are a lie if his life does not show that he is right with God. I John 3:9 says, "Whosoever is born of God doeth no sin." This doesn't mean that a saved person will be perfect as some would have us believe, but it means that when a person has had a true experience with Christ he will not keep on sinning and know about it. He will not practice sin because when a person has met Jesus in a true experience his life is changed. He is a new creation. His ideas are different, his thinking is different, and his life is different.

II. *The second lie.* (See 1:8.) The second liar is the man who claims to "have no sin," that is, he says he has never sinned.

(a) Many world leaders are asking, "What's wrong with the world?" Many parents of rebellious teenagers are asking, "What's wrong with our country?" The Bible tells us what is wrong. Man has a spiritual disease called "sin." Some would like to call it mistakes or bad judgment, but our problem is sin and the cure is the Lord Jesus.

(b) Man must recognize and realize this. He must face reality, come to Christ, and confess his sin, and then Christ will save him, forgive him, and wash him as clean as snow.

III. *The third lie.* (See 2:4.) The third liar is the man who says, "I know God," but doesn't keep his commandments. Here John moves from the more general "walking in the light" to the specific responsibility to obey the commandments God has given. Obedience to God's commandments are not optional. One who practices deliberately the violation of God's commandments and says, "I know God," is lying.

IV. *The fourth lie.* (See 2:9.) The fourth liar is the man who says, "I am in the light," but does not show his love for his brother in Christ. We as Christians must show love and concern toward the lost and toward fellow Christians. The Bible teaches us that if our brother has anything against us we should get things right with him and then come to God. If we will not forgive our fellow man, neither will the Father forgive us. We cannot be right with God if we are not right with our fellow man. If we say, "I am in the light," but we are not right with our fellow man, we lie. —Sherman Barnette.

SUNDAY: OCTOBER TWENTY-EIGHT

MORNING SERVICE

Topic: Can Death Rob You of Life?
TEXT: I Cor. 15:54–55.

How are we to deal with the fact of death so that we can know the truth of Paul's statement of faith in life's victory over death? Does the Christian faith have the answer? Can it enable us to master death? How can we experience the truth of the statement, "Learning to die is a part of living"?

I. How to react to the certainty of death. (a) One does not have to live very long before he learns that most of us react negatively to the certainty of death.

(1) Some of us are *terror-stricken by the contemplation of death*. We run scared. Dr. Elisabeth Kubler-Ross says, "Death in itself is associated with a bad act, a frightening happening, something that in itself calls for retribution and punishment." Looking at the people in our day, she comments, "Death is still a fearful, frightening happening, and the fear of death is a universal fear even if we think we have mastered it on many levels."

(2) Some of us are *burdened with deep anxiety* when we realize the certainty of death. That may not be anxiety about our own death but the concern about the possible death of loved ones.

(3) Our culture seems caught in a *universal conspiracy to deny the fact of* death. Because we fear it and dread its coming, we do many things to deny that it is real. We seek to camouflage death in so many ways. We make the dead look as if they were only asleep.

(4) There is a *conspiracy of silence about death in our time*. We avoid mention of death because it makes us overly anxious and fearful. We shut our minds to its certainty, choosing to think "less morbid thoughts" about life and living.

(5) Some persons approach the certainty of death with *fatalism*. They sing the old song, "Whatever will be, will be!" We cannot prevent it. We can only let it happen.

(b) There are positive ways of dealing with the certainty of death. (1) We can frame our life in the larger dimension of a faith in life to come. The Christian faces the certainty of death just like anyone else. But he faces it with the assurance that the God who has given us this life will provide for our life beyond the grave. The Christian joins Paul in his song of triumph because he knows he is not alone. God is here. He has the companionship of Jesus as a partner in the process of living and dying and living again. Because of Jesus, the Christian is assured that God has conquered death and that each of us shares in that victory. "Death is swallowed up in victory!"

(2) None can deny the certainty of death. All can be released from its slavery through the faith which believes Jesus when he says, "Because I live, you shall live also." His reference was to life beyond death.

II. How to deal with the fact of death. Accepting the certainty of death is a fact of our life. How are we to deal with this fact of death?

(a) There are many temptations in this regard. (1) We are tempted to accept a *dream-like reaction* which refuses to believe death has come, for instance, to a person dear to us.

(2) The fact of death may well induce a *negative reaction to life*. The temptation is to

"eat, drink, and be merry for tomorrow we may die." Why not live it up now?

(3) There are people who resign themselves to the fact of death and *passively wait for the end.* Some take the way of self-destruction, while others may live and move and breathe but life's significance has gone, and they have experienced a living death of meaning and purpose in life.

(4) Some persons react with *hyperactivity.* Their motto is "So little time and so much to do." All of us are under the sentence of death. "I must keep busy because there is so much to get done before I pass on!" This is often a negative rather than a positive reaction to the fact of death.

(5) Some persons seem determined to *know only negation, anguish, and despair* in the face of death. This is especially true for those who realize their death date is near. It is so easy then to settle for anguish, and despair for death seems to suggest little more than doom, despair, separation, and loneliness.

(b) How can one think positive thoughts in the face of all this?

(1) The Christian is called to think positive thoughts in his response to the fact of death. He will refuse to gloss over the fact of death by denying its existence. He refuses to keep death out of conversation or to disguise the fact of death when it comes to a friend or loved one.

(2) Some people have set the pattern for us by seeking to find a cause greater than their own survival. Tom Dooley is remembered because of this. He threw his life into medical missions by serving the people of southeast Asia. Then he learned he had terminal cancer and gave the last ounces of his energy and the last days of his life in serving this cause which meant more to him than his own comfort and survival.

(3) The Christian learns how to deal with the fact of death by a lifetime of study of the life and teachings of Jesus. As one in his Bible study and devotion moves through the days of Jesus' years among us as one of us, he finds insight into the Christian faith in life and death.

III. Master death through faith. (a) It is a faith you can find in various parts of the Bible. There are some classical chapters of instruction and comfort. Here are accounts of God's dealings with people over the centuries. Here is the unfolding of God's own acts of self-revealing love. Here is the story of how mankind has discovered the basis for assurance that there is life beyond death, and that we will find a Father's welcome into a heavenly home where life continues in his presence. Here are some chapters which have given the religious perspective on life and death to a host of persons.

(b) We master death through faith that life is eternal here and now as well as in the hereafter. The life God has given you is eternal from its inception. We do not wait until our physical death to inherit eternal life. Jesus constantly stressed the importance of your life and mine here and now because it bears the imprint of the divine. You have been created in the image of God. You have been created to be in constant fellowship with the Father through life, through death, and through the life that lies beyond death. When we can have this kind of perspective on life and death, then we can accept death as an integral part of a continuing experience of life.

(c) We master death through faith when we see that the biggest death-threat is not what we call death—the cessation of earthly living—but the death of meaning. The person to be pitied is not the one who faces death in a physical sense but the person for whom all meaning has gone in life. He is the dead one. His is the hopeless situation, if there is such. For until he can once again recapture the glorious joy of being alive in God through Christ and find the meaning and significance which God has given him as a person, he will suffer death without release.

(d) We master death through faith as we share the resurrection hope. The early church was built on the resurrection fact. Listen to those early Christian apostles and you hear them declaring themselves as witnesses of the risen Lord who conquered death and gave life to all persons who would follow in his way. It was the fact that there is a living Lord among us that kept the church alive in an alien and hostile world. It was the assurance that there was life beyond the grave that enabled Christians to be martyred by the thousands rather than to deny their Christ. For some of them it was an experience long desired, for it brought them "home to be with Jesus."

(1) Can death rob you of life? Yes, if you let it. But it need not because Jesus has come to share God's life with us and to give us an understanding about life and death and life beyond death.

(2) Can death rob you of life? Not if your life is "hid with God in Christ," as Paul put it, and not if you have claimed the life that is eternal here and now and beyond the grave in the hereafter.—Hoover Rupert.

Illustration

MISSING BOND. We are living in a culture that is secular. Religion does not play the role that it used to play. This is particularly true for people under forty years of age in this society. When a strong religious bond is missing, there are few things that can hold the culture together.—Richard Hofstader.

Sermon Suggestion

DON'T WORRY. Text: Matt. 6:34. (1) Face up to your worries realistically. (2) Face up to your worries actively, which is to say, do something. (3) Face up to your worries constructively. (4) Face up to your worries presently, that is, now, at the present time. (5) Face up to your worries faithfully.—Charles L. Copenhaver.

Worship Aids

CALL TO WORSHIP. "O love the Lord, all ye his saints: for the Lord preserveth the faithful. Be of good courage, and he shall strengthen your heart, all ye that hope in the Lord." Ps. 31:23–24.

INVOCATION. O heavenly Father, who hast given us a true faith and a sure hope: help us to live as those who believe and trust in the communion of saints, the forgiveness of sins, and the resurrection to life everlasting; and strengthen this faith and hope in us all the days of our life.

OFFERTORY SENTENCE. "God is not unrighteous to forget your work and labor of love, which ye have showed toward his name, in that ye have ministered to the saints, and to minister." Heb. 6:10.

OFFERTORY PRAYER. Our Father, help us who claim to be Christians to bring forth fruit consistent with our profession of faith. May these tithes and offerings be so used that others may hear the glad story of thy redeeming love.

PRAYER. O thou who hast made of one blood all nations of men to dwell on all the face of the earth: forgive us that we have so often shed our blood in conflict rather than in peace. Forgive us for our hatreds, fears, distrust, and divisiveness and for the deeper sins that have caused them. Forgive us for the bad blood of our weaknesses. May the good and redeeming blood of Christ cleanse us, renew us, and unite us with thee and with our fellow man. We pray for peace on earth and for goodwill among men. May the United Nations ever speak and act with patient and productive boldness. We pray for peace on earth and for goodwill among men. May America dare to be Christian in itself and in every world relationship. We pray for peace on earth and for goodwill among men. Most of all we pray that the church of Christ in our land and every land may so proclaim and demonstrate the ways of divine peace and Christian unity that all men shall be saved and all nations shall be ruled by thee.—Charles T. Leber.

EVENING SERVICE

Topic: How to Attend Church
TEXT: Ps. 55:14.

Our church services are not by any means all that they ought to be. One finds there poor preaching, bad music, antiquated theology, ugly architecture, hypocritical people, and almost anything you wish to say. But one finds there also sincerity, beauty, devotion, depth, earnestness about God, and goodness. What you find in a church depends in part, though not wholly, on what you look for.

I. The first principle for attending church is to go in a receptive and appreciative, not in a critical, attitude. The fault-finding spirit will drive out the worshiping attitude more quickly than will anything else, and it is hardly fair then to blame the church for not leading you into worship. It is the same as with friendships. The more you pick flaws in people from the outside, the less you get into the inside of their lives.

II. A second requirement is to shut distractions from your mind. You may not be able to do this wholly. But remember you are there to worship, not to look around at people's clothes or to go over in your mind what you did last night or to plan out your week's work. There are other occasions for such matters.

III. Enter into all the hymns and responses. There is little enough opportunity in a church service for personal participation, but people often cut themselves off from what there is by passively looking on.

IV. You should, if possible, connect yourselves with the work of the church in some way other than attending the Sunday service. You need to do this for the help you can give, but you also need to do it in order to feel yourself a part of it.

V. You ought, if you are free to do so, to choose the church best suited to your temperament. When you have been reared in a certain church and have many ties there, it is usually unwise to break them. But if you are in a new environment where you are free to choose, attend the church where you find you can worship best.—Georgia Harkness.

SUNDAY: NOVEMBER FOURTH

MORNING SERVICE

Topic: A Letter to Laodicea
Text: Rev. 3:14, 17.

I. *The one who speaks.* (a) It was more than coincidence that the Lord describes himself to this church as "The Amen, the faithful and true witness." We have almost lost the impact of the word "amen," using it only as a concluding word to tie a bow on our prayers. It was the Greek word "amen, amen" which Jesus so often used to introduce something of dramatic importance and which the KJV translates "verily, verily" or "truly, truly." The word means "So be it" or "This is verily so!" It suggests here that there are established truths. There is an authority; the "Amen" speaks, and Jesus Christ is that authority. This is something we need to remember today as well. Not only is he the authority, but he is faithful above all. "Great is thy faithfulness," the psalmist said. Though every man be a liar, God is true.

(b) The one who speaks here is "the beginning of God's creation." The word in the Greek, here translated beginning, is

arche. Unfortunately we get our word "archaic" from it, which generally designates something that is old, worn out, and decrepit. More correctly understood, *arche* means the origin, the initiator. Christ was the creating hand. (See John 1:1–3; Col. 1:15–16.) Our word "archeology," the study of original things that substantiate history, gives a better clue. This is the one who speaks, the Amen, the true witness, the originator of all created things.

II. *The harsh indictment.* (a) "I know your way of life," he said. "I know your works, that you are neither cold nor hot. Would that you were cold or hot!" They had lost the zeal. The Greek word for hot is *zestos,* which means not only hot but kept at the boiling point. It suggests that what God wants in the church and in every Christian is "boiling poing" zeal. Christianity requires enthusiasm. The church at Ephesus had "left its first love." The church in Laodicea had lost its first zeal. We might find ourselves uncomfortably in both of these places or somewhere in between.

(b) "Would that you were cold or hot, but because you are lukewarm, I will spew you out of my mouth." The word "vomit" is not too strong. Jesus was saying to that church, "You make me sick!" There is nothing so unpalatable as something tepid. Cold? Yes. Hot? Yes. But lukewarm? No. Christianity without zeal is repugnant, fit only to spit out. Christ does not mean by this that "I will cast you into hell"; he is, after all, speaking to believers. But there are times when even the beloved child of a family becomes so revolting that parents must apply harsh discipline in order to bring about renewal. God may discipline harshly, even removing his blessings, to bring the lukewarm church to its senses.

III. *The redemptive teaching.* (a) "You say, I am rich, and have prospered, and have need of nothing." The wealth of that community apparently must have come into the church as well. There is a risk in having too much of material good and of being too successful in the world. A church begins as a small, zealous flock, seeking to win others, anxious to tell the community about Jesus Christ, so filled with love for their fellow men and driven by the love of God that is within them that the little church grows in numbers. Then a strange transformation takes place. Little by little it becomes an established organization, and the first thing you know they have a tremendous building complex. The work goes well and they are "self-supporting," but the old zeal is gone. Advertising techniques and other means replace personal witness and invitation. The organization is so busy that it takes all of their energies just to keep the machine moving, whether or not it is producing anything. That was Laodicea; they were rich and had need of nothing. But Jesus said, "You are wretched, pitiable, poor, blind, naked." Like the king in Hans Christian Andersen's "The King's New Clothes," their religious garments were figments of imagination and having no reality at all. We need to apply this to ourselves. There are so many things that seem to spell success —buildings, program, activity, even stewardship. We seem to be well off. We even have a reputation of being spiritual. But we may indeed be empty. That is what the Lord was saying to Laodicea. Is he saying it to us?

(b) "Therefore I counsel you to buy from me gold refined in fire that you may truly be rich." Get the currency that has value in eternity. But how can I buy? I have "nothing in my hands to bring." You must come and "buy without money and without price" (Isa. 55:1). Your need is the most precious gift to bring. Come like that, and you will have "treasure in heaven."

(c) Come also to receive "white garments to clothe your nakedness." You boast, said Jesus to Laodicea, about your clothing industry; you drape your body well; you have just the right cut of style. But that which clothes the soul you know nothing of. There is a garment of righteousness. That, Christ said to the Laodiceans, you need more than anything else, and so do we.

IV. *The loving purpose.* (a) This letter, which starts out in a more harsh way than any of the others, ends in the most tender way. Jesus follows the sober analysis with a purpose behind his critique: "Those whom I love I reprove and chasten; so be zealous and repent." His purpose is not judgment but rather helpfulness and redemption.

(b) Almost always when the New Testament speaks of God's love, the Greek word *agapao* is used. This is that highest self-giving, sacrificial love. But in this instance Jesus uses the word of warm affection, *phileo*. He says: "I love you with affection; I hold you as a dear friend. That is why I rebuke and chasten you. I want you to be what will be most purposeful and most satisfying." While he was harsh with them, he showed his concern. How sad would be our state if God ceased to discipline us as the children of his affection.— Paul P. Fryhling.

Illustrations

CHURCH WELLS. Churches are like cisterns or wells, an old saint once observed. There are cistern churches. They don't provide water at all; they just store the water that is piped into them. And what is worse, they sometimes leak and lose even the water that is put in them. Then there are shallow well churches. They do all right until dry weather comes, and then they go dry. Many churches are like this. A deep well church is better. It never goes dry, but of course one has to keep pumping to get any water. Finally there is the artesian well church. It just keeps pouring out its water day and night the year around without any pumping. The Jerusalem church was like this. And because it was like this, it continued to grow as the Lord added persons to it daily.—John W. Wade.

DEEP IN THE EARTH.   In the critical days of World War II, England faced the necessity of increased coal production. Winston Churchill called a meeting of labor leaders to give them the facts and to enlist their support. He closed his presentation by picturing in their minds a parade which he was sure would be held in Piccadilly Circus after the war. He said there would come the men of the Royal Navy whom everyone would know had kept the vital sea lands open. There would come the men of the Army who had come home from Dunkirk and then gone on to defeat Rommel in Africa. Then there would come the men of the Royal Air Force who had driven the Luftwaffe from the sky and beat it at its own game. Then, he said, last of all would come a long line of sweat-stained, soot streaked men in miner's caps. Someone would cry from the crowd, "And where were you during the crucial days of our struggle?" And from ten thousand throats would come the answer, "We were deep in the earth with our faces to the coal." The English are well known for their reserve, but those men wept and cheered when Churchill sat down. Churchill had convinced every man that he was needed and that England would not win without him. —Allen D. Montgomery.

Sermon Suggestions

WHEN LOVE IS A SIN.   Text: Heb. 4:12. (1) The love of things which lowers our sights so that we look at the creature and not the Creator. (2) The love of men which makes us content with something less than God. (3) The love of self which is often the reality of our love for things and men because things and men satisfy our ego.—Albert E. Day.

WHY CHRISTIANS FORGIVE.   Text: Matt. 6:14. (1) Because an unforgiving spirit is injurious to ourselves. (2) Because an unforgiving spirit is unjust to others. (3) Because an unforgiving spirit is offensive to God. (4) Because Christ specially requires us to forgive injuries done to us. (5) Because he makes our forgiveness of others the condition of being forgiven ourselves. —Wilson T. Hogue.

Worship Aids

CALL TO WORSHIP.   "Trust in [God] at all times; ye people, pour out your heart before him: God is a refuge for us." Ps. 62:8.

INVOCATION.   Eternal God, who committest unto us the swift and solemn trust of life, since we know not what a day may bring forth but only that the hour for serving thee is always present, may we wake to the instant claims of thy holy will, not waiting for tomorrow but yielding today. Consecrate with thy presence the way our feet may go, and the humblest work will shine, and the roughest places be made plain.— James Martineau.

OFFERTORY SENTENCE.   Every man hath his proper gift of God, one after this manner, and another after that." I Cor. 7:7.

OFFERTORY PRAYER.   God of all good, who hath rewarded our labors, we acknowledge thankfully thy favor and do now dedicate a share of our material gains to the even more satisfying ministries of the spirit.

PRAYER.   God our Lord, we rejoice in the fierce joy of living in a revolutionary time when victims of oppression and contempt are achieving the stature of manhood and human dignity. Amid the shaking, grant that our desire for the courage to do thy will will be greater than our creature-longing for security. Give us a proper loathing for the false security of looking down at others and a proper pride to stand level-eyed with all who fight for truth and justice. May we trust thee enough to be glad when thou dost destroy the shoddy and corrupt things we have loved and replace them with the clean and true things thou wouldst have us learn to love. Give us the strength to be with thee where thou art, and bless us there.—Truman B. Douglass.

EVENING SERVICE

Topic: Faith or Fear?
TEXT: Mark 4:40 (RSV).

What kind of faith is it that Jesus invites his disciples to partake in the challenge of this story of the storm on the waters? Does Christian faith make a scrap of difference? For certainly there are many whose lives are sorely afflicted and wounded, whether they are Christians or not.

I. The Christian religion and the Christian faith are not states of life lived away from the storm. Christ is in the boat, in history, incarnate, in it with us. Strong faith is not the absence of doubt or fear; it is rooted in the same experience. Christianity is not life aboard a luxury liner in calm and untroubled waters; it is life aboard a lifeboat precisely where the storm is, seeking to rescue and save but never to evade or avoid the storm and the waves.

II. Christian faith is not belief in any thing at all, but belief in some one, the person of Christ. All else will pass away, and in a sense all else is only secondary and ephemeral. "Heaven and earth shall pass away but my word shall not pass away." Most of us are not too concerned about the "word," so long as heaven and earth remain stable.

III. You and I were not promised stability or security; we were promised an ever deepening love relationship with God in Christ, such as would take us through suffering rather than get us round it. Why do we continue to ask when faced with a problem, What is the way round it? whereas the truly Christian response is, What is the way through it?

(a) The bald fact is that we cannot have security and maturity. It is only through times of deep unrest and storm that we learn the maturity of love. The securities of life become secondary as our inner life becomes deeper and richer.

(b) Paul's promise is the fruit of his own bitter experience of storm and tempest and great trial. "I am convinced," he says, "that nothing can separate us from the love of God in Christ Jesus." The boat may well sink; all may well be lost except faith; and to possess this is to possess all things.

IV. "Why are you afraid?" This is the daily question of true love and true faith and is always the question on the lips of Christ who invites us to more adventure, to more trust, and to greater maturity. Faith and love cannot remove you from life and risk, but faith and love mean that risk enriches life.—Michael Marshall.

SUNDAY: NOVEMBER ELEVENTH

MORNING SERVICE

Topic: Why Should I Pledge? (Stewardship Day)
TEXT: Deut. 14:22.

Somewhere in the Bible there is a rule that I am supposed to give ten percent of my income. But I think John Wesley said it better than Deuteronomy: "Gain all you can, without hurting either yourself or your neighbor in soul or body; save all you can by cutting off every expense which serves only to indulge foolish desire; and then give all you can, or in other words give all you have to God. Render unto God not a tenth, not a third, not a half, but all that is God's, be it more or less." If I'm not moved by the Old Testament rule, then why do I give?

I. Because I am as an American a relatively wealthy man and the head of a most affluent household. Without checking the statistics I am sure that our family must easily rank in the top ten percent of the world's wealthy. Seldom has anyone in my family gone to bed hungry. We eat well, too well. I have seldom had to worry about the danger of winter's cold or icy rain. My only concern about clothes has been deciding whether I would be fashionable enough for the occasion. I've got a garage, almost as big as my house, filled with bicycles and cars. I don't even have to walk next door if I don't want to. I can ride a half dozen different ways. But I need to remember that my neighbors who suffer in poverty are my brothers and sisters. I need to remember this when I fill out my pledge card and not just when I write platitudinous editorials.

II. Because I'm grateful for what God and his people have done for me. I realize that the church is not his one and only earthly agent, but I also know that through that imperfect agent God gave me life anchored in a power greater than any earthly force. In God through Christ I found reason for life, or, better still, reason for life found me and gifted me with purpose and meaning. I want to be an active participant in that kind of enterprise which is the church's business. I want to give because I am grateful.

III. Because I believe in the work and the ministry of the church, and because I am thrifty I want to make certain that my money is spent wisely.

(a) I have had opportunities to see the church in mission and ministry at the local level and in wider areas. I am not always pleased. More times than I would like to admit, I have seen my brothers and sisters take their stewardship standards from the prosperous world around them rather than the New Testament. But so have I, and along with many in the church we need to be less hypocritical in following Christ.

(b) What I've seen in the church is far better than the alternatives I've found. I find in the church hope. I find in the church people who are for others rather than for themselves. I find sinners in the church, but I also find saints. I know good people and their good work. I believe my money spent by such Christians in such work helps build a sane world where there are people who still care. I give because if I didn't I wouldn't have much left to hope for or dream for.—Keith I. Pohl.

Illustrations

DEDICATION. Christian stewardship is the dedication of all I am and have, under the control of God's spirit in Christ, to the doing of his will in recognition of his lordship, in gratitude for his love, in every area of my life, and in the service of his redemptive fellowship.

UPDATING OUR GIVING. The ten cent cup of coffee has gone the way of the penny postcard. We cannot mail a postcard for one cent, and we cannot buy a cup of coffee for a dime. We know it. We accept it. We have adjusted our lives to it. When it comes to philanthropy, we simply have not advanced with the times. This does not mean that we are not giving more than when a postcard was a penny and a cup of coffee was one thin dime. It does mean however that we have spread our philanthropic dollars so thin that often they neither fill stomachs nor communicate deep concern for needy people. Much of our giving simply does not make a difference! Perhaps you ought to give more. That is something only you can decide. Whether or not you give more is not the issue. What does your giving accomplish? That is the important question, and if you are among the hundreds of thousands who must reply, "Not very much," it is time to consider some new models for creative giving. It is exciting to realize that as individuals we sometimes give more than corporations, more than foundations, more than other people. In fact at times we give enough to make a real difference. As individuals we can make many differences, for there are many courses we can take in philanthropic giving, and whether or not we use them we should know what they are and how we can respond to human need and a personal desire to do good in the very best possible way.—Raymond B. Knudsen.

ARE PEOPLE THANKFUL FOR US? Most of us express our gratitude to our heavenly Father around Thanksgiving time. Perhaps we should ask the question, "Are we the kind of persons that others express their gratitude for?" Do we do the little extras that brighten the lives of others? When we make a deposit at the bank, do we make out the deposit slip ourselves or do we make a hurried teller do it while the line behind us grows longer?

When we go to church do we sit on the last pew in the back or do we fill a pew toward the front so that latecomers can have those in the rear?

Do we have our minds made up at the restaurant so that a tired waitress doesn't have to wait an eternity for our order or do we change our minds so often that she's waiting for us to make our request known?

Do we play our part in community and civic organizations or do we sit back and expect them to serve us? Are we constantly harping about the "good ole days" yet never do anything to chart a better future?

Do we put others first or do we always look out for "number one"?

Are we willing to go the second mile or are we always afraid that someone will take advantage of us?

Do we leave the working world each day a better world than it was in the morning when we first greeted it or do we make the situation worse?

Do we look at a difficulty as a problem or as a challenge?

Do we lift loads from other's shoulders or do we put weights on those who are already heavy laden?

Yes, thank God for what he's done for us. Yet at the same time let us be the kind of persons that others can thank God for. —*Wesleyan Christian Advocate.*

Sermon Suggestions

THE DIVINE APPRAISER. Text: Mark 12:-41. (1) The divine appraiser would have us consider the source of what we possess. (2) The divine appraiser would have us appreciate the value of our possessions. (3) The divine appraiser would have us appreciate not only the source of our possessions and the value of them but also the cost of our gifts.—Ralph W. Sockman.

LESSONS FROM THE HARVEST. Text: Mark 2:23. (1) Harvest helps us to recapture the thought of God in the common things of nature. (2) Harvest reminds us of the faithfulness of the Creator. (3) Harvest reminds us that man cannot live by bread alone. (4) Harvest reminds us that God requires the service of man.—George H. Morrison.

Worship Aids

CALL TO WORSHIP. "Wait on the Lord: be of good courage, and he shall strengthen thine heart: wait, I say, on the Lord." Ps. 27:14.

INVOCATION. Our Father, we thank thee for thy word and for the eternal truths which guide us day by day. We thank thee most of all for the living word, Jesus Christ, and the sureness of his presence. Teach us how to turn unto thee so that thy thoughts may be our thoughts and thy ways our ways.

OFFERTORY SENTENCE. "Seek ye first the kingdom of God, and his righteousness, and all these things shall be added unto you." Matt. 6:33.

OFFERTORY PRAYER. O Lord Jesus Christ, who hast taught us that to whomsoever much is given, of him shall much be required: grant that we, whose lot is cast in this Christian heritage, may strive more earnestly by our prayers and tithes, by sympathy and study to hasten the coming of thy kingdom among all peoples of the earth, that as we have entered into the labors of others, so others may enter into ours, to thy honor and glory.

PRAYER. O God, we have known and worshiped you as a God of peace, and yet our own efforts in this area have been so feeble and few. We have seen and known something of the beauty of your creation. We have seen and known also the tragedy of its destruction by war. Help us now to discern our need for a world community at peace where refugees will have no need to wander across the face of the earth, where children will no longer become orphans because of the ravages of war, where men's value of other men's lives will no longer be cheapened, and where men and women and children the world over will be united in the high adventure still of building that idea of one world that has been lost from our vision. Work with us, Lord, in this as we ask it in the name of him who came and suffered for peace and love for all the people of his world.—Edler G. Hawkins.

EVENING SERVICE

Topic: Where Do You Put the Accent?
SCRIPTURE: Luke 15:11–32.
The key phrase in the parable of the prodigal son is "make me." The basic lessons to be learned from this dramatic record come into sharp focus by the way the accent is placed on a part or all of this phrase.

I. *The voice of stubbornness:* "Give me the portion of goods that falleth to me" (v. 12).

(a) The accent in this case is on the word "give" in the phrase "give me." In other words the prodigal son was saying that he was tired of the restraints of the home, the rules of the family circle, and the authority of his father. He raised a rebel flag into the face of the father and defiantly said: "Make me obey your commands if you think you can. I'm my own boss. I'll do as I please. Nobody is telling me what to do."

(b) The son felt that there was no rapport or understanding between him and his father, and the son was ready to declare his independence by running away from home. The son was ready to assert his identity as one who knew who he was by sarcastically saying to his father: "I'm

fed up with having you try to make me do what you want me to do. So I'm getting out on my own."

II. *The voice of selfishness:* ". . . and took his journey into a far country, and there wasted his substance with riotous living" (v. 13).

(a) At this juncture in his life when he was really living it up, he was putting the accent on the "me" in the phrase "make me." He wanted to know: What will this activity do for me? What thrill will come to me by what I am doing? What will I get out of this for my own enjoyment?

(b) He was ready to spend any amount to get some kick out of life, to find some way to gratify his passions, and to indulge in those activities that would give him a faster heartbeat. His only concern was: How will this give me more pleasure? What will this do for me in satisfying my personal interests?

III. *The voice of submission:* ". . . make me as one of thy hired servants" (v. 19).

(a) When the prodigal son came to himself and saw what was happening to his life, he started the process of making a comeback. He was ready to humble himself and acknowledge that he was wrong. At this point his expression was "make me" with an equal accent on each word. This is turned into the voice of submission or obedience or yielding. He has turned around 180 degrees from his previous attitude. He is ready to be a part of the family circle instead of standing outside the circle and objecting to everything that happened in the circle.

(b) This is the profile of a person making a change for the better in his way of life. He moves from rebellion against God and from the life-style of being self-centered to the point of being surrendered and submissive to God's will for his life. This means that he is a transformed person.—Mendell Taylor.

SUNDAY: NOVEMBER EIGHTEENTH

MORNING SERVICE

Topic: The Chivalry of Thanksgiving (Thanksgiving Sunday)

TEXT: II Sam. 23:15–17.

I. *Unearned values.* (a) The chivalry of thanksgiving makes clear that a large part of life is composed of values we have not earned. They are part of our legacy from our predecessors. These values we call our heritage. Strictly speaking a heritage is a portion allotted to an individual or community. It comes from the past. The good and great of the ages are the true creditors of the race. What they leave us is the true "unearned increment."

(b) I would not glorify the past indiscriminately, but I would celebrate those institutions and faiths and ideals which we take for granted. "The plain fact is that the biggest part of our lives is our heritage. By long and patient process as aspiring, thinking, trying, daring, and sacrificing, mankind has accumulated a cultural inheritance!"

(c) The pioneers in realms of government, science, social relationships, and religion have gone "in jeopardy of their lives" to bring us purer water to refresh and liberate our spirits. "Ye are bought with a price." To saunter through life as if everything we possess belonged to us "in fee simple" to possess is to be inwardly impoverished.

(d) There are some things of the past which need to be left behind. There are customs and traditions which impede mankind's progress. But there are other things like "the principles of Jesus, the power of applied science, the idea of democracy" we escape from only at our peril. "Far be it from me, O Lord, that I should do this: is not this the blood of men that went in jeopardy of their lives?"

II. *Recognition of values.* (a) Recognition of values should awaken within us humility and thanksgiving. I suspect that when David held that water up to the light and realized what it stood for, he was moved to profound humility and thanksgiving. Humility is the mark of the discerning mind. It is the response of the appreciative soul. Pride rules our wills for the simple reason that we concentrate our attention upon the things we have done.

(b) Humility is the garden in which the forget-me-nots of thanksgiving grow. When you encounter a man or woman who is grateful for the tradition of the home and the old-fashioned fidelities of family life; for basic moral convictions like courage, self-sacrifice, and decency; and for the tradition of liberty and democracy and the Christian tradition of faith and life, you do not find a person who is arrogant and self-complacent. Rather you meet in these persons men and women who are humbly grateful for the great movements of thought and life which enrich and liberate the present.

(c) You cannot choose your heritage, but you can choose your attitude toward it. We can drink all the draughts from the well of God without a second thought as to what they signify. Or like David we can lift them up until their sacramental significance shines through them, transfiguring our heritage and transforming us.

III. *Response to values.* (a) The chivalry of thanksgiving is always expressed in determined and enthusiastic action. "Freely ye have received, freely give." "We ought to lay down our lives for the brethren because Christ first laid down his life for us." In Heb. 11 the writer carves out of the illustrious names of the past what has been fittingly called "The Westminster Abbey of the scriptures." But after the roll call he does not ask for new songs of gratitude for the past. He does not commission his people to erect new and greater monuments. He challenges them to build on, not only to uphold worthy traditions bequested to them but to make new ones.

(b) Our churches must be more than symbols of an ancient faith. Religion has its roots in the long past, but it is vastly more than an antique. It is a power through which we recover moral greatness and spiritual quality. Down in Plymouth churchyard where the Pilgrims are buried, there is this line on the tombstone of Governor William Bradford: "What our fathers with so much difficulty secured do not basely relinquish."

(c) Are we concerned about maintaining and expanding the idea of democracy? Do we display any of the courage and fortitude of our fathers' religion? Do we sacrifice to maintain the glory of their cause? Do we put heart and soul into the cultivation of a vigorous church life in our community? Do we have a vivid sense of God's presence to guide and guard our lives?—David A. MacLennan.

Illustrations

GOD'S GOODNESS.   Governor Edward Winslow, writing about the Thanksgiving of 1621, stated, "Although it be not always so plentiful as it was at this time with us, yet by the goodness of God we are so far from want that we often wish you [in England] partakers of our plenty." The settlers harvested twenty acres of Indian corn and six acres of barley. A party of four hunters in one day brought in enough game for Chief Massasoit and ninety men to feast for a week. Their seacoast bounty included lobsters in abundance, eels, oysters, salad herbs, grapes, strawberries, gooseberries, raspberries, and plums. Winslow added, as if writing to us, "These things I thought good to let you understand that you might on our behalf give God thanks, who hath dealt so favorably with us."—Charles T. Klinksick.

DIVINE IMPRINT.   Travel wherever you may in the world, you will find the civilization of the people ranks with their belief in the teachings of the Bible. No other book has played such an important part in the making of civilization as the Bible. It deals with the terrestrial as well as the celestial affairs of life. It proclaims the past and foretells the future. It is the only book that gives man a place and a purpose in the world. It furnishes to him a code, fixes for him a goal, and bids him "subdue the earth." It is no common book. It bears the divine imprint on every page.—Pat M. Neff.

SOMEONE TO THANK.   If I were to wake up one morning and find I was an atheist with my faith in God completely gone, I think I would miss almost more than anything else having someone to thank. The loss of what we call grace, the recreating and refreshing power that comes through Christ, would of course be devastating, but what a deprivation it would be to plunge on to the end of one's days with no one to thank. I can hardly conceive what it would be like never, never being able to say in a moment of exhilaration, of unexpected happiness, or of rescue from deep distress, "O God, you're good to me!"—David H. C. Read.

Sermon Suggestions

WHY WE GIVE THANKS.   Text: Eph. 5:20. (1) Because it is a part of our religious heritage as given us by our Hebrew-Christian tradition, as recorded in the Bible, and as perpetuated by our religious customs. (2) Because we feel a great thirst which can be quenched only as we drink freely from the fountain of our national heritage. (3) Because it is the mark of a people of character to want to express an inner feeling of gratitude for all the gifts of life which come to them so full and free.—Homer J. R. Elford.

PAGES OF POWER.   Text: II Tim. 3:16–17. (1) We should read the Bible with understanding. (2) We should read the Bible with integrity. (3) We should read the Bible with an open mind. (4) We should read the Bible with imagination. (5) We should read the Bible with a listening heart and a resolve to act.—Everett W. Palmer.

Worship Aids

CALL TO WORSHIP.   "Ye shall know truth, and the truth shall make you free. God is a Spirit: and they that worship him must worship him in spirit and in truth." John 8:32; 4:24.

INVOCATION.   O God our Father, giver of all good things, we are grateful for the Thanksgiving season of the year when we come with gratitude for bountiful harvests filling granary and bin. Give us such a spirit of thankfulness that every day and every season and all thy continuing gifts may be occasions for thanksgiving, and all the year be blessed with an ever-continuing gratitude. As thy mercies are new every morning, so may our praise rise to thee each day and hour.

OFFERTORY SENTENCE.   "Thou crownest the year with thy goodness. . . . Samuel took a stone, and set it between Mizpeh and Shen, saying, Hitherto hath the Lord helped us." Ps. 65:11; I Sam. 7:12.

OFFERTORY PRAYER.   Dear God, help us to become unobstructed channels that thy love may flow through us to others and our gifts may be used for the proclamation to all men of thy saving goodness.

CALL TO THANKSGIVING.   Let us offer thanksgiving to God at this season for all his blessings upon our nation and for all those persons and movements in our heritage which have reflected a commitment to God's will and a commitment to those values that enhance human liberty, dignity, growth, and fulfillment. Thanksgiving however becomes only hollow ceremony unless it motivates us to repentance and new commitments. Let our thanksgiving for the natural resources of this land become the motivation for a new dedication to the way of Christian stewardship. Let our thanksgiving for the contributions of ethnic minorities compel us to make adequate amends for past injustices and to make a new commitment of our total resources to full equality for all persons. Let our gratitude for our material goods be expressed in an active concern to feed the hungry everywhere in our world. Let our gratitude for our spiritual heritage motivate us to share the good news of Christ,

whom to know is life abundant.—W. Kenneth Goodson.

EVENING SERVICE

Topic: The Religion of the Bible (Bible Sunday)

TEXT: Isa. 28:14, 17 (NEB).

What are some of the fruits of the religion of the Bible?

I. The first is freedom. The Bible is the first book in the history of the world to enunciate the proposition that human beings have a God-given right to live in liberty. No one had ever thought of that idea before the day when Moses stood before the Egyptian pharaoh and pronounced those words that have echoed down the ages: "Thus says the Lord, the God of Israel, 'Let my people go.' " Until that moment no one had ever questioned the universally accepted belief that the power of the king over his subjects, like the power of the master over his slaves, was an absolute power. But once the question had been voiced, it was never to be silenced, and it became one of the fundamental themes of the Bible.

II. The second has been justice. One of the reasons why the Bible is so hard to read is that large parts of it are composed of codes or laws. No legal code makes easy reading. But easy to read or not, law is the expression of the biblical belief that God is a God of righteousness and justice, that is, he is ultimately concerned that the basic principle on which the social and political order rests shall be the principle of fairness. The moral standards of the Bible's law are the ten commandments. God says over and over, as in Isaiah, "I will use justice as a plumb line and righteousness as a plummet." Indeed the call to social justice is the heart of the message of the prophets.

III. The third has been the belief that human intelligence and human effort are the ultimate means by which the course of history is determined. Until the Bible came along, most religions were the sort that might have written over the doors of their temples, "Come in, but leave your brains outside." Such religions trade largely in superstition, prejudice, and fear, and their power is directly proportional to the ignorance and weakness of the people whom they seek to hold in thrall. Contrast with such religions the faith of the Bible. It assumes almost from the beginning that true understanding of the nature of things must be based on that experience which can be grasped by the human mind and dealt with by human reason. It also assumes, again from the beginning, that human effort is what makes the ultimate difference in determining the kind of world we are to live in. This is no religion of submission and resignation, despairing of the possibility of changing things for the better; it is a religion of engagement, of struggle, and above all of hard work.

IV. The fourth is hope not only for a better life for all people here on earth but also for a larger life for every individual in the world beyond the horizon of this earthly existence. The Bible does not only answer the questions, "Where did I come from? and What ought I to be doing here?" It also answers the deepest question of all, "Where am I going?" And the answer it gives is unequivocal. Beyond this earthly life there is another life in the spirit where we shall be together again and where we shall be with Jesus. That is the heart of religion of the Bible.—Charles H. Buck, Jr.

SUNDAY: NOVEMBER TWENTY-FIFTH

MORNING SERVICE

Topic: The Second Touch
SCRIPTURE: Mark 8:22–26.

I. Mark told about a man who received a second touch. He had to have it because the first was inadequate. With the first touch he went from blindness to sight but his sight was distorted. He said, "Yes, I see men, but they are like trees walking." Life like that would have been almost as miserable as life without sight. To have a blurred vision is only a step away from no vision at all. What afflicts so many people is a blurred vision and a distortion of sight.

(a) The first touch gives sight; the second touch gives clarity. The first touch gives life; the second touch gives meaning to that life. The first touch gives hearing; the second gives understanding.

(b) Job had the first touch when he said, "I have heard of thee by the hearing of the ear." He had the second touch when he said: "But now my eye seeth thee. Therefore, I melt away; I repent in dust and ashes."

II. The second touch assumes that there has been a first touch. God has come to us in Christ, but as we walk with the Lord in the light of his word we arrive at a place in this venture where our sight, our vision, becomes clear, and we can accept God's reality with more understanding.

(a) The second touch does not change the reality; men are not trees after all. They never were. They just seemed to be trees. But it does change the way we see reality.

(b) Sometimes nothing will actually change except the viewer himself. There are so many things that we cannot alter. Some matters seem to be fixed. Whereas we cannot change them, we can do as Paul did and find that "God's grace is sufficient" to allow us to live with the problem.

(c) We can see with understanding. We can see with greater commitment to the God who can make all things clear.

III. What are some distinct areas of our lives where the second touch is needed?

(a) We need that touch in our concept of God, our thoughts about God, and our relationship with him through Jesus Christ.

(1) One day you and I brought to Christ a sinful life. At that time we felt much like the disciples who brought a lunch for the feeding of the 5,000 and said to Christ, "What is this among so many?" I have felt that my life wasn't much to give to Christ. But to us Jesus said, "It's just as big as we make it."

(2) Now time has elapsed, and just as time and circumstances can remove the gleam from a cherished relationship, so can it also happen to the Christian experience. The joy of the beginning vanishes. The thrill of the adventure declines. The

confidence of victory eludes us. We can settle down into the dull routine of mediocrity without any excitement. Like David of old, many of us need to say, "Restore unto me the joy of thy salvation." Touch me again! The salvation is there, but the joy is not. The sight is there, but it is blurred.

(b) We need the second touch as we look at life. The farther we go in life, the more we see its raw side and the more disillusioned we are tempted to become. Someone has said that "a man is abnormal unless he is a radical at the age of 21 and a conservative at the age of 35." Idealism seems to wane in the wake of oppression and disappointment. When we have been hurt, abused, misused, or failed by someone in whom we had placed our confidence, we tend to block out the vision of Christ who can calm the waves, and we find ourselves being swallowed up by the sea. We need the second touch.

IV. Something great happens whenever a person can suddenly see clearly and can begin to put life into its proper persepctive.

(a) If you want to see life as you ought to see it, look at it through the eyes of Christ. Let him "create in you a clean heart and renew a right spirit within you." Even if you are a Christian, remember that Paul wrote to the Romans and spoke about a constant "renewing of the mind" that was necessary because life changes and we change. We must go through this renewing process, allowing God to make us new by giving us a fresh outlook at every juncture of life.

(b) If something is distressing and defeating you, Jesus Christ can touch your life and help you to become the victor and not the victim. Turn your life over to him. Confess that you "see, but not clearly." You've got life in Christ, but you're not living it abundantly. That's what he wants us to have. (See John 10:10.)

(b) Jesus saw life more clearly than any human being before him or since that first century. Yet he lived a positive, abundant life because he lived it with hope in God. He knew that God was greater than any problem he would ever have to face.—Jerry Hayner.

Illustrations

THIS FAR. Not until death can we be wholly free from sin; but we can come this far, that it reigns not in us, sits not on a throne, holds no parliament within us, and gives us no laws. To die to the dominion of sin; that by the grace of God, we may. —Lancelot Andrewes.

DAILY PRAYER. In this evil world each day some altar should be set up where the prayer may be lifted, "God make me good." But added to that must always be this prayer: "God make me good for something. Deliver me from the guilt of the good and from cowardly and complacent silence and inaction."—Frederick Brown Harris.

Sermon Suggestions

HOW DO YOU RECEIVE CHRIST? Text: John 1:12. (1) Whenever you worship in his name. (2) Whenever you do something you would not do if it were not for your commitment to be his disciple. (3) Whenever you keep quiet moments of thinking about him and reading of his life. (4) Whenever you have a second thought and go back seeking reconciliation where you might have lived in tension. (5) Whenever you greet another as though he is your brother. (6) Whenever you reorder your living and your giving, your work and your play.—Gene E. Bartlett.

BELIEVING IN PEOPLE. Scripture: Luke 5:27–32. (1) We must redefine what is really important about people. (2) As Christians we must discourage all those things which tend to take away the humanity of people and encourage those things which work for people. (3) As Christians within the fellowship of the church we have the unique opportunity to demonstrate by what we are just what people are.—John W. Abbott.

Worship Aids

CALL TO WORSHIP. "Whatsoever things are true, whatsoever things are honest, whatsoever things are just, whatsoever things are pure, whatsoever things are lovely, whatsoever things are of good report; if there be any virtue, and if there be any praise, think on these things." Phil. 4:8.

INVOCATION. As we begin another day, most gracious Father, make us to know that we never drift out of thy love and care. Faces may change and conditions may alter, but thou art never so near to us as when we need thee most.

OFFERTORY SENTENCE. "Upon the first day of the week let every one of you lay by him in store, as God hath prospered him." I Cor. 16:2.

OFFERTORY PRAYER. Our Father, help us to trust thee more fully and to accept our responsibility toward thy work and thy children who are our brethren in Christ.

PRAYER. Almighty God, in whom is calmness, peace, and concord: heal the divisions which separate your children from one another and enable them to keep the unity of the spirit in the bond of peace. Where there are diversities of knowledge and faith and we cannot all be of the same mind may we be one in brotherly love and in devotion to your holy will. Deliver us from all blindness and prejudice, from all clamor and evil speaking, that by the charity of our temper and thought and life we may show forth the power and beauty of the faith we profess.—Chester E. Hodgson.

EVENING SERVICE

Topic: Guidelines for Love and Service
TEXT: Mark 12:31.

We love and serve when we do things to benefit others just because we think and decide that they are worth doing things for. We use people when we do for them only what is necessary in order to gain from them or by them values and things which are of more worth to us than they are.

I. Things are to be liked and used. They are correctly loved when they are appreciated, used carefully, and not rated as more valuable than persons. God has given and provided humanity with things beyond measure for us to like, use, manage, and enjoy. Failure or refusal to enjoy what God has given is a denial of love. Nevertheless things are not to be rated as more valuable than God himself.

II. Persons are to be loved but never used. At no time is a follower of Jesus exempt from having concern for another human being as a person—even strangers, enemies, and unlikables. Since we are to love neighbor as self, not to permit others to use us is equally as important as not permitting self to use others.

III. The basic nature of love is to serve, even when one doesn't like to do what is needed or asked. It is the basic nature of love to be completely voluntary. This recognizes one's own freedom to serve or not serve and likewise recognizes another's freedom to serve or not to serve. How much to serve, when to serve, and who is to be served are all questions decided in each relationship. Each situation gives equal consideration to the interests of all persons involved including self.

IV. All human beings have three options with regard to their relationship to God: to disregard him completely; to try to use him to get what they like, want, or need; or love him and seek always to serve him. People who completely disregard God do not participate in religious activities. In Matt. 6 Jesus points out that even sincere and deeply religious people can use God instead of loving and serving God.

V. Religious activity is the same in appearance, whoever participates; but the mind, heart, and soul of the doer can be quite different. When any activity such as praying, singing, Bible reading, evangelism, and giving money is done to gain admiration for self, to create and maintain an exclusive fellowship with those doing them in the same way, or to secure a home in heaven, that is using God. Yet those same activities can serve God when done as an expression of love. These are love and service when God's work is recognized and the only self-benefit desired is the joy of serving him.—Klahr Raney II.

SUNDAY: DECEMBER SECOND

MORNING SERVICE

Topic: What's the Point of It All? (Advent)

SCRIPTURE: John 1:9–30.

To miss the point of a pun or a frivolous joke may be embarrassing, but it can hardly be called a disaster. What is disastrous is to miss the point of a lesson to be learned or an insight to be gained or a value to be discovered or an event to be understood. It's more than a parson's solemn worry that this is precisely what millions of people are doing with Christmas. What is the point of it all—this massive, votive, festive, and superlative celebration that the world calls Christmas and the church calls Advent? If we ask why Christ came, John is ready with answers.

I. He came *to give God a new visibility*. (See v. 18.) (a) To Moses God said, "I AM." No predicate. No descriptive adjectives. The "I amness" of eternal, independent, and sovereign self-existence.

(b) When Jesus came, he gave the subject a predicate: "I am the good shepherd," "I am the bread of life," "I am the water of life," "I am the door," and "I am the way, the truth, and the life." William Temple wrote, "The supreme revelation is given in the life and person of Jesus." In him the revealing "word became flesh and dwelt among us" (v. 14). In a space and time framework we are permitted to see what God is like.

II. Jesus came *to give people a new possibility*. (See v. 12.) (a) Like it or not, we are all the creatures of God, for "without him was not anything made that was made" (v. 3). But because we are spoiled, self-centered, and rebel creatures, we need a new beginning, a new life, and a new orientation toward God, the neighbor, and ourselves. The rebel creature must become the obedient child.

(b) Man the creature is convertible. What he is not is self-convertible. Self-improvable, yes. But that is not radical enough. He needs the gift of new life that goes to the root of his egocentric death.

III. Jesus came *to give grace a new immensity*. After declaring in v. 14 that our Lord was "full of grace," John adds in v. 16, "And from his fulness have we all received, grace upon grace."

(a) "Grace," says James Stewart, "means something completely and forever undeserved." Stanley Jones wrote, "It is love favoring us when we are not favorable, loving us when we are not lovable, accepting us when we are not acceptable, and redeeming us when by all the rules of the book we are not redeemable."

(b) Here of course is where Christmas points to Good Friday. The ground and guarantee of this vast and inexhaustible grace is the atoning event of the cross, whereon Christ the sinless "was made sin for us" that "in him we might become the righteousness of God" (II Cor. 5:21, RSV).

IV. Jesus came *to give truth a new vitality*. Return to v. 14: "full of . . . truth."

(a) Truth is that which squares with reality, whether you can package it in a neat sentence or not. "People are bipeds" is a fact. Yet it falls absurdly short of the truth about people.

(b) Our Lord did more than express truth; he embodied it. "I am the truth," he affirmed. With a perfection denied to us, he closed the gap between "is" and "ought," between hypocrisy and honesty, and between deceit and straightforwardness. More than something to be believed, truth is something to be lived.

(c) Think of the empty cliches, the smirking slurs, and the cheap half-truths that we toss around with smug complacency when we are "paying our respects" or lack of them to groups or classes or races against which we are prejudiced. Christ came to embody truth-at-all-costs in his own life and to enthrone it in the lives of his confessors.

V. He came *to give glory a new identity*. "We have beheld his glory" is John's way of saying it in v. 14. The very human life of the divine Christ has a glory all its own.

(a) The glory of the *commonplace*. A stable as well as a star. An infant's smile no less than an emperor's splendor. Thus, when seen through Christian eyes, "earth's crammed with heaven."

(b) The glory of *compassion*. In which the real heroics belong not to priest or prelate but to the good Samaritan; not to feuding apostles, arguing over "who is the greatest," but to the man wearing the slave's apron and washing the feet of his imperceptive friends.

(c) The glory of a *cross*. The innocent taking guilt. Suffering love become redemptive. The undeserving offered pardon and peace. That's glory—in Christian definition.—Paul S. Rees.

Illustrations

INEXHAUSTIBLE SOURCE. The Nile River struggles through the labyrinth of the jungle swamp, which consumes millions of gallons of water; pushes itself through the limitless miles of the semi-desert, which absorbs it like a sponge; carries upon its bosom the commerce of a continent and sings its way at last to the great sea. Why does it succeed? From whence does it derive such power? How does it survive such drain upon its life? It is born from an inexhaustible source; it flows out of Lake Victoria, the watershed of a continent, on beyond where the country rises, terrace upon terrace, to the lofty mountains of the moon! It is born in the hidden springs of the hills, the mother of all mighty rivers. Because of its inexhaustible source, it has the power to push through jungle and desert.—Leonard Cochran.

MAKING OF PERSONS. It is characteristic of Christianity that choice is made not of principles but of a person, of the living God, of Christ. It does indeed bring with it all the moral principles that can be discovered by reason. But it makes us something more than mere machines applying principles. It makes us persons. It brings us more than a code of ethics. It brings us personal relationship, a current life springing from the very source of all life and true liberty.—Paul Tournier.

Sermon Suggestion

WHY HE BECAME LIKE US. Scripture: II Cor. 5:18–21. (1) The word made flesh: incarnation. "God was in Christ." (2) The way made clear: salvation. "God was in Christ reconciling the world unto himself." (3) The world must know: participation. "And hath committed unto us the word of reconciliation."—Frank Pollard.

Worship Aids

CALL TO WORSHIP. "Arise, shine; for thy light is come, and the glory of the Lord is risen upon thee. Lift up thine eyes round about and see." Isa. 60:1, 4.

INVOCATION. Dear Christ, who art the light of the world, shine, we pray thee, so that all who walk in darkness and dwell in the land of the shadow of death may have the light of life. May thy word at this season be for us a lamp unto our feet and a lamp unto our path.

OFFERTORY SENTENCE. "To do good and to communicate forget not: for with such sacrifices God is well pleased." Heb. 13:16.

OFFERTORY PRAYER. O God, who didst give to us the gift of thy Son, stir us with such love toward thee that we may gladly share whatever thou hast entrusted to us for the relief of the world's sorrow and the coming of thy kingdom.

PRAYER. O God, by whose hand all living things were made and by whose blessing they are nourished and sustained: we give thee hearty thanks for all the bounties of thy providence wherewith thou hast enriched our lives, and we humbly pray that, enjoying thy gifts in contentment, we may be enabled by thy grace to use them to thy praise. Especially we thank thee for thy great love in sending thy Son to be the savior of the world and in calling us out of our sins into fellowship with him, and we beseech thee to grant us always thy Holy Spirit, through whom may we grow continually in thankfulness toward thee, as also into the likeness of thy Son, Jesus Christ our Lord.—Louis F. Benson.

EVENING SERVICE

Topic: Three Doors (Advent Communion)

TEXT: John 10:9.

I. *The door of opportunity.* (See Rev. 3:8.) (a) This door, when opened by God, cannot be closed except he close it. For those faithful to him it is kept open. In its context this verse promises an open door of reward, fulfillment, and blessing watched over by God himself.

(b) Through this door of opportunity the faithful may pass. Jesus in his earthly ministry spoke about his own contribution; he then said to his listeners, "He who believes in me will also do the works that I do; and greater works than these will he do, because I go to the Father." Jesus was talking about expanded opportunity and about increased service and endeavor on the part of his disciples. Our Lord repeatedly offers limitless possibilities of spiritual greatness and glory to all those who remain true to him.

II. *The door of relationship.* (See Rev. 3:-20.) (a) There is no picture of intimacy more striking than that of sitting at a common table and breaking bread together. This is the picture seen through that door of relationship as an individual comes to God in response to the presence of Jesus Christ. There is nearness, there is satisfaction, there is understanding, and there is fellowship. The unity between a believer and his Lord is dramatized by the sharing of a meal together. Christ seeks admission to each individual's life; he knocks at the door. Wherever he is welcomed in, the outcome is a relationship of love and joy.

(b) If the relationship is real, the opportunities are boundless. God puts no limits on himself or ourselves when faith is strong and trust is sure. If we are darkly pessimistic about what our church can do or about our own personal influence as Christians in the world today, the reason may well be that the door of relationship is yet unopened. We have yet to sit at table with the Christ whose feast is abundant and whose grace is overflowing. Our need is to swing wide that door to let the Master in.

III. *The door of life eternal.* (See Rev. 4:1.) (a) It is the passage available for all of those whose entries through the door of relationship and subsequent doors of opportunity have shown them to be faithful, steadfast, and true. Obviously it is not the first door; one comes upon it as a result of a continuing pilgrimage. But we are assured that it is a glorious threshold to cross, and God has prepared it for his own.

(b) Further reading in the book of Revelation enhances our understanding of what lies beyond that door. Its importance to us however always must be seen in the perspective of those other doors. Entrance into the life eternal is predicated upon responsible living in the life at hand. There is no short-cut to that third door. One must open first the door of relationship, then show himself trusting enough to walk through various doors of opportunity. Only then, in God's time, will there be revealed the door of life eternal.—John H. Townsend.

SUNDAY: DECEMBER NINTH

MORNING SERVICE

Topic: A Fresh Look at Christmas (Advent)

SCRIPTURE: Matt. 3:23–26; Gal. 1:17–23.

Our exchanging of gifts is predicated on its calling attention to the gift that makes Christmas something to celebrate. It is to remind us that God cared enough to give the very best. He gave all he could. He gave himself. Emmanuel, God with us. As we struggle together for fresh insight into the meaning of Christmas, we are all too prone to give easy explanations of difficult situations. When it comes to interpreting the coming of Christ, we deal in the realm of mystery and faith. A God small enough for us to understand completely would not be big enough for us to worship.

I. What we can understand is that God, seeking to bridge the gap between himself and us, came himself. God entered the world through a human mother and took on a robe of flesh like yours and mine with all of its weakness and frailty. God's fleshly entry into our world had a definite theological purpose. Just saying he was "with us" is not enough. It is significant to see how God was to reveal himself to us, that is, as prophet, priest, and king.

II. God, as Jesus of Nazareth, came as prophet. The prophets of old had spoken for God. They had told of what God approved and disapproved. The law, which was prophetically given through Moses, had embodied God's demands. It was, in Paul's words, our "schoolmaster," "our custodian." God's new message is likewise prophetic. As Jesus speaks as prophet and we believe by faith, we become the children of God. Jesus as prophet has a message that is truly good news. God will give us what we need, not what we deserve. He has seen our plight, and he has come to call us to himself.

III. Jesus came as priest. By his own words he had made this clear. "I came not to be ministered unto, but to minister" (Matt. 20:28).

(a) He was to be a priest, one who serves as an intermediary between man and God. But he was a special kind of priest who would "give his life as a ransom for many." We are an Easter people, and Christmas has no real meaning apart from the crucifixion and resurrection. The giving is fulfilled at the cross.

(b) When Joseph is informed of the uniqueness of the child Mary is carrying, he is given some very specific instructions about the name the child was to be given. "You shall name him Jesus (meaning Savior) for he will save his people from their sins."

(c) Because of his priestly function, Jesus becomes the hinge of history. All of time is divided into the time before his coming and after Advent. And salvation history is likewise divided, the period under the law and the period under grace.

Covenant religion moves in Christ from laws and requirements to relationships that are predicated on faith.

IV. Jesus came as king. This baby born in such lowly estate in Bethlehem is worshiped even in infancy. Shepherds came to fall down and worship. Wise men, kings, came to give gifts to a king greater than themselves.

(a) His kingdom was not the materialistic dream that most Jews dreamed of in their expectation of the messiah. How difficult those thirty long years must have been for Mary. She had conceived by the Holy Spirit as foretold. The child was born and worshiped. Then for all those years Jesus was just a carpenter in Nazareth. How many times must she have doubted it all. It is Peter, not Mary, who proclaims to the world, "Thou art the Christ, the Son of the living God." It is only after the resurrection that Mary worshiped him as king.

(b) Some of us are like Mary. We have been exposed to all the facts about his coming, but we have yet to encounter him as King of kings and Lord of lords, the Lord of our life. Perhaps this year we will discover Christmas in the truest sense of what it is. Perhaps as we sing, "O come let us adore him," we can lift our hearts as never before and worship "the Mighty God, the Everlasting Father, the Prince of Peace."—Edgar H. Ellis, Jr.

Illustration

SPEAKING OF ANGLES.   Whenever in the Bible an event takes place unable to be explained by rational considerations, the writers introduce an angel. What the angel says in effect is: "Do not attempt to go any further. This thing is beyond you. You are at the frontier of another world. Powers are at work here which belong to God alone." So the angel is a symbol of the existence of a world which is no less real. —D. W. Cleverley Ford.

Sermon Suggestions

CHRIST'S MESSAGE TO THE MODERN WORLD.   Text: Luke 2:10. (1) There is at the heart of things a God who loves every human being dearly, so dearly that all of us can trust God in life and at death. (2) All human beings, irrespective of race or creed or color, are the children of God. As such they are entitled to unfailing consideration and respect. (3) Because all human beings are God's children and possess infinite value, each of us owes active kindness to everyone he meets. (4) The measure of our greatness is not the extent of our wealth or power but the extent of the service we render other people.—James Gordon Gilkey.

JESUS WAS DIFFERENT. Text: Phil. 2:9. (1) His difference in birth. (2) The difference in what he became. (3) The difference in what he did.—Leslie D. Weatherhead.

Worship Aids

CALL TO WORSHIP. "O Zion, that bringeth good tidings, get thee up into the high mountain; O Jerusalem, that bringeth good tidings, lift up thy voice with strength; lift it up, be not afraid; say onto the cities of Judah, Behold your God!" Isa. 40:9.

INVOCATION Our Father, help us during this special season to remember the many ways thou hast pointed out to us the coming of our Lord Jesus Christ. May we be ever mindful that thou wilt not let us sit in darkness, but if we are receptive we will see the light of thy many signs in the prophets, in the lives of our neighbors, and in the eyes of our family.

OFFERTORY SENTENCE. "I will freely sacrifice unto thee: I will praise thy name, O Lord; for it is good." Ps. 54:6.

OFFERTORY PRAYER. We praise thee, O God, for thy countless blessings and pray that thou wilt accept these gifts in gratitude in Jesus' name.

PRAYER. O Desire of nations, long-expected Jesus, when will you appear among us in your glory? Your coming in humility brought great gladness and peace to those who waited for the kingdom, but how few of all mankind know that you have come, and fewer still have learned to walk your ways. Something more than this was promised, something more has kept the Advent hope living in our hearts. Yet the centuries pass, and we ask, "Where are the signs of your coming?"

Yet, O God, we feel that you are at hand. Hope still is strong. The highway is being exalted. The stones are being cast out. The people lift their heads, and we believe that redemption draws near.

May your coming not be to us as a thief in the night, may we not be numbered among those who are unprepared for your coming, and may your coming be like the daybreak at the end of a dark night, that our lives and all of life may be illumined by your presence.—William E. Orchard.

EVENING SERVICE

Topic: The Magnificat and the Coming Revolution

SCRIPTURE: Luke 1:46–55.

I. There was to be the general revolution: "He has scattered the proud in the imagination of their hearts." The proud were the enemies of Israel, primarily the Romans, but evil persons among the Israelites are not excluded, particularly those who set themselves up above others with an overwhelming estimate of their own means or merits, despising others, or it may be treating them with scorn or contempt. "He has scattered the proud with their purposes" (MOFFATT).

II. There was to be political revolution: "He has put down the mighty from their thrones." If the rule of princes should cut across this new kingdom, their rule would be terminated. In the kingdom of God, God is the sole ruler. And only as princes fit into and embody this rule are their thrones permanent.

III. There is to be social revolution: "He has exalted those of low degree." This new kingdom was to be a kingdom of man as man. There would be a canceling of all privileges based on birth, property, and social standing. It was to throw open the gates of life and opportunity to all.

IV. There was to be economic revolution: "He has filled the hungry with good things and the rich he has sent empty away." Economically the first concern for this new kingdom is for the poor, not that they should be comforted by promise of future rewards but that poverty should be banished by providing the good things God has provided for all.—E. Stanley Jones.

SUNDAY: DECEMBER SIXTEENTH

MORNING SERVICE

Topic: How Far to Bethlehem? (Advent)
SCRIPTURE: Luke 1:26–35.

I. How far to Bethlehem? It depends upon where you are and how you travel. Our answers are confused because it is easier to think of geography than soul distance. It isn't much of a distance by steamship or jet. It is quite a journey by sailing ship and camel. Some are much nearer than others. For those who cannot even understand why we make so much of Bethlehem, it is a very long way. To those who feel unworthy of walking where Jesus walked, it is very, very near.

II. How far to Bethlehem for Mary and Joseph? It must have been a difficult and a long journey for them. They may have answered differently. Several days of walking or riding a donkey was commonplace in their time. Since they had never leaned against the soft upholstery in an automobile that smoothed the rough places with cushioned tires, they did not expect what we do. Then too they were going to the city of their fathers. There was the promise their child would be born there. There was much to convince them that God was quite near and had been good to them, and they likely would have answered, "It was not very far to Bethlehem."

III. How far to Bethlehem for the shepherds? They had no overnight journey; they were just outside keeping watch over their sheep. But because they were out in the fields with their sheep they certainly were removed from any main thoroughfare to the town. They were probably in the area still known as the Shepherds' fields. This is at the south side of Bethlehem near the Dead Sea. From there to the town is a difficult climb up a steep slope. It was not easy for them to even begin, for you do not just walk away from your sheep in the middle of the night without concern for their safety. When you remember the centuries of tradition that a good shepherd will lay down his life for his sheep, he would not leave them in the middle of the night; and when you recall the steep climb, it may have seemed quite a distance to the shepherds. Bethlehem was close enough for the shepherds so that they "came with haste and found . . ."

IV. How far to Bethlehem for the wise men? Tradition says it took them thirty days to make the journey. There are those intellectuals who always start further off. It would seem they must take a longer road than the simple and intuitive who come directly. Some thinking persons must first find room for Jesus in their philosophy. There are those who can never start to Bethlehem until they are convinced the journey makes sense and is intellectually respectable. This fact is not criticism, for the way for them is often rough and hard and made easier for us because they travel it all the way. The wise men are often detoured by cruel kings whose political tyranny is the result of other philosophers who never found the homeland. The journey undoubtedly was a longer, harder one for the wise men, but there are some of us who would not consider Bethlehem worth seeking if the wise men had not also traveled there.

V. How far to Bethlehem for Herod? It was too far. Even though the palace was less than five miles away and even though he said he wanted to come and worship the Christ Child, the journey was too much for him. Herod had power. In this world even wise men do stop and stay awhile with power. But those ancient wise men recognized two things more in Herod: fear and tyranny. It is these which still make the journey too far for some. His fear was of a kingship that might take his sovereignty from him. His fear of losing something kept him from giving himself.

VI. How far to Bethlehem for those who lived there? In the middle of the geography of Christmas they were separated from the experience of Christmas by their utter indifference. The light of the star brightened their landscape but not their minds or hearts. Some of them should have heard the first faint cries of the child, but they yawned and talked about the high tax rate and went about their petty concerns with no room for God, not even a God as small as a baby. I cannot believe there was literally no room in Bethlehem that night. It was lack of heart room that caused Jesus to be born in a cave where the cattle were stalled. Those without heart room for God are always those furtherest from Bethlehem. This is true if they are in Bethlehem or in a Christian church.

VII. How far to Bethlehem for you? Where are you now and how will you travel? Where in the story of Bethlehem do you find yourself? As for Mary and Joseph, does the promise of Bethlehem more than compensate for the hurt and discomfort of the journey? Do you come to Bethlehem with the simple faith and haste of the shepherds? Is your journey that of the intellectual striving of the wise men, and do you still follow the star? Like Herod, do you verbalize your desire to see this child and worship him and yet stay walled up in your place of fear and tyranny? Do you find you are too busy for the journey, or like the townsfolk is your indifference so pronounced that you would not recognize Bethlehem if you were there?—Harry N. Peelor.

Sermon Suggestions

THE JOURNEY'S GOAL.　　Text: Heb. 12:2. (1) Without a goal to aim at, we never really get things done. (2) To have a goal is the only way to have a test of progress. (3) If we have a goal, it is essential that that goal should be beyond our attainment, for that is the very essence of an ideal.—William Barclay.

PREPARING FOR HIS COMING.　　(1) The promise. (See Luke 1:26–31.) (2) The prediction. (See Luke 1:32–33.) (3) The plan. (See Luke 1:34–35.) (4) The perplexity. (See Matt. 1:18–19.) (5) The proclamation. (See Matt. 1:20–21.) (6) The prophecy. (See Matt. 1:22–23.)—H. C. Chiles.

Worship Aids

CALL TO WORSHIP.　　"Lo, the star, which they saw in the east, went before them, till it came and stood over where the young child was. When they saw the star, they rejoiced with exceeding great joy." Matt. 2:9–10.

INVOCATION.　　Hushed be our hearts, O God, by the mystery and the wonder of the birth of the Christ Child. Make us truly wise with the wisdom of a little child that once again the highest truth may be born afresh in our hearts. Let not our souls be busy inns that have no room for thy Son, but this day throw wide the doors of our lives to welcome our holy guest.

OFFERTORY SENTENCE.　　"Offer the sacrifices of righteousness, and put your trust in the Lord." Ps. 4:5.

OFFERTORY PRAYER.　　May we find it to be a joyful experience, O Lord, to offer these gifts in the name of Jesus. Grant unto us the wisdom of the men of old who found a token in a star, worshiped the child as a newborn king, and made offerings at his feet.

PRAYER.　　O God, our Father, whose Son Jesus Christ was born into a simple home, living the life of a simple peasant, loving simple things, save us, we pray thee, from such an entanglement in the complexities of life that we lose our simplicity of spirit, our sense of wonder, our taste for simple pleasures, and our joy in little things. Grant that no wealth of possession or learning of mind or pride of soul may take away our taste for lowly things or make the song of a bird or the trust of a child or humble, quiet friendship merely dull or boring. Amid all the distractions of this complicated modern life of ours, keep our hearts childlike and simple so that the gates of the kingdom, closed to the merely clever and the conceited, may be always open unto us.

EVENING SERVICE

Topic: The Word Became Flesh
SCRIPTURE: John 1:1–18.
I. What a profound mystery! (a) Jesus is God. (See vv. 1–2.) He is not merely in God or an emanation from God but one who reveals God so that no one can know God except through him. (See v. 18.)
(b) Jesus is the creator. (See v. 3.) His wisdom and might are displayed in the depths of the seas, in the heights of outer space, and in the way in which we hear and see and think. He is lord of the universe.
(c) Jesus is also a man. (See v. 14.) A helpless infant who developed and grew up in human fashion, he was a friend of sinners and was numbered with the transgressors. Confronted with temptations and acquainted with sorrow, he suffered and died. He became like us, except that he was without sin. He partook of our humanity in the fullest sense. A mystery indeed: the word became flesh.

(d) Through this word become flesh God has something of eternal import to say to us. Here in the incarnation is God's own testimony.
II. What a unique testimony! (a) God uses men to bring his testimony to the world. He used John the Baptist. (See vv. 6–8.) John was a fine witness, but many nevertheless rejected his testimony. (See vv. 9–11.) Today God uses pastors as well as lay Christians. Are our ears open to God's testimony?
(b) The testimony is that Jesus Christ is full of grace and truth. Full of grace toward you. You can leave with him your sins and burdens. Full of truth toward you. In a deceitful world you can still rely on him.
(c) God enables us to receive the testimony. No man can receive it by his own powers. (See vv. 5, 10.) The Spirit creates faith through the testimony concerning Jesus. (See vv. 9, 13.) To believe in Jesus is to be born of God.
(d) Nothing is more unique than the word becoming flesh, for in the assuming of our humanity by the Son of God we see a mighty wonder and receive a saving testimony. Our birthday was the prelude to our rebirth in baptism through which we have the joy of salvation. That joy is a reality because the word became flesh.—Gerhard Aho.

SUNDAY: DECEMBER TWENTY-THIRD

MORNING SERVICE

Topic: The Christmas Star (Advent)
SCRIPTURE: Matt. 2:1–12.
I. *It was a guiding star.* (See v. 2.) (a) Those wise men would never have been able to find, see, and know the young King Jesus had it not been for the star. Have you ever sat down with your Bible and a map and tried to work out the journey taken by those magi?
(1) Those ancient pilgrims had to face vast distances. We read that "there came wise men from the east to Jerusalem" (v. 1). Had they not been guided by that providential star they never could have traveled the vast distances which are implied in the phrase "the east to Jerusalem."
(2) These magi had to face varied dangers. Brigand bands thronged the highways. There were doubtless areas that were almost unchartered and where travel was bound to be arduous, but guided by the star they traveled on until they met the Christ.
(b) God has given us a Christmas star, which is Christmas Day, to guide our thinking about and our believing in King Jesus, the savior of the world. Will you do

what the wise men did and follow the guiding star, that is, follow the meaning of Christmas until it leads you to the savior? Whatever distances you have to travel in your thinking or dangers you have to encounter in terms of experience, do not tarry until you have met Jesus Christ, the Son of God.

II. *It was a guarding star.* (See v. 9.) (a) King Herod was a wicked man. If he had had his wish, he would have done away with the young child. The fact is that Herod was like so many people today. He tried to ignore what the scriptures say about the Lord Jesus Christ and did not want the savior to live; he was determined to do away with the reality of the coming king.

(b) As soon as the wise men had finished listening to Herod and had left his presence, God's guarding star appeared. Instead of being influenced by what Herod had said, their minds and steps were guarded, and they reached the place where the young child was. The guarding star demonstrated the veracity of the scriptures.

(c) Even the chief priests and scribes had to admit it was written in the prophecy of Micah that out of Bethlehem "shall come a Governor, that shall rule my people Israel" (v. 6). God still has his guarding star: it is Christmas Day. People can say that the Bible is not true, but what about Christmas? Christmas is the fulfillment of at least 333 prophecies concerning the birth, life, death, and victory of our Lord Jesus Christ.

(d) The guarding star vindicated the reality of the savior. The story tells us that the star "which they saw in the east, went before them, till it came and stood over where the young child was" (v. 9). Whatever Herod or the chief priests and scribes had to say about the birth of Christ did not alter the fact that Jesus had really come. Men and women today try to tell us that Jesus is not alive, but what about Christmas? The fact that we celebrate Christmas signifies that Jesus was born as your savior and mine.

III. *It was a gladdening star.* (See v. 10.) (a) Up until then the star had been moving, but suddenly it stood over where the young child was. To these wise men it became the gladness of finding Christ. Any doubt or fear as to whether Jesus was a real person, a real king, and a real savior vanished immediately, and joy and gladness filled their hearts. Without delay they fell down and worshiped him, "and when they had opened their treasures, they presented unto him gifts; gold, and frankincense, and myrrh" (v. 11).

(1) Scholars have speculated on the meaning of these gifts. It is generally agreed that the presents were intended to symbolize that which they recognized in the being and nature of the king before whom they bowed and worshiped. The gold was a recognition of his sovereignty. The frankincense was a recognition of his sovereignty. The frankincense was a recognition of his deity. The myrrh was the recognition of his humanity. They had found the Christ and his sovereignty had claimed their allegiance, his deity had commanded their reverence, and his humanity had compelled their acceptance, and their hearts were full of joy and gladness.

(2) Will you not do what the wise men did and open the treasures of your heart to him and own his sovereignty, deity, and humanity in your life? He waits for this allegiance, reverence, and acceptance. If only you will respond to the Christ of Bethlehem, you will know the gladness of the Christmas star.

(b) There is the gladness of following Christ. We read that "being warned of God in a dream that they should not return to Herod, they departed into their own country another way" (v. 12). What they had seen, heard, and experienced of the child Jesus determined their future action. Despite Herod's invitation to return to Jerusalem, they departed into their own country another way. What mattered to them was following God's leading, cost what it would.—Stephen F. Olford.

Illustrations

WHAT IS CHRISTMAS? Christmas is God's answer to those who would write his obituary.

Christmas is God walking down a celestial staircase as a little baby nestled in a woman's arms.

Christmas is starlight dancing in a little girl's eyes as she looks forward to the fulfillment of a gentle and lovely Christmas wish.

Christmas is overworked store clerks trying to smile when their backs ache and their feet hurt.

Christmas is concern for the neglected and the poverty stricken of the community and the last minute search by busy people to see that no one has an empty Christmas.

Christmas is a candlelit altar with people coming and going in attitudes of prayer.

Christmas is a heavy laden postman wishing that so many people did not send so many Christmas cards.

Christmas is red ribboned gifts, Christmas trees, family gatherings, fruitcake, and mistletoe.

But above all it is the birthday of the King of kings and Lord of lords. It is God's entrance into human history in the form of a person who would live and die as no man ever did.

It is the joyous assurance God has not left his universe but has entered into the experiences of humankind in order that they might understand him and he might be near them.

Christmas is the greatest truth of eternity and is the light that ultimately will dispel the darkness around the world.—*Wesleyan Christian Advocate.*

ANGELS SINGING. There must be always remaining in every man's life some place for the singing of angels and some place for that which in itself is breathlessly beautiful and, by an inherent prerogative, throws all the rest of life into a new and creative relatedness. Despite all the crassness of life, despite all the hardness of life, and despite all the harsh discords of life, life is saved by the singing of the angels.—Howard Thurman.

Sermon Suggestions

WE NEED CHRIST THIS CHRISTMAS. Text: Heb. 4:16. (1) We need his love to drive out our hate. (2) We need his truth by which we may chart our course. (3) We need his courage that we may face life unafraid. (4) We need his compassion that we may not pass by on the other side. (5) We need his presence that we may walk life's road with assurance.—W. Wallace Fridy.

THE GOODWILL WE PROFESS. Text: Luke 6:32–33. (1) True Christian goodwill extends to people we don't like. (2) True Christian goodwill extends to people who can't pay back. (3) True Christian goodwill extends to people who most need it.—Frank H. Epp.

Worship Aids

CALL TO WORSHIP. "Behold, I bring you good tidings of great joy, which shall be to all people. For unto you is born this day in the city of David a Savior, which is Christ the Lord. Glory to God in the highest, and on earth peace, good will toward men." Luke 2:10–11, 14.

INVOCATION. Grant, O Lord our God, we beseech thee, that now and every time we come before thee in worship and in prayer we may be vivedly aware of thy presence, become conscious of thy power and a sense of thy protection, and finally know in our hearts and minds and souls the wonder and the grace of thy peace.

OFFERTORY SENTENCE. "When they were come into the house, they saw the young child with Mary his mother, and fell down, and worshiped him. And they presented unto him gifts; gold, and frankincense, and myrrh." Matt. 2:11.

OFFERTORY PRAYER. Our Lord Jesus Christ, whose birthday has become a season of benevolence and giving, bless these our gifts which we offer in thankfulness for thyself, God's unspeakably precious gift.

PRAYER. Eternal Spirit, to whom all souls belong, we lift our adoration and our praise to thee. Thanks be to thee for every gift of grace that elevates and enlightens life. Thou who didst surprise the world at Bethlehem, coming in a little babe when none was so expecting thee, surprise us with some unforeseen arrival of thy help today. Amid the confusions of an anxious earth we meet to celebrate the Christ Child's coming. Light of the world, who didst shine that first Christmas in a dark generation and didst come to a strange and humble place where shepherds gathered at a manger, shine on us in our darkness and come to us in our humble estate that, while we sing of our Lord's birth long ago, our hearts may rejoice because his spirit has been born anew in us.

We need thy strengthening presence to sustain us through these troubled days and to keep unspoiled the Christlike spirit of goodwill amid violence and hate. Thanks be to thee for all the happy and cleansing memories of Christmas, for the renewed faith they bring in friendship's fidelity and love's power, for names recalled of old and young upon whose remembrance we praise thee for affection given us more than we deserved. For those who long ago made Christmas beautiful; for little children, like the child whom Christ put in the midst of his disciples; and for all true friends, whose affection and faithfulness have sustained us, we thank thee at Christmas time.

We pray for the welfare of the world. Upon all who seek it grant wisdom and determination, patience and final triumph. Give to the world in our time, O God, a fresh evidence of thy victorious power. Let the angels' song of goodwill among men come down from heaven to earth and be the song of the nations too. May he who came first as a little child come now as more than a child—the savior, the victor over sin and death and hell, the redeemer of the world, and the prince of peace.

Especially for all homes we pray in every nation under heaven, for all mothers who cradle their infants, for all hungry and all unwanted children, and for the innocent upon whom fall the iniquities of the world, for them we pray. And as we pray, enlarge our sympathies, and with our generous support may the missionaries be enabled to carry the ministry of thy church to the ends of the earth. Today when we joyfully call Christ, "Lord, Lord," may we remember his warning and do the will of his Father in heaven.

Now visit those especially in this company who feel beyond the reach of the radiance that Christmas brings; bereaved, tempted, and perplexed, in whatsoever ill estate we be, let thy strength be sufficient for us now. Come to us in some unexpected insight or some invasion of unlooked-for power, and work thy transforming miracle in our hearts, providing faith for fear, courage for cowardice, strength for weakness, and victory for defeat. Increase our confidence in thee, burnish again our ideals that the fingers of the world have tarnished, give us brave hearts, and send us, who came here with plumes shorn and armor dented, into the world again rearmed with faith and strength for tomorrow's battles.—Harry Emerson Fosdick.

EVENING SERVICE

Topic: Words of Glory
TEXT: John 1:14.

I. These words sing. They are not pedestrian, prosaic, ordinary words like dog, cat, mouse, barn, dirt, and hay. They are rather singing, celebrating, lifting, and soaring words. They are poetic words so put together that they point to a truth that can never be captured simply by words.

(a) Sometimes if you want to express a deep truth that arises out of a personal experience so that you know exactly what you are talking about—like describing what happened to you when you saw your first-born child for the first time or when you fell in love—you say the experience is so remarkable and so glorious that it just cannot be expressed in words. You only can sing, "Hallelujah, it is indescribable." You say: "I cannot tell you what it means. It is beyond description." So you sing in celebration or you dance in celebration. The fact is that the glory of it goes through your whole being, and you live in celebration.

(b) You are transformed as a person,

and that is what shows when the transcending experience of life, which cannot be put into words but which are real, true, and honest experiences, are lived. Those transforming experiences, like love and the birth of a new person who comes out of absolute mystery into this world, usually can only be sung or danced and lived.

(c) This is true of all the profound experiences we live through, not only of birth and love but also of death and bereavement; not only those wonderfully inspiring experiences that seem to lift us when we are at one with another person or when we share something very deeply but also in those other experiences when we are utterly alone and misunderstood and alienated.

(d) These are experiences of the pain of life, the pain sometimes of just enduring life when it seems at certain moments that as the wheel of life turns everything goes wrong. Who is not changed when a loved one dies? There are times when we apparently can only hold on to the agony of separation and seek to find in pain a transcendent meaning that changes us, makes us stronger, more accepting, less judgmental, more gentle, and maybe more lovable. These moments that arise out of the depths can never be expressed in words.

(e) The songs that express the deep truths of life, those truths which affect and change us, may be songs of gladness at one time and infinitely sad songs at other times. There is truth in sadness as in happiness, and both truths are sung, cried, and lived. The deeper we live through those experiences, the more transformed, renewed, and changed we become.

II. The words of the text have to be lived

to be believed. And they are lived only in a down-to-earth way.

(a) Those words of glory are pointing to an earth-bound event—a birth of a baby, flesh, breathing, cows, dirt, a barn, hay, and smells—they are pointing to the flesh and the pain of the flesh, to rejection and no place to lay his head. They are pointing to the earth-bound taxes the people pay, to oppression and to the down-trodden, and to torture and the killing of innocent babies. If you look far enough ahead, you see the baby born in a manger now grown to manhood and dying on a cross, and you see soldiers' indifference, women's tears, and disciples' fears.

(b) The words of the text were written and sung after the event. They were written by people who sang them and lived the spirit of the one born, died, and raised again. They were transformed by his spirit of love, compassion, righteousness, and steadfastness. That life, they said, is eternal. It is the word made flesh. He dwelt among us. He lives among us. We live in him. That glory is the glory of God. He is full of grace and truth. When we live in love and compassion through all the experiences of life, we take on his nature, and we become graceful and authentic human beings. We begin, more and more, to ring true and to reveal in our nature God's eternal and true nature.

(c) The words are singing, celebrating words—glory, grace, and truth—and they are lived in our flesh, where we are, just as we are in all the glad and in all the sad experiences of life from birth to death and through death to an eternal life of glory with him made flesh for us, Jesus Christ our Lord.—John B. Coburn.

SUNDAY: DECEMBER THIRTIETH

MORNING SERVICE

Topic: When Do You Stop Living?
TEXT: II Cor. 4:16.

Life cannot possibly be measured by the things of the spirit which are quite independent of markings upon a calendar. The truly vital life-signs are spiritual. The important question is a spiritual question: When do you stop living? Or to turn the question around a bit: What are the vital life-signs of the spirit?

I. A vital life-sign of the spirit is to enjoy life with an undiminished enthusiasm. It is to look upon life as something interesting and exciting and to face days with a degree of expectancy. It is to be alive with anticipation.

(a) To possess this vital life-sign is to retain some of the wide-eyed eagerness of the childlike spirit and to escape the deadening boredom of those who profess to have been everywhere and to have seen everything.

(b) To live life to the full with joy, finding unsuspected rewards in every day and unanticipated pleasures in every experience, is a clear and vital life-sign, an indication that one has not stopped living.

(c) This is the very heart of religion. This is why I say that the most important vital life-signs are inescapably the matters of religion. J. Leuba is correct when he contends, "Life, more life, a larger, richer, more satisfying life, is in the last analysis the end of religion. The love of life, at any and every level of development, is the religious impulse."

II. A vital life-sign is to retain a satisfying and fulfilling relationship with others.

(a) We think of the recluse as being abnormal and rightly so. We consider the hermit to be queer and with good reason. A sign of our wholesomeness is our involvement in the lives of others. To be alive is to care about others, to be interested in others, and to have a concern for others.

(b) We begin life as totally self-centered creatures, physically alive but spiritually as yet unborn. We cannot even focus our eyes on others, and it takes us some time to get accustomed to the voices of others. But then as we mature we become conscious of the presence of others, and we become aware of their responses to us. It takes the better part of a lifetime to grow to the spiritual level where we really think of the needs of others and hold a concern for them, and alas for some this level is never achieved. So it is that our spiritual aliveness is marked by a vital life-sign of involvement with the lives of others.

(c) To continue to be involved with others, sharing their joys and sorrows and caring for them in countless ways, is to be useful to others. This is life, for as Goethe said, "A useless life is an early death," not necessarily of the physical being but most certainly of the spiritual being.

III. If we are to accept positively the admonition of Jonathon Swift who said, "May you live all the days of your life," we shall have to escape the jaws of the past tense which can lock us into the days gone by and hold us back from the fulfillments of the present tense and the hopes of the future tense.

(a) A vital life-sign demanded of us at every point where there is change is a willingness to embrace the future as a friend rather than as an enemy. It is a vital life-sign to enter into the future tense cheerfully and without resentment, no matter what may be a person's fondness for the present and his sentiment about the past.

(b) Herbert Spencer saw this clearly: "A living thing is distinguished from a dead thing by the multiplicity of the changes at any moment taking place in it."

IV. A vital life-sign of the spirit is present when there is a firm faith that dwells within the mind and heart of a person.

(a) Paul was right when he made a distinction between physical life-signs and spiritual life-signs. He wrote, "Though our outward man perish, yet the inward man is renewed day by day."

(b) A person may be enormously fit and yet may experience a death of the inner spirit. Conversely a person may be broken in body and yet have a buoyant and radiant spirit within that broken body.

(c) There is not necessarily an interdependence of mind and body, for we have all witnessed in our lifetime giants of the spirit who lived within, as Paul phrased it, "broken vessels." We have also seen those who were physically fit and energetic and who were strangely empty and lacking in inner depth of mind and heart.

(d) God made us physical beings, but he also made us spiritual beings. We have a destiny and a dignity above the dust. For the moment we are held down by the earth, but there is something within us that pulls us up to the stars. Do you not know this? Have you not felt this? And does this not give you the assurance that as a human soul you have not stopped living?—Charles L. Copenhaver.

Illustration

SPIRITUAL JOURNEY. Suppose you are driving down a strange road. It is a narrow, winding highway in the hills. You are looking for a poorly-marked side road which you must take to reach your destination.

First, imagine that you are making this journey at night. With only the headlights of the car to guide you, the trip can be nerve-racking. You may find your way with great difficulty and only after making mistakes.

Now suppose instead that you are taking the same trip in the early evening as the sun is beginning to set. You are driving west, and at just the crucial moment you are blinded by the blazing sun in front of you. So you miss the side road you have been hunting.

Finally, imagine that you are taking the same journey in the afternoon when the sky is blue and the air is clear. What a difference that makes! How much more easily you reach your goal.

So it is with our spiritual journey. 'We might search for God with our feeble headlights and flashlights. But God has not left us to the frustration of that task. Instead he has sent his light upon our way, not the blinding light of his full glory but the saving light of Jesus Christ. God's desire is not to dazzle us but to guide us. He conceals all that would distract and confuse us but reveals all that we need in order to find our way.—Laurence H. Stookey.

Sermon Suggestions

THE MANTLE OF ELIJAH. Text: II Kings 2:13. (1) The mantle of Elijah is a trust to be handled with reverence and responsibility. (2) The mantle of Elijah is a challenge. It is there not to be looked at and admired but to be adapted and worn. (3) The mantle of Elijah is the symbol of a spirit that must be kept alive.—R. Leonard Small.

ON THE DAY AFTER CHRISTMAS. Scripture: Matt. 2:1–12. (1) Our celebration of Christmas can bring a new perspective on our work. (2) Our celebration of Christmas can give us a new confidence that God can help us face and handle the unexpected in life. (3) Our celebration of Christmas can give us a new commitment to Christ and Christian living.—Lewis R. Rogers.

Worship Aids

CALL TO WORSHIP. "We have thought of thy lovingkindness, O God, in the midst of thy temple. According to thy name, O God, so is thy praise unto the ends of the earth." Ps. 48:9–10.

INVOCATION. Mysterious God of creation, we are forever awed by the wonder of life here and now, beyond and forever. The more we learn of nature and existence, the more we ponder the puzzle of your conceptions. Through science and technology we have conquered boundaries unimaginable to our father's father. Yet every answer leaves unknown, though sharper in its reality, the inexpressible nature of your word. The more we discover of the discernible, the more we anticipate our need of the eternal.—Richard D. Bausman.

OFFERTORY SENTENCE. "Therefore, as ye abound in every thing, in faith, and utterance, and knowledge, and in all diligence, and in your love to us, see that ye abound in this grace also." II Cor. 8:7.

OFFERTORY PRAYER. Dear Father, help us to be ever concerned to find thy way for our lives, and may we never be satisfied to give thee our second best in return for thy great gift of love.

PRAYER. O God, in whom we live and move and have our being, in thy merciful providence thou hast brought us to this good hour. We bow before thee with grateful hearts for thy care and goodness during the days passed. We thank thee for thy guiding hand which has been ever ready to direct us and restrain us, for thy watchful eye which has protected us, and for thy love which has been a constant source of concern in all our affairs.

O thou gracious one, through this new year help us to be diligent in use of time, to be faithful to every trust, to be extravagant in thy service, to be watchful of words we utter, to be generous in our criticism of others, to be courageous in time of testing, to be aware of the needs of men, to be slow to expose, to be quick to believe the best, to be responsive to thy voice, to be dependent upon thy strength, and to be accompanied by thy presence.—W. Wallace Fridy.

EVENING SERVICE

Topic: The Lure of Yesterday

SCRIPTURE: Gal. 2:11–21 (NASV).

The Bible teaches that God is not behind us but in front and urging us to move on. A person will either grow in grace or he will stagnate in yesterday. Like the pull of a magnet, the lure of yesterday will draw you away from the responsibilities of today, and it will greatly limit your usefulness. Why is yesterday so dear to most people?

I. *It is familiar.* No one prefers the unknown to the known. Even the most adventuresome person will find this true when he is honest with himself. This is one reason why death holds such fear for many. It is a state "from whose bourne no traveler returns," and we know so little about it. The cautious traveler would rather go ten miles out of his way to follow a highway he knows than to take a chance on some professed new short cut. We use products of a given brand name as over against some new and perhaps equally good brands because we know them from experience. Our psychological and spiritual patterns develop along the same lines.

II. *It never offends anyone.* Few people get offended over their "long agos." But today demands change if we are going to be able to meet the needs of tomorrow, and that is uncomfortable. To ask a man to change his thinking or his ways is to question the value or the lasting value of his yesterdays, and that is an offense to some people, particularly those who have prepared little for today and expect to do less for tomorrow.

III. *It costs nothing.* Yesterday demands nothing of today, no struggle and no discipline. If we live all the time in yesterday, we can live a long time on the work we used to do, and we do not have to do anything now. Peter's relapse into yesterday at Antioch did not cost him anything at the moment, and until called into question by Paul, he was able to maintain a comfortable friendship with the gentile Christians and the ceremonial Jewish Christians. Had he not had this relapse, it might have cost him the alienation of some friends in Jerusalem who were unwilling to live in today. Had Peter graciously but firmly insisted upon friendship and love for the gentile Christians that were equally as warm and meaningful as for the Jews, it might well have severed some relationships that had lasted through the years.

IV. When the lure of yesterday settles in one's life, he begins to develop a "yesterday psyche."

(a) We see this in church life when an individual decides he has served his time and now he is going to take it easy. "I've served my time" is another way of saying: "I've had all I want of tomorrow. I've had all I want of today. Now I want to live in yesterday." That is a serious sickness.

(b) Peter was a great man, and his greatness was evident even here in this error. Paul said Peter did not need an accuser; he stood condemned by his own act. But when rebuked, Peter accepted in humility and changed his ways. That is a characteristic of greatness. He broke the hold that yesterday had on him and became a man of great tomorrows.—Fred R. Skaggs.

SECTION XI. A Little Treasury of Illustrations

X-RATED SALAD.   A mother was preparing a green salad for dinner. She had thrown unacceptable portions of vegetables into the sink to be sent down the garbage disposal. Her teen-age daughter came to tell her that she and some friends were going to see an X-rated movie. To try and gain her mother's consent she used the time-worn arguments about art and educational value. As she talked her mother began to pick up the discarded vegetables and put them in the salad. Seeing this, the daughter exclaimed: "Why, mother, what are you doing? You are putting garbage in the salad!" The mother replied, "Well, I figured that if you did not mind putting garbage in your mind, you would not mind eating it in your salad."—Herschel H. Hobbs.

CANDLE FOR THE DEVIL.   In a church in Russia an old peasant woman set a candle before a picture of the last judgment. "Why do you do that?" somebody asked. "No one seems to pray for him. We ought to pray for him too." She meant the Devil.

BLESSING.   In *Fiddler on the Roof*, Tevye, the father and principal character in the show, is a generous man. In fact he is much more generous than his wife, Golde, would like. In one of his outbursts of generosity, Tevye says a beautiful thing. He offers the newcomer named Perchik a chunk of cheese from his dairy cart. Tevye has little else to offer a stranger, and the audience is aware of the kindness represented by such a gift. Perchik, the stranger, at first refuses, insisting that while he also is poor, he is no beggar. Tevye insists on giving him something to eat however and says simply, "Here—it's a blessing for me to give."—John H. Townsend.

PAYMENT.   Some American tourists helped a young Irish girl with a heavy burden she was carrying. They chatted with her while giving assistance, but she, being overwhelmed by such kindness, was unable to speak. Finally, when the tourists had completed their good deed and turned to leave, the girl said, "I cannot repay your kindness, but I can pass it on."—Allan J. Weenink.

EVERYONE FIRST.   Like any ordinary tourist the Prince of Wales on visiting Vienna wanted to see the sights and asked particularly to see the palace where the Congress of Vienna was held. It was that Congress that was supposed to make peace in Europe after the defeat of Napoleon. He was shown a building whose most striking feature were five doors all leading into the main entrance hall. There, precisely at the stroke of noon, the five ambassadors from the victor nations could enter the chamber at the same time and find their places at the conference table. Everybody except the loser nation could be first. Nobody needed to be second. No nation would be affronted in its national honor by having to bring up the rear. Was it for this, one wonders, that the Light Brigade rode so gallantly into the jaws of death? Was it for this that the Battle of Waterloo was fought, so that somebody could sit down first at a conference table?—John W. Rilling.

DARK HOURS.   Our highest hopes are often destroyed to prepare us for better things. The failure of the caterpillar is the birth of the butterfly; the passing of the bud is the becoming of the rose; the death or destruction of the seed is the prelude to its resurrection as wheat. It is at night in the darkest hours, those preceding dawn, that plants grow best and most increase in size. May this not be one of nature's gentle showings to man of the times when he grows best, of the darkness of failure that is evolving into the sunlight of success? Let us fear only the failure of not living the right as we see it, leaving the results to the guardianship of the infinite.—William George Jordan.

QUIET TIME.   The scene is a baseball game in which Lucy is playing in the outfield. A ball drops beside her, but Lucy made no move to catch it. Charlie Brown, the manager, rushes out in anger to ask why she had not caught the ball. He points out that she did not even have to take a step but just hold out her glove. And Lucy answers simply, "I was having my quiet time."

AT THE GATE.   In *The Trial* by Franz Kafka, Mr. K, the hero, wanders into a church and hears a priest tell a parable. A man was told to enter a kingdom through a certain gate. When he arrived he found the gate, but he noticed a sentinel guarding the entrance. So he sat down and waited for the sentinel to give him instructions or to grant permission to enter. But the guard did nothing and said nothing. So the man continued to wait for something to happen or for someone to come. For a whole life he sat there. Then the guard closed the door. He said to the man: "The door was made for you and for you alone. And because you chose not to enter

it, it is being closed forever."—Mark Trotter.

FORESIGHT.   Sigmund Freud told about a sailor who was shipwrecked on a South Sea Island. When he saw the natives emerging from the jungles, he knew for that evening he would perhaps become the soup or at least the main dish for supper. But it was not so. To his astonishment they put him on a throne and gave him a crown for his head. They actually proclaimed him as their king, and every native became his slave. The sailor enjoyed his new station in life but soon discovered that it would only last for one year. After that he would be banished to an island where he would starve to death.

Obviously he did not like that idea, so he ordered the natives to build boats, and he started transplanting fruit trees to the island. He sent carpenters to the island to build comfortable houses and farmers to clear the land and plant crops. He was making plans for the next year when his reign would end, and if then he were banished to the island, he would have a place in which to live, fruit and vegetables to eat, and protection from the merciless sun.—Jerry Hayner.

DIVINE APPAREL.   A minister was performing a marriage in a home. The bride's young sister was fascinated by the long black robe he wore. When the service was over, the minister took off the robe and put on a jacket. Unable to restrain herself, the little girl burst out: "Why, you're not God. You're just wearing his clothes!"—Stephen Mark Heim.

HOLDING ONE'S OWN.   A man was driving his mule to Memphis. He was not at all sure of the distance, so he asked a passerby. "About seven miles" was the reply. So he drove on. After a considerable drive he had not reached Memphis, so he asked again. "About seven miles" was the answer. This experience was repeated several times with the same answer. Finally the drive slapped the mule with the reins and exclaimed, "Thank goodness, we're at least holding our own."

WHICH SIDE? Michael Faraday when he was a boy sold newspapers. On one occasion while he was waiting for his papers in front of the iron gates of the newspaper office, he put his arms and head through the bars. Thoughtfully he began to philosophize concerning his position. With his arms and head on one side of the gate and his heart and body on the other side, on which side of the gate was Michael Faraday? At this point somebody opened the gate and nearly jerked his head off, so, as he says, he learned the hard way that there is no profit in trying to be on two sides at once. Both wisdom and safety lie on the side of decision.—Harold Blake Walker.

CABLE. A Belgian who had been sent by his firm to a country in South America to close a business deal which had been pending for thirteen years received, after six months, an imperative cable from his home office asking why he didn't settle the affair promptly and return to the home office. He replied by cable with this revealing sentence: "Everything here is very simple except the difficulties which are enormous!"—Charles L. Copenhaver.

SIGN. The sign of the truly religious man is not that he comes to church to find God but that he finds God everywhere, not that he makes a great deal of sacred places but that he sanctifies common places.—William Barclay.

THE SAFE WAY. An amateur mountain climber and his guide neared the summit of a lofty peak in the Swiss Alps. The guide knew that from this great height they would behold an inspiring view—a vast panorama of nature's victories and defeats. In the amateur's eagerness to reach the summit, he tried to pass his guide. Knowing the danger and treachery of the howling winds that blustered across the towering peak, the guide stretched forth a restraining hand and said, "The only safe way to reach the top and gaze out upon the world is upon your knees."

MISSING ELEMENT. Howard Maxwell was a man in tune with the times. His four-year-old daughter Melinda acquired a fixation for "The Three Little Pigs" and asked that her daddy read it to her night after night. Mr. Maxwell, very pleased with himself, tape recorded the story. When Melinda next asked for it, he simply switched on the playback. This worked for a couple of nights, but then one evening Melinda pushed the storybook at her father. "Now, honey," he said, "you know how to turn on the recorder." "Yes," said Melinda, "but I can't sit on its lap."—James L. Pleitz.

SHARING. The throwing of a bone to a hungry dog, as Jack London pointed out, is not true sharing. Rather it is human-inspired benevolence. It is only when one is himself hungry and then shares his meal with someone who also is hungry that he exercises the genuine act of sharing. It involves the spirit of giving oneself in what is shared.—E. Paul Hovey.

NEIGHBOR. A little girl, told that the church on the corner was God's house, said to her mother, "We are really lucky to live in the same neighborhood with God." —Brian L. Harbour.

GETTING AND GIVING. Men should not come to church to get but to give. If anybody asked me the one supreme justification for church-going, I should reply, "An opportunity to give—the giving of money, yes, as a symbol of a dedication of the whole life, but equally important, a giving of one's talents and one's whole self to the cause and to the teachings of Jesus."—William Marston.

INVESTMENT. Benjamin Franklin is reported to have left at his death an amount equal to about $5000 each to the cities of Boston and Philadelphia. The money was to be held in trust for 200 years. In the year 1991 it may be used. The two cities administered the trusts differently, and the final distribution will not be the same. It has been estimated that the accumulated interest on the money in the

Boston trust will have increased the amount to three and one-half million dollars. More than $300,000 was paid out in 1891 as directed by the will.—Jonas L. Stewart.

TWO MATTHEWS.   Michelangelo Caravaggio, an Italian painter of the closing years of the sixteenth century, was commissioned to paint a picture of St. Matthew for the altar of a church in Rome. He was instructed to portray Matthew writing his gospel with an angel to be shown giving him inspiration and direction. Caravaggio painted Matthew as the gospel record suggested to his artist's imagination. He showed a bald, roughly-bearded, rudely-clothed, and barefooted old man. He is writing in a book which he holds rather awkwardly, and as he writes his brow is anxiously furrowed. By Matthew's side the artist painted a youthful angel who carefully guides the old man's hand as a teacher guides the hand of a child learning to write.

When Caravaggio took his picture to the church and affixed it to the altar, the authorities were shocked by what they deemed to be his great disrespect for Matthew. They demanded that he do another painting. The second one shows a rather different Matthew—self-assured, well-scrubbed, benign, and with his head crowned by a delicate halo. And the angel—this time an ethereal creature —hovers over him. Caravaggio was a good painter, and his second picture is technically a good one. But it lacks the force and the sincerity of the first one. The first painting represents the real Matthew of the gospels, whereas the Matthew of the second one is a character in a pious fable.

The Matthew of Caravaggio's first painting was made of common clay redeemed by the touch of Jesus Christ. He was one of us. He had the same mixed motives and confused aims that you and I have. He was the amalgam of saint and sinner, of angel and beast that you and I are. In his inner life he knew the tensions we know. "Jesus saw a man named Matthew"—a very ordinary man, a man made of the stuff we are made of, and Jesus made a disciple of him.—J. A. Davidson.

WILL THEY CARE?   Edward Askew Sothern, an American actor in the last century, saw a small boy who wanted to go outdoors to join his older playmates but feared they would not accept him. When the children started to return to the house, Sothern said playfully, "Let's hide behind the curtain and they won't know where we are." The boy looked at him disconsolately and said, "Suppose they don't care?"—William C. Heffner.

ENTRUSTED WITH THE GOSPEL.   Such an immense and shining splendor entrusted to such poor, pathetic, and broken instruments. Such an infallible truth committed to very fallible man. Such an amazing gospel committed to such an ordinary church. It is so frightfully incongruous; in fact it is all wrong! Yet it is God's doing, and somehow it must be right.—James S. Stewart.

SECURITY.   All the way from the carpenter's shop to the cross Jesus was the securest man who ever lived, talking about peace when his situation was not peaceful, about joy when the circumstances were not joyous. His was the security of life in God, the only permanent security there is. He promises to give us that security as we identify ourselves with him and surrender our lives to God in trust and obedience.

INDEBTEDNESS.   Comes the dawn and the unsuspecting patriot, garbed in pajamas, a garment of East Indian origin, wakes up with a glance at the clock, a medieval European invention, rushes to the bathroom to shave, a rite developed by the priests of Egypt, looks in a glass also invented by the Egyptians, washes with soap invented by the ancient Gauls, and dries himself with a Turkish towel. He pulls on his garments, many of which are from Japan and Australia, fastens them with buttons which first appeared in Europe at the close of the stone age, puts his feet into leather tanned in Argentina, and ties about his neck a strip of colored cloth which is a survival of shoulder shawls worn by the seventeenth-century Croats. And so to breakfast. Before him in pottery vessels known as China is an orange domesticated around the Mediterranean, a cup of coffee from Brazil, and waffles originally served in Scandinavia.

Breakfast over he reaches for a piece of moulded felt invented by the nomads of eastern Asia, and takes his interurban train, an English invention. He buys a newspaper with coins invented in ancient Libya and reads the news in letter characters invented by the Semites and provided for him by a printing process invented in Germany on paper material invented in China. As he scans the terrible news of foreign lands he gives utterances of fervent thanks to a Hebrew God in language borrowed from England that he is 100 percent (decimal system coming from the Greeks) independent American, the word American taken from Amerigo Vespucci, an Italian geographer.—Ralph Linton.

SHARED KNOWLEDGE. There is no atheism at once so stupid and so harmful as fancying God to be afraid of any knowledge with which he has enabled man to equip himself.—James Russell Lowell.

ONE NOTE. A man bought a cello and sat all day playing one note. Finally his wife said, "I don't know much about music, but I do know that others who play the cello keep moving their fingers up and down the strings." "Ah," said the husband, "they are searching for the note. I have found it!"—Harry N. Peelor.

FAITH CROSSING. A Talmudic interpretation of the Red Sea crossing tells how the sea waters did not part and allow Moses to pass simply because God looked down from heaven and saw that unless he opened the waters they would all be drowned. This interpretation suggests that the reason the sea opened was in response to Moses putting his toe into the water, risking that the seas would drown him but being that determined and filled with that much faith. The story ends as does each Talmudic interpretation with a moral: "Do not just stand there on the dry land praying for miracles!"—William L. Dols, Jr.

SENSITIVITY. President Lincoln at the height of the battle of Shiloh went into the war department office for some up-to-date information and was confronted by the brother and sister-in-law of General Lew Wallace, who was in the thick of the fighting. The sister-in-law blurted out, "We had heard that a General Wallace was among the killed, and we were afraid it was our Wallace—but it wasn't." To which Lincoln replied, "Ah, but it was somebody's Wallace."—Alfred T. Davies.

FRANK'S SON. In October of 1932 twenty-nine men were involved in an all-day prayer meeting near Charolette, North Carolina. "At first our prayers were for revival in Charlotte," one participant recalls, "but soon we were praying that God would send a revival that would spread over the state and even to the ends of the earth." Two more days of prayer and fasting were held in 1933, and a fourth day of prayer was scheduled for May, 1934, on the farm of Frank Graham. On that day someone asked God "to raise up somebody to preach the gospel around the world." Little did they know that God would call Frank's son Billy to preach the gospel to packed stadiums in North America and abroad, including a presentation to a million people on one single occasion in Seoul, Korea.—*Decision.*

GIFT. Andrew Fuller went into his native town seeking gifts for the cause of missions. One of his old acquaintances said, "Well, Andrew, I'll give you five pounds, seeing it is you." "No," said Mr. Fuller, "I can't take anything for this cause, seeing it is for me." And he handed the money back. Feeling reproved, the man hesitated a moment and then said: "Andrew, you are right. Here are ten pounds, seeing it is for the Lord Jesus Christ."—G. Ray Jordan.

SOUND THEOLOGY. Lucy and Linus were looking out the window at a steady downpour of rain. "Boy," said Lucy, "look at it rain. What if it floods the whole world?" "It will never do that," Linus replies confidently. "In the ninth chapter of Genesis, God promised Noah that would never happen again, and the sign of the promise is the rainbow." "You've taken a great load off my mind," says Lucy with a relieved smile. "Sound theology," pontificates Linus, "has a way of doing that!"

THROUGHOUT THIS DAY.   As I enter this new day, God himself goes with me. His love, his care, his guidance, and his protection surround me. They surround me as the silent sunlight surrounds a tree. If I encounter a difficult task, I can trust God to give me, through the processes operating within my body, the physical strength I must have. If I encounter a hard problem, I can trust God to give me, through the operations of my mind, the wisdom I need. If I must endure hardship because there is no honorable way of escape from it, I can trust God to give me the strength, the patience, and the inward quietness which my difficult situation demands. I need never be afraid. I need never feel confused, bewildered, or inadequate. Whatever happens, God's love and care encompass me. Secure within them I can face life and any situation which life may create undismayed.—James Gordon Gilkey.

HIDDEN FORCES.   One of the most dramatic scenes in European history occurred when Charles VIII demanded ransom from the free city of Florence. Piero Capponi, the mayor, refused to make the payment. Charles thundered, "I will have my trumpets blown, and my army will overtake your city." Capponi's answer is immortal: "Blow your trumpets, and we will ring our bells." Charles was silent, for he knew that at the ringing of the bells the hidden army of Florence would spring into being.

PREACHING LOVE.   Albert Schweitzer, asked how he found it possible to preach so effectively to the natives of Africa, replied: "Oh, these people are born scared, live scared, and die scared of evil spirits. I limit myself to preaching to them that, in spite of all appearances to the contrary and behind all the seeming mystery and cruelty of life, there is not terror but love, the Father of Jesus Christ."

FORETOPMAN'S PRAYER.   When the ships of the British Navy had more yards and masts than they have now, at the order "Way aloft" the men raced up the rigging to carry out the duty specified aloft. On one of the ships on two successive days a man was killed. Each had been captain of the foretop and had fallen from aloft to deck. Seamen sometimes are rather superstitious, and when a third captain of the foretop in that week was named, they were sorry for him. He was a hard man and sometimes drank more than he should. Billy Hicks had sense enough to know that this made things more dangerous for him. When the time came, he went through the evolution without a single mishap, and the crew breathed more easily when it was over and there was no accident.

A week later an officer of a sister ship came aboard. He said to the captain: "Have you a man called Hicks? I want to see him." When Hicks came the officer began to read a line or two out of a little notebook he carried. Hicks became very red in the face. On a dark night that officer on his ship had seen lights flashing a signal, and it was the signal he was reading out of his book. "You are making fun of me, sir," said Billy. "No," said the officer, "but tell me about it." Then Hicks said: "It was like this, sir. I was made captain of the foretop when two men had been killed. I asked the officer if I might go up to the top and practice some signaling, and he said to me, 'Go ahead.' When I got my light going, I just said my prayer with it. I've quit drink and lowdown things and stand on my own feet now, sir."

This is what the officer took down when he read the signal: "God, this is Billy Hicks signaling. I've been promoted cap of the foretop, God. I ain't much feared of death, but, your holiness, when I go up tomorrow give me nerve to play the man and, God, give me what I used to feel when I knelt at my mother's knee and said, 'Our Father.'

Good night, God. Yours truly, Billy Hicks."—Homer J. R. Elford.

THE GIFT OF MEMORY. Memory makes it possible for time to be used more than once. The memory of a heartening or beautiful thing recalls the time that it happened. That time has gone by, but it can be used again when the memory comes back. Think how many times people have been refreshed and fortified by memories of some shining hour in the past. It is a wise way of living to store the mind with high and lovely things to remember and to call them often to mind.—Halford E. Luccock.

THE LEAST IN THE KINGDOM. Who are the least in the kingdom of heaven? The following are pretty small: those who are saving themselves at the expense of the church, those who are engaged in the business of saving institutions because those institutions support them, those who are fighting old battles that do not need to be fought over again, those who are giving their best energies to the defense of methods that no longer fit the problem, those who are trying to turn the hands of the clock back, and those who are fighting other good people who disagree with them. There are other small ones in the kingdom, but these cause some of the worst trouble.—Roy L. Smith.

FRAME. The difference in human life depends for the most part not on what people do but on the meaning and purpose of their acts. Outwardly the experiences of life are much the same. All of us are born and all die. All lose loved ones, nearly all marry, and nearly all work. The question is not what happens to me, at least in the big experiences of life. All these things happen to all of us. The question is in what frame do I put the things that happen to me?—Elton Trueblood.

DAY OF JUDGMENT. The preacher was describing the Day of Judgment. "Lightning will crackle," he said, "thunder will boom, rivers will overflow, flames will shoot down from the heavens, the earth

will quake violently, and darkness will fall over the world." Whereupon a small boy in the front pew turned to his father and asked, "Do you think they'll let school out early?"—The Baptist Record.

THE HEART'S CAPACITY. William Allen White in his autobiography wrote of a boyhood friend and playmate, Temple Friend, who was kidnaped by the Indians when about one year of age. Temple's grandfather was an itinerant missionary to the Indians. He persisted in his faith that his grandson was alive.

Coming to an Indian village, he made it a practice to line up all the boys near the age of his grandson. Whispering quietly in the ear of each boy so as not to startle him, he repeated the name of his grandson, "Temple, Temple." Time went by and his faith seemed hopeless.

About eight years later he came to an Indian village remotely situated from his usual circuit. There were about a dozen boys eight to ten years of age. Gathering them together as he had done many times before, he once more whispered in the ear of each boy the name of his grandson Temple. At the middle of the line one boy's face lighted up suddenly, and he responded, "Me, Temple!"

No explanation can be satisfactorily given as to how, across the intervening years since his kidnaping at such an early age, this boy retained the memory of a name long unheard. But the story reveals both the capacity of a heart to remember a heritage and the persistent search love makes for its own.—William F. Keucher.

THE CHRISTMAS GUEST. Kenneth I. Brown tells of an American botanist searching in Colombia, South America, for a rare plant specimen to add to his botanical museum. A native Carib guide named Pedro is engaged to assist with the search, and as a guide he begins by leading the way into the Colombian wilderness. At nightfall on Christmas Eve the botanist and Pedro arrive at an isolated Indian village named Cispatia, inland on the Mulatto River. Pedro, before their arrival, indicated that no white man has visited

Cispatia for twenty years. The botanist thus expects an unusual reception but in no way is prepared for the overwhelming respect, reverence, and even worship that is accorded him the moment he sets foot in the village. Language being a problem, the botanist can only behave graciously and responsively to the exaggerated attention he receives.

After a lavish meal is served him—from the hands of the tribal chieftain—a partially paralyzed young muchacha seeks him out. As the other villagers watch intently the girl walks awkwardly toward the American, drops her staff, and stumbles and falls into his arms. A moment later she leaps from him into the shadows, and the villagers suddenly raise their voices in haunting, unmusical, but somehow joyous refrains.

The next morning, Christmas Day, the American is wakened by the same strange chanting, only to discover himself surrounded by gifts and trinkets brought by the natives. Perplexed, upset, and anxious to depart, the botanist finds Pedro and gives the order to leave. Before he can go, however, the chieftain makes a request of him, translated by Pedro. "Bless," he is asked, "bless the people." Bewildered, unused to religious expressions of any kind, the American obliges by repeating over them a scripture verse remembered from childhood, and then swiftly he and his guide make their exit.

"Pedro, what did it all mean?" he asks after they are beyond the village. "You know," Pedro replies. "I don't know," the American says. "Tell me."

Slowly, reverently Pedro answers, "Christ come." Stunned by the thought, the American, who had taken the villagers' homage as the white man's due, hears Pedro explain: "Old miss'nary tell—Christ come. He come day 'fore Christmas; come up river at shade-time in dugout with hombre. He stay at Cispatia. They know at Cispatia." And then in the hush of the jungle, the distant chanting of the villagers ceasing, Pedro leans forward to ask, "It is true, no es verdad, you are, you are —he?"—John H. Townsend.

TWO STAGES. Carl Michaelson told of an actor who appeared on the stage in New York City. In one play he died in the first act. After the curtain was pulled, he arose, dressed, and went across the street to another theater where he had a part in another play. In a real sense this is what happens to us in this life. We lie down in death, but when the curtain is rung down upon our life upon this stage, we rise and go off to live in some other place. Human consciousness and human personality do survive.—Thomas A. Whiting.

CHRIST'S POOR BOOKKEEPER. Some years ago there was a missionary, an Englishman, stationed in India who never could keep his accounts and finances in order. He was many times chided and rebuked by the home board but always in vain. He simply could not keep his books straight. So the home board relieved him of his position and sent a man in his place who was a good bookkeeper. The missionary who was dismissed, instead of going home to England, went off on his own account in a new section of India where no missionary had ever gone before.

Many years passed and the mission station where this good man but poor bookkeeper had once lived reached out into adjoining fields and sent missionaries into the section where this man had gone unaided and alone. One missionary began to tell the people the story of Jesus, how he was the poor man's friend, how he loved little children, and how he healed the sick, and to his surprise the people seemed to understand at once. Their faces were aglow, and one of them said: "Sahib, we know this man of whom you tell us. He has been living here for years." The missionary then discovered that the man who had been dismissed by the home board because of his poor bookkeeping had come into that section and lived among the people, visiting them in their sickness, ministering to them in their times of need, and incarnating the very spirit of Christ. Perhaps this particular missionary was not even up to the average in ability, but in fidelity he was a star of the first magnitude.—Edgar DeWitt Jones.

EXPERIENCING GRACE.   We may still see today men delivered from the chain of their natural reactions after experiencing the grace of God. We see sick people regain physical vitality. We see neurotics delivered from psychological inhibitions on which sometimes even the best treatment has had no effect. But we also see the strong becoming gentle. We see them throwing off the armor plating which imprisons them, their armor of health, insensitiveness,   and   self-confidence.—Paul Tournier.

TWO QUESTIONS.   There are many questions asked in the Bible, but one in Genesis and another in Matthew are, I think, greatest of all. God asked Adam, "Where art thou?" Wise men from the east asked "Where is he that is born king of the Jews?" In one, God was searching for the sinner; in the other, men were searching for the savior of the world.—B. J. Ratnam.

THE LIVING PRESENCE.   Through nineteen centuries Christians have shared in an experience which they have felt they could best describe as being with a Presence which they have associated with the historic Jesus seen in the pages of the New Testament and with the eternal God. Of their honesty in reporting that enduring and repeated experience there can be no doubt. Nor can there be doubt that through that experience they themselves have been transformed. Through it they have been lifted out of moral defeat and impotence into victory and from despair to triumphant hope. Through it they have found power to go through suffering, disappointment and the loss of loved ones, of health and of worldly goods, and to face physical death not only unafraid but also with quiet confidence and joy. Through it strength has come to them in battle, single-handed or with a small company of kindred spirits, against enthroned wrong and age-long evils, and yet to do so in humility, without vindictiveness, and in love.—Kenneth Scott Latourette.

WITNESSING COMMUNITY.   The church is not an institution parallel to that of the state or the nation. It is rather a witnessing community. It is the community that speaks for the kingdom and not only by words but also by a life-style where we dare to practice a love for which the world is not yet ready.—Krister Stendahl.

REVERENT UNDERSTANDING.   I well recall the day when I stepped for the first time within the Church of St. Croce in Florence. It is my favorite church in Italy. Perhaps this is because its architecture is of that pure gothic type of which one sees so little in Italy. One wearies of the heavy baroque of the Roman churches. Or it may be because of the lovely chancel windows whose glass is reminiscent of Chartres or Bourges. It is a treasure-house of art and sculpture. In its crypts and chapels lie some of the greatest men of Italy.

As you enter, a dim but beautiful light rests upon all that half-hidden, mysterious wealth of sacred beauty with which you are surrounded. You stand still for a moment, hushed by the solemn splendor. Then slowly you advance along the sculptured pavement, stopping now and again to examine some exquisite carving, some wonderful bit of sculpture, until at last you arrive at the transcepts. There on the walls are the famous frescoes of Giotto illustrating different episodes in the life of St. Francis. They are half obliterated, and one hopes no hand will seek to restore them.

All around one is a beauty which appeals powerfully to the imagination. But that beauty reveals itself only to the inquiring mind. One needs one's Ruskin to understand the meaning of these delicate sculptures on the pavements, many of them so effaced that one can barely trace the beautiful lines and figures. One needs patience and much reverent curiosity if one is to make out the delicate carvings on the pavement or trace in their relation to each other the different figures of the frescoes.

No hurried tourist understands St. Croce. But the reverent mind, after once it has caught the beauty and the appeal of that glorious interior, delights to spend long hours and even days within these walls, moving with curious, intent, and inquiring interest from spot to spot, finding always something to delight, to fascinate, to inspire.

Such, I believe, was the mood of the psalmist. To dwell in the house of the Lord, to behold the beauty of the Lord, to inquire in his temple—this cannot mean that he wanted to live within the walls of a building all the days of his life. It can mean only that he found life, existence, experience, when once it had been permeated with the life of God, so incomparably rich, so inexhaustibly beautiful, that he asked nothing more for himself than that he should make fresh, constant discoveries of its richness and its significance. Precisely, that is, as the lover of St. Croce inquiries in that temple, so the psalmist declares that the "one thing," the one controlling and dominant desire of his life, is to discover for himself with grave and reverent curiosity the meaning and the beauty of a world, a life, an experience that is permeated with the life of God.—Raymond Calkins.

THE DOOR THAT OPENS. In the construction of the usual wooden door there are four panels separated by a long upright center board and a shorter horizontal board. These two boards form a cross. This standard plan for making doors comes from a carpenter's guild in England in the Middle Ages which took as its motto the words, "I am the door." They worked this sign of the cross into every door, and so it is still done today. The cross and the door are a combination of symbols that have real meaning for us. The cross itself is a bleak and forbidding thing. On the first dismal Good Friday the disciples must have felt as if the cross was as a door slammed in their faces. But it turned out to be as a door opening to new joy and to a new power for living.—Charles M. Crowe.

TWO FACES. A legend tells us that a powerful king commanded legions of soldiers and with them conquered vast domains. He was wise, brave, and feared by all, but no one loved him. Each year he grew more severe and also more lonely. His face reflected his greedy soul. There were deep lines about his cruel mouth and deep furrows on his forehead.

In one of the cities of his kingdom lived a beautiful girl. He wanted her for his queen and decided to speak to her of his love. Dressing in his finest robes and placing a crown on his head, he looked into the mirror to see what kind of picture he would make for the beautiful girl. He saw only that which brought fear to his own heart—a cruel, hard face which looked even worse when he tried to smile.

Quickly he called for his court magician. "Make me a mask of the thinnest wax so that it will follow every line of my features, but paint it with your magic paints so that it will make me look kind, pleasant, and true. Fasten it to my face so that I shall never have to take it off. Make it handsome and attractive. Use your greatest skill, and I will pay you any price you ask."

The magician replied: "This I can do on one condition. You must keep your own face in the same lines which I paint, or the mask will be ruined forever, nor can I replace it."

"I will do anything you ask," said the king, "to win the admiration and love of the girl. Tell me how to keep the mask from cracking."

"You must think kindly thoughts, and to do this you must perform kindly deeds. You must make your subjects happy. You must replace anger with understanding and love. Build schools for your subjects instead of forts, hospitals instead of battleships. Be gracious and courteous, and above all you must be honest with all men."

So the wonderful mask was made, and no one would have guessed that it was not the true face of the king. So handsome was it that the beautiful girl became the queen of the realm. Months passed, and though the mask was often in danger of ruin, the king fought hard with himself to keep it intact. The subjects wondered at the miraculous change which had been wrought and attributed it to his lovely wife who, they said, had made him like herself.

Since gentleness and thoughtfulness had entered the life of this man, honesty and goodness were his also, and soon he regretted having deceived his beautiful wife with the magic mask. At last he could bear it no longer and summoned the magician. "Remove this false face of mine!" he cried. "Take it away. This is not my true self."

"If I take it away," said the magician, "I can never make another, and you must wear your own face as long as you live."

"Better so," said the king, "than to deceive one whose love and trust I have won dishonorably. Better that I should be despised by everyone. Take it off, I say, take it off!"

As the magician took off the mask, the king with fear and trembling sought his reflection in the mirror. His eyes brightened and his lips curved into a radiant smile, for the ugly lines were gone, the frown had disappeared, and his face was the exact likeness of the mask he had worn. His face had come to reflect the attitude of his heart. He had become a living witness to the proverb, "As a man thinketh in his heart, so is he."—Homer J. R. Elford.

ABIDING PRESENCE. You do not so much as touch the threshold of religion, so long as you are detained by the phantoms of your thought. The very gate of entrance to it, the moment of its new birth, is the discovery that your gleaming ideal is the everlasting Real, no transient brush of a fancied angel wing but the abiding presence and persuasion of the Soul of souls. Short of this there is no object given you, and you have not even reached the specified point of admiration.—James Martineau.

THE JANUS-QUALITY. Janus is the spirit of the threshold, poised forever on that razor edge between outward and inward life where every object in the universe has its secret center and where man himself must learn at last to stand. In varying measure all forms of being radiate this Janus-quality. The greater the being, the more intense the radiation. In none is this more evident than in the greatest being the Western world has known. Jesus Christ has a Janus-face. On the one hand is the Jesus-face, gentle pastor of his sheep, wise moralist, golden sun of the noonday world; on the other, the terrible Christ-face, numinous, indecipherable, eyes fixed irrevocably on the abyss of the timeless. No wonder the parson and his little flock stick to the Jesus-face. The Christ-face once seen, if only for a moment, would empty as by magic all those prosperous pews.—Alan McGlashan.

HE GAVE HIMSELF. In his *Dialogues in Limbo* George Santayana pictures a stranger from earth, presumably a Christian, speaking with one of the spirits of antiquity about Jesus. Says the stranger: "If you asked me for my own opinion, I should say that there is one great gift which our prophet has bestowed upon us, and that is himself. . . . It was divine love free from craving or decay. The saint and the blackguard alike were known to him at their true worth; in both he could see something disfigured or unattained, perhaps hidden from their eyes, and yet the sole reason and root of their being, something simple and worthy of love beneath their weakness and perversity; and the assurance of this divine love. . . lent them courage not wholly to despise themselves but to seek and to cleanse the pure pearl in their dunghill, on which his own eye rested, and not without reason to call him the savior of their souls."

NOT FOR OURS ONLY. Young Henry Holland, a son of an Anglican country parson, was born in 1875. Like some men born in clergymen's families, he was not as attached to the church as his father might have wished, and when he was in the early twenties he went to Edinburgh to study medicine. He said later that he decided to "go into medicine to get out of the church." When he got to Edinburgh he was surprised to find quite a number of students who were preparing to be medical missionaries. He also found that some of the most brilliant doctors on the faculty were active Christians and taking part in the activities of the University Christian Medical Association. All this made him think, although he didn't say anything about it and didn't change his course.

He had seen day after day over the mantelpiece in the common room a cryptic motto: "Not for ours only." Finally he got up the courage to ask one of the students what it meant, and the student pointed out that it was the completion of I John 2:2. In a way which we cannot understand and certainly cannot explain, a flash of light illuminated the mind and spirit of that young, potential doctor. It changed the course of his life. He became a doctor, as he had planned, but for a different reason and with a different purpose. He was a medical missionary and was sent to the border country between Afghanistan and Pakistan and to a town called Quetta. There was no hospital, no doctor, nothing in the way of medical light or service.

He responded to the light. He went and was there for fifty-six years, the builder of a hospital, the great eye surgeon of India. In those fifty-six years it is estimated that he gave sight to 100,000 persons. An American doctor who went to see him, as a great many did, said when he came home: "I was not prepared to grasp at once the stimulating, striking character of this dynamic and expert eye surgeon. But in a few moments his simple and compassionate nature, radiating from his inner warmth, embraced me, and I knew that here was a very good and great man." He had become a son of light.—Theodore P. Ferris.

TOUCH OF THE GALILEAN.　The most wonderful work in all the world is not to take iron and steel and make a locomotive or a watch. Nor is it to take pen and paper and write an *Iliad*. Nor is it to take paint and brush and paint an "Angelus." An infinitely greater task than all this is to take an ignoble man and transform him into an upright man. Here we touch the creative power of the Galilean and bow before the mysteries of God.—George E. Wellington.

SCHOOL OF SUFFERING.　Those who heard Jenny Lind, the sweet singer of Stockholm, told of the wonderful quality of her voice and the charm of the songs she sang. Yet few knew that she owed as much to the school of suffering and of sorrow as to the academy where her powers were developed. Her childhood was full of sadness. She was an orphan. The woman with whom she lived used to lock her in the room each day while she went out to work. The only means of whiling away the long hours was for the child to sit by the window and sing to herself.

One day a passerby, who happened to be a music master in the city, heard the voice of the unseen singer. He detected in it possibilities. He called a friend to his side, and together they listened to the wonderful voice within. Getting in touch with the child's guardian, they subsequently made arrangements for the almost friendless girl to be given a chance. There were many difficulties to be overcome, but step by step she mounted the ladder of fame. She captured London, Paris, Vienna, Berlin, and New York. Some say there never was such a voice, thrilling like the thrush, pure as the notes of the lark. But those who knew her best realized how the sorrows of her childhood gave a richness and depth to her songs that otherwise were unattainable.—J. W. G. Ward.

ONE MAN'S EFFORT.　There is only one way in which one can endure man's inhumanity to man and that is to try in one's own life to exemplify man's humanity to man.—Alan Paton.

FIRST DEMAND.　The only way in which the church can defend her own territory is by fighting not for it but for the salvation of the world. Otherwise the church becomes a "religious society," which fights in its own interest and thereby ceases at once to be the church of God and of the world. And so the first demand which is made of those who belong to God's church is not that they should be something in themselves, not that they should, for example, set up some religious organization or that they should lead lives of piety, but that they should be witnesses to Jesus Christ before the world. It is for this task that the Holy Spirit equips those to whom he gives himself.—Dietrich Bonhoeffer.

STORY OF FOUR MEN.   The three men of Lincoln's cabinet who did most to help him sustain the burden and win through to victory—Seward, Chase, and Stanton—had treated him with contempt and even insult.

Soon after Lincoln's inauguration, Seward wrote him an amazing letter, expressing in thinly veiled terms his feeling that Lincoln was incompetent to deal with the great issues confronting the country and offering himself to assume the responsibility of national leadership. Lincoln gently but firmly showed him that that could not be, and they worked together in loyal friendship to the end.

While yet a member of the cabinet, Chase sought to be nominated for the presidency in Lincoln's place, but Lincoln cherished no resentment and soon thereafter appointed him chief justice of the Supreme Court of the United States.

Stanton openly insulted Lincoln when they first met at a court of law in Illinois, refused to continue with a case if Lincoln were to be associated with him, and profanely called him a "gawky, long-armed ape." But in time Lincoln said, "The War Department has demonstrated the great necessity for a secretary of Mr. Stanton's great ability, and I have made up my mind to sit down on all my pride—it may be a portion of my self-respect—and appoint him to the place." His trust was justified, and in the end it was Stanton who stood by Lincoln's deathbed and in reverent awe pronounced the solemn verdict: "Now he belongs to the ages."—Luther A. Weigle.

MESSAGE.   A boy five years of age attended Sunday school for the first time. Returning home he excitedly showed his mother a card on which was a picture of the Savior as the good shepherd. Underneath were the words: "God is love." His mother asked the child what was written

and what the teacher said about it. The child thought for a moment and then replied, "I think, Mummie, teacher said it was 'God has sent his love to you.' "—W. P. Hares.

HARDENED VIRTUE.   When a man has won most of the battles against the world, the flesh, and the devil and when he has made himself a walking embodiment of the ten commandments and is highly disciplined in virtue, he often loses sympathy with those who have failed in the fight. He grows hard toward sinners. His very passion for righteousness makes it hard for him to adopt any attitude which seems to lessen the gravity of sin, and the man, who of all others should be showing tenderness to penitents, seems concerned only to tax them with the enormity of their wrong doing.—W. E. Sangster.

MIRACLE OF LOVE.   Do you remember the great trial scene in Sir Walter Scott's *Waverley* in which the Highland chieftain, Fergus Mac Ivor, is condemned to death for the crime of treason against his sovereign, King George? It is after the judge has put on "the fatal cap of judgment," that Evan Maccombich, one of Fergus' retainers, rises up in the court and asks to be heard. When given permission he addresses the judge: "I was on'y gangin' to say, my lord . . . that if your excellent honor and the honorable court would let Vich Ian Vohr gae free just this once, and let him gae back to France, and no' trouble King George's government again, on'y six of the very best of his clan will be willing to be justified in his stead; and if ye'll just let me gae doon to the Glennaguoich, I'll fetch them up to ye mysel', to head or hang, and ye may begin wi' me the very first man."

There was a ripple of laughter through the court at this quixotic suggestion. Whereupon the clansman turned to the spectators, and he said: "If the Saxon gentlemen are laughing because a poor man such as me thinks my life, or the life or six of my degree, is worth that of Vich Ian Vohr, it's like enough they may be right; but if they laugh because they think I would not keep my word and come back to redeem him, I can tell them they ken neither the heart of a Hielandman nor the honor of a gentleman."

Here was a humble clansman whose love for his chief moved him to look into the face of death without a tremor. This is the miracle of love.—John Haynes Holmes.

COMPASS. God speaks to us through the Bible not because we can look up, as in an encyclopedia, what he has said but because, as we read and meditate upon the Bible, he speaks to us directly through it. He speaks to us through the words of Jesus Christ, but we cannot without thinking apply these words to our immediate questions. We are given a compass, not a map.—Nathaniel Micklem.

DAWN IN THE PYRENEES. Hilaire Belloc was not only a philosopher and a well-known writer but also an experienced mountaineer. On one occasion he invited a friend quite unfamiliar with mountaincraft to go with him on a walking tour over the Pyrenees into Spain. On the journey they were unexpectedly compelled to spend a night near the summit of a lofty peak. Belloc recorded that they lay down on a narrow ledge and, covering themselves with their meager garments, they waited for the day. Toward morning a storm arose and the fierce wail of the wind aroused his inexperienced fellow traveler from a troubled sleep. In a frenzy of fear he shook Belloc into wakefulness and cried, "I think it is the end of the world." "Oh, no," replied the veteran Belloc, shouting above the fury of the wind, "this is how the dawn comes in the Pyrenees." —Theodore Cuyler Speers.

STRENGTHENED BY PRAYER. Henry M. Stanley was a strong man. As a reporter he was sent to Africa to find the missionary David Livingstone. In his diary he wrote: "On my expeditions prayer made me stronger than my non-praying companions. It did not blind my eyes, nor close my ears, nor dull my mind, but on the contrary it gave me confidence. It did more. It gave me joy and pride in my work and lifted me hopefully over 1500 miles of forest track, eager to face the day's perils and fatigue. By prayer the road sought for has become visible and the dangers immediately lessened, not once or twice or thrice but repeatedly, until the cold unbelieving heart was greatly impressed."

IMPLORING ARMS. The sculptor Auguste Rodin in one of his masterpieces, "The Centauress," depicts in its lower part, near the base, the feet of a beast that is being sucked down by the mud. The upper part of this being is not a beast but a manlike figure struggling to be free from the mud. He stretches imploring arms heavenward as if reaching for the helping hand of God.—Herbert E. Hudgins.

TWO INVITATIONS. While visiting America, Henry Drummond received two invitations to dinner at the same time. One was from Oliver Wendell Holmes to meet Henry Wadsworth Longfellow, and the other was from Dwight L. Moody to meet Ira D. Sankey. Drummond loved the poems and the books of Holmes and Longfellow, but he believed that he knew where truer poetry was to be found. To his mind it lay in that story of the good shepherd and his lost sheep which Elizabeth Clephane and Sankey and Moody had made real to him in the song, "The Ninety and Nine." Drummond accepted Moody's invitation.—C. Elsie Harrison

WESLEY'S ANSWER. John Wesley began his ministry at a time of religious depression, social evils, political and economic inequalities, at a time when, according to one observer, "the light looked like the evening of the world." But Wesley offered his discouraged generation just one answer. His answer was often recorded in his journal: "I simply offered Jesus Christ to the people." At the Christmas Conference in 1784, when the Methodist Church in America was organized, the following question was placed in the discipline: "What is the best general method of preaching?" The answer: "To offer

Christ." Circuit riders in the frontier days of our country's development had only one answer to the question, "What shall I do to be saved?" That was, "Believe in the Lord Jesus."—W. Wallace Fridy.

ADMISSION. A woman with a grudge wrote a number of crank letters to Muriel Lester's school in England. The superintendent of the school guessed her identity and asked her to give up the libelous habit. At first the woman vowed innocence, but when the letters were produced she broke down, dropped her head, wept many salt tears, and remarked, "Oh, Miss, I am as good a woman as God ever made, only I cannot live up to it!"

ADVICE. A centipede, suffering from arthritis, went to the wise old owl for advice. The owl thought for a long time and then replied: "Centipede, you have one hundred legs swollen with arthritis. My advice is that you change yourself into a stork. With only two legs you would cut your pain 98 percent. Then by using your wings to stay off your legs you wouldn't have any trouble at all." The centipede was delighted with the suggestion and asked the wise old owl how he could change into a stork. The owl quickly replied: "Oh, I wouldn't know about the details. I offer only general policy."—William P. Gray.

EMBROIDERED BOOKMARK. Some years ago in a mine disaster in England forty miners lost their lives. The families, grief-stricken and bewildered, gathered about the entrance to the mind. Someone asked Bishop Edward Stanley to say something that would help these hapless folk, and this is what he said: "We stand today in the face of mystery, but I want to tell you about something I have at home. It is a bookmark embroidered in silk by my mother and given me many years ago. On one side the threads are crossed and re-crossed in wild confusion, and looking at it you would think it had been done by someone with no idea of what he was doing. But when I turn it over I see the words beautifully worked in silken

threads, 'God Is Love.' Now we are looking at this tragedy from one side, and it does not make sense. Someday we shall be permitted to read its meaning from the other side. Meanwhile let us wait and trust."—John A. Redhead.

GLORY AND GRACE. Justice William O. Douglas recalled how at the age of seven or eight his mother told him how wonderful his father had been. They had moved from a little town in Washington to Portland for an operation which proved to be fatal. Before the operation his father had said: "If I die, it will be glory. If I live, it will be grace." These words were beyond the understanding of a small boy, but years later they came back with meaning to interpret a great crisis in his own life. To die is glory. To live is grace. They could only mean that beneath the changes of this present life, beneath our toil and love, beneath our laughter and tears is the great foundation of the unchanging goodness of God. And if life carries us into open sunlit fields, this is God's grace that overflows the cup of life. And if the pathway turns toward the valley, even this is appointed in a divine wisdom for a glory not yet seen.—Harold E. Nicely.

INVOLVEMENT. A businessman, whose parents and wife were sincerely and actively involved in the worship and projects of their church, never had become involved himself. His philosophy was: "If I lead an honest, decent, and useful life, that is all that is required."

One night he had a vivid dream in which he died and knocked at the door of heaven. St. Peter answered and asked his name. He gave it and waited. At last St. Peter said, "I'm sorry, but your name isn't here."

Excitedly he asked: "Is my wife's name there? It should be. She never missed a worship service unless she was ill. She was active in all the church organizations. I never complained when dinner was late because she came in from church work just before I arrived. I gave her all the money she asked for the church and never be-grudged it. She was good enough for the both of us."

With a sad smile, St. Peter said, "Yes, she was good enough for both of you."

He awakened with his pulses throbbing madly. Recalling the dream and thinking it through, he said: "I never looked at it that way. I must get personally involved."—John N. Link in *The Northern Light.*

WHAT GOD CAN DO.   In 1872 Dwight L. Moody attended a meeting conducted by Henry Varley in a hay mow in Dublin. He heard the speaker say quietly, "The world has yet to see what God can do with and for and through and in a man who is fully and wholly consecrated to him."

Back in London the next Sunday, as he thrilled to the preaching of Charles H. Spurgeon, the words of Varley repeated themselves in his mind. "The world has yet to see . . . with and for and through and in a man!"

Moody pondered: "Varley meant any man! Varley didn't say he had to be edu-cated, or brilliant, or anything else—just a man! Well, by the Holy Spirit in me, I'll be one of those men."

UNASSAILABLE CASTLE.   On a certain hilltop in Europe there stands an ancient castle which emerged from the feudal wars unscathed and impregnable. But if you ex-amine this age-old structure carefully, you will find evidences in the masonry that it was not always impervious to attack. More than once in earlier times its walls were breached, but always its defender turned defeat into future advantage, building more massively the bit that had crumbled, pushing out flanking towers, investing the bulwarks with cunningly devised slopes and angles, until at last, defying the full force of the invader, it stood unassailable. —Carl Hopkins Elmore.

SPIRITUAL EMPTINESS.   Why is it true that people are drinking more and more? Is it not because there is an unnamed anxi-ety springing from a spiritual emptiness? We are trying to be cheerful with cocktails because the truth about us is that we are cheerless. We are trying to exude confi-dence because deep inside there are fears that gnaw at us. We seek the security of genial companions around the bar be-cause we are so terribly insecure about the things that are really important.—Charles L. Copenhaver.

FOR PEOPLE.   The church must decide what it is for. It exists for more than build-ing an institution or an organization. It exists for more than the maintenance of its clergy. It exists in the name of God and in the name of Jesus Christ for people. It exists for the salvation, happiness, and well-being of people.—John F. Havlik.

BEGINNING.   Whatever else the Bible has to say, it makes it quite plain from the outset that life will have neither meaning nor purpose unless we begin with God. The first four words of the story the Bible tells are not "Once upon a time" but "In the beginning God."—William Neil.

THE RIGHT WORDS.   A few months after moving to a small town a woman com-plained to a neighbor about the poor ser-vice at the local drug store. She hoped the new acquaintance would repeat her com-plaint to the owner.

Next time she went to the drug store, the druggist greeted her with a big smile and told her how happy he was to see her again. He said he hoped she liked their town and to please let him know if there was anything he could do to help her and her husband get settled. He then filled her order promptly and efficiently.

Later the woman reported the miracu-lous change to her friend. "I suppose you told the druggist how poor I thought the service was?" she asked.

"Well, no," the woman said. "In fact—and I hope you don't mind—I told him you were amazed at the way he had built up this small town drug store and that you thought it was one of the best run drug stores you'd ever seen."

ON THE NATURE OF GOD.   God is un-wearied patience, a meekness that cannot be provoked; he is a never-ending mercifulness; he is unmixed goodness, impartial, universal love; his delight is in the communication of himself, his own happiness to everything according to its capacity. He does everything that is good, righteous, and lovely. He is the good from which nothing but good comes, and resisteth all evil only with goodness. William Law.

NO CHOICE.   Several years ago John Coventry Smith told the story of a conversation between Howard Lowry, president of Wooster College, and Dr. Sarvepalli Radhakrishnan, the Hindu philosopher. Lowry remarked that he was sometimes embarrassed by the Christian claim of uniqueness of Jesus Christ, which is at the heart of evangelistic preaching. To say to India, "Jesus Christ is the light of the world"—isn't that arrogance? Is not that a subtle form of exalting ourselves, as if to say, "We only have the light." Dr. Radhakrishnan paused and replied: "Yes, but the Christian has no choice. This is what your scriptures say. You cannot say less. You are saved from arrogance when you say it in the spirit of Jesus Christ."—Samuel H. Moffett.

POTENCY.   Christian education is informed by Christian love, and Christians believe that the loving presence of God in human life is so potent that if it were taken seriously the entire world would be refashioned.—Wayne R. Rood.

GENIUS AND DEMON.   Charles H. Spurgeon related an experience he had when he visited the library of Trinity College. His attention was arrested by a statue of Lord Byron. The librarian said to him, "Stand here, sir." He did as he was directed, and as he looked at the statue, he said: "What a fine intellectual countenance! What a grand genius he was!" Then the librarian suggested that he take a look from the other side of the statue. As he did, he said: "Oh, what a demon! There stands the man who could defy God!" Then the librarian explained that the sculptor had designed the statue to show the two characters—the most superhuman

qualities—that Byron possessed and "yet the enormous mass of sin that was in his soul."

The human heart carries and perhaps "will always carry, its cruelty and its springtime in his heart."—Charles F. Jacobs.

REALIZATION.   Self-respect cannot be hunted. It cannot be purchased. It is never for sale. It comes to us when we are alone, in quiet moments and in quiet places, and when we suddenly realize that knowing the good, we have done it; knowing the beautiful, we have served it; knowing the truth, we have spoken it.—Whitney Griswold.

SOURCE OF STRENGTH.   It is an ironic fact that in this nuclear age, when the horizon of human knowledge and human experience has passed far beyond any that any age has ever known, that we turn back in this time to the oldest source of wisdom and strength—to the words of the prophets and the saints, who tell us that faith is more powerful than doubt, that hope is more potent than despair, and that only through the love that is sometimes called charity can we conquer those forces within ourselves and throughout the world that threaten the very existence of mankind.—John F. Kennedy.

SOMEBODY CARED.   One season a class of young people in the church where I served decided that on Christmas morning they would take bags of popcorn, candy, and fruit to each of the children in the wards of one of our county hospitals. They found that most of the children already had received some gift, but as they went down the wards they discovered one lad who had nothing to show that anyone had visited him. His face shone as they gave him the colored bag of dainties. Most of the other children began devouring their fruit at once, but as the young people came back through the ward they saw that this little fellow had placed his fruit and candy out on the pillow, in plain sight, without having eaten any of it.

"Why don't you eat it, son?" asked the teacher of the group as she came up to the bed.

"Nope," said the boy, with a quiver in his voice, "I'm going to keep it out there so all the kids can see that somebody did care about me when it was Christmas."—Albert W. Beaven.

GUIDING CANDLES.   Long ago there lived a shoemaker. Though he was poor, each night he placed a lighted candle in his window to welcome travelers seeking shelter.

War came to his nation, followed by famine. The shoemaker suffered less than some others. His neighbors believed it might be because of his lighted candle. On Christmas Eve every house had a candle burning in the window.

By morning a mantle of snow covered the village. Soon a messenger, bringing news of peace, came riding into the village. "It was the candles," the villagers whispered to one another. "They have guided Christ to our doors."—E. Paul Hovey.

DIVINE LOVER.   The journey which our divine lover took was from heaven to earth to win his bride. In his people he found a bride deep in debt and paid it all; under sentence of death and died in her place; a lost creature, clad in rags, and took of his own royal robes to cover her. To wash her, he shed his blood; to win her, he shed his tears; finding her poor and miserable and naked, he endowed her with all his goods; heir of all things, she was to enjoy everything that he possessed as his Father's Son, and to share all things with himself; for are not his people "heirs of God and joint heirs with Christ"?—Thomas Guthrie.

READY.   During World War II Helmut Thielicke was pastor in Stuttgart, Germany. The city was ravished by Allied bombing. One morning Thielicke stood in combat boots and military fatigues before a gaping hole. It was a cellar which had sustained a direct bomb hit the night before. Some twenty men had been seeking shelter there. A woman approached to ask, "Are you Pastor Thielicke?" When he replied in the affirmative, she said: "My husband was down there last night. All they found of him was his cap. We heard you preach. I want to thank you for getting him ready for eternity."

INDEX OF CONTRIBUTORS

SERMON TITLE INDEX

(Children's stories and sermons are identified cs; sermon suggestions ss)

SCRIPTURAL INDEX

INDEX OF PRAYERS

INDEX OF MATERIALS USEFUL AS CHILDREN'S STORIES
AND SERMONS, NOT INCLUDED IN SECTION IX

INDEX OF MATERIALS USEFUL FOR SMALL GROUPS, NOT INCLUDED IN SECTION V

INDEX OF SPECIAL DAYS AND SEASONS

TOPICAL INDEX